A reference grammar for students of English
R A Close

Longman

Longman Group Limited
Longman House.
Burnt Mill, Harlow,
Essex CM20 2JE.
England.

First published 1975
Sixth impression 1982

ISBN 0 582 52277 3

Filmset by Keyspools Ltd, Golborne, Lancs.

版權所有
翻印必究

中 華 民 國 七 十 三 年 八 月 初 版
新聞局登記證局版台業字第１４５２號

發行人：戴　奕　煌
負責人：劉　燈　明
發行所：文 鶴 出 版 有 限 公 司
　　　　台北市和平東路一段１０９號６Ｆ
電　話：３９３４４９７・３９４１７９１
印刷所：合　興　印　刷　廠

Printed in Hong Kong by
Wing Tai Cheung Printing Co. Ltd.

Foreword

Students of English are fortunate in having this further opportunity to share the insights of R. A. Close into the complexities and delicacies of English grammar. He brings to the task of writing the present book an enviable and scarcely surpassed experience of forty years' advanced English teaching in many countries with widely ranging language backgrounds – notably Japan, China, Chile, Greece, Czechoslovakia and France. The impact of his work in the classroom is measured in part by the successful pursuit of his aims and methods by the countless teachers who have had the benefit of studying under him. But his influence has happily made itself felt to an even wider extent through the printed page. He has generously given his advice to writers on English language teaching in many countries, and their books have been immeasurably better in consequence. More importantly still, he has himself written numerous articles and several books, all of them informed by a clarity, profundity, and subtlety of mind, and written with a pen which with surgical keenness probes and dissects problems that had previously seemed so entangled and obscured as to merit despairing abandonment in the no-man's land of 'idiom'.

A reference grammar for students of English demonstrates another of his notable gifts: the ability to compress analyses, learning, and pedagogical counsel with rigorous but ever readable economy. And it is an economy which leaves him room both to reflect the thinking of other linguists and also – a striking feature of the book – to endorse his statements with liberal and enlightening examples. As a result, he has provided an invaluable guide to students and teachers of English alike.

Randolph Quirk
University College London

Contents

Part Two

Chapter Fifteen
Adverbials

Appendix One
Summary of spelling rules

Appendix Two
Notes on punctuation and the use of capital letters

Bibliography

Index

Preface

With the rapid advance of linguistic science, there has been a revolution in English grammar. 'Traditional' grammar is now considered to be obsolete, to have been forced into a mould originally intended for Latin, and to be dominated by dogma about what should and should not be said. New theories, or 'models', of grammar are constantly being developed. Yet the facts of English usage remain; and people need to know what the facts are.

English grammar is largely a matter of sentence construction. It is information that we can apply, consciously or unconsciously, to form sentences that are acceptable as a whole or in detail. *Part One* of this book will explain how an English sentence is built up. In the process, it will briefly describe the grammatical system as a whole and will introduce the terminology with which we can label its component parts. The description will include much that is still valid in the old style of grammar, as well as innovations that seem likely to last. Some of the terminology may be new; most of it is well known, though the revolution has obliged us to redefine terms whose meaning has become blurred. In any case, the terminology and the concepts behind it are broadly in accordance with those of *A Grammar of Contemporary English*,[1] which is without doubt the English Grammar of our times.

Part Two will deal with the detail. It is mainly to this part of the book, together with the Index, that readers will turn for reference. However, an understanding of the information given in *Part Two* may depend on a careful study of *Part One*.

This Grammar is, relatively, 'short'. It aims at concentrating on frequently-used constructions. Lists of verbs and adjectives, for example, have been taken, with few additions, from *A General Service List of English Words*.[1] The adverb 'normally' often occurs in this book. That expression has not been used loosely; it points to a norm from which deviation can occur in the haste of modern times, in the continuance of regional tradition, and, especially, in creative writing.

A bibliography is provided, on page 305, not only as a guide to further reading, but also in acknowledgement of works I have consulted and used.

I owe a great debt of gratitude to Professor Randolph Quirk, with whom I have been personally associated since 1958, especially since my election as an Honorary Research Fellow at University College, London, where I have had the privilege of drawing on the facilities of the Survey of English Usage and of benefiting from contact with its staff.

I am particularly grateful to Mr John Bright for so conscientiously

[1] See Bibliography on page 305.

working through a draft of this book, and for making many suggestions for improvement which I have gladly adopted; also to Mr Peter Clifford, Mr D. K. Swan, Miss Delia Halnon and Mrs Eileen Mohr of Longman Group Ltd, for their unfailing and very efficient help throughout the arduous process of converting a much-revised manuscript into publishable form.

For years, my wife has been telling me that a short English reference grammar is badly needed. I would like to think that the result is worthy of her inspiration and encouragement.

R A C

English vowel and consonant sounds, and their spellings

Vowels

PHONETIC SYMBOL	VOWEL SOUND AS IN:
iː	*see*, *sea*, *me*, *these*
i	*it*, ver*y*
e	*get*
æ	*cat*
ɑː	*car*
ɔ	*hot*
ɔː	*horn*, *saw*
u	*put*
uː	*too*, *June*, *blue*, *new*
ʌ	*up*
əː	*her*, *bird*, *burn*
ə	*better*, *actor*, *collar*
	DIPHTHONG SOUND AS IN:
ei	*day*, *rain*, *date*
əu	*go*, *toe*, *note*, *coat*
ai	*fly*, *fine*, *high*
au	*how*, *house*
ɔi	*boy*, *noise*
iə	*here*, *hear*, *cheer*
ɛə	*chair*, *care*

Note: All vowel and diphthong sounds are 'voiced'.

Consonants

Voiced

PHONETIC SYMBOL	CONSONANT SOUND AS IN:
b	*burn*
m	*moon*
w	*we*
v	*voice*
ð	*this*
d	*day*
n	*no*
l	*look*, *feel*
r	*run*
z (sibilant)	*zoo*, *pens*
ʒ (sibilant)	*measure*
j	*yes*
g	*gate*
ŋ	*long*
h	*here*

Voiceless

p	*pen*, sto*p*
f	*f*ull, roo*f*
θ	*th*in
t	*t*ea, ca*t*
s (sibilant)	*s*ee, book*s*
ʃ (sibilant)	*sh*ip, bru*sh*
k	*c*at, *k*i*ck*

Also sibilant are the combinations tʃ as in ma*tch* and dʒ as in ju*dge*.

Relation between pronunciation and spelling

The spelling in the words given as examples above may be called 'standard'. That is to say, it would be assumed by a speaker of English that a word spelt *heed* would be pronounced with vowel /iː/, that *hid* would be pronounced with vowel /i/, *led* with vowel /e/, and so on. When this assumption cannot be made in the case of some of the irregular verbs, the pronunciation is indicated by phonetic symbols.

Stress

When the pronunciation of a word of more than one syllable is given, the sign ' indicates that the following syllable is stressed, as in be'ginning, 'offering. In compound nouns and in nominal groups, stress is indicated thus:

a 'good `friend, 'boiling `water: stress on both parts

a `school ˌfriend, a `bathing ˌcostume: stress on the first part.

The element marked ` has what is called NUCLEAR STRESS, and it is here that the voice falls (or rises) in pitch.

Conventions and abbreviations used

/feis/	phonetic transcription
'offer	syllable following ' is stressed
You { should / =ought to } be	both *should be* and *ought to be* are acceptable in the example given, without change of meaning
He { does / did } not go	both *does not* and *did not* are acceptable in the example given, but with different meaning
I said (that) it was	a word in round brackets in an example is optional
cp	compare
eg	for example
ie	that is
viz	namely
[1] after a sentence	this refers to a footnote
* before a sentence	the sentence following * is unacceptable

Part One
Chapter One
Constructing the sentence

1.1

We tend to speak, and we normally aim at writing, in COMPLETE SENTENCES. In spoken English, we often give short responses, which can be recognised as *parts* of complete sentences (1.60); and writers of advertisements, for example, sometimes deliberately produce 'sentences' that are not complete (2.36). To be complete, a sentence needs at least one FINITE, INDEPENDENT CLAUSE. In this chapter, we shall see what a clause in English consists of and what makes it finite.

A Finite clauses and simple sentences
1.2

a We can best see what a finite clause is by examining examples of a SIMPLE SENTENCE. A simple sentence contains only one finite clause, so that the structure of a finite clause is identical with that of a simple sentence. Here are ten one-clause sentences from a short story:

  1 **I** *have* just *telephoned* George Lamb.
  2 **He** *was* my best friend.
  3 **This** *is* his photograph.
  4 **We** *were placed* in the same class twenty years ago.
  5 At nine o'clock, **we all** *assembled* in the hall.
  6 **The boys** *were waiting* for the headmaster to come in.
  7 **The headmaster's desk** *stood* on a high platform.
  8 **He** *did not like* us, George and me, very much.
  9 **Everyone in our class** *could see* that.
  10 Yet **George** always *did* his work perfectly.

b Each of those one-clause sentences has a SUBJECT, which is in bold type. Except for *yet* in [10] the rest of each sentence is the PREDICATE, *ie* what is said about the subject. If either of those two parts, subject or predicate, were missing, the sentence would not be complete. However, in an IMPERATIVE, as in [13] and [14] below, the subject is usually unstated. Note that the subject often is, but need not be, the first part of the sentence.

Statements, questions and imperatives
1.3

a Examples [1] to [10] are all STATEMENTS. A clause may also take the form of a QUESTION, as in:

  11 *Have* **you** *seen* George Lamb today?

12 *Did* **you** *know* him well?

In [11] and [12], the subject is again in bold type, and the rest of the sentence is the predicate, part of which now comes before the subject. The subject of a question like [11] or [12] can be easily found, because it comes immediately after the first part of the predicate (1.26, 2.3).

b A clause may take the form of an IMPERATIVE, as in:

13 *Have* this seat.   14 *Be* careful.

In those two examples, only the predicate is stated. If the subject of an imperative clause is absent, we assume it is *you*, the person or persons addressed, since *you* occurs if we expand [13] and [14] to:

13a You have this seat.   13b Have this seat, will you?

14a You be careful.   14b Be careful, will you?

However, a subject other than *you* can be actually stated, as in:

15a Somebody take this seat.

15b $\begin{Bmatrix} \text{All} \\ \text{Everybody} \end{Bmatrix}$ stand up please.

c An imperative often expresses a command; it can also express an invitation, a request or a warning (3.10).

Affirmative, interrogative and negative
1.4

We can make AFFIRMATIVE statements, as in

16 I have found some mistakes already;

or we can avoid an affirmative statement, as in the INTERROGATIVE

17 Have you found any mistakes yet?

or as in the NEGATIVE

18 I haven't found any yet.

The distinction between affirmative on the one hand, and interrogative and negative on the other, is marked in a number of ways in English: note, for example, the use of *some* and *already* in [16] as opposed to *any* and *yet* in [17] and [18]. Other examples are *I have found some mistakes too* and *I haven't found any either*.

B The noun phrase
1.5

The subject of a clause is usually (2.8, 2.18, 3.17, 3.24) A NOUN PHRASE. 'Noun phrase', often abbreviated to NP, is a convenient term for any one of the following:

a a NOUN, such as *George, boys*;

b a NOMINAL GROUP, such as *the boys, the headmaster's desk*, in which a noun (*boys, desk*) is the HEAD, and in which the other words (*the, the headmaster's*) MODIFY the head;

c a PRONOUN, which may be one of the seven so-called PERSONAL PRONOUNS (*I, you, he, she, it, we, they*[1]) or an INDEFINITE PRONOUN like *everyone* or *something*, or one of the words like *this* and *that* which can be used as pronouns and which are listed in 6.2. A pronoun is a PRO-FORM, *ie* a form used instead of another form. Various types of pro-form will be mentioned in this book;

d a PRONOMINAL GROUP, such as *we all, everyone in our class*, in which a pronoun (*we, everyone*) is the head.

Besides being the subject of a clause, an NP can have other functions (1.33).

Nouns
1.6

a A noun is a word that we can use at certain points in the structure of a sentence. Thus, *work* is a noun if it fills the gap in *He always did his – perfectly*. It is a VERB (1.13) if it fills the gap in *His brothers – in a factory*.

b A noun may be a PROPER NOUN (*George, George Lamb, New York*) or a COMMON NOUN (*friend, desk, bird, air*).

c Both proper nouns and common nouns can refer to something ANIMATE (*George, friend, bird*) or INANIMATE (*New York, desk, wing*).

d A proper noun is the name of someone or something that is usually imagined as UNIQUE: the speaker in example [1] is assuming that there is only one George Lamb. On the other hand, a common noun is a name given either to one example, or more, of a CLASS OF THING or to the CLASS AS A WHOLE. *Friend* refers to one example of a class in *George was a good friend*, but to the class as a whole in *A friend is somebody we like and know well*. A common noun is often found in a nominal group, and by modifying the head (1.5b) the speaker can say which particular example of a class he has in mind. The MODIFIERS *the*, in [6], and the *headmaster's*, in [7], help to DETERMINE which examples of the classes of thing called 'boy' and 'desk' the speaker is talking about. A proper noun will not normally be modified in this way.

Note: It is true that the sun, for example, is unique, in so far as for most of us it is the only thing of its kind. But we can talk of *other suns* and we often use *sun* as the head of a nominal group, *eg the rising sun*. For such reasons, we may classify *sun* as a common noun. We can also imagine more than one George Lamb and say *That is not the George Lamb I mean*. However, there would no doubt be general agreement that a name like *George Lamb* or *New York* does not normally need to be modified.

---

[1] We should add to these seven the indefinite personal pronoun *one*, as in *What does one do now?*

Modifiers
1.7
a We can have PREmodifiers, coming before the head, or POSTmodifiers coming after it, thus:

PREMODIFIERS	HEAD	POSTMODIFIERS
a good	friend	
my school	friends	
the	headmaster	of the school
the headmaster's	desk	
several	boys	
we		all
	everyone	in our class

When the head is a noun, modifiers usually precede it. Phrases on the pattern *of the school* (1.36d) follow it. When the head is a pronoun, modifiers normally follow it, too.[1]

b In the column headed PREMODIFIERS above, there are three main classes of word:

i *good*, which is an ADJECTIVE. In *a good friend* both the adjective and the noun are stressed: NUCLEAR STRESS is then on *friend* (see p xii).

ii *school*, which is a noun modifying another noun, and which here refers to a SUBCLASS of the class of person called 'friend'. In *a school friend*, nuclear stress is on the modifier.

iii *a, my, the, the headmaster's* and *several*, which are DETERMINERS. Determiners can be IDENTIFIERS (6.16), telling us, either definitely or indefinitely, which friend or which school friends or which headmaster, the speaker means; or they can be QUANTIFIERS (6.33), telling us, again either definitely or indefinitely, what quantity. Thus, both identifiers and quantifiers can be indefinite (*eg a*) or definite (*the*). We can subdivide the definite determiners into those that SPECIFY and those that do not.

For example:

George went to a school: *a* is indefinite;

He went to the school: *the* is definite, but it still does not specify, by itself, exactly *which* school;

He went to this school: *this* is both definite and SPECIFYING: it tells us exactly *which* school.

Determiners
1.8
a Identifiers include:

i THE ARTICLES – the INDEFINITE ARTICLE, *a*, and the DEFINITE ARTICLE, *the*;

---

[1] There are a few exceptions to this rule. Here is one:
A I've finished all my work.   B Lucky you!

ii the DEMONSTRATIVES, *this* and *that*, *these* and *those*;
iii the POSSESSIVE form of the personal pronouns. (*my, your, his, her, its, our, their, one's*.)

b Quantifiers include NUMERALS, and *much* and *many* which are freely used in negative and interrogative sentences but usually avoided in affirmative sentences in informal style, as in:

19 A Were there many boys in George's class?

   B No, there weren't many.

   but Yes, there were a lot.

Count nouns and mass nouns
1.9

a *Much* and *many* also illustrate the distinction between COUNT NOUNS (also called UNIT NOUNS or COUNTABLES) and MASS NOUNS (or UNCOUNTABLES). Count nouns such as *friend*, *desk*, can be preceded by *one*, and may have a separate plural form which can be preceded by *How many* or by a numeral higher than one. Mass nouns, like *bread*, *milk*, cannot be preceded by *one*, they cannot have a separate plural form, but can be preceded by *How much*.

b Just as a word like *work* can act as either a noun or a verb, so a number of nouns may be used either as mass or as count according to the speaker's exact meaning: *light* is a mass noun in *Light travels much faster than sound*; it is a count noun in *I have a light by my bed*.

Person, number and gender
1.10

Nouns and pronouns, besides being animate or inanimate, can also be PERSONAL (human) or NON-PERSONAL (animal or inanimate object). We say *Who was on the platform?* if we expect a personal noun as the answer, *What was on the platform?* if we expect a non-personal one.[1] The traditional term PERSONAL PRONOUN, still in use today, employs 'personal' in a different way. The words *I, you, he*, etc., are called 'personal' because they can be classified thus:

Table 1

		SINGULAR	PLURAL
1ST PERSON		I	we
2ND PERSON		you	you
3RD PERSON	MASCULINE	he	
	FEMININE	she	they
	NEUTER	it	

[1] But *who* can be used with reference to a domestic animal, as in *Who is that scratching at the door? Danny* (our dog) *or Tom* (our cat)?

Table 1 introduces three grammatical categories which are found in many languages – PERSON, NUMBER and GENDER.

a PERSON decides the speaker's choice of *I/my, you/your, he/his, etc.*, and it may affect the form of the verb (1.16.2).

b NUMBER – SINGULAR (NUMBER) OR PLURAL (NUMBER) affects the form of almost all words used as count nouns, and of the demonstratives (1.8a): *this* and *that* are used in a nominal group when the head is a singular count noun or a mass noun; *these* and *those* are used when the head is a count noun in the plural. Whether the subject is singular or plural may affect the form taken by the verb (1.12).

c GENDER – MASCULINE (GENDER), FEMININE (GENDER), NEUTER (GENDER) – affects the form of the 3rd person singular of the personal pronouns, as shown in Table 1. *He* refers to a person or animal regarded as male; *she* to a person or animal regarded as female; *it* to an inanimate object, or to a person or animal not yet regarded as male or female (*eg Who is it?*). The distinction between male and female may affect our choice of LEXICAL ITEMS – words or phrases that could fill a 'slot' in the structure of a clause. For example, of the lexical items *friend, headmaster, actress, hospital matron*, only the first two could fill the 'slot' in *He was a good –* . The SUFFIX *-ess* is found in a number of words referring to women; but many words referring to women do not have this suffix. Thus, *friend* could fill the slot in *She was a good –* . Words like *friend, neighbour, cousin*, etc., may refer to male or female.

The plural of nouns
1.11

1 Almost all words used as count nouns have a plural form which follows a rule. This rule applies to all new additions to the language, such as *bus, motel, jeep*.

Pronunciation[1]

a Add the SYLLABLE /iz/ to any BASE (*ie* singular form) ending in a SIBILANT (page xi). What is added to the base is called an INFLEXION or ENDING: face/feis/, faces/ˈfeisiz/; page/peidʒ/, pages/ˈpeidʒiz/; bus/bʌs/, buses/ˈbʌsiz/; match/mætʃ/, matches/ˈmætʃiz/.

b Add the VOICED /z/, with no extra syllable, to any base ending in any voiced (page xi) sound except a sibilant: boy/bɔi/, boys/bɔiz/; friend/frend/, friends/frendz/; motel/məuˈtel/, motels/məuˈtelz/.

c Add the VOICELESS /s/, with no extra syllable, to any base ending in any

---

[1] The traditional view was that grammar was something that affected the way in which a language was written. It is now widely recognised that grammar concerns the spoken language as well as the written.

voiceless (page xii) sound except a sibilant:

desk/desk/, desks/desks/; jeep/dʒiːp/, jeeps/dʒiːps/.

Spelling

d Add the letter *s* to the base, *eg boy, boys,* except as in e and f.

e Add the letters *es* to any base ending in the letters *ch, s, sh* and *x,* and normally to a base ending in the letter *o*:

matches, buses, bushes, boxes, potatoes.

f When the base ends in the letter *y* preceded by any consonant letter, change the *y* to *i* and add *es*:

country, countries; fly, flies.

2 The same rule applies to the form taken by the verb when the subject is 3rd person singular (1.10, 1.16.2), and to the pronunciation of the possessive form of nouns (1.8a, iii). Thus *'s* will be pronounced /iz/ in *George's* or *Thomas's,* /z/ in *Tom's* and /s/ in *Jack's.* Similarly, the CONTRACTION *'s* for *is* will be pronounced /z/ in *Tom's away* and /s/ in *Jack's here;* while the contraction will not occur after the sibilant in *Thomas is away* or *This is his place.*

3 For irregular plurals, see 5.14–23.

Agreement, or concord, with the subject

1.12

a The relation between the number of the subject and the form taken by the verb is known as AGREEMENT or CONCORD. Simple examples of agreement are *He was ...* in example [2] and *The boys were ...* in [6]. Note also the following examples; and note that when the subject is a nominal group, as in [25], [26] and [27], it is the head that decides what form the verb should take:

Examples

Notes

20 I am your friend. You and I are very good friends.

You and I form one plural subject. Note that *I* comes at the end of the phrase, *You and I.*

21 I was placed in George's class. George and I were placed ...

Similarly, *George and I* form one plural subject.

22 Either George or John was responsible for the damage.

Either George was, or John was: alternative subjects.

23 George, as well as John, is away today.

George, only, is subject.

24 Ten pounds is too much.

ie That sum is too big.

25 The pages of this book are numbered.

Pages is the head; *book* is part of the postmodifier.

26 The cost of these repairs is too high.

Cost is the head; *repairs* is part of the postmodifier.

27 The employment of young chil-   *Employment* is the head; *of young*
dren, in most countries, is against   *children* is the postmodifier. *In*
the law.   *most countries* is an adjunct, as in
1.47.

b A COLLECTIVE NOUN (5.24) – like *school*, when it refers to a *group of persons*, or *family, government, team* – may be followed by a singular verb (*eg is*) or a plural verb (*eg are*). It may be associated with a singular possessive form (*its*), or a plural one (*their*). However, it is reasonable to be consistent within the same sentence or two, and to say either

28   Our team plays best on its own ground,
    or
28a Our team play best on their own ground.

Everyone, someone and *no one* will only take a singular verb but are associated with either *his* or *their, eg*

29   Everyone likes to go his own way,
    or
29a Everyone likes to go their own way.

In [29a], *their*, like *everyone*, might be regarded as indefinite rather than definitely singular or plural. An example like [29a] will often be heard, though it is more likely to occur in informal than in formal style. In everyday speech, examples like [29] might sometimes sound pedantic.

The same remarks apply to *everybody, somebody* and *nobody*.

C The verb phrase
1.13

While the subject of a clause is a noun phrase (NP), the predicate is a VERB PHRASE (VP). Every finite clause has the following basic structure:

    NP (subject) + VP (predicate)

in which VP consists sometimes of a FINITE VERB only, as in *We all waited*, but much more often of a group of words with a finite verb as its head, as in all the examples in 1.2. We shall see when a verb is or is not finite from the examples given in 1.14–1.21. For a clause to be finite, there must be a finite verb in it.

Verbs, finite and non-finite
1.14

In the examples in 1.2, that part of the predicate which is in italics is a finite verb. The verb is either SIMPLE, consisting of one word (*was, is, assembled, stood, did*), or COMPLEX, consisting of a VERBAL GROUP (*have telephoned, were placed, were waiting, did not like, could see*).

1.15

What are commonly classified as 'verbs' include the ten MODALS:

will	shall	can	may
would	should	could	might
must	ought		

The modals cannot be used as FULL VERBS: that is to say, they cannot be the
only verb in a sentence, but must be used with another verb as in *Everyone
could see that*. However, they can stand alone in, for example, a short
response, as in the dialogue:

    30 A Could anyone see it?

        B Oh yes, everyone could (see it).

The modals will be discussed further in 1.17, 1.22 and Chapter 14.

1.16

Every verb except the ten modals and *used to* (1.30c) can be used as a full
verb, with THREE SIMPLE FINITE PARTS and THREE SIMPLE NON-FINITE PARTS,
as follows:

FINITE

1 The IMPERATIVE:

    Please *be* quiet. Somebody *take* this seat.

The imperative (1.3b) has only one form, which is the same as the BASE.
We shall use the base, printed in capital letters, when referring to a verb
independently of any of its parts: thus, we say that *have* is the imperative of
the verb HAVE, and *be*, of the verb BE.

2 The SIMPLE PRESENT TENSE:

    This *is* his photograph. We *assemble* in the hall.

The simple present tense of BE has three forms (*am, is, are*). The simple
present tense of every full verb except BE has two forms. One, which is
always the same as the base, is used for all subjects except the 3rd person
singular. Whenever the verb is 3rd person singular, an inflexion – the same
one in pronunciation and spelling as that used for the plural of nouns (1.11)
– is added to the base, thus:

I miss George	He misses/misiz/me
I always stand here	George stands/stændz/there
I take this seat	Somebody else takes/teiks/that one[1]
I try hard	He tries hard too
I go home with him	He goes home with me

Apart from *am, is* and *are*, there are only three exceptions to that rule: the
3rd person singular of HAVE is *has*/hæz/; the 3rd person singular of SAY
and DO is regular in spelling (*says, does*), but irregular in pronunciation,
/sez/, /dʌz/. A regular pronunciation of *says*/seiz/, is also current.

3 The SIMPLE PAST TENSE:

    He *was* my friend. We *assembled* in the hall.

---

[1] Contrast this example with the imperative in example [15].

The simple past tense of BE has two forms, *was*, *were*.

The simple past tense of every verb except BE has one form only.

With REGULAR verbs – the great majority of verbs in the language are regular, including recent additions to it like *telephone* and *televise* – the simple past is formed as follows:

Pronunciation

a Add the syllable /id/ to any base ending in /d/ or /t/:
mend, mended/mendid/; wait, waited/weitid/.

b Add the voiced /d/, with no extra syllable, to a base ending in any voiced sound except /d/ itself:
play, played/pleid/; assemble, assembled/əsembld/.

c Add the voiceless /t/, with no extra syllable, to a base ending in any voiceless sound except /t/ itself:
like, liked/laikt/; ask, asked/ɑːskt/.

Spelling

d Add the letter *d* to any base ending in the letter *e*, as in *assembled*, *telephoned*;

e Add the letters *ed* to any base not ending in *e*, as in *played*, *mended*, *waited*.

f When the base ends in a single consonant letter preceded by a single vowel letter (*a, e, i, o* or *u*), the consonant is doubled. This rule applies to all words of one syllable, *eg stop, stopped*, and to words of more than one syllable when the final syllable is stressed, *eg oc'cur, oc'curred*. It does not normally apply when the final syllable is unstressed, *eg 'offer, 'offered* (9.4).

g When the base ends in a consonant letter + *y*, the *y* changes to *i* before *-ed* is added; *eg try, tried; occupy, occupied*.

NON-FINITE

4 The INFINITIVE, as in

   6 The boys were waiting for the headmaster *to come* in.

   9 Everyone in our class could *see* that.

The infinitive, too, has the same form as the base, although it is often preceded by the INFINITIVE MARKER, *to*, as in *to come*. In *could see* the infinitive is BARE. The infinitive is non-finite; thus, while *for the headmaster to come in* has a subject, *the headmaster*, it has no finite verb and is therefore not a finite clause.

5 The PRESENT PARTICIPLE (or *-ing* participle), as in

   6 . . . *waiting* for the headmaster to come in.

The part of example [6] that has just been quoted does not constitute a finite clause either, because the participle, *waiting*, is not, by itself, a finite verb. The present participle is formed, in every case, by adding the sound /iŋ/, and the spelling *ing*, to the base. However, if the base ends in a single letter *e*, the *e* is omitted in the spelling before the *ing* is added; and a single consonant letter preceded by a single vowel letter is doubled in a stressed syllable, as in the past tense (1.16,3f) *eg*

write, writing; stop, stopping; be'gin, be'ginning, but *'offer, 'offering.*

For exceptions to this rule, see 9.3.

6 The PAST PARTICIPLE (or *-ed* participle), as in

I have just *telephoned* George Lamb.

With regular verbs, and a number of irregular ones as well, the past participle has the same form as the past tense (1.16,3). *Assembled* is the past tense, and finite, in example [5]. The same form is the past participle, and non-finite, in: *Assembled in the hall, we all waited for the headmaster to arrive.*

The modals
1.17

The modals (1.15) are traditionally called 'defective' in that they have only one form each. They have no inflexion even when the subject is 3rd person singular; they have no imperative, and no non-finite parts. A verbal group can contain only one modal at a time: to express the idea of MUST + CAN within one verbal group, the speaker has to replace CAN by a PARAPHRASE beginning with a full verb, thus:

31 You *must be able* to speak English fluently.

Modals have tense, in so far as *can* and *may* are present tense, while *could* and *might* are past;

32a Everyone can see it now.   32b Everyone could see it then.

But *could* and *might* very often do not refer to the past at all, as in

33 Perhaps I could see you tomorrow.

All verbal groups beginning with a modal are finite.

Time and tense
1.18

a PRESENT TENSE (13.1) is the name given to a verb form like *stands*, and PAST TENSE (13.16) is the name given to a form like *stood*. The past tense is normally used when the speaker is referring to an act or state occurring in time that he considers to be no longer present. The idea 'no longer present' is often marked by an ADVERBIAL of past time, such as *twenty years ago* (example [4]) or by some other means, including the whole context in which one is speaking or writing. When the meaning 'no longer present' is not intended, then a present tense is normally used. However, a past tense form does not always refer to past time, nor a present tense form to present time, as in:

34 It's time you went to bed now.

35 At that moment, Jim rushes in and shouts 'They're coming!'

b Reference to FUTURE time in English is made in a variety of ways (13.25).

Will+infinitive is often used to refer to the future, though it has other functions as well (14.2).

c The non-finite parts of a verb have no tense, nor are they affected by the person and number of the subject. *See* remains unchanged in *I want to see, he wants to see, we wanted to see*; *waiting* remains unchanged in *I am waiting, he is waiting, we were waiting*; and *telephoned* is unchanged in *I have telephoned, he has telephoned, we had telephoned*. Thus both the 'present participle' and 'past participle' can be used with the present tense and both with the past tense: that is why modern grammarians prefer terms like the '*-ing* participle' and the '*-ed* participle'.

Irregular verbs
1.19
The term 'irregular' is applied to verbs that do not form the past tense and past participle according to the rule in 1.16.3. There are three main types of irregular verb:

Type 1, like PUT, for which the past tense and the past participle are both the same as the base;

Type 2, like HEAR, for which the past tense and the past participle, *eg heard*, are the same as each other but different from the base;

Type 3, like WRITE, for which the past tense and past participle are different from each other (*wrote, written*).

Summary of verb forms
1.20
All the forms that a full verb can take may be summarised in the following table:

Table 2

	REGULAR	IRREGULAR			
		Type 1	*Type 2*	*Type 3*	BE
1 Imperative; infinitive; present tense, except 3rd person singular	wait	put	hear	write	be am, are
2 Present, 3rd person singular	waits	puts	hears	writes	is
3 Past tense	waited	put	heard	wrote	was were
4 *-ing* participle	waiting	putting	hearing	writing	being
5 *-ed* participle	waited	put	heard	written	been

Thus, REGULAR verbs have four different forms. An irregular verb may have three, four or five – or eight in the exceptional case of BE.

Verbal groups
1.21
Verbal groups can be of five types:

Type 1   MODAL + INFINITIVE: *could see, ought to see*
Type 2   HAVE + PAST PARTICIPLE: *have telephoned*
Type 3   BE + PRESENT PARTICIPLE: *were waiting*
Type 4   BE + PAST PARTICIPLE: *were placed*
Type 5   DO + INFINITIVE: *did not like, Did you know?*

The first four of those types can be combined with one another to form more complex verbal groups like:

36 George *will have finished* that book by Friday.   (Types 1 & 2)
37 He *has been learning* English for four years.   (Types 2 & 3)
38 By next October, he *will have been learning* it for
   five years.   (Types 1, 2 & 3)
39 The headmaster *could be seen* by everyone.   (Types 1 & 4)
40 The roll *is being called* now.   (Types 3 & 4)

All such groups are formed in the order 1,2,3,4, thus:

1   2   3   4
Modal + HAVE-*ed* + BE-*ing* + BE-*ed*

What is called the LEXICAL MEANING is contained in the *last* word, which is the LEXICAL VERB; but only the *first* word is affected by person, number and tense (as in [37], [39] and [40]), and it is the first word that makes the group finite.

TYPE 1, MODAL + INFINITIVE
1.22
The full verb which follows a modal will always be in the bare infinitive, except in the case of *ought*, thus:

   can see, could see, must see, but *ought to see*

With regard to meaning, the modals express a variety of MOODS or attitudes towards a possible action or state to which the lexical verb (*eg see*) refers, as we shall see in Chapter Fourteen.

TYPE 2, HAVE + PAST PARTICIPLE
1.23
a HAVE is used as a full verb in a sentence like *That man has a gun.*
b HAVE + past participle is an expression of PERFECTIVE ASPECT (see c below), and here HAVE is used as an AUXILIARY. The auxiliary is finite and changes according to person, number and tense.
c If the present tense of the auxiliary is used, the PRESENT PERFECT (13.9) is formed, as in
   1 I *have* just *telephoned* George Lamb.
   In using the present perfective aspect, we refer to an action or state occurring in a PERIOD OF TIME WHICH WE IMAGINE AS CONTINUING UNTIL

NOW. We do not say anything, *eg* by using an ADVERBIAL OF PAST TIME (1.47), to suggest that the period of time is no longer present. We can, however, use other adverbials, such as *just, in the last few minutes, for the last two hundred years*, to indicate the DURATION of the period which we imagine as continuing until now, or to indicate, by a phrase like *till now* or *so far*, that the period does continue until now.

d *Had* + past participle produces the PAST PERFECT (13.21), as in
  41 The headmaster entered. The boys *had* already *assembled.*
In using the past perfective aspect, the speaker refers to an action or state occurring in a period which he imagines as continuing until THEN – 'then' in [41] being the time in the past when the headmaster entered.

e All the modals can precede HAVE + past participle, *have* now being the infinitive in accordance with 1.22. We can thus find examples like:
  36 George *will have finished* that book by Friday.
  which means 'On Friday, he will be able to say, "I have finished this book"'. It is convenient to refer to this use of *will have -ed* as the FUTURE PERFECT. However, *modal + have -ed* more often refers to the past: *you could have seen George* means 'you had the opportunity of seeing him but you did not see him'. Examples of that kind will be discussed in Chapter Fourteen.

f The infinitive, though it does not have tense (1.18,c), can have perfective aspect. The infinitive is simple, in
  42 I am happy (now) *to be* George's friend (now).
    and
  43 I was happy (then) *to be* George's friend (then).
  It has perfective aspect in
  44 I am happy (now) *to have been* George's friend (before now).
    and
  45 I was happy (then) *to have been* George's friend (before then).

TYPE 3, BE + PRESENT PARTICIPLE
1.24
a BE is very often used as a full verb, as in *He was my best friend.*
b BE + present participle is an expression of PROGRESSIVE ASPECT (13.1), in which BE is an auxiliary. *Am, is* and *are* + the participle make up the PRESENT PROGRESSIVE (*eg They are waiting*); *was* and *were* help to make up the PAST PROGRESSIVE (*eg They were waiting*). In using the progressive aspect, whether in the present tense or in the past, the speaker is normally concerned with action in progress, with action that has begun but not ended, or with uncompleted activity or with a temporary state of affairs. Verbs referring to activity[1] which can easily be imagined in these ways

[1] Activity in this context does not necessarily imply movement, as in the example *He was lying on the ground.*

and which can therefore be used freely in the progressive form, are called
ACTION VERBS: they include WALK, RUN, READ, WRITE, WORK,
PLAY, LOOK, LISTEN and so on. Other verbs, referring to states,
and called STATIVE VERBS, do not normally occur in the progressive form.
Notice the use and the avoidance of the progressive in:

46 A What are you doing here? (DO: action verb)
    B I'm waiting for George Lamb. (WAIT: action verb)
    A I know him. I see him. (KNOW, SEE: stative)

Stative verbs include:
  i BE, and HAVE in the sense of 'hold' or 'possess';
  ii Verbs that express the meaning of BE and HAVE more elaborately,
    eg RESEMBLE (= be like), POSSESS, OWN;
  iii Verbs like SEE and HEAR that refer to an involuntary reaction of the
    senses; and
  iv Verbs like KNOW and BELIEVE that refer to a state of the mind.

Verbs in group iii are often preceded by CAN or COULD, as in *I can see
him, Everyone could see that.* For other stative verbs (13.2).

c The progressive can be combined with a modal, or with the perfective or
with a modal and perfective together:

47 George is playing football now. He *will be playing* again tomorrow.
37 He *has been learning* English for four years.
38 ... he *will have been learning* it for five years.

Will be playing, in [47], indicates 'action in progress in the future'; *has
been learning*, in [37], indicates 'action in progress in a period continuing
until now'; and *will have been learning* indicates 'action in progress in a
period ending at some time in the future'. Action in progress before
'then' (past) can be indicated thus:

48 The headmaster entered. The boys *had been waiting* for him.

d The infinitive of action verbs can have progressive aspect, as in

49 Why are you playing? You $\left\{ \begin{array}{l} \text{should } be \\ = \text{ought } to\ be \end{array} \right\}$ *working*.

TYPE 4, BE + PAST PARTICIPLE

1.25

a The auxiliary BE + past participle produces the PASSIVE VOICE, in contrast
with the ACTIVE (VOICE). The verb is 'active' in

50 The headmaster placed George and me in the same class,
but 'passive' in
51 George and I *were placed* in the same class.

In [51], 'what happened to George and me' is given greater prominence
than 'who caused it to happen', either because who caused it to happen is
unknown, or is felt by the speaker to be relatively unimportant, or
perhaps because the speaker prefers not to mention the cause. The

passive enables the speaker to choose, as the grammatical subject and the logical THEME of his sentence, the person or thing affected by the action.[1]

b The passive can be used in the following combinations:

i in the present tense (*People are killed on the roads daily*);

ii in the past tense (*We were placed in the same class*);

iii in the progressive aspect, as in

52 Hurry. The roll *is being called.*

53 We were nearly late. The roll *was being called.*

iv in the perfective aspect, as in

54 You're late. The roll *has been called.*

55 We were late. The roll *had been called.*

v with a modal, as in

56 This work $\left\{ \begin{array}{l} should \\ = ought\ to \end{array} \right\}$ be corrected.

vi with a modal + perfective, as in

36a That book *will have been finished* by Friday.

The roll will be being called, though possible, is rarely found.

Operators
1.26

At the end of 1.21, we saw that it is the first word in a verbal group that makes the group finite. We shall call this first word an OPERATOR since it is the key word in six important operations performed on the VP. Let us illustrate these operations with the group *could see.*

1 THE NEGATIVE OF THE VERBAL GROUP is formed by putting *not* immediately after the operator: *could not see.* When this *not* is unstressed in fluent speech, it has a reduced, or contracted form, pronounced /nt/ (1.31). In informal writing, /nt/ is written *n't* and joined to the operator: *couldn't see.*[2]

2 The INTERROGATIVE is formed from the affirmative by placing the operator *before* the subject and leaving the rest of the sentence unchanged:

They could see it. (affirmative) Could they see it? (interrogative)

When the subject is a group, all the group must come immediately after the operator:

57 Could *everyone in the class* see that?

58 Was *the headmaster of the school* fond of George?

3 The NEGATIVE-INTERROGATIVE will then be produced, informally, by placing the operator + *n't* before the subject:

---

[1] The grammatical subject is not always the logical theme. See example [125] in 1.57d.

[2] In the unreduced form, the operator and *not* are written as two separate words, except in the case of *cannot*. But compare *You cannot (can't) stay here: you must go*, where *can* is negated, with *You can not stay: you may go if you want to* where the lexical verb is negated. *Can not* is not reduced to *can't*. A similar comment could be made about all the modals.

59a Couldn't they see it?

   b Couldn't everyone in the class see it?

   c Wasn't the headmaster of the school fond of George?

There is another form of the negative-interrogative:

60a Could they not see it?

   b Could everyone in the class not see it? etc.

but this is usually reserved for either formal or deliberate style. *Could not everyone see it?* also occurs in formal style.

4 TAG QUESTIONS as in

61a George could see that, couldn't he?

   b You couldn't see that, could you?

   c You could see that, could you not? (formal)

5 An EMPHATIC AFFIRMATIVE, as in the second line of the following:

62 A They couldn't see that, surely?

   B I'm afraid you're wrong. Everyone *could* see it. (the operator here is stressed.)

6 A PRO-FORM FOR THE WHOLE VERB PHRASE (see 1.5c for this meaning of 'pro'). Instead of repeating the whole verb phrase, we can use the operator alone, as in [63B] and [64]:

63 A Could anyone see that?

   B Oh yes, everyone could. (= could see that)

64 I could see that and so could George. (*ie* George could see it too.)

1.27

The operators are a CLOSED SET,[1] namely:

a the ten modals (1.15);

b *have, has* and *had* as auxiliaries for verbal group Type 2 (1.23), and sometimes as parts of the full verb HAVE (1.29);

c *am, is, are, was* and *were,* both as parts of the full verb BE and as auxiliaries forming verbal groups of Types 3 and 4;

d *do, does* and *did* as auxiliaries for verbal group Type 5 (1.28);

e *need, dare* and *used to* (1.30).

TYPE 5, DO + INFINITIVE
1.28

a Not counting the full verbs BE and HAVE, there is no operator in the affirmative of the simple present and simple past of full verbs, *eg He stands, he stood.* For the six operations in 1.26, DO is supplied as an operator. The present tense of DO is regular (1.16.2). except for the pronunciation of does/dʌz/; the past is *did.* Hence, the six operations are

---

[1] A group of items to which new additions to the language cannot be made: *cp* 1.11.

performed on simple tenses as follows:

Operation 1: The headmaster $\begin{Bmatrix} \text{does} \\ \text{did} \end{Bmatrix}$ not like us.

Operation 2: $\begin{Bmatrix} \text{Does} \\ \text{Did} \end{Bmatrix}$ he like George? $\begin{Bmatrix} \text{Do} \\ \text{Did} \end{Bmatrix}$ you (like him)?

Operation 3: $\begin{Bmatrix} \text{Doesn't} \\ \text{Didn't} \end{Bmatrix}$ he like him? $\begin{Bmatrix} \text{Don't} \\ \text{Didn't} \end{Bmatrix}$ you (like him)?

Operation 4: He $\begin{Bmatrix} \text{likes} \\ \text{liked} \end{Bmatrix}$ George, $\begin{Bmatrix} \text{doesn't} \\ \text{didn't} \end{Bmatrix}$ he?

Operation 5: He $\begin{Bmatrix} \text{does} \\ \text{did} \end{Bmatrix}$ like him. I $\begin{Bmatrix} \text{do} \\ \text{did} \end{Bmatrix}$ like him.

Operation 6: He $\begin{Bmatrix} \text{likes} \\ \text{liked} \end{Bmatrix}$ George and so $\begin{Bmatrix} \text{do} \\ \text{did} \end{Bmatrix}$ I.

Remember that every verbal group of Type 5 is formed with the operator (DO) + *infinitive*, so that the negative of *he likes* is *he doesn't like*, and the interrogative of it is *Does he like*; and the affirmative *he liked* becomes *he didn't like* and *Did he like?*

b DO is also used for the negative and emphatic imperative, *eg Do not park here. Don't stop. Do go on. Do be careful.*

THE SPECIAL CASE OF HAVE
1.29
With the full verb HAVE, we must distinguish between HAVE meaning 'hold' or 'possess', as in *That man has a gun*, and HAVE meaning something else, as in *Most people have a bath every day*. HAVE meaning something else requires DO in the six operations in 1.26. Thus:

  65 I don't have a bath on a cold morning.
      or
  66 I have tea for breakfast and so does my wife.

HAVE meaning 'hold' or 'possess' can either act as its own operator or take the operator DO. Thus:

  67 Have you any money on you?
  68 I have some money and so has George.
      and
  69 I asked John for some money but he hadn't any.
      or
  70 Do you have any money? Does John?
  71 I didn't have any – nor did George.

In the past interrogative, DO is now commonly preferred even when HAVE means 'hold' or 'possess', as in

  72 Did you have enough money?

Generally speaking, examples [67], [68] and [69] would be typical of British English rather than American.

NEED, DARE AND USED

1.30

a NEED and DARE are used both as full verbs, with the four regular forms given in 1.20, Table 2, and as modals with one form each. As modals, NEED and DARE tend to occur only in the negative and interrogative and their use is usually restricted to the following operations:

Operation 1: You need not wait.   I dare not go yet.
Operation 2: Need we wait?   Dare we go yet?
Operation 4: We need not go yet,   We dare not go yet, dare we?
need we?

With operation 4, We $\left\{ \begin{array}{l} need \\ dare \end{array} \right\}$ *not go yet, do we?* is also found.

b Alternatively, we can use the full-verb pattern, thus:

(1) You don't need to wait.   I don't dare (to) go yet.
(2) Do we need to wait?   Do we dare (to) go?

and so on, as in 1.28.

A modal must be followed immediately by the infinitive of a full verb, so NEED must be used in the full-verb pattern in a sentence like *Do you need anything?*

c USED, /juːst/, which is followed by the infinitive with *to*, fits into the same pattern as OUGHT. It functions only as an auxiliary to make up a past tense, indicating a past state of affairs or past habitual action, generally in contrast with a different state of affairs or different habit in the present.

73 I used to write my letters by hand, but now I type them (14.30).

THE OPERATORS SUMMARISED

1.31

The bigger numbers refer to the five types of verbal group in 1.21:

Table 3

OPERATOR	CONTRACTED NEGATIVE	OPERATOR	CONTRACTED NEGATIVE
1 will ('ll)[1]	won't /wəunt/	2 have ('ve)	haven't
would ('d)	wouldn't	has ('s)[4]	hasn't
shall	shan't /ʃɑːnt/	had ('d)[5]	hadn't
should	shouldn't	3, 4 am ('m)[6]	—
can	can't	is ('s)[7]	isn't
could	couldn't	are ('re)	aren't
may	—[2]	was	wasn't
might	mightn't	were	weren't
must	mustn't /mʌsnt/	5 do	don't /dəunt/
ought to	oughtn't[3] to	does	doesn't
		did	didn't

Table 3a

OPERATOR	CONTRACTED NEGATIVE
need	needn't
dare	daren't
used to	use(d)n't/juːsnt/[3] to

Notes:

1 The contracted forms in brackets are commonly used in fluent speech and informal writing, and can be followed by *not*, eg *It's not here.* These reduced forms cannot act as the first nor as the final syllable of a clause: thus *'ll* cannot replace *will* in *Will you have some tea?* nor in *I won't have any but George will.* A clause can end with *'ll not* etc.; but *'ll not* etc., cannot replace *won't* etc. in the negative-interrogative, as in *Won't you sit down?* Whether the contracted form is used or not may also depend on the sound before: thus *'ll* is unlikely to replace *will* in *The hall will be full.* Regard *'s not* and *isn't* etc. as equally acceptable.

2 *Mayn't* occurs rarely in modern English.

3 *Didn't ought to* is commonly heard in substandard English. Similarly, the informal *didn't use(d) to* is commonly heard instead of *usedn't to.*

4 *He's, she's, it's* can be a contracted form of *he has* etc., or of *he is* etc. The contracted form is commonly used when HAVE is an auxiliary (*He's been away*) but is generally avoided when HAVE is a full verb, as in *He has a gun.*

5 *He'd* and *she'd* can be a reduced form of *he would* etc., as in verbal group Type 1, or of *he had* etc., as in Type 2. The infinitive follows *He'd* in Type 1, the past participle follows it in Type 2.

6 *'m not* is used as a reduced negative (*I'm not ready yet*) but is replaced by *aren't* in the negative-interrogative (*Aren't I good enough? I'm good enough, aren't I?*)

7 Distinguish between *it's*, with apostrophe *s*, reduced form of *it is* or *it has*, and the possessive *its*, no apostrophe (1.8a, iii).

Agreement with the verb
1.32

Compared with other European languages, English provides very few cases where the form of the verb depends on the number and person of the subject. These few cases can be summarised as follows:

Table 4

SUBJECT	PRESENT TENSE	PAST TENSE
I	am, have, do, know	was
he, she, it	is, has, does, knows	was
you, we, they	are, have, do, know	were

D Different functions of the noun phrase
1.33
In addition to being the subject, NP can also be:

a the COMPLEMENT of the subject + BE (COMPLEMENT – that which COM-PLE*tes*). *George was my best friend* can be analysed into

SUBJECT	PREDICATE	
	Verb	*Complement*
George	was	*my best friend*

The verb in such an example merely serves to join the subject and the complement together. For that reason, the full verb BE is known as a COPULA (= that which joins): it is often omitted in newspaper headlines, telegrams and notes; and in some languages there is no literal translation for it. There are other copulas, such as BECOME: (10.3). When the complement is a noun, it must agree with the subject in number and gender:

74 George was *a good actor*.
75 Jane and Mary were *good actresses*.

b the DIRECT OBJECT of a verb, as in

SUBJECT	PREDICATE	
	Verb	*Direct object*
I	knew	*George Lamb*
George	finished	*his work*

A verb that takes an object is called TRANSITIVE; or, to be more accurate, we could say that it is used transitively. Some verbs, like the full verbs DO and ENJOY are only used transitively. Others, like TELEPHONE can be used transitively, as in example [1], or intransitively, as in *George has just telephoned*. Others, like RISE and LIE are only used intransitively;

c the INDIRECT OBJECT, as in

SUBJECT	PREDICATE		
	Verb	*Indirect Object*	*Direct Object*
76 The headmaster	gave	*George*	a new book
77 He	found	*George*	a seat

[76] could be re-worded *The headmaster gave a new book to George*; [77], *He found a seat for George*.
Either or both of the two objects can be a pronoun, as follows:

A The headmaster $\left\{ \begin{matrix} gave \\ found \end{matrix} \right\}$ George $\left\{ \begin{matrix} a \text{ a new book} \\ b \text{ the book} \end{matrix} \right.$

B The headmaster $\left\{ \begin{matrix} gave \\ found \end{matrix} \right\}$ him $\left\{ \begin{matrix} a \text{ a new book} \\ b \text{ the book} \end{matrix} \right.$

C The headmaster $\begin{Bmatrix} \text{gave} \\ \text{found} \end{Bmatrix}$ George $\begin{Bmatrix} \text{a one} \\ \text{b} \text{ —} \end{Bmatrix}$

D The headmaster $\begin{Bmatrix} \text{gave} \\ \text{found} \end{Bmatrix}$ him $\begin{Bmatrix} \text{a one} \\ \text{b it } (\text{or gave it him}) \end{Bmatrix}$

although *gave it him* for Db would be more widely acceptable.

For Cb, we would have to say The headmaster $\begin{Bmatrix} \text{gave} \\ \text{found} \end{Bmatrix}$ it $\begin{Bmatrix} \text{to} \\ \text{for} \end{Bmatrix}$ George.

d the COMPLEMENT OF THE OBJECT, as in

SUBJECT	PREDICATE		
	Verb	*Direct object*	*Complement*
78 He	found	$\begin{Bmatrix} \text{George} \\ \text{him} \end{Bmatrix}$	*a bright pupil.*

Note that the SURFACE STRUCTURE of [77] and [78] is the same: both sentences are constructed on the pattern NP + *verb* + NP + NP. But while [77] can be re-worded *He found a seat for George*, [78] can be re-worded *He found George to be a bright pupil*. The presence of BE in the re-wording of [78] suggests that what the headmaster actually thought, and probably said, was *George is a bright pupil*.

e the OBJECT OF A PREPOSITION, as in

4 . . . in *the same class*.

7 . . . on *a high platform*.

In [4], the NP, *the same class*, is the object of, or is 'governed' by, the PREPOSITION *in*: in [7], the NP, *a high platform*, is governed by the preposition *on*;

f in APPOSITION to another NP, as in

79 Your friend *George Lamb* has just telephoned.

80 George Lamb, *your old school friend*, has just telephoned.

In [79], the NP *George Lamb* is in apposition to the NP *your friend*; and in [80], *your old school friend* is in apposition to *George Lamb*. There is a distinction between those two examples which is found in other parts of English grammar (2.26). In [79], *George Lamb* is RESTRICTIVE; it restricts the meaning of *your friend* by providing a definite answer to the question *Which friend?* Note the absence of commas in [79], and the continuity of the intonation. In [80], *George Lamb*, being unique (1.6d), does not need to be modified; *your old school friend* is NON-RESTRICTIVE; it does not tell us which George Lamb has telephoned but merely adds information about him. In [80], the NP in non-restrictive apposition is placed between commas and breaks up the intonation of the sentence.

The objective case
1.34

a As direct object or indirect object of a verb, or as object of a preposition, five of the personal pronouns have a separate form and are then said to be in the OBJECTIVE CASE. The second member of each of the following pairs is in the objective case:

I/*me*; he/*him*; she/*her*; we/*us*; they/*them*

You, it and *one* remain unchanged. Notice the difference between

[8] He did not like us, George and me, very much

and

[51] George and I were placed in the same class.

George and I is the subject of sentence [51]. In [8], *George and me* is the object of *did not like*, in apposition to *us*.

b When the direct or indirect object has the same reference as the subject, a REFLEXIVE PRONOUN is used as follows:

SINGULAR	PLURAL
I have hurt *myself*	We have hurt *ourselves*
You have hurt *yourself*	You have hurt *yourselves*

He has hurt *himself* ⎫
She has hurt *herself*   ⎬   They have hurt *themselves*
The dog has hurt *itself* ⎭

One can hurt *oneself* doing that.

An example of a reflexive pronoun as indirect object would be

George found himself a new book;

and an example after a preposition:

The headmaster often talked to himself.

However, the ordinary personal pronoun, objective case, is used in examples like

I enjoy having my friends $\begin{Bmatrix} around \\ by \\ near \end{Bmatrix}$ me.

I'm going to take this book up to bed with me.[1]

Either the ordinary pronoun or the reflexive (emphatic) one can be used in examples like

The headmaster put George and $\begin{Bmatrix} me \\ =myself \end{Bmatrix}$ in the same class.

c Note that the emphatic pronoun ending in -*self* can also be used to focus attention not only on the object but also on the subject, as in

We spoke to the headmaster himself, not to his secretary.

The headmaster $\begin{Bmatrix} himself\ met\ us\ at\ the\ door. \\ =met\ us\ at\ the\ door\ himself. \end{Bmatrix}$

d The only other examples of objective case in English are found in *whom*, and in the absence of the relative pronoun, as explained in 2.29.

---

[1] One way of explaining these two examples is the following: A contrast is made in 'I've not hurt *him* but I've hurt *myself*'; but no such contrast is likely between *I enjoy having my friends around me* and **I enjoy having my friends around him*.

E Prepositional phrases
1.35

a A preposition normally precedes an NP. It can be separated from its NP as in:

81 *What* was the headmaster's desk standing *on*?

82 The *platform* that the headmaster's desk stood *on* was very narrow and he often fell off it.

But the association between preposition and NP is always there.

b A primary function of an English preposition is to express a relationship in SPACE between one thing (*eg the desk*) and another (*eg the platform*) (8.1). It can refer to POSITION or to MOVEMENT IN ONE DIRECTION OR ANOTHER. It can express position or movement in relation to something that the speaker imagines as a POINT or place (with no dimension, or with dimensions that do not matter); or as a LINE (with one dimension); or as a SURFACE on which something can rest (with two dimensions); or as a SPACE in which something can be enclosed (with three dimensions). Commonly-used English prepositions can therefore fit into the following scheme:

Table 5

	POINT	LINE OR SURFACE	SPACE OR AREA
Movement ——→ X	to X	on *or* onto[1]	in or into
Resulting position OX	at X	on	in
Movement ←—— X	(away) from X	off	out of
Resulting position O X	away from X	off	out of

Similarly, we can have movement (or position) ALONG a line, ACROSS a surface, or THROUGH a space; or position after one has gone across a line or surface, or through a space.

c Note that *to* can be either the infinitive marker, as in *to come*, or a preposition, as in

83 The headmaster walked slowly to the door.

d Prepositions can also express relationships in time (8.7), as in *at nine o'clock, on Saturday, in 1964*; and can express other ideas, such as DESTINATION or PURPOSE (*for*, as in *This parcel is for George*), AGENCY (*by*,

[1] This preposition can be written *onto* or *on to*. See 1.41a.

as in *It was left here by his mother*) or INSTRUMENT (*with*, as in *He cut the string with his penknife*).

1.36

A preposition + NP forms a PREPOSITIONAL PHRASE, which can be

a an ADVERBIAL OF PLACE (POSITION) answering the question *Where?*, as in

   7 The headmaster's desk stood *on a high platform*;

   or an adverbial of place (MOVEMENT) answering the question *Where to?*:

   83 The headmaster walked slowly *to the door*;

b an ADVERBIAL OF TIME, answering the question *When?*;

   84 I first met George *in 1968*;

c SOME OTHER ADVERBIAL PHRASE, *eg* (*Handle this*) *with care*;

d a POSTMODIFIER (1.7) in an NP, as in

   85 The desk *on the platform* was covered with books;

e the COMPLEMENTATION OF AN ADJECTIVE, as in

   86 George was good *at arithmetic*.

We often have a choice of preposition according to the exact relationship in space between, say, the desk and the platform. Thus:

87 The desk was $\begin{Bmatrix} \text{on} \\ \text{in front of} \\ \text{beside} \end{Bmatrix}$ the platform

Sometimes, as in [86], there is no choice: we have to learn – or to consult a reference book such as this to find out – what prepositions are normally associated with what adjectives: (7.20).

Verbs followed by prepositions
1.37

Constructions on the pattern of verb + preposition + NP are very common in English. They are of four main kinds:

1 First, we can use a verb in a LITERAL sense, often expressing physical action, and can follow it with a prepositional phrase, also using the preposition literally, as in 1.35, *eg*:

Table 6

	VERB	PREPOSITIONAL PHRASE	
		Preposition	NP
	1	2	3
We	ran	across	the road

The verb phrase *ran across the road* falls into three separate parts. We could substitute other verbs for *ran*, other prepositions for *across*, other noun phrases for *the road*, expanding Table 6 as follows:

Table 6a

1	2	3
a go, come, walk, run, step, climb	to, at, away from	c that spot, the door
b stay, stand, wait, live, work, play	on, onto, off	d the road, the roof
	in, into, out of across, along, through	e this room, a town

From Table 6a, we can make up many different verb phrases; *eg*

> *come to the door*   *work in a town*
> *wait at that spot*   *walk across the road*
> *climb onto the roof*   *stay away from the door*
> *run along the road*   *stay out of this room*

However, there are restrictions on what we can do with that table. Verbs expressing movement from one place to another (1a) have to be used with prepositions expressing·movement as in Table 5. Verbs not expressing movement from one place to another (1b) have to be used with prepositions expressing position. The choice of preposition will depend on whether the NP following it refers to a point on the map of our environment (*that spot, the door*), or to a line or surface (*the road, the roof*), or to a space or area (*this room, a town*).

2 Second, we have verbs like LOOK and LISTEN which can either be intransitive (*Look! Listen!*) or transitive. If transitive, with a direct object, they require a preposition (*Look at this. Listen to me.*). We shall call LOOK AT and LISTEN TO PREPOSITIONAL VERBS. Some prepositional verbs can only be used transitively, *eg The boys were longing for the holidays.* Thus, instead of Tables 6 and 6a, we have a two-part Table 7:

Table 7

	PREPOSITIONAL VERB	DIRECT OBJECT
You	look at	this
You	listen to	me
They	were longing for	the holidays

3 Third, verb + preposition may form an IDIOM, *ie* a phrase whose meaning is different from the combined literal meaning of its separate parts, as in
    88 I came across an interesting example the other day.
We shall call *come across*, as used in [88], a PHRASAL VERB OF TYPE 1. Phrasal verbs of other types will be introduced in the following paragraphs.
4 As well as the three kinds of construction mentioned above, we have the pattern *verb + object + preposition + NP* as in
    89 Everyone congratulated George on his success.

F Adverb particles
1.38
In is a preposition if it 'governs' an NP (*eg in the same class*). The same word has a similar meaning but fits into a different pattern in *the headmaster came in*. There, *in* does not govern any NP and in that case we call it an ADVERB PARTICLE.[1] Some words, like *in* and *on*, can be either prepositions or adverb particles; some, like *into* and *onto*, are only prepositions; others, like *away* and *back*, function as adverb particles but not as prepositions: see 8.1.

Verbs followed by adverb particles
1.39
a Phrases on the pattern of *come in*, as in example [6], are very common in English. They consist of verb + adverb particle as two separate lexical 'items. *Come* could be replaced by *go, walk, run*, etc.; *in* by *out, up, down*, etc. In those phrases, *in, out, up, down*, etc. have their basic physical meaning.

b The same pattern is frequently used but with the adverb particle having some secondary meaning. For example, *on* can mean 'forward', as in *go on, keep on, play on*; *up* can indicate completion of an act, as in *eat up; drink up, wake up*, or a stop, as in *give up*; *in*, collapse, as in *give in*; *off*, departure, as in *set off*; *out*, departure, or spreading, or disappearing, as in *get out, set out, spread out, die out*; *away*, disappearing, as in *die away*.

c Combinations like *give up, give in* (both meaning 'surrender') or *come about* (=happen) are idioms, and we shall call these PHRASAL VERBS OF TYPE 2, which are intransitive.

1.40
a Verb + particle can form a transitive group as in
90 George took his coat off. He took it off.
The particle can also come between the verb and the object, but not if the object is a personal pronoun, as in
91 He took off his coat. He took it off.
The meaning of many such constructions need cause no trouble so long as the primary meaning of the verb and of the particle is understood. Other constructions on that pattern are *put on, give back, throw away, break down*.

b Again, the particle can have a secondary meaning, as in *keep a light on, give something up* (=abandon it), *send a letter off*.

c Idioms on this pattern include combinations like *bring a boy up* (=educate him). We shall call them PHRASAL VERBS, TYPE 3. A distinction

---

[1] Also called 'prepositional adverb'.

should be made between LITERAL and IDIOMATIC meanings; *bring up* is used literally in *Bring the visitor up*, ie bring him upstairs, but idiomatically in *They brought George up as their own child*. Furthermore, a distinction should be made between a phrasal verb of Type 2, *eg break down*, meaning 'collapse' (*She broke down when she heard the sad news*) and one of Type 3, *eg break down* as in *Please break these figures down*, meaning 'analyse them'.

d Note that the preposition in 1.37, if it is a monosyllable, is unstressed. The particle in 1.39 and 1.40 is stressed.

Go up to my office
1.41

a A direction may be indicated twice or even three times in the same phrase, thus:

92a' Go up to my office.

 b Go on (=forward) up to my office.

Up in [92a], and both *on* and *up* in [92b], are adverb particles, stressed; and *to* is a preposition, unstressed, governing an NP (*my office*). Note the difference between *run out onto the pitch* as in 1.35 and 1.37, and *walk on* (=forward) *to the end of the road*.

b One or more parts of a phrase on the model of [92], may have a secondary meaning, *eg on* in [92b] or in *Get on with your work*.

c Idioms on this pattern include *put up with* (=tolerate), and *run out of* as in *We've run out of bread* (=exhausted our supplies of it). We shall call phrases like *run out of*, in that sense, and *put up with*, PHRASAL VERBS OF TYPE 4.

Phrasal verbs summarised
1.42

We can now summarise the four types of phrasal verb as follows:

Table 8

TYPE	STRUCTURE	EXAMPLE
1	Verb + preposition	We *came across* an old man.
2	Verb + adverb particle	Don't *give in*.
3	Verb + object + adverb particle	*Bring* a child *up*. *Bring up* a
	or Verb + adverb particle + object	child. *Bring him up* well.
4	Verb + adverb particle + preposition	We've *run out of* bread.

See Chapter Twelve.

G Adjectives
1.43
a In *a good friend*, the adjective is used ATTRIBUTIVELY. In *George was very good at arithmetic*, the adjective occurs in the predicate as an OBLIGATORY complement of subject + BE, and there it is used PREDICATIVELY. Many adjectives can be used in both those ways; but some, *eg afraid, asleep, awake*, are only used predicatively, while others, *eg chief, principal*, only occur attributively. In a few cases, the meaning of the adjective differs according to its position in the clause. Thus:

93 George was late (= he was not early).

94 The late George Lamb (= George Lamb, who is now dead).

b An adjective that can be used predicatively may also complement the direct object, as in

95 He found George intelligent.

ie He found George to be intelligent. The construction in [95], can also be used to indicate the RESULT of the activity to which the verb refers, as in

96 All the people on the island paint their houses white.

In that case, *to be* cannot be inserted before the adjective.

c A few adjectives, particularly *open*, can combine with a verb expressing physical action, like *break*, to form a construction which follows the same patterns as phrasal verb type 3 (1.40), thus:

97 The thieves broke the safe open. They broke it open.

or They broke open the safe. (*Cp* [90] and [91])

1.44
a Some adjectives express a condition or a quality of which there are degrees, in which case we may call them GRADABLE. *Good* is gradable: there are degrees of goodness. We can have a HIGH DEGREE (*very good*), an EXCESSIVE DEGREE (*too good*), a SUFFICIENT DEGREE (*good enough*) or an INSUFFICIENT DEGREE (*not good enough*). We can COMPARE *good*: it can have a POSITIVE DEGREE (*good*), a COMPARATIVE (DEGREE) (*better*) and a SUPERLATIVE (DEGREE) (*best*). Adjectives like *complete* and *unique* are not gradable; they are not normally compared, nor modified by *very, too* or *enough*.

b Certain adjectives, *viz* those referring to shape (*round, tall*) or size (*big, narrow*) can only modify count nouns.

c Adjectives, like verbs, can refer to action, although they are more often stative (1.24). *Foolish* refers to action in

98 George was being rather foolish,

for the fact that BE is, exceptionally, used in the progressive in that sentence indicates that the meaning is 'George was acting rather foolishly'. A 'stative' adjective, like *tall*, could hardly replace *foolish* in [98].

H Adverbials
1.45
An adverbial can be a single-word adverb, *eg here, there, now, then, often,* or an adverb particle, as in 1.38, or an ADVERBIAL PHRASE, like *twenty years ago*. In the sentence *The desk was on a high platform*, the prepositional phrase *on a high platform* is also an adverbial phrase used as an adverbial of place.

1.46
In the sentence *The desk* $\begin{Bmatrix} was \\ stood \end{Bmatrix}$ *on the platform,* the adverbial is OBLIGATORY. The sentence could not end at $\begin{Bmatrix} was \\ stood \end{Bmatrix}$ and something must be added to finish it. An adverbial is usually required after SIT, *eg We sat down*, and is obligatory after LIE in *We were lying down*, as well as after LIVE, which can be followed by an adverbial of place or of time or of manner, *eg He lived* $\begin{cases} in\ Rome. \\ two\ hundred\ years\ ago. \\ happily. \end{cases}$

An adverbial, or an adjective, is also obligatory after certain commonly-used verbs + object, as in

99 The headmaster put George and me in the same class.

*He put George and me would be incomplete. PUT, like PLACE and LAY (in the sense of 'put down'), therefore requires something after its object: it could be a prepositional phrase, or an adverbial phrase like *over there*, or an adverb particle, *eg down*, or sometimes an adjective, as in *Put your desk straight*.

1.47
Many adverbials are ADJUNCTS: they provide additional information, are part of the structure of the clause, but are OPTIONAL, *ie* not essential to the structure. Adjuncts include adverbials of

a PLACE (POSITION)   telling us where (*eg in the hall*)
b PLACE (DIRECTION)   telling us where to (*eg to the door*)
c TIME WHEN   telling us when (*eg at nine o'clock*)
d TIME, DURATION   telling us how long (*eg for 10 days*)
e RELATIVE TIME   telling us how long ago (*eg just*)
f FREQUENCY   telling us how often (*eg always*)
g DEGREE   telling us to what extent (*eg almost*)
h MANNER   telling us in what way (*eg carefully, with care*)

Adverbs of manner
1.48
a Adverbs of manner are normally formed by adding the SUFFIX *-ly* to an

adjective, so that *His work was careful* can be re-worded *He did his work carefully*. A few adverbs of manner have the same form as the adjective; for example, *hard* is an adjective in *This is hard work* but an adverb of manner in *George works hard*. Note that *hardly* is an adverb of degree, as in *I hardly know him*.

b Adverbs of manner can be gradable (1.44a), *eg carefully*, or not gradable, *eg perfectly*. Gradable adverbs can be compared: *more carefully, most carefully*.

Position of adverbials
1.49
a Adverbials can be found in three main positions – at the end, at the beginning or in the middle of a clause.

b The END POSITION is a very common one, as in

8 He did not like George and me *very much*.

10 George did his work *perfectly*.

16 I've found some mistakes *already*.

18 I haven't found any *yet*.

100 I met George $\begin{cases} \textit{twenty years ago/then.} \\ \textit{at school/there.} \\ \textit{several times a week.} \end{cases}$

101 I met him $\begin{cases} \textit{here.} \\ \textit{today.} \end{cases}$

c An adverbial is not normally placed between a verb and its object. This rule is broken only if there is a good reason, as in

102 I remember *very clearly* the morning that George first came to school.

where the object is much longer than the adverbial, and where, for the sake of clarity, *very clearly* should come closer to *remember* than to *came to school*.

d We often put certain adjuncts, *eg* adverbials of place (position), time and frequency, at THE BEGINNING of a clause, so as to focus attention on the location, time or frequency of an occurrence. Thus:

103 $\left.\begin{array}{l} \textit{Twenty years ago,} \\ \textit{At school,} \end{array}\right\}$ George was inclined to be fat.

104 *Sometimes* George and I went swimming together.

1.50
Single-word adverbs of frequency, *eg always, never, often, sometimes*, the adverbs of relative time *just* and *still*, and adverbs of degree (15.25) *eg almost, hardly, quite*, normally occupy a MEDIAL POSITION. This is immediately *after* the operator (1.26) in any complex verbal group (1.21), immediately *after* the full verb BE, and *before* any other simple verb:

105   We {
have often seen him.   We have seen him often.
are still waiting.
are quite tired.
still have a little money.
sometimes go to Spain. }   Sometimes we go to Italy.

Already can also occur in the medial position, and so can *yet*, which will then follow *operator + not or n't*. *Often* and *sometimes* may occur at the end of the clause, to emphasise the frequency of an event, or may occur at the beginning to make a contrast with something that has already been said, as in [105]. *Ever* and *never* normally remain in the medial position, though *never*, followed by an obligatory INVERSION of subject and operator, may come at the beginning:

106   Never have I seen him so angry!

Very; very much
1.51

a Traditionally, *very* is classified as an adverb. It is certainly an optional adjunct (and often an unnecessary one). It is used as an INTENSIFIER (15.28) premodifying a gradable adjective or adverb, *eg very good, very carefully, very often*. It can be used before an adjective in the superlative, *eg the very best*, but not immediately before a comparative. *Much, very much* and *far* can be used instead before a comparative, *eg (very) much better, far better*.

b *Very* cannot modify a verb; but a gradable verb can be modified by *very much*, as in

[8] He did not like us very much.

Other adverbs: conjuncts and disjuncts
1.52

a *Yet*, as used in example [10], (*Yet George always did his work.*) falls outside the structure of that sentence. Its function there is to form a logical link between what is said in one sentence (example [9], and what is said in the next [10]. We shall therefore call it a CONJUNCT (15.31). Other typical conjuncts are *Besides* and *Therefore*. Note that the conjunct *Yet* begins the sentence; but the *adj*unct (1.47) *yet* comes at the end of example [18] (*I haven't found any yet*).

b If we begin example [8] (*He did not like us very much*) with the adverb *Naturally*, that would also fall outside the structure of the sentence. It would express the speaker's attitude towards the statement he is about to make and would be equivalent to *It seems to me natural that ...* We shall call such an adverb a DISJUNCT (15.30). Other typical disjuncts would be *Honestly* and *Of course*. Note that the disjunct *Naturally* would normally begin the sentence, while the adjunct would end it, as in *He did not speak naturally*, *ie* in a natural way.

I Co-ordination
1.53

Each separate part of the structure of a clause can be duplicated or further added to by CO-ORDINATION. The subject is duplicated in

    107 George and I were good friends,

the two parts of the subject being joined by the CONJUNCTION *and*. There are three parts to the subject in

    108 George, Robert and I were always together.

In such a case, it is usual to separate the parts by commas, using the conjunction to join the last two parts only. Similarly, the predicate has more than one part in

    109 We always worked and played together.

    110 We ran, jumped and shouted for joy.

We can have similar co-ordination between two or more parts of the object, between two or more prepositional phrases, and so on. Alternative co-ordination is effected by the conjunction *or*:

    111 We take our holidays in July or August.

1.54

Co-ordination can sometimes be ambiguous. *He spoke to George and me* may mean that he spoke to both of us together or to each of us separately. We could express the idea of 'separately' by saying

    112 He spoke both to George and (to) me.

Similarly, *or* serves two different functions in

    113 The desk stood on a dais or platform

        and

    114 Your book is in your desk or on that shelf.

In [113], *or platform* explains the meaning of *dais*. In [114], there are two alternatives which we can make clearer by saying

    114a Your book is either in your desk or on that shelf.

A negative form of [114a] would be

    115 Your book is neither in your desk nor on that shelf.

J Types of clause structure
1.55

In making up a clause in English, we have a choice of FIVE BASIC SENTENCE PATTERNS in which all the elements are obligatory. Each follows the fundamental pattern NP + VP (1.5, 1.13). In each, the subject comes first and is followed by a verb: it is only the composition of the VP that changes. The VP may contain the following elements: VERB, INTRANSITIVE (referred to as *Vi* below); VERB, TRANSITIVE (*Vt*): BE or another COPULA (1.33a); ADJECTIVE (*Adj*); ADVERBIAL (*Adv*); COMPLEMENT (*C*); DIRECT OBJECT (*dO*); and INDIRECT OBJECT (*iO*). These symbols are used in Table 9 below.

Table 9

THE FIVE TYPES OF CLAUSE STRUCTURE

Type	*Structure of VP*		*Examples*
1	*Vi* +	a —	We waited
		b *Adv*	We sat down
2	BE + *C*	a NP	He was {my friend
		b *Adj*	intelligent
		c *Adv*	in my class}
3	*Vt* + *dO* +	a —	I made a mistake
		b *Adv*	I put the key in the lock
4	*Vt* + *iO* + *dO*	a (to)	I gave him an answer
		b (for)	He made me a suit
5	*Vt* + *dO* + *C*	a NP	I found him a bore
		b *Adj*	I found him dull

Each of those basic patterns can be expanded by modifiers, optional adjuncts and co-ordination, to form a great variety in the superstructure of the clause. We shall see in the next two chapters how clauses can be combined within a sentence to make that variety much greater; and we shall see in Chapter Ten how the five basic patterns can be further subdivided.

1.56

Producing 'good grammar' is often a question of fitting a verb into the pattern or patterns appropriate to it. For example, TELL will fit into basic pattern 3 (*He told the truth*) and 4 (*He told me the truth*). SAY and EXPLAIN will fit into 3, with or without the optional addition of a prepositional phrase, as in

116 I {said 'Good morning'} / {explained the answer} (to him);

but neither SAY nor EXPLAIN will fit into 4. Lists of commonly-used verbs will be found in Chapter Ten arranged according to the patterns in which they fit.

Common variations on the basic patterns
1.57

a   Pattern 1 in Table 9 is avoided if the verb is BE meaning 'exist'. To re-word *Three exceptions exist*, using BE, we should have to use the pattern *There* + BE + subject, as in

117 There are three exceptions (*There BE* unstressed).

b   Similarly, pattern 2 is usually avoided when the subject is indefinite

(1.7b), so that while it is grammatical to say

118 $\begin{Bmatrix} \text{A desk was} \\ \text{Some books were} \end{Bmatrix}$ on the $\begin{Bmatrix} \text{platform} \\ \text{shelf} \end{Bmatrix}$

it would be more idiomatic to say

119 $\begin{Bmatrix} \text{There was a desk} \\ \text{There were some books} \end{Bmatrix}$ on the $\begin{Bmatrix} \text{platform} \\ \text{shelf} \end{Bmatrix}$

The pattern in [119] is also used with NUMERALS, as in

120 There were thirty-six (boys) in our class.

There BE is unstressed in [119] and [120]. An alternative to [119] and [120] in narrative style would be a complete reversal of the normal word-order, as in

121 On the platform, $\begin{Bmatrix} \text{was} \\ \text{stood} \end{Bmatrix}$ a strange-looking old man.

c Pattern 2c is reversed when *Adv = Here* or *There*, stressed, and when the speaker is drawing attention to the presence of a person or thing:

122 $\begin{Bmatrix} \text{Here} \\ \text{There} \end{Bmatrix}$ is $\begin{Bmatrix} \text{Uncle Jack.} \\ \text{an interesting example.} \end{Bmatrix}$

But a personal pronoun subject comes before BE when *Here* or *There* begins the sentence:

122a There they are. Here I am;

though *Here am I* is possible in literary style or in contexts like

122b Here am I, trying to help you and what thanks do I get?

d Pattern 1b may take the form:

123 In walked the headmaster. Here comes the train. There goes my bus.

This variation requires an intransitive verb of motion, and does not occur in the progressive. A personal pronoun subject will, again, come before the verb:

124 Away they went. There they go. Here I come.

Patterns 2, 3, 4 and 5 can be varied, especially in informal speech, so as to bring to the fore an element that the speaker wishes to stress, as in the second part of

125 (I can take your suitcase.) Heavy trunks I *can't* take.

Similarly, *Very intelligent he was. In the lock I put it. Five dollars I gave you. Rather charming I found her.*

The subject of a sentence like [125] can be identified by converting the sentence into a question requiring the answer *Yes* or *No* in which case the subject comes immediately after the operator, thus: *Can't I take heavy trunks?*

K Types of question
1.58
a YES/NO QUESTIONS require an answer in which either *Yes* or *No* is stated or implied, as in

126 Have you met George Lamb? (Yes, I have *or* No, I haven't)
YES/NO QUESTIONS begin with an operator (1.26) and follow the pattern operator + subject + rest of the verb. They normally end on a rising intonation. A *Yes/No* question can also be formed simply by giving a rising intonation to an affirmative construction, as in
127 You've met George Lamb?
Notice how a *There*-sentence is converted into a question:
128 Was there a desk on the platform?
    Were there any books on the shelf? (*Cp* [119])
Contrast [128] with *Was George there?* which is the interrogative form of *George was there.*

b *Yes/No* questions are frequently asked, particularly in conversation, by means of a statement followed by a TAG QUESTION (1.26,4). A commonly used tag question is one in which an affirmative statement is followed by negative or vice versa. In either case, both the statement and the tag will have a falling intonation, marked ` in these examples:
a You've met George Làmb, hàven't you?
b You lìke him, dòn't you?
c You haven't met his còusin, hàve you?
d You don't know his bròther, dò you?
In those examples, the tag question asks for confirmation of the statement just made. Other tag questions have a rising intonation:
e You've met George Lamb, háven't you?
f You haven't met his cousin, háve you?
In e and f the tag expresses some doubt about the truth of the statement and invites the hearer to say what the truth is. We can also have an affirmative statement followed by an affirmative, but with a rising intonation. This can express a wide range of attitudes on the part of the speaker, from casual enquiry, as in
g You've locked the dóor, háve you?
to heavy sarcasm or threatening anger, as in
h You've done that agàin, háve you?
Whatever the meaning of the tag, its verb must echo the operator in the statement: *have..haven't, was..wasn't, could..couldn't* etc. If there is no operator in the statement, then *do, does* or *did* must be used in the tag. In a *There*-sentence, *there* acts as the subject of the tag, as in
i There was a desk on the platform, wasn't there?
If an indefinite pronoun is the subject of the statement, then *they* is generally used in the tag:
j Everyone has been told what to do, haven't they? (1.12b).

c WH-QUESTIONS begin with a '*Wh*-question word', *What, Who, Which, Where, When, Why, How, How many*, etc. *Who* can only be used as a pronoun, but *What* can be used both as a pronoun and as a noun modifier:

129 A Who is that?   B George Lamb.
    A What is that?   B A screwdriver.
    A What boy, *or* What make of car, is that?

Which can be used both as a pronoun and as a noun modifier, and it can refer to both personal and non-personal nouns. Whereas *What* $\left\{ \begin{array}{l} boy \\ car \end{array} \right\}$

means *What one of all the* $\left\{ \begin{array}{l} boys \\ cars \end{array} \right\}$ in general, we say *Which* $\left\{ \begin{array}{l} boy \\ car \end{array} \right\}$ in trying to identify one of a limited set, as in

130 I can see several cars. Which (car) is yours?

Wh-questions can be subdivided into (i) those asking for the subject of a sentence, and (ii) those asking for any part of the sentence except the subject.

  i TARGET, SUBJECT. Simply replace the subject of an affirmative sentence by *Who, What, Which* or *Whose*, or by *What, Whose, Which* + noun:

AFFIRMATIVE	QUESTION
Somebody broke the window.	*Who* broke the window?
Something broke the window.	*What* broke the window?
Somebody's window was broken.	*Whose* window was broken?

  ii TARGET, ANY PART EXCEPT THE SUBJECT. Begin with the *Wh*-question word or phrase, then use the interrogative pattern: operator + subject + rest of the VP.

ANSWER REQUIRED	TARGET	QUESTION
(That means) X.	NP, object	What does this mean?
(He was reading) a paper.	NP, object	What was he reading?
(He was reading) 'The Times'.	NP, object	What paper was he reading?
(He was) reading a paper.	VP	What was he doing?
(It was) on the platform.	*Adv* place	Where was the desk?
(I met him) yesterday.	*Adv* time	When did you meet George?
(He did his work) carefully.	*Adv* manner	How did he do his work?
(I see him) twice a week.	*Adv* frequency	How often do you see him?
(I gave it to) George.	Object of prep	Who did you give it to?
(He made it for) me.	Object of prep	Who did he make it for?
(There were) thirty-six (boys in the class).	Quantifier	How many boys were there in the class?
(I have known him) since 1968.	Prep phrase with *since*	How long have you known him?

Questions on the pattern *Who did you give it to?* are very frequently heard. All the commonly-used prepositions could fit into that pattern, except *since* and *during*, which are placed before the *Wh-* question word, *eg Since when have you known him?* The pattern *To whom did he give it?* can be used with all prepositions though it is typical of formal style. But *like* usually occurs at the end of a complete sentence, *eg What does it look like?* though we may hear *Like what?* in informal speech.

L Negation
1.59
a As we have seen, a sentence can be made negative by *not*, which we may call a NEGATOR. A sentence can be made negative by other negators: *never, hardly, scarcely, hardly ever, scarcely ever, seldom, rarely,* the quantifier (1.7b) *no*, its pro-form *none*, and its compounds *nothing, nobody, no one, nowhere.* A clause should contain only ONE of those negators. Thus:

131 I have $\begin{cases} \text{not} \\ \text{never} \\ \text{hardly (ever)} \\ \text{scarcely (ever)} \\ \text{seldom} \\ \text{rarely} \end{cases}$ spoken to George's sister.

132 I have $\begin{cases} \text{not said anything to anybody} \\ = \text{spoken to nobody } or \text{ no one} \\ = \text{said nothing to anybody} \end{cases}$ about you.

133 George $\begin{cases} \text{isn't anywhere} \\ = \text{is nowhere} \end{cases}$ here.

134 I $\begin{cases} \text{haven't any money.} \\ = \text{have no money.} \end{cases}$ I $\begin{cases} \text{haven't any.} \\ = \text{have none.} \end{cases}$

b *Neither* and *nor* can be used as negators, as follows:

135 A I haven't spoken to George's sister either.

B $\begin{cases} \text{Neither} \\ = \text{Nor} \end{cases}$ have I.

Neither and *nor* are interchangeable in [135].

c *Neither* and *nor* can also be used as NEGATIVE CO-ORDINATORS (1.53) in the following ways:

136 Neither George nor I broke the window.

137 We neither want nor need any help from you, thank you.

138 We had neither food nor water for three whole days.

As co-ordinators, *neither* comes first, *nor* second.

d The prefix *un-*, or *in-*, negates a single word and can be used in the same clause as one of the negators, thus:

139 That sentence is ungrammatical, isn't it?

140 This sentence is not ungrammatical, is it?

M Short responses
1.60
Short responses, as in column 2 below, occur frequently in normal conversation. Note how such responses can be identified as parts of a complete sentence:

1	2	3
QUESTION	RESPONSE	PART OF THE SENTENCE
1 Who was reading a newspaper?	George's father (was)	NP, subject, with optional addition of the operator.
2 What newspaper was he reading?	'The Times'	NP, direct object.
3 What was he doing?	Reading ('The Times')	Lexical verb in VP, (+direct object).
4 Where was the desk?	On the platform	Prepositional phrase, acting as adverbial of place.
5 When did you first meet George?	Twenty years ago	Adverbial phrase of time.

Subject + operator is very typical of a short answer. A phrase like *reading* (*a newspaper*) is also typical; but *was reading* (*a newspaper*) would not normally occur without a subject.

N Exclamations
1.61
We may often hear and make utterances which are not complete sentences as defined in this chapter. Such utterances include EXCLAMATIONS, *eg*
   141 What wonderful weather! What a beautiful day!
   142 How beautiful! How interesting!
We could expand those exclamations into complete sentences, thus:
   141a What wonderful weather we're having! What a beautiful day it is!
   142a How beautiful it is! How interesting this is!
Notice the difference between [142a] and the question *How interesting is this?*

Chapter Two
Expanding the sentence

In this chapter we shall see how a sentence can be expanded so that it contains more than one finite clause.

A Co-ordinate clauses
2.1

a A COMPOUND SENTENCE has two or more clauses which are linked by co-ordination in the same way as the separate parts of a single clause can be (1.53). Thus:

1 /Everyone was in the hall/ *and* /the doors had been closed/.

1a /Most of us were in the hall/, the doors had been closed/ *and* /late-comers had to wait outside/.

2 /He did not like us/ and everyone knew/, *but* /no one admitted it/.

3 (Either) /he did not like the way we dressed/, *or* /we had offended him in some other way/.

The oblique stroke, /, marks the beginning and end of each clause. All of the clauses are CO-ORDINATE, *ie* of equal rank.

b In [1] above, the two clauses are linked by the CO-ORDINATING CONJUNCTION, *and*: in that sentence, either clause could come first, but *and* must come between the two. In [1a], the first and second clauses are linked by a comma, the second and third by *and*: in that example, the third clause could not change places with the second, if the meaning is that late-comers had to wait after the doors had been closed. In [2], the second and third clauses are linked by the co-ordinating conjunction *but*: the order of the clauses could not be changed, since *knew* in the second clause refers to what has been said in the first, and our understanding of the third clause depends on our having heard or read the two previous ones. In [3], the two clauses are linked by the co-ordinating conjunction *or*; and the first clause is introduced, optionally, by *either*.

c Co-ordinate clauses, therefore, tend to follow either a logical or a chronological order. REFERENCE words such as personal pronouns, *eg it* in [2], must come after the words to which they refer. This need not happen in a SUBORDINATE CLAUSE (2.5), as in the sentence *Although he tried to hide it, the headmaster took a strong dislike to George and me*.

d In examples [1], [1a] and [2], we could replace the commas and conjunctions by full stops, so as to have a sequence of simple sentences. We could convert [3] into simple sentences by replacing both *Either* and *or* by *Perhaps*. However, all the examples are effective as compound sentences, since there is a close logical connection between the separate clauses in each sentence.

2.2
When the subject of two or more co-ordinate clauses refers to the same person or thing, it need not be re-stated (4.45):

   4 The headmaster did not like us very much and seldom gave us any praise.

We could insert *he* before *seldom*, but that is not necessary. We would not repeat *the headmaster* in any case. In a subordinate clause the subject cannot be omitted. Hence:

   4a It was clear that the headmaster did not like us, because he seldom gave us any praise.

Conjunctions and conjuncts (1.52)
2.3
a *So* and *yet* are commonly used as co-ordinating conjunctions, as in

   5 /George was good at arithmetic/, *so* /he was put straight into the second class/.

   6 /George was very good at arithmetic/, *yet* /he was never given full marks/.

After *so* and *yet* the same subject is less likely to be omitted than it is in an example like [4]. *So* and *yet* can also be used as conjuncts: in that case, either (a) *so* will be preceded by *and*, and *yet* will be preceded by *and* or *but*, or (b) we can put a full stop after *arithmetic* and begin a new sentence with *So* in [5] and *Yet* in [6].

b *And* and *but* can also be used as conjuncts, especially in informal style, as in

   7 Cars are very dangerous machines. And they are expensive.

   8 Thousands of accidents happen every day. But we all imagine that nothing will happen to *us*.

In [7], *And* could be replaced by the conjunct *Besides*; and, in [8], *But* could be replaced by the conjunct *However*. Similarly, *Or* could begin a sentence, forming a link with a previous sentence, and could be replaced by a conjunct like *Alternatively*. On the other hand, *besides, however* and *alternatively* cannot be used as co-ordinating conjunctions in examples like [1–3].

Neither, nor; not only
2.4
a The negative co-ordinators, *neither* and *nor* (1.59c) can be used to join co-ordinating clauses. If the subject is the same in both clauses, we can say:

9 He neither liked the way we spoke, nor approved of the way we
dressed.

If the subject in the second clause is stated, the clause can begin with
neither or *nor* with inversion of subject + operator as in 1.50 example
[106], thus:

10a He did not like the way we spoke, $\left\{\begin{matrix} \text{neither} \\ =\text{nor} \end{matrix}\right\}$ did he approve of
the way we dressed.

b Co-ordinate clauses are often linked by *not only* and *but also*:

10b He not only disliked the way we spoke, but also disapproved of the
way we dressed.

Not only can begin the sentence, with inversion as in [10a]:

10c Not only did he dislike the way we spoke, but he also disapproved
of the way we dressed.

B Subordinate clauses
2.5

A COMPLEX SENTENCE has two or more clauses, at least one of which is
SUBORDINATE to a main clause. A main clause is one that can stand alone,
ie is not dependent on another clause. A clause can be subordinate[1] by
being able to replace an NP in the other clause, or by modifying an NP
in the other clause, or by being able to replace an adverbial in it. Thus:

11 /Everyone could see $\left\{\begin{matrix} \text{a that/.} \\ \text{b (that)/he was frightened/.} \end{matrix}\right.$

12 /I often see $\left\{\begin{matrix} \text{a my old school friends/.} \\ \text{b =friends /who were at school with me/.} \end{matrix}\right.$

13 /I met George Lamb $\left\{\begin{matrix} \text{a twenty years ago/.} \\ \text{b when /I was at school/.} \end{matrix}\right.$

In [11a], *that* (pronounced /ðæt/) is an NP, a demonstrative pronoun (1.8a),
and the object of *see*. In [11b], *that he was frightened* can replace the NP and
is called a NOUN CLAUSE, object of *see* in the MAIN CLAUSE: in that sense, the
noun clause is subordinate to the main clause. In [12b], *who were at school
with me* is a RELATIVE CLAUSE, 'relating' to and modifying *friends* in the
main clause. In [13b], *when I was at school* is an ADVERBIAL CLAUSE OF TIME,
or a temporal clause, equivalent to an adverbial adjunct, *eg twenty years ago*.

2.6

A subordinate clause is usually – and always can be – introduced by a
SUBORDINATING CONJUNCTION, *eg when* or *that* (pronounced /ðət/ in fluent
speech), or by a RELATIVE PRONOUN, *eg who. He was frightened* and *I was at
school* are independent clauses and complete sentences by themselves; but

[1] Or DEPENDENT.

that he was frightened and *when I was at school* are subordinate clauses and cannot be complete sentences on their own: a main clause must be added, as in [11b] and [13b], before a complete sentence can be made from them.

C Noun clauses
2.7
We can subdivide noun clauses into THAT-CLAUSES, like [11b], and WH-CLAUSES like

14 No one knows what caused the accident.

A *wh*-clause can begin with any *wh*-question word (1.58c).

That-clauses
2.8
A *that*-clause can have *four* of the functions of an NP (1.33). It can be:
a the SUBJECT of a verb in another clause, as in

15 That the driver could not control his car was obvious.

The conjunction *that* is obligatory when the clause is subject. However, [15] is formal in style: it could be replaced in formal style, and generally would be replaced in informal style, by

16 It was obvious (that) the driver could not control his car,

in which case the ANTICIPATORY *it* refers to the *that*-clause.
b the OBJECT of a verb in another clause, as in [11b]. When the clause is object and comes after its verb, *that* is optional, and is usually omitted in a short sentence. *Everyone could see he was frightened* would be normal idiomatic English.[1] In longer sentences, especially when the *that*-clause is separated from the verb of which it is the object and when there is more than one subordinate clause, *that* is usually obligatory, as in

17 Everyone could see, I believe, that he was terrified.

18 Everyone could see what was happening and that poor George was really scared.

Sometimes, the *that*-clause, as object, can come before the clause it depends on, and in such a case *that* is obligatory:

19 That George was really afraid, I can't believe.

Compare this reversal of the normal order with example [125] in 1.57.
c the COMPLEMENT of subject + BE, as in

20 The truth is (that) he was very shy.

Again, *that* is optional in a short sentence of such a kind, but usually obligatory in a more complicated one.
d in APPOSITION (1.33f) to a noun like *fact, truth, explanation*:

21 We must face the fact that we have spent all our money.

---

[1] However, *that* would be required in a short response (1.60), eg

A What did you assume from his attitude?

B That he was frightened.

22 The hard truth, that they had spent all their money, was a great shock to her.

In [21], the apposition is RESTRICTIVE (1.33) and answers the question *Which fact?* There is no comma and no break in intonation in [21]. In [22], the apposition is NON-RESTRICTIVE: it merely reminds us of what the truth was: the *that*-clause interrupts the intonation pattern of the sentence and is put between commas. *That* can sometimes be omitted in an example like [21], but not in one like [22].

2.9

A *that*-clause, unlike an NP, cannot be governed by a preposition. This has two consequences:

a Certain adjectives, which refer to personal feelings or states of the mind, *eg afraid, certain, delighted, glad, interested, pleased, positive, satisfied, surprised,* (7.18) and which can be followed by preposition + NP, can also be followed by a *that*-clause, but then the preposition is deleted. This also happens after certain nouns, *eg (take) care.* Thus, *I'm afraid of fire* and *Take care of the baby* can be contrasted with

23 I'm afraid (that) the house will catch fire, *and*

24 Take care (that) nothing happens to the baby.

b When the *that*-clause refers to a statement of fact, the words *the fact* are inserted between the preposition and the clause, *eg*

25 The fire was due to the fact that someone had dropped a lighted cigarette.

2.10

We must distinguish between an example like [19], *That George was really afraid, I can't believe,* where the *that*-clause is the object of *believe,* and one like

26 He was really afraid, I believe.

in which *He was really afraid* is the main clause, not introduced by *that,* and *I believe* is a COMMENT CLAUSE. In [19], intonation rises on *afraid:* it normally reaches a high pitch on *can't* and falls on *believe.* In [26], it falls on *afraid,* and the comment clause is spoken on a flat, low level pitch. The main clause in [19] tends to be negative; though it can also make an affirmative CONCESSION, *eg That George was frightened, I agree.* The comment clause in [26] is normally affirmative, though a negative is possible, as in

27 You can't lend me any money, I (don't) suppose(?).

which could be a question ending with a rising intonation.

Indirect speech: reported statements

2.11

DIRECT SPEECH, quoting the actual words spoken, is written between inverted commas, as in

28   The guard says, 'The road is closed'.
   or
28a 'The road is closed,' the guard says.

Note the conventional punctuation in those two examples. INDIRECT SPEECH would be:

29   The guard $\begin{Bmatrix} \text{says} \\ \text{tells me} \end{Bmatrix}$ (that) the road is closed.
   or
29a The road is closed, the guard $\begin{Bmatrix} \text{says.} \\ \text{tells me.} \end{Bmatrix}$

In [28] and [29], the quotation and the *that*-clause are objects of *says*. In [28a] and [29a], *the guard says* is a comment clause, as in [26], with exactly the same intonation. Note that SAY occurs in both [28] and [29]. Some verbs, *eg* SHOUT, can replace SAY in [28] but not in [29], while others, *eg* DENY could replace SAY in [29] but not in [28]. See 10.4, B11.

2.12
The tense of the verb in direct speech normally changes when indirect speech is reported as a PAST EVENT. The change of tense follows this rule:

i $\begin{Bmatrix} \text{PRESENT TENSE in a simple verb (1.14)} \\ \text{or in an operator in a verbal group (1.26)} \end{Bmatrix}$ becomes PAST; and

ii PAST TENSE in a simple verb becomes PAST PERFECT (1.23d).

eg DIRECT SPEECH	INDIRECT SPEECH
a 'The road is closed.'	I tell you the road is closed.
	I told you the road was closed.
b 'They are repairing it.'	I tell you they are repairing it.
	I told you they were repairing it.
c 'The bridge has collapsed.'	I tell you the bridge has collapsed.
	I told you the bridge had collapsed.
d 'No one can cross it.'	I tell you no one can cross it.
	I told you no one could cross it.
e 'The floods weakened it.'	I tell you the floods weakened it.
	I told you the floods (had) weakened it.

In indirect speech, *had* is obligatory in c but optional in e. *Hope* and *hoped* could replace *tell you* and *told you* respectively, with the same sequence of tenses: *cp wish*, 2.16.

2.13
While the tense-change shown in 2.12 is normal, it need not be made if, for example, the speaker wishes to emphasise that the situation described in the actual words spoken still exists. Thus:

30 I told you (that) $\begin{Bmatrix} \text{the road is closed} \\ \text{the bridge has collapsed} \\ \text{no one can cross it} \end{Bmatrix}$.

[30] could be re-worded: *The road is closed*, etc., *I told you that before.*

2.14

Other changes in the *that*-clause may be necessary in reported past speech. Note the effect on personal pronouns, possessives and certain adverbials of time:

DIRECT SPEECH	INDIRECT SPEECH
a 'Jack, you've passed your exam.'	I told Jack he'd passed his exam.
b 'Your parcel arrived yesterday, Mary.'	I told Mary her parcel had arrived the day before.
c 'Mr X will be back tomorrow.'	They told me Mr X would be back the next (*or* the following) day.

d 'I'll telephone $\left\{\begin{array}{l}\text{today}\\\text{this evening}\end{array}\right\}$.'   He said he'd telephone that $\left\{\begin{array}{l}\text{day}\\\text{evening}\end{array}\right\}$.

e It happened two $\left\{\begin{array}{l}\text{hours}\\\text{days}\\\text{weeks}\end{array}\right\}$ ago.   They told me it (had) happened two $\left\{\begin{array}{l}\text{hours}\\\text{days}\\\text{weeks}\end{array}\right\}$ before.

However, like the tense in 2.13, the adverb of time need not always change. *They told me Mr X will be back tomorrow* is correct if the *tomorrow* referred to in the actual words spoken has not yet come. If, at six o'clock, I say *'They told me the plane arrived two hours ago'*, that is correct if I mean that the plane arrived at four.

2.15

No change of tense will occur in indirect past speech when the verb in the actual words spoken is already past perfect, or when it begins with a modal in past tense form (1.17) or with *ought*. Thus:

'The bridge had collapsed.'	I told you the bridge had collapsed.
'I could see you at eight.'	I said I could see you at eight.

Must can remain unchanged or be replaced by *had to*.

'You must go.'   He said we $\left\{\begin{array}{l}\text{must}\\\text{= had to}\end{array}\right\}$ go.

2.16

a The rule for tense-change given in 2.12 applies in *that*-clauses following WISH. Thus:

The road is closed,	but I wish it wasn't (closed).
It isn't open,	but I wish it was (open).
They aren't repairing it yet,	but I wish they were (repairing it).

The bridge has collapsed,	but I wish it hadn't (collapsed).
We can't cross it,	but I wish we could (cross it).
I stopped for tea,	but I wish I hadn't (stopped for tea).
I'll help you.	Oh, I wish you would (help me).

The same rule applies when I'd $\left\{\begin{array}{l}rather\\=sooner\end{array}\right\}$ is followed by a *that*-clause,

as in *I'd* $\left\{\begin{array}{l}rather\\=sooner\end{array}\right\}$ *we stopped now*. What is happening after *wish* and *I'd rather* is that the speaker imagines a NON-FACT to be a reality. The idea of 'non-fact' is marked by the use of the SUBJUNCTIVE *were* even with a 1st or 3rd person singular subject, as in *I wish it weren't, I wish I were*. Compare the tenses that follow *wish* with those that follow *hope*, as in 2.12.

b Past tense for present non-fact also occurs in *It's time we went. It's time the children were in bed.*

That-clauses with should
2.17
a Verbs like SAY, THINK, HOPE (10.4, B11) can be followed by *that*-clauses in which present, past or future can be reported: see the examples in 2.12. But verbs like PROPOSE and RECOMMEND (10.4, B12a) refer only to imagined action in the future, as in

31 We $\left\{\begin{array}{l}\text{propose}\\\text{recommend}\end{array}\right\}$ that Mr X $\left\{\begin{array}{l}\text{a should go.}\\=\text{b goes.}\\=\text{c go.}\\\text{a should be dismissed.}\\=\text{b is dismissed.}\\=\text{c be dismissed.}\end{array}\right.$

Of the three active (*ie* not passive) possibilities after 'Mr X', and of the three passive possibilities, (a) might be regarded as normal, (b) as informal and (c) formal and typical of official style, especially in American English. The (c) forms (*go* for 3rd person singular, and *be dismissed*) are traditionally called SUBJUNCTIVE.

b *Should* also occurs in *that*-clauses after verbs and adjectives expressing personal feelings, judgements, etc., as in

32 $\left\{\begin{array}{l}\text{We regret}\\=\text{We are sorry}\end{array}\right\}$ that you should feel obliged to resign.

33 It is right that he should be punished.

Should could be omitted in [32], but not in [33]. Adjectives which could replace *right* in [33] include *better, essential, important, necessary, wrong*.

Wh-clauses
2.18
A *wh*-clause can have four of the functions of an NP. It can be:

a the SUBJECT of another clause:

34 What caused the accident is a complete mystery.

As in [16], this can be converted into a sentence beginning with *It*:

35 It is a complete mystery what caused the accident,

though a *wh*-clause is more likely than a *that*-clause to occur at the beginning of the sentence.

b the OBJECT of a verb in another clause, as in

14 No one knows what caused the accident.

As in example [19], a *wh*-clause acting as object can come before the main clause:

36 What caused the accident, I can't imagine.

c the COMPLEMENT of subject + BE:

37 The question is what caused the accident.

d the OBJECT of a preposition, as in

38 It depends on what you really mean.

2.19

Compare [19] and [36]:

[19] That George was really afraid, I can't believe.

[36] What caused the accident, I can't imagine.

Those two examples have the same intonation as each other (2.10); and in both the first clause is the object of the second. On the other hand, in

[26] He was really afraid, I believe

and

39 What caused the accident, I wonder?

which also have the same intonation as each other (2.11), the first clause is the main and the second is a comment clause.

Indirect questions
2.20

Wh-clauses are usually INDIRECT QUESTIONS, which are formed as follows:

a TARGET, SUBJECT OF THE SENTENCE (1.58c, i):

Statement	That man caused the accident.
Direct question	Who caused the accident?
Indirect question	Tell me who caused the accident.

In this case, the only difference between the direct question and the indirect is that the latter is preceded by a clause containing a verb like TELL (me), ASK (somebody), (I) WONDER.

b TARGET, ANY PART EXCEPT THE SUBJECT (1.58c, ii)

Statement	Mr X will return on Monday.
Direct question	When will Mr X return?
Indirect question	Tell me when Mr X will return.

The direct question now has the order 'operator + subject', while the indirect question returns to the normal order 'subject + verb'.[1]

c Direct YES/NO QUESTIONS (1.58) have no *wh*-question words and this gap is filled in indirect questions by *if* or *whether*, thus:

Statement   You have met George Lamb.
Direct question   Have you met George Lamb (or not)?

Indirect question   I wonder $\left\{\begin{array}{l} \text{if} \\ =\text{whether} \end{array}\right\}$ you've met him (or not).

If is normal when the subordinate clause is object and follows the main clause, but it can be replaced by *whether*, especially if the speaker feels that the answer is doubtful. *Whether* is obligatory in

40 Please tell me whether or not you agree.

It is also obligatory when the *wh*-clause precedes the main clause or is the object of a preposition:

41 Whether we can really help you, I don't know yet. (object)
42 Whether we can help you is a difficult question. (subject)
43 It depends on whether we have enough money. (object of prep.)

2.21

The difference between direct and indirect questions appears if we choose examples in which the target is not the subject of the sentence (2.20). Thus:

44 Where was the boy standing, I wonder? (direct question)
44a Have you met George Lamb, I asked you? (direct question)

Compare those examples with:

45 Where the boy was standing, I don't really know. (indirect)
45a Whether you have met George Lamb or not, I can't remember. (indirect)

2.22

The rules for sequences of tenses given in 2.12 and 2.15 apply equally to indirect questions, *eg*

'Who caused the accident?'   Someone asked me who (had) caused the accident.

'Have you met George Lamb?'   You wanted to know if I had met George Lamb.

What (meaning 'the thing that'), and whatever
2.23

Notice the difference between

[34] What caused the accident was a complete mystery,   *and*

---

[1] The order OPERATOR + SUBJECT will sometimes be found in indirect questions when the operator is the full verb BE, as in (*What's the matter?*) *Tell me what's the matter*, instead of *Tell me what the matter is.*

46 What caused the accident was a broken bottle.

In [34] the whole question (*What caused the accident?*) was the mystery. In [46], a certain *thing* that caused the accident was found to be a broken bottle. We could change [34] to

34a What $\begin{Bmatrix} \text{ever} \\ \text{on earth} \end{Bmatrix}$ [1] caused the accident, nobody knows.

and [46] to

46a Whatever caused the accident has not yet been found.

What in [46] = the definite thing that; *whatever* in [46a] = the indefinite thing that – it might be anything.

2.24

Who is not used in modern English as *what* is used in 2.23, example [46]. *Who caused the accident was a complete mystery* is acceptable, the mystery being the whole question, *Who caused the accident?* But we could not say **Who caused the accident was very careless*. We should have to say

47 $\begin{Bmatrix} \text{The person who} \\ =\text{Whoever} \end{Bmatrix}$ caused the accident was very careless.

2.25

However, 'when it happened' in

48 I remember when it happened

can either be an indirect question or mean 'the time when it happened'. The same applies to clauses beginning with *where*. Notice the difference between

49 I remember when my father was born,

    and

50 I'll never forget $\begin{Bmatrix} \text{when} \\ \text{where} \end{Bmatrix}$ I first met you.

We can assume that [50] means 'I'll never forget the $\begin{Bmatrix} \text{time when} \\ \text{place where} \end{Bmatrix}$ we met', while [49] can only mean 'I know the answer to the question "*When was your father born?* See also 2.35.

D Relative clauses
2.26

Just as one NP in apposition to another (1.33f) can be RESTRICTIVE or NON-RESTRICTIVE, so a relative clause (2.5) can be RESTRICTIVE (or DEFINING) or NON-RESTRICTIVE (or NON-DEFINING). *I met your old school friend George Lamb* can therefore be matched with

51 I met a friend who was at school with you,

---

[1] *Ever*, as a separate word, can be used after *what, who, when, why* and *how* to give the impression that a *wh*-question is a real puzzle.

in which *who was at school with you* is a defining relative clause, answering the question *Which friend?*[1] And *I met George Lamb, your old school friend* can be matched by

52 I met George Lamb, who was at school with you I think,

in which *who was at school with you* is a non-defining clause. In [52], George Lamb needs no defining; the clause only gives additional information about him, and this additional element is separated from the rest of the sentence by a break in intonation and by a comma or commas in writing.

2.27

A relative clause always follows its ANTECEDENT, *ie* the NP to which it relates; and it must follow as soon as possible if the speaker's exact meaning is to be understood. *I put the books in the cupboard which you bought yesterday* suggests that it was the cupboard rather than the books that you bought. Sometimes a relative clause may appear to be separated from its antecedent, as in

53 George was the only boy at school that I really liked.

But there, the antecedent of the clause *that I really liked* is the whole nominal group *the only boy at school*, in which *boy* is the head and *at school* a postmodifying phrase. In any case, if *at school* came after *I liked* in [53], it might suggest that I only liked George at school or that I liked other boys out of school. Separation would be normal, and would not cause misunderstanding, in an example like

54 A war broke out which lasted for forty years.

2.28

Since the relative clause has to follow its antecedent so closely, it often separates the head-word in the subject from the verb, *eg*

55 Be careful. The car *that overtook us a few minutes ago* has now been stopped by the police. (defining clause in italics)

The car that overtook us ... should be seen as a nominal group composed of *The car* (head) + *that overtook us ...* (postmodifier). A non-defining relative clause often splits up the clause to which it is subordinate, as in [56]:

56 A red sports car, *which seemed to be doing at least a hundred miles an hour*, shot past us. (non-defining clause in italics)

2.29

Whether the relative clause is (A) defining, or (B) non-defining, its antecedent can be (1) personal or (2) non-personal; and the relative pronoun

[1] Note the short response (1.60):

A Which friend did you say?

B {A friend / One} who was at school with you.

beginning the clause can be (a) the subject of the clause, (b) the object of a verb in the clause, (c) the object of a preposition, or (d) a possessive. We can illustrate (a), (b), (c) and (d) as follows:

a That is the man. *He* hit me.   = That is the man *who* hit me.
b That is the man. I saw *him*.   = That is the man *whom* I saw.
c That is the man. I spoke to *him*. = That is the man *to whom* I spoke.
d That is the man. *His* car crashed. = That is the man *whose* car crashed.

Whom and *to whom* are normally reserved for formal occasions; and that raises the question: which relative pronoun should we use? The rules answering that question are not rigid, but they can be systematised as in the Table below.

Table 10
RELATIVE PRONOUNS

	(A) in defining clauses		(B) in non-defining clauses	
	(1) *Personal*	(2) *Non-personal*	(1) *Personal*	(2) *Non-personal*
a SUBJECT	*who* or *that*	*which* or *that*[1]	*who*	*which*
b OBJECT	*(whom)*[2], *(who)*[3] or *(that)*	*(which)* or *(that)*[1]	*who(m)*	*which*
c OBJECT OF PREPOSITION	*to whom*; or *(whom)*, *(who)* or *(that)...to*[4]	*to which*; or *(which)* or *(that)*[1]*...to*	*to whom*; or *who(m)...to*	*to which* or *which...to*
d POSSESSIVE	*whose*	*whose*[5] or *of which*	*whose*	*whose*[5] or *of which*

Notes:
1 In a few cases (2.31), only *that* is acceptable.
2 As elsewhere in this book, a word in round brackets can be considered optional: the relative pronoun, object, is usually omitted in short sentences, but only in defining clauses.
3 Consider *whom* as formal, or as obligatory after a preposition, or as desirable in any style in a sentence like *Who beat whom?* where the object is contrasted with the subject.
4 The preposition will normally come at the end of the clause in informal style, as in *That's the man I was speaking to.*
5 Not all writers would be happy about using *whose* when the antecedent is non-personal, while *of which* can sound formal. See the example for A2d in 2.30.

2.30
Examples of the use of relative pronouns, illustrating Table 10:

(A1) DEFINING CLAUSES, WITH PERSONAL ANTECEDENT

a There is the driver $\left\{\begin{array}{l}\text{who}\\ =\text{that}\end{array}\right\}$ overtook us five minutes ago.

b Where is the man $\left\{\begin{array}{l}\text{(whom)}\\ =\text{(who)}\\ =\text{(that)}\end{array}\right\}$ I saw this morning?

c Is that the man $\left\{\begin{array}{l}\text{to whom you handed your application form?}\\ =\text{(whom)}\\ =\text{(who)}\\ =\text{(that)}\end{array}\right.$ you gave your tickets to?

d That is the boy whose father is an astronaut.

(A2) DEFINING CLAUSES, WITH NON-PERSONAL ANTECEDENT

a There is the car $\left\{ \begin{array}{l} \text{which} \\ =\text{that} \end{array} \right\}$ overtook us five minutes ago.

b Where is the book $\left\{ \begin{array}{l} \text{(which)} \\ =\text{(that)} \end{array} \right\}$ I bought this morning?

c Is that the address $\left\{ \begin{array}{l} \text{to which you sent the telegram?} \\ =\text{(which)} \\ =\text{(that)} \end{array} \right.$ you sent the telegram to?

d He mentioned a book
$\left\{ \begin{array}{l} \text{whose title} \\ =\text{the title of which} \end{array} \right\}$ $\left\{ \begin{array}{l} \text{has slipped my memory.} \\ \text{I can't remember now.} \end{array} \right\}$ [1]

(B1) NON-DEFINING CLAUSES, WITH PERSONAL ANTECEDENT

a The driver, who was very young, had only just got his licence.

b The driver, who(m) I had never seen before, insisted that he knew me.

c Sergeant Brown, $\left\{ \begin{array}{l} \text{to whom I showed my licence,} \\ =\text{who(m) I showed my licence to,} \end{array} \right\}$ was very polite.

d The injured pedestrian, whose leg had been broken, was carried away on a stretcher.

(B2) NON-DEFINING CLAUSES WITH NON-PERSONAL ANTECEDENT

a They soon repaired the car, which had not been badly damaged.

b The front bumper, which the other car had twisted a little, was soon put straight.

c Martin's garage, $\left\{ \begin{array}{l} \text{to which the car had been taken,} \\ =\text{which the car had been taken to,} \end{array} \right\}$ was not far away.

d This book, $\left\{ \begin{array}{l} \text{whose author} \\ =\text{of which the author} \\ =\text{the author of which} \end{array} \right\}$ is a woman of eighty, is very amusing.

Which or that?

2.31

a *That*, not *which*, is used for (A2), a and b in the following cases:

i when the antecedent is an indefinite pronoun (1.5c), as in

57 $\left\{ \begin{array}{l} \text{All} \\ \text{Everything} \\ \text{Anything} \end{array} \right\}$ $\left\{ \begin{array}{l} \text{that remains} \\ \text{(that) you see here} \end{array} \right\}$ can be divided between you.

---

[1] *Of which the title has slipped my memory* also occurs in formal style. In informal style, *of which* could be avoided thus: *He mentioned a book – I can't remember the title of it now.*

ii when the antecedent is modified by a superlative (1.44a); including *first* and *last*, and by *next*, as in

58 Which was the $\begin{Bmatrix} \text{first} \\ \text{fastest} \\ \text{next} \end{Bmatrix}$ steamship that crossed the Atlantic?

b *That* can be used instead of *which*, and *vice versa*, to avoid repetition, provided that the writer is free to choose; *eg*
59 Which is the car that overtook us?

Of which, of whom, of whose
2.32

a Two simple sentences on the pattern *I can lend you* $\begin{Bmatrix} \text{two} \\ \text{several} \end{Bmatrix}$ *books.*

$\begin{Bmatrix} \text{Both} \\ \text{Five} \end{Bmatrix}$ *of them are very good,* can be re-worded as main clause + relative

clause on the model:

60 I can lend you $\begin{Bmatrix} \text{two} \\ \text{several} \end{Bmatrix}$ books, $\begin{Bmatrix} \text{both} \\ \text{five} \end{Bmatrix}$ of which are very good.

or I can lend you $\begin{Bmatrix} \text{two} \\ \text{several} \end{Bmatrix}$ books, of which $\begin{Bmatrix} \text{both} \\ \text{five} \end{Bmatrix}$ are very good.

If the second of those two simple sentences were *I can recommend* $\begin{Bmatrix} \text{both} \\ \text{five} \end{Bmatrix}$

of them, we could produce

61 I can lend you $\begin{Bmatrix} \text{two} \\ \text{several} \end{Bmatrix}$ books, $\begin{Bmatrix} \text{both} \\ \text{five} \end{Bmatrix}$ of which I can recommend,

or I can lend you $\begin{Bmatrix} \text{two} \\ \text{several} \end{Bmatrix}$ books, of which I can recommend $\begin{Bmatrix} \text{both} \\ \text{five} \end{Bmatrix}$.

b The two simple sentences *Thank you for your letter. I sent you the following telegram in answer to it,* could be combined to produce:
62 Thank you for your letter, in answer to which I sent you the following telegram.
c *Whom* would replace *which* in [60], [61] and [62] if the antecedent were personal. Distinguish *of whom* from *whose* and *of whose*:

63 That is the boy $\begin{Bmatrix} \text{whose father is an astronaut.} \\ \text{of whom we have just been speaking.} \\ \text{of whose father we have just been speaking.} \end{Bmatrix}$

The three relative clauses in [63] could be replaced by the simple sentences

His father is an astronaut, We have just been speaking of him and *We have just been speaking of his father*, in that order.

2.33

A change in the normal word-order, subject + verb, often occurs in RELATIVE CLAUSES, especially in formal writing, when there is a short intransitive VP and a comparatively long subject, as in

64 He is a man $\begin{cases} \text{on whom} \\ \text{on whose shoulders} \end{cases}$ falls a heavy responsibility.

Cp 1.57, example [121].

More than one relative clause in a sentence
2.34

a There are two defining clauses in the sentence
65 She is the only girl I know who can play the guitar.
The clause *I know*, with its relative pronoun omitted, restricts the meaning of *girl*, and the clause *who can play the guitar* then restricts the meaning of *the only girl I know*.

b When two relative clauses within the same sentence are independent of each other, it is clearer to begin each with its own relative pronoun, as in
66 He was a man whom all his friends admired and who won the respect even of his enemies.

Relative clauses with antecedents referring to time, place, manner
2.35

In the sentence *I shall never forget (the time) when George first came to school*, we could be more precise by replacing *(the time) when* by, *eg the day (that)*:

67 I shall never forget the $\begin{cases} \text{day} \\ \text{morning} \end{cases}$ (that) George first came. etc.

Similarly, *(the place) where* can be replaced as in

68 Can you show me $\begin{cases} \begin{cases} \text{(the place) where} \\ \text{the house in which} \end{cases} \text{Shakespeare lived?} \\ \text{the house} \begin{cases} \text{(that)} \\ \text{(which)} \end{cases} \text{Shakespeare lived in?} \end{cases}$

Note also:
69 I admired the way (in which) you answered his questions.
70 That is (the reason) why so few people come here.

The reason why is often heard, though *why* is sufficient in [70]. Remember that *the thing that* is replaced by *what*, as in [46] (2.23) and in

71 This is $\begin{cases} \text{the thing that} \\ = \text{what} \end{cases}$ I can never understand.

Relative clauses with a whole clause as antecedent
2.36
The whole of the main clause is the antecedent in
  72 He arrived half an hour late, which annoyed us all very much.
In some styles, *eg* in advertising, a relative clause of this kind is sometimes written as a separate sentence:
  73 Every bottle of 'BUZZ' has been tested in our laboratories. Which is why we're so sure of our guarantee.

E Adverbial clauses: time, place and manner
2.37
There are various types of adverbial clause. Three of them can clearly be related to the adverbials of time, place and manner (1.47). Thus:

74 I met George Lamb $\begin{cases} \text{in 1954.} \\ \text{when I was at school.} \\ \text{whenever I went into town.} \end{cases}$ (time)

75 You may park your car $\begin{cases} \text{under the trees.} \\ \text{where there is a parking sign.} \\ \text{wherever you like.} \end{cases}$ (place)

76 George writes $\begin{cases} \text{carefully.} \\ \left\{ \begin{matrix} \text{as} \\ \text{the way} \end{matrix} \right\} \text{his father did.} \\ \text{as if he} \left\{ \begin{matrix} \text{is} \\ \text{was} \\ \text{were} \end{matrix} \right\} \text{left-handed.} \end{cases}$ (manner)

Notes: i Clauses of time and place may follow or precede the main clause. Clauses of manner usually follow.
      ii *When*, as in [74], = at the (definite) time that; *whenever* = at any (indefinite) time. *Where*, in [75], = at the (definite) place that; *wherever* = at any indefinite place.
     iii Distinguish between the subordinating conjunction *as* (in [76]), introducing a clause, and the preposition *like*, governing an NP, as in *George writes like his father.*
     iv *The way his father did* is typical of informal style. *As if he is left-handed* suggests that he really *is* left-handed; *as if he was* suggests that he might be; *as if he were* suggests that he is not (see 'non-fact', 2.16).

2.38
a When a complex sentence containing a time (or temporal) clause has future reference, future is normally indicated in the main clause by

will ('ll) (or by *shall*[1] with *I* or *we*), but not in the subordinate clause. The two simple sentences *Mr X will return soon. Then he will telephone you* can be combined to form

77 Mr X will telephone you $\left\{ {\text{when} \atop \text{as soon as}} \right\}$ he returns.

(Contrast [77] with the indirect question in 2.20b, where *will* may occur in the noun clause.) Similarly, the two sentences *I will return your book on Monday. I will have read it by then* (see 1.23e) can form

78 I will return your book on Monday $\left\{ {\text{when} \atop \text{as soon as}} \right\}$ I have read it.

By the rule given in 2.12, the tense in past reported speech would be

79 Mr X said he would telephone you $\left\{ {\text{when} \atop \text{as soon as}} \right\}$ he returned.

80 I promised I would return your book $\left\{ {\text{when} \atop \text{as soon as}} \right\}$ I had read it.

b The rules stated in 2.38a will apply to temporal clauses with future reference introduced by *after, before, till, until, whenever,* and by other expressions that could replace *when* or *as soon as,* eg *once, immediately, the moment, the day,* etc., as in

81 He will telephone you $\left\{ {\text{immediately} \atop \text{= the moment}} \right\}$ he comes back.

c The main clause in (a) and (b) could be an imperative:

82 Come and see me $\left\{ {\text{as soon as you get back.} \atop \text{when you have finished.}} \right\}$

2.39

Till and *until* (the two words are inter-replaceable) mark the end-point of a period of time. They are associated with a verb denoting an action or lack of action which can continue during the period ending at that point.

83. Wait here till I come back.

84 $\left\{ {\text{Don't leave} \atop \text{You mustn't go}} \right\}$ till I return.

In [83] the waiting, and in [84] the not-going, will continue throughout the period. LEAVE and GO in the affirmative could not replace WAIT in [83], since they denote actions performed at a *point* of time, not continuing through a period.

2.40

On the other hand, *since* (when it introduces a time clause) can mark the beginning of a period of time continuing until NOW (1.23c) or until THEN

---

[1] When *will* appears in examples in this chapter, the reader may assume that *'ll* can be substituted for it in informal style (but see 1.31, Note a) and that it can be replaced by *shall* with *I* or *we*. A similar remark applies to *would,* when it can be replaced by *'d,* or by *should* with *I* or *we*.

(1.23d). In a temporal clause, a verb in the past tense can mark the beginning of the period, while the verb in the main clause is present perfect if the period continues until NOW, or past perfect if it continued till THEN:

85 Since I left school (till NOW), I have only seen him once.

86 I met George last week. Since we left school (till THEN), we had often written to each other.

Since followed by a verb in the present or past perfect referring to activity having duration and still continuing, means 'during the period when', as in

87 Since we have lived here, we have made many friends.

LIVE in [87] could not be replaced by a 'point-of-time' verb, *eg* COME.

2.41

While can mean 'during the period that':

88 George arrived while I was having a bath.

89 He was playing while I was doing my homework.

90 $\begin{cases} \text{George waited} \\ \text{I did my homework} \end{cases}$ while $\begin{cases} \text{I had my bath.} \\ \text{he played.} \end{cases}$

Those three last examples could be illustrated by a stress mark (') representing an event occurring at a point in time; by a straight line (——) representing an action in progress; and by an asterisk (*) representing an action completed, thus:

91 $\begin{cases} \text{George arrived} \\ \text{while I was having a bath.} \end{cases}$ ——

92 $\begin{cases} \text{He was playing} \\ \text{while I was doing my homework.} \end{cases}$ ——

93 $\begin{cases} \text{George waited} \\ \text{while I had my bath.} \end{cases}$ * *

In [91] and [92], *while* could be replaced by *when* and *as*; in [93], *while* could be replaced by *as* but not usually by *when*.

F Other adverbial clauses

Conditional clauses – clauses introduced by if, unless, . . .

2.42

What are traditionally called CONDITIONAL CLAUSES are adverbial clauses beginning with *if* or with conjunctions having similar meaning, like *unless*. We can divide such clauses into five groups – a neutral type, three BASIC TYPES, and a mixed group – according to the sequence of tenses that they attract. In every group, the conditional clause can come before or after the main clause.

NEUTRAL TYPE: SAME TENSE IN BOTH CLAUSES

94 If the wind blows from the north, this room is very cold.

95 If the wind blew from the north, we moved into the other room.
In those two examples, the *if*-clause could be replaced by *sometimes*, and *if*
itself could there be replaced by *when*. But *when* could not replace *if* in
  96 If you never have a cold, you're very lucky,
where the *if*-clause could be replaced by *in that case*.

TYPE 1: PRESENT TENSE in the IF-CLAUSE, WILL or IMPERATIVE IN THE MAIN
In this type, what is said in the main clause is CONTINGENT, *ie* dependent, on
something that may not happen, though this 'something' is assumed by the
speaker to be a real possibility:

97 If you park your car there, $\begin{cases} \text{a lock it and leave the key here,} \\ \text{b the police will take it away.} \end{cases}$

The sequence of tenses in [97] is the same as in [77]; and [78] can be matched
by
  98 I will let you have your book back on Monday, if I have finished it by
  then.
Can, like *may* and *must*, is acceptable in the *if*-clause when *will* is not:
  99 Park your car under a tree, if you can find a space.
Should can occur in the *if*-clause, as in

100 If you should be interested, $\begin{cases} \text{I will send you a copy of my book.} \\ \text{please let me know.} \end{cases}$

The effect of *should* in such a case is to suggest that the 'something that may
happen' is itself dependent on chance or some other unpredictable factor.
[100] can be re-worded thus:

100a Should you be interested, $\begin{cases} \text{I will send you a copy etc.} \\ \text{please let me know.} \end{cases}$

The idea of dependence on chance or on someone else's wishes can be
emphasised by stressing *should* in [100] and [100a]. A conditional clause,
type 1, can be seen in both [101] and [102]:
  101 Drop that, and I'll kill you.
  102 Drop that, or I'll kill you.
which can be re-worded
  101a $\left.\begin{matrix} \text{If you drop that} \\ \text{If you don't drop that} \end{matrix}\right\}$ I'll kill you.
  102a

TYPE 2: PAST IN THE IF-CLAUSE, WOULD IN THE MAIN
Here, what is said in the main clause is an imaginary consequence of a
PRESENT NON-FACT (2.16, 2.37, Note iv). The *if*-clause states the non-fact
and its verb is accordingly in the past tense. The sequence of tenses is the
same as in [79]:

103 If you parked your car there (now), $\begin{cases} \text{they would tow it away.} \\ \text{we could keep an eye on it.} \end{cases}$

Were is commonly used, even with 1st and 3rd person singular subjects, to
emphasise non-fact (2.16). Thus:

104 If I were you, I would keep quiet.

105 If John were here now (but he isn't), we could play tennis.

As in [100a], the operator can begin the subordinate clause:

106 Were I in your place, I would be very worried,

though this construction would be less typical of plain English than *If I were in your place*, etc. Note also:

107 $\begin{cases} \text{If it wasn't} \\ \text{If it weren't} \\ \text{Were it not} \end{cases}$ for the fact that X is 20 miles away, I would walk there.

Were it not could begin the clause, but *Was, Wasn't* or *Weren't,* could not. Regard *Were it not* as formal.

TYPE 3: PAST PERFECT IN THE IF-CLAUSE, WOULD + PERFECT IN THE MAIN

What is said in the main clause is now seen as an imaginary consequence of PAST NON-FACT – something that did not happen, and the past tense in [103] becomes the past perfect (2.12).

108 If you had parked your car there (but you didn't),

$\begin{cases} \text{they} \\ \text{we} \end{cases}$ $\begin{cases} \text{would have towed it away.} \\ \text{could have kept an eye on it.} \end{cases}$

Again, the operator can begin the subordinate clause in formal style:

109 Had you informed us earlier, we would have taken the necessary steps.

110 Had we not been delayed, the accident would never have happened.

Had . . . not is not contractable to *Hadn't* in this construction.

MIXED GROUP, USING ANY OTHER SEQUENCE OF TENSES AND ASPECTS

Four of the commonest combinations are:

a *If*-clause with *will*, replaceable by *'ll*, not *shall*, with 2nd or 3rd person subject, and containing a suggestion of willingness:

111 If you will write me a letter about it, I will attend to it at once.

Would could be used in the *if*-clause, with *will* or *would* in the main, to produce a more hesitant or a politer effect:

112 If you would write me a letter . . ., I will attend to it. . . .

113 If you would write me a letter . . ., I would be most grateful.

The construction in [113] is frequently used in business or official correspondence, where *should* is generally preferred with *I* or *we*, if only to prevent a repetition of *would*.

b *If*-clause with *will*, *'ll* or *would*, with no suggestion of willingness:

114 I $\begin{cases} \text{can} \\ \text{could} \end{cases}$ lend you five pounds, if that $\begin{cases} \text{will} \\ \text{would} \end{cases}$ help.

This is an exception to the rule followed by Type 1. It can be seen as

meaning either *I* $\begin{cases} can \\ could \end{cases}$ *lend you five pounds.* $\begin{cases} Will \\ Would \end{cases}$ *that help?* or

'My loan depends on whether, at some time in the future, a loan will help'. In other words, it depends on whether helpfulness can be predicted.

c Past tense in the *if*-clause, not referring to present non-fact, as in Type 2, but assuming actual fact in the past:

115 If you parked your car there (then), $\left\{\begin{array}{l}\text{where is it now?}\\ \text{you were very foolish.}\\ \text{the police would have}\\ \quad\text{removed it.}\end{array}\right.$

d *Were to*+INFINITIVE in the *if*-clause making a supposition about the future:

116 If $\left\{\begin{array}{l}\text{I}\\ \text{you}\end{array}\right\}$ were to touch that wire, $\left\{\begin{array}{l}\text{I}\\ \text{you}\end{array}\right\}$ would be killed instantly.

As in [106], *were* could begin the clause in formal and rather old-fashioned style:

117 Were this enterprise to fail, it would be a disaster for us all.

Was could replace *were* in [116] (in informal style) with 1st and 3rd person singular subjects, but not in [117].

2.43

A conditional clause, coming before or after the main, can also be introduced by the conjunctions listed in this paragraph, with the same sequence of tenses as in *if*-sentences.

a *Unless*, meaning 'if . . . not' or 'except on condition that'.

118 You won't catch the train $\left\{\begin{array}{l}\text{if you don't hurry.}\\ \text{unless you hurry.}\end{array}\right.$

119 Your parcel will be despatched this evening, unless you (would) prefer to take it with you now.

120 Goods will not be despatched unless they are paid for in advance.

[120] implies that the goods will only be despatched on that condition.

b *Whether*, not replaceable by *if* before *or not*:

121 Whether you lock your car or not, the police will tow it away.

Compare this with examples [40–43], which are of noun clauses.

c *On condition (that)*, $\left\{\begin{array}{l}provided\\ providing\end{array}\right\}$ *(that)*, $\left\{\begin{array}{l}so\\ as\end{array}\right\}$ *long as*:

122 I will let you drive $\left\{\begin{array}{l}\text{on condition (that)}\\ =\text{provided (that)}\\ =\text{providing (that)}\\ =\text{so}\\ =\text{as}\end{array}\right\}$ you have a valid licence.

On condition (that) normally requires a human agent, *eg you (have)* as in [122]. With the other conjunctions in [122], the agent can be animate or inanimate, *eg*

123· We'll be all right so long as it doesn't pour with rain.

d $\begin{Bmatrix} Suppose \\ Supposing\ (that) \end{Bmatrix}$, making a supposition about the future or the past:

124 $\begin{Bmatrix} Suppose \\ =Supposing\ (that) \end{Bmatrix}$ I $\begin{Bmatrix} had \\ were\ to\ have \end{Bmatrix}$ an accident, who would pay? (future)

125 $\begin{Bmatrix} Suppose \\ =Supposing\ (that) \end{Bmatrix}$ I had had an accident, who would have paid? (past)

e *In case*

126 Make a note of my telephone number, in case you want to ring me up.

Distinguish this construction from *In case of fire, ring the alarm bell,* where *in case of* is a preposition governing an NP. In [126], *of* is deleted, as in (2.9).

Comparison clauses – clauses introduced by than . . .
2.44
Than, as . . . as, the same . . . as

a A gradable adjective or adverb (1.44 and 1.48) in the comparative degree is often followed by a clause beginning with the conjunction *than*:

127 George is $\begin{Bmatrix} quicker \\ a\ quicker\ worker \end{Bmatrix}$ than I am.

128 He writes more neatly than I do.

b A gradable adjective or adverb can also fit into the constructions:

129 George is $\begin{Bmatrix} as\ quick \\ as\ quick\ a\ worker \end{Bmatrix}$ as John is.

130 Jack is not $\begin{Bmatrix} so \\ =as \end{Bmatrix}$ quick as John is.

131 Jack is not such a quick worker as John is.

132 George writes as neatly as John does.

133 Jack does not write $\begin{Bmatrix} so \\ =as \end{Bmatrix}$ neatly as John does.

c A comparison of manner can be made thus:

134 George wrote (in the same way) as his father did;

and a comparison of quantity (see 1.8b) can be made thus:

135 George $\begin{Bmatrix} has & as\ much\ money \\ does\ not\ have\ \begin{Bmatrix} so \\ =as \end{Bmatrix} many\ books \end{Bmatrix}$ as I have.

d Note that, in subordinate clauses of this type, the operator is used as a pro-form (1.26, 6) as in [128]. The operator is often omitted after *than* and *as*; eg

136 George is quicker than $\left\{\begin{array}{l} I \\ =me \end{array}\right\}$. John is not $\left\{\begin{array}{l} so \\ =as \end{array}\right\}$ quick as $\left\{\begin{array}{l} I \\ =me \end{array}\right\}$

A speaker saying $\left\{\begin{array}{l} than \\ as \end{array}\right\}$ I, which is acceptable but rather pedantic, may be assuming that *than* introduces the clause $\left\{\begin{array}{l} than \\ as \end{array}\right\}$ I am. $\left\{\begin{array}{l} Than \\ As \end{array}\right\}$ me is quite acceptable, at least in informal style, and can be regarded as an example of a preposition followed by the objective case.

Reason clauses – clauses introduced by because . . .
2.45

a A clause of reason or cause may begin with *because, since, seeing (that),
now (that)*, or *as*, and may precede or follow the main clause. BECAUSE is
normally used in answer to *Why?* especially when the reason clause is
given as a short answer.
137 A Why don't you open the door?
  B Because I've brought the wrong key.

b SINCE, besides being used as in 2.40, can mean 'in consequence of the fact
that', as in
138 Since I was in the same class as George, I know him very well.

c SEEING (THAT) could replace *since* in [138], but it would be reasonable to
restrict its meaning to 'in view of the fact that', as in
139 Seeing (that) the hall is already full, I think the meeting should now
  begin.

d NOW (THAT) could replace *seeing (that)* in [139] but could not replace
since in [138]. However, we could say
140 Now (that) I was in the same class as George, I used to be with him
  all day long.
in which case *now that* would mean 'at the time in the past that'. *As* could
replace all the conjunctions used in examples [137–140], though to keep
the meaning of [140] exactly unchanged one would have to say *As I was
now* etc. *As* has other uses (2.37 and 2.41), and it may sometimes be
clearer to replace it by *while* (time) or *because* (reason).

e All the complex sentences in 2.45a–d could be re-worded, in informal
style, so that the subordinate clause became a main clause followed by a
co-ordinate clause beginning with *so* (2.3), thus:
I've brought the wrong key, so I can't open the door.

f In 2.45a–d, the subordinate clause could precede or follow the main. A
clause of reason or cause introduced by *for* will only follow, as in
141 Too much money makes a country poor, for it sets a dearer price on
  everything. (Proverb)

Also, a *because*-clause cannot precede when it expresses the speaker's reason for making the statement contained in the main clause, as in
142 He went home early, because I saw him leave
(which is only likely to occur in informal style).

Contrast clauses[1] – clauses introduced by though . . .
2.46
a The complex sentences in this section could be re-worded by two co-ordinate clauses joined with *but*. Thus *I was in the same class as John for four years, but I never knew him very well*, can become

143 $\left\{\begin{array}{l}\text{Though}\\=\text{Although}\end{array}\right\}$ I was in the same class as John for four years, I never knew him very well.

THOUGH and ALTHOUGH, as conjunctions, are interchangeable.

b EVEN THOUGH emphasises the idea of contrast between the two clauses, and also implies 'in that as well as every other circumstance':
144 Even though he sat next to me, we never said a word to each other.
Though is not normally replaceable by *although* after *even*; and *though* not *although*, can be used as a conjunct coming at the end of the sentence:
145 We were in the same class for four years. I never knew him very well, though.

c EVEN IF adds the idea of contrast to an *if*-clause and implies 'under that as well as every other condition':
146 Even if an icy wind blew from the north, we always slept with our windows wide open.
147 Even if you lock your car, they will still tow it away.

d WHILE, besides being used as in 2.41, can express contrast and be replaced by WHEREAS, as in
148 I prefer the country to the town. The air in the country is pure, $\left\{\begin{array}{l}\text{while}\\=\text{whereas}\end{array}\right\}$ the atmosphere in the town is stale and polluted.

e The sentence *Although he is a good student and tries hard, he will never be top of his class*, could be re-worded in the following ways:
149 Good as he is, he will never be top of his class.

150 Try as he $\left\{\begin{array}{l}\text{does,}\\\text{will,}\\\text{may,}\\\text{might,}\end{array}\right\}$ he will never etc.

151 However hard-working he is, he will never etc.
152 However hard he tries, he will never etc.
153 However he tries, he will never etc.

---

[1] Also called CONCESSION CLAUSES.

The reader may find other variations of this kind, especially in formal and literary style. For example, *though* may be substituted for *as* in [149]; and *may be* will often occur instead of *is* in examples like [151].

f All the subordinate clauses in 2.46 may precede or follow the main.

2.47

The use of *however* in [151–153] is similar to the use of *whatever* etc. in the examples below:

154 Whatever caused the accident, it was not a broken bottle.

155 Whoever was responsible, it was not the poor pedestrian.

156 Whenever it happened, it was certainly not yesterday.

157 Wherever you met her, it was not in *my* house.

Contrast those examples with [46a] in 2.23. In [154], we can replace *whatever* etc. by

No matter what (caused the accident, it was not etc.);

and in [155] we can replace *whoever* etc. by *No matter who* etc. A clause beginning with *No matter* could also follow the main, as in

158 *You* are not responsible, no matter who caused the accident.

Purpose clauses
2.48

a Purpose is commonly expressed by an infinitive (3.12). It can also be expressed by finite clauses beginning with *so that, in order that, lest, for fear (that)*. SO THAT, purpose, must be distinguished from *so that*, result: see 2.49.

159 They shut the window, so (that) the neighbours $\begin{cases} \text{wouldn't} \\ \text{shouldn't} \\ \text{couldn't} \end{cases}$ hear the radio.   (purpose)

160 He spoke so clearly (*ie* as clearly as he did) so that everyone could understand.   (purpose)

IN ORDER THAT is more formal and suggests a more deliberate purpose:

161 In order that there should be no misunderstanding, we propose to issue these instructions to every employee, in writing.

FOR FEAR THAT combines the idea of purpose with that of 'afraid that':

162 We issued these instructions in writing, for fear that a spoken message might be misunderstood.

The formal LEST could replace *for fear that* in [162]; but *for fear that* would not replace *lest* in

163 We erected this memorial, lest our children (should) forget,
    nor

164 We issued the instructions in writing, lest a spoken message (should) be misunderstood (*cp* 2.17a, example [31]),

ie when the conjunction simply means 'so that . . . not' or when the verb after it takes the subjunctive form. (2.17a)

If . . . BE to . . . can express purpose, as in

165 If everyone is to hear you, you must speak up.

b A purpose clause may precede or follow the main.

Result clauses
2.49

a Result clauses will usually *follow* the main. Note the difference between [166] and [167], and the ambiguity of [168]:

166 So that everyone $\begin{cases} \text{could} \\ \text{should} \\ \text{would} \end{cases}$ hear the announcement, we turned the radio up to the maximum volume.   (purpose)

167 We turned the radio up, so that everyone heard the announcement. (result)

168 We turned the radio up so that everyone could hear the announcement.   (purpose *or* result)

So $\begin{cases} +\text{ADJECTIVE} \\ +\text{ADVERB} \end{cases}$ $+ that$ . . . will only follow the clause on which it is dependent, and it refers only to result:

169 $\left.\begin{array}{l} \text{His speech was so clear} \\ \text{He spoke so clearly} \end{array}\right\}$ that we could understand every word.

Such (*a*) $(+\text{ADJECTIVE})+\text{NOUN}+that$ . . . will produce a similar sentence to [169]:

170 He $\begin{cases} \text{made such a (good) speech} \\ \text{advanced such convincing arguments} \\ \text{showed such (great) courage} \end{cases}$ that he was elected unanimously.

In literary or elaborate style, the nominal group in [170] could have the following variations:

$\begin{cases} \text{He} & \begin{array}{l} \text{made} \begin{cases} \text{a speech so remarkable} \\ \text{so remarkable a speech} \end{cases} \\ \text{advanced arguments so convincing} \\ \text{displayed courage so unshakable} \end{array} \\ \text{So convincing were his arguments} \end{cases}$ that he was elected, etc.

b A result clause could precede the main in informal style, as in *We could see Mont Blanc clearly, the visibility was so good.*

Qualifying clauses
2.50

These qualify the main clause, in the sense of limiting its application to specified cases. For example,

171 Monday will be a good day for the meeting, as far as I am concerned,
means that Monday will be convenient, at least in one particular case.
Similarly,

172 Our protest was successful, $\begin{Bmatrix} \text{in that} \\ \text{in so far as} \end{Bmatrix}$ the Minister agreed to
reconsider the matter.

The old-fashioned *inasmuch as*, in place of *in so far as*, will sometimes be
found in formal style.

G Cleft sentences
2.51

a A CLEFT SENTENCE is a device for focusing attention on a particular piece
of information. Thus, if we start with

173 Mr Turnbull gave George this ticket on Saturday,

we can focus attention in these different ways:

173a It was Mr Turnbull who gave George this ticket.

b It was George (that) he gave this ticket to.

c It was this ticket that he gave (to) George.

d It was on Saturday that he gave George this ticket.

b We can also focus attention by using a *wh*-clause:

173e What Mr Turnbull gave George was this ticket.

Note that while the *it*-type of sentence focuses attention by putting the
'particular piece of information' at the beginning of the sentence, the
wh-type puts it at the end.

H Length of sentences
2.52

The number of clauses in a sentence can, in theory, be infinite, so long as
they are all linked together grammatically. We had sentences with three
co-ordinate clauses in 2.1. Here is a sentence with two co-ordinate clauses
and with one subordinate dependent on the second of them:

174 George was late, and the roll had already been called when his
father brought him into the hall.

Here is a sentence with three clauses, the third being subordinate to the
second, which is subordinate to the first, which is the main clause:

175 He was late because his father had been told that school did not
begin until nine o'clock.

Both [174] and [175] are clear enough. But a sentence that contains more
than two or three clauses linked together grammatically requires very
careful construction and is often difficult to read. If we try to make up such
a sentence on the spur of the moment in speech, we often end up with
something that cannot be identified as a sentence at all. That often happens

when we have not carefully thought out what we are going to say. In practice, therefore, when we are trying to write grammatically and intelligibly we need to keep the number of clauses in a sentence small.

Chapter Three
Infinitive, -*ing* and -*ed*

A sentence can not only be expanded, as in Chapter Two, it can also be condensed. The following chapter discusses the main functions of the non-finite parts of the verb, which play an important part in making a sentence as compact as possible.

A The bare infinitive
3.1
The infinitive without *to* follows the modals (1.15) *will, shall, would, should, can, could, may, might* and *must*, and also *need* and *dare* when they are used as modals (1.30).

3.2
The bare infinitive also follows:

a *had better, had best, would (or had) rather, would sooner and might (just) as well* (14.32): eg
  1 We'd better try again. (*meaning* I think we should)
  2 Better (*usually meaning* You'd better) try again.
  3 You'd best try again. (*This is now rather old-fashioned.*)
  4 I'd $\left\{ \begin{array}{l} \text{rather} \\ =\text{sooner} \end{array} \right\}$ stop now. (*meaning* I'd prefer to stop now)
  5 We might (just) as well walk.
  Had better etc. can be followed by the progressive infinitive, as in *We'd better be going*, but cannot be negated, though we can negate the infinitive, eg *We'd better not stop, I'd rather not wait. We might (just) as well not have a car at all*;

b *Let's* (formally *Let us*) as in *Let's go*, meaning 'I suggest we go'. Negative: *Let's not go*, or more informally *Don't let's go*;

c HELP, LET, MAKE, also HEAR (tell), as in
  6 Will you help carry this trunk? *But see* (3.5a).
  7 Let go (of that rope). Don't let go (of my hand).
  8 We must make do (=manage) (with what we've got).
  9 Men have heard tell (=have heard stories) of a strange land far away to the west (*typical of narrative style*);

d HAVE, HELP, LET (=allow) and MAKE + object, as in
  10 I'll have you know I'm the boss here.   (informal)
  11 Will you help me carry this trunk? *But see* (3.9a).

12 Please let us (=allow us to) go with you.[1]

13 Don't make me laugh.

KNOW is also used in this pattern, but usually only with perfective aspect; and BID occurs in it in old-fashioned narrative style:

14 We $\begin{Bmatrix} \text{have} \\ \text{had} \end{Bmatrix}$ never known him lose his temper before.

15 The knight bade the traveller enter.

Note that after LET and MAKE the infinitive can be omitted if it is understood, *eg Please let us. Don't make me*; and that the infinitive with *to* is used when examples like [13] and [14] are put into the passive, *eg He was made to resign. He has never been known to lose his temper.*

e The infinitive without *to* occurs after *Why, Why not,* as in

16 Why worry? Why not relax?

and after *ráther than*, which can also be followed by *-ing*:

17 Let's finish the job now rather than $\begin{Bmatrix} \text{leave} \\ \text{=leaving} \end{Bmatrix}$ it till tomorrow.

3.3

Either the bare infinitive or *-ing* can occur after FEEL, HEAR, NOTICE, SEE, WATCH + object; and here we can see a distinction in the functions of the infinitive and *-ing*.

18a I saw that man break the window. (I saw the complete act)

  b I watched the fishermen hauling their boats up onto the shore. (I watched while the activity continued)

19a Did you hear a dog bark? (give one bark)

  b I heard that dog barking all night. (going on barking)

20a I didn't notice you raise your hand. (complete act)

  b But I noticed several people leaving the room. (I noticed them while they were on their way out)

The distinction is comparable to that between progressive aspect, with *-ing* (1.24), and non-progressive aspect, here indicated by the infinitive.

B The infinitive with *to*
The infinitive after verbs
3.4

An important function of the *to*-infinitive is to indicate a future action or state:

21 The best item on the programme *is still to come*.

22 If we *are to win* this match, we must all do our very best.

23 It was 1491. Columbus *was to reach* America a year later.

---

[1] *Let us* is not contractable to *let's* when *let* means *allow*. Note that the infinitive, when it is monosyllabic, can come immediately after *let* and before a comparatively long object, as in *He let slip a very unfortunate remark.*

24 He $\left\{\begin{array}{l}\textit{grew (up)}\\\textit{came}\\\textit{got}\ \text{(informal)}\end{array}\right\}$ *to be* rather selfish.

BE *to*, as in examples [21], [22] and [23], is often used to refer to the future. It can serve as a kind of future tense, as we shall see in 13.33a (*The Prime Minister is to speak on television this evening*), or to express a command or prohibition regarding future action, as in 13.33b (*You are (not) to stand here*), or to refer to a future in the hands of fate, *eg I don't know what is to happen to us.*

I hope to see you
3.5

a The idea of something that is 'to come' is apparent in

25 I hope to $\left\{\begin{array}{l}\text{see you this evening.}\\\text{be invited to the party.}\end{array}\right.$

There are a large number of verbs, including EXPECT, HELP, PROMISE and WANT, that can replace HOPE in that pattern. A list of them will be found in Chapter Ten (10.4, B3).

b In *I hope to see*, the subject of *hope* and the subject of *see* are the same: *I hope that I will see. See* in *I hope to see* refers to the future as seen from the present, while *see* in *I hoped to see* refers to the future as seen from the past. If the subjects of *hope* and *see* are different, or if *hope* is present while *see* refers to the past, the construction *hope to see* cannot be used. Instead, we would say:

26 *I* hope (that) *you* will see him this evening,[1]   or

27 I *hope* (that) $\left\{\begin{array}{l}\text{I}\\\text{you}\end{array}\right\}$ *saw* the right man.

c Just as the infinitive after HOPE, EXPECT, PROMISE, refers to a future act or state, so the perfect infinitive stands for the future perfect (1.23e) as in

28 I $\left\{\begin{array}{l}\text{hope}\\\text{expect}\\\text{promise}\end{array}\right\}$ $\left\{\begin{array}{l}\text{(that) I will have read}\\=\text{to have read}\end{array}\right\}$ this book by next Tuesday.

d We can also use HOPE, EXPECT and PROMISE with a *that*-clause, but not WANT; so WANT cannot replace HOPE in example [26]. However, we can use WANT in a different pattern, *eg I want you to see him this evening.* This again (1.56) illustrates the importance of using a verb in the pattern(s) appropriate to it.

e After a small set of verbs, *eg* LIKE, HATE, PREFER, the *to*-infinitive refers not to a future state or action but to a habit or a course of action that is liked, not liked or preferred. Thus: *I like to go for a walk on*

---

[1] Present tense is also frequently used in the *that*-clause after HOPE. *eg I hope you see him this evening.*

Sundays. I hate to see you cry. I prefer to go to bed early. These verbs can also be followed by *-ing*, when emphasis is on the activity rather than on the habit, *eg I like going for a walk* = I am content when I am walking. When these verbs are preceded by *would*, then the following *to*-infinitive *does* refer to a future action or state, as in

29 A Would you like to go for a walk?

    B Yes, I *would* like to (go for a walk).

Note how *would have liked to* is used:

I would like (now) to see that film (now or later)

I would have liked (then, past) to see it (then)

I would like (now) to have seen it (before now)

I would have liked (then) to have seen it (before then)

Cp 1.23f.

He seems to be ill
3.6

SEEM, APPEAR and HAPPEN can also be followed by the *to*-infinitive, but the effect is not the same as it is with HOPE. For example, the statements *He is ill. He is sleeping. He has been hurt. He was knocked down by a car* can be QUALIFIED (*ie* made less definite) in the following way:

30 He $\left\{\begin{array}{l}\text{seems} \\ \text{appears} \\ \text{happens}\end{array}\right\}$ to $\left\{\begin{array}{l}\text{be ill.} \\ \text{be sleeping.} \\ \text{have been hurt.} \\ \text{have been knocked down by a car.}\end{array}\right.$

Note that 30 could be re-worded as

30a It $\left\{\begin{array}{l}\text{seems} \\ \text{appears} \\ \text{happens}\end{array}\right\}$ that he $\left\{\begin{array}{l}\text{is ill.} \\ \text{is sleeping.} \\ \text{has been (*or* was) hurt.} \\ \text{has been (*or* was) knocked down by a car.}\end{array}\right.$

I don't promise to; I promise not to
3.7

In the pattern *I promise to go*, we can negate either the first verb or the second, or both. Thus:

31 I don't promise to see Mary again (so I may not see her).

32 I promise $\left\{\begin{array}{l}\text{not} \\ \text{never}\end{array}\right\}$ to see her again (so I won't).

Similarly,

33 The poor old widow can't afford to have a telephone.

34 A busy doctor can't afford *not* to have a telephone.

3.8

We can end short responses in this pattern with the infinitive marker *to*, leaving the rest of the infinitive understood, as in

35 A You mustn't see Mary again.

    B I want to, but I promise not to.

However, *be* is usually retained even in a short response, as in *Are you on holiday today? – No, but I'd like to be.* or *Have you been vaccinated? – No, I don't want to be yet.*

I want you to go
3.9

a WANT, TELL and other verbs, including HELP (10.4, B4), fit into a different pattern from the one in 3.5, though it also contains an infinitive referring to the future:

36 I want you to $\begin{cases} \text{go to the party. I want you to.} \\ \text{be invited. I want you to be.} \end{cases}$

37 I didn't tell you to do that. I didn't tell you to.

38 I told you not to do that. I told you not to.

b In those examples, the subject of *want* and *tell* is *I*, while the subject of the verb in the infinitive is *you*. A similar comment would apply to every verb that fits into this pattern except PROMISE. In

39 I promise (you) not to see her again,

I give the promise to you, and it is I who will not see her again.

c EXPECT and WISH are among the verbs that fit into this pattern. They can also be followed by a *that*-clause. But while *I expect (that) he'll come* means 'I think he'll come', *I expect him to come* can mean either 'I think he'll come' or 'My orders are that he should come'. Similarly, *I wish he'd come* expresses a wish, while *I wish him to come* is an order.

d Notice the difference between B's responses in [40]:

40 A May I go out this evening?

    B Yes, I'll allow you to go. I'll allow you (to).

      or

      No, I'd hate you to go. I'd hate you to.

To may perhaps be omitted after *allow you*, but certainly not after *hate you* without an important change of meaning. It is therefore advisable not to omit the *to* after verbs in this pattern in short responses. (See 10.4, footnote to B4.)

e This pattern can be combined with the construction beginning *There is . . .* (1.57b) to produce a sentence like

41 I want there to be no mistake.

3.10

Told someone to do something is an INDIRECT IMPERATIVE:

DIRECT IMPERATIVE   INDIRECT IMPERATIVE

Go away.   I $\begin{cases} \text{told} \\ \text{ordered} \end{cases}$ him to go away.

Don't go yet.   I told him not to go yet.

Have a seat.   I $\begin{Bmatrix}\text{asked}\\\text{invited}\end{Bmatrix}$ him to have a seat.

Be careful.   I $\begin{Bmatrix}\text{advised}\\\text{warned}\end{Bmatrix}$ them to be careful.

The use of *advised, asked, invited, warned* in the 'indirect' column indicates some of the various functions of the imperative (1.3c).

I'm longing for you to come
3.11
I'm longing can replace *I hope* in *I hope to go*, but it cannot replace *I tell* in *I tell you to go*. But LONG, and some other verbs (10.4, B5a) can fit into a different pattern:

    42 We're longing for you to come here again,

where once more the infinitive refers to the future.

The infinitive expressing purpose (2.48)
3.12
a The infinitive with *to* frequently expresses PURPOSE, indicating that one action will follow another:

    43 I have come to apologise. (*Contrast this with* [24].)

    44 I sent Mrs Bacon a bunch of flowers to thank her for the party.

b A more elaborate expression of 'purpose + consequent action' can be made by putting *so as* or *in order* before the infinitive with *to*, and this can help to avoid confusion with other uses of the infinitive. Note the difference between [45] and [46], [47] and [48] and [49] and [50]:

    45 Some people $\begin{Bmatrix}\textit{refuse}\\\textit{hesitate}\end{Bmatrix}$ to say what they think.

    46 Some speakers *hesitate* $\begin{Bmatrix}\text{(so as)}\\=\text{(in order)}\end{Bmatrix}$ to choose the right word.

    47 The lecturer stopped talking at last (see 3.25a).

    48 He stopped $\begin{Bmatrix}\text{(so as)}\\=\text{(in order)}\end{Bmatrix}$ to talk to me after the lecture.

    49 Our host left us, $\begin{Bmatrix}\text{(so as)}\\=\text{(in order)}\end{Bmatrix}$ to pay the bill. (He paid it)

    50 He invited us to a restaurant then left us to pay the bill. (We had to pay it)

The infinitive expressing consequence
3.13
The infinitive expresses purpose in *He went home to get his coat*, but unexpected consequence in

    51 He went home to find his old friend George waiting for him.

In [51], *to find* could be replaced by *and found*, and what he found was pleasant. It was unexpectedly unpleasant in

52 He went home (only) to find his house in ruins.

The infinitive after adjectives
3.14

The idea of consequence is also present in

a 53 Walter was $\left\{ \begin{array}{l} \text{too weak} \\ = \text{not strong enough} \end{array} \right\}$ to climb the wall.

ie he could not climb it because *he* was too weak, or not strong enough.

Example [53] could be re-worded with $\left\{ \begin{array}{l} so \\ such \end{array} \right\}$ ... *as to*, on the following pattern:

54 He was $\left\{ \begin{array}{l} \text{so weak} \\ \text{in such a state} \end{array} \right\}$ as to be unable even to feed himself.

b 55 The sea was $\left\{ \begin{array}{l} \text{too cold} \\ = \text{not warm enough} \end{array} \right\}$ to swim in,

ie people could not swim in the sea because *the sea* was too cold;

c 56 The bridge was $\left\{ \begin{array}{l} \text{too narrow} \\ = \text{not wide enough} \end{array} \right\}$ for the truck to cross,

ie the *truck* could not cross the *bridge* because the bridge was too narrow.

He is anxious to see her
3.15

The infinitive in the pattern BE + adjective + infinitive will sometimes indicate a future action or state, sometimes not:

a 57 *He is anxious to see her* = He wants (very much) to see her.

To see in [57] is 'something that is to come', as in 3.4. Adjectives that could replace *anxious* in this kind of construction include *(un)able, afraid, anxious, apt, ashamed, bound, curious, determined, eager, free, inclined, keen, prepared, ready, reluctant, willing*, all expressing a personal attitude to something that has not yet happened.

b 58 *He is likely to see her* = *It is likely that he will see her* = He probably will see her.

Again, *to see* is 'something that is to come', but here the adjective is an indication of the *speaker's* attitude towards the future. This attitude is clearer in other adjectives that could replace *likely, eg certain, sure.* In *George is sure to see Mary*, it is the speaker rather than George who is sure.

c 59 *He is happy to see her again* = He is happy $\left\{ \begin{array}{l} because \\ when \end{array} \right\}$ he sees her *or* has seen her again.

Happy in this construction could be replaced by *content(ed)*, *delighted*, *excited*, *fortunate*, *glad*, *grateful*, *honoured*, *(un)lucky*, *pleased*, *proud*, *relieved*, *sad*, *sorry*, *surprised*, *thankful*, *thrilled*. Again, these adjectives are indications of personal attitudes or conditions, but this time in relation to something that *has* taken place. Note this variation of [59]:

60 He must be happy to sing like that. (=I assume he's happy if he sings . . .)

As in 3.5b, *I am sorry to hear* = *I hear* it and *I am* sorry, while *I was sorry to hear it* = *I heard* it and *I was* sorry. If the subject or time reference is different, we must say *eg I am sorry that you feel that way* or *I am sorry I was rude to you*. However, we can say

61 I am sorry to have missed him. (=I am sorry (that) I $\left\{\begin{array}{l}\text{have missed}\\\text{missed}\end{array}\right\}$ him)

d 62 *He is foolish to meet her again* = *It is foolish of him to meet her again*

or He is $\left\{\begin{array}{l}\text{being foolish}\\\text{acting foolishly}\end{array}\right\}$ by meeting her again.

Only 'action' words (1.44c) could replace *foolish* in this construction: they include *brave, clever, cruel, generous, good* (in the sense of 'kind' or 'well-behaved'), *kind, polite, reasonable, rude, selfish, sensible, silly, stupid, wicked, wise*.

e 63 *George is quick to take offence.* (=He takes offence quickly)

Similarly, *hesitant, prompt, reluctant, slow, willing*.

f 64 *He is easy to teach.* (=He is an easy pupil to teach *or* It is easy to teach him)

We could replace *easy* in this construction by *agreeable, amusing, difficult, hard, hopeless, interesting, nice, pleasant*. The subject of the sentence could also be inanimate, *eg*

65a This rule is easy to remember.

b $\left\{\begin{array}{l}\text{This car}\\\text{It}\end{array}\right\}$ is $\left\{\begin{array}{l}\text{easy}\\\text{expensive}\end{array}\right\}$ to drive.

g Note the difference between *It is easy to drive* as in [65b], when *It* refers to *This car*, and the same sentence when the anticipatory *It* stands for *To drive (a car)*. Similarly, in

66 *It is important to remember this rule*,

It there stands for 'to remember this rule'. *Important* in [66] could be replaced by *advisable, better, best, convenient, desirable, difficult, essential, (un)necessary, (im)possible* and by *well* (formal style) or *(just) as well* in less formal style.

The infinitive after nouns
3.16

a Nouns corresponding to the verbs that fit into the pattern of *wish to*

(3.5) are usually followed by the infinitive with *to*, as in
67 I have no wish to quarrel with you (=I don't wish to).
68 They will make another attempt to cross the river tonight.
Exceptions: *We have no hope of finding him. Some people have a preference for eating out* (=They prefer to eat at a restaurant).
b Nouns corresponding to the adjectives that fit into the pattern of *anxious to* (3.15) are likewise followed by the infinitive. *He was anxious, determined, etc., to please* could be re-worded

69 He showed $\left\{ \begin{array}{l} \text{an anxiety, a determination} \\ \text{an inclination, a readiness} \\ \text{a reluctance, a willingness} \end{array} \right\}$ to please.

Nouns corresponding to other adjectives in 3.15 may either be followed

by the infinitive, *eg it was* $\left\{ \begin{array}{l} an\ honour \\ a\ pleasure \\ a\ relief \\ a\ surprise \end{array} \right\}$ *to see her*

or may fit into a different pattern, thus:

70 His $\left\{ \begin{array}{l} \text{delight, excitement} \\ \text{pleasure, pride} \\ \text{relief, surprise} \end{array} \right\}$ at seeing her again was tremendous.

Infinitive as subject, complement and object
3.17
a The infinitive can be the subject of the sentence as in

71 To hesitate is $\left\{ \begin{array}{l} \text{fatal.} \\ \text{a pity.} \end{array} \right\}$

but modern English tends to prefer the ANTICIPATORY *it* construction, as in 2.8 (example [16]), 3.15 (example [66]) and

72 It is $\left\{ \begin{array}{l} \text{fatal} \\ \text{a pity} \end{array} \right\}$ to hesitate.

It was $\left\{ \begin{array}{l} \text{good} \\ \text{a great pleasure} \end{array} \right\}$ to see you.

b The infinitive is the complement of subject + BE in
73 Your mistake was to write him that letter.
Notice the difference between
74 Your mistake was not to write that letter. (You failed to write)
and
75 Your mistake was not to write a letter but to write so rudely. (You did write: your mistake was to write rudely)
Possible confusion between [74] and [75] could be avoided if [75] were worded *Your mistake was not so much to write a letter as to write so rudely.*
c The infinitive is used as object of the verb in the *hope to* pattern (3.5).

d The infinitive is not used immediately after a preposition: *-ing* is used instead in an example like

76 We can depend on finding him there.

Nor is it used as the object in a sentence on the pattern *I found him dull* (basic sentence type 5, 1.55). We can say *We consider meeting her foolish*; but if an infinitive were used in place of *-ing* in that sentence, we should have to say

77 We consider it foolish (of him) to meet her.

The passive infinitive
3.18

a The passive infinitive is found in *Women like to be admired, I want this to be done again, He is not strong enough to be moved yet, He is determined to be obeyed.* It is used in

78 The boy was nowhere to be seen. (= One couldn't see him anywhere)

79 You are to be congratulated. (= One must congratulate you)

80 Jack's work leaves much to be desired. (*LEAVE much to be desired* being a fixed expression meaning 'BE very unsatisfactory')

b Only the active is normally used, though the meaning is passive, in

81 This house is to let. (= Someone wishes to let it)
and

82 You are not to blame for what happened. (= No one should blame you)

Infinitive with perfective and progressive aspects
3.19

a Examples of the perfect infinitive have been given in 1.23f. (*I am happy to have been George's friend*), 3.5c (*I expect to have read this book*) and 3.15c (*I am sorry to have missed him*).

b The infinitive can occur in the progressive aspect, as in

83 $\left\{\begin{array}{l} \text{I don't want} \\ \text{I don't} \left\{\begin{array}{l}\text{want} \\ \text{expect}\end{array}\right\} \text{you}\end{array}\right\}$ to be sitting here all day.

After WANT + object, *to be* can be omitted, as in

84 I don't want you (to be) sitting here all day.

The progressive infinitive can also occur after an adjective:

85 We are sorry to be leaving so soon.

C The *-ing* participle and gerund
3.20

When it is used in conjunction with BE to express progressive aspect (*eg We're waiting*), the *-ing* form has a verbal function and is traditionally called a participle. It is a participle in commonly-used constructions like *Let's go swimming. Come dancing with us.* It can also function as an NP, in which case it is traditionally called the GERUND, as in *I like* $\begin{cases} chocolate. \\ swimming. \end{cases}$

In [86], *standing* can therefore be called a participle; in [87], it can be called a gerund:

86 Standing here all day, I see some very strange people.

87 $\begin{cases} \text{Standing (here all day)} \\ \text{This kind of work} \end{cases}$ makes me very tired.

3.21

Running is a participle in *a running stream* and here *running* acts as an adjective, describing *stream.* The same word is a gerund in *running shoes*, 'shoes used or intended for running': and here *running* is the label for a subclass (1.7b, ii) of shoe and could be replaced by a noun, *eg sports shoes.* Note that *a running stream* has the same stress pattern as *a good friend* (1.7b, i) while *running shoes* has the same stress pattern as *a school friend* (1.7b, ii). Other examples of phrases on these two patterns include:

a -*ing as participle, nuclear stress on the noun*

ˈboiling ˋwater	ˈliving ˋpeople
ˈchanging ˋcircumstances	ˈsliding ˋdoors
the ˈfollowing ˋexample	a ˈmoving ˋstaircase

The first stress falls on *hard, fast, long* in examples like ˈhardworking ˋstudents, ˈfast-moving ˋtraffic, ˈlong-playing ˋrecords, *ie* students that work hard, traffic that moves fast, records that play for a long time.

b -*ing as gerund, nuclear stress on the -ing form*

a ˋbathing costume	= a costume used or intended for bathing (in)
ˋworking clothes	= clothes used or intended for working (in)
ˋwriting paper	= paper used or intended for writing (on)
ˋboiling point	= point at which a liquid boils
a ˋchanging room	= room where one changes one's clothes (for sports)
a ˋliving room	= room where one lives when not sleeping

The -ing participle as adjective
3.22

a The -*ing* participles in 3.21a are not 'full' adjectives, in that they cannot be modified by *very* or *too*, nor can they be compared (1.44). A number of -*ing* participles can, however, be used as 'full' adjectives, *eg*

88 That is a $\begin{Bmatrix} very \\ more \end{Bmatrix}$ $\begin{Bmatrix} interesting \\ exciting \\ amusing \\ entertaining \end{Bmatrix}$ story.

A list of *-ing* participles used as adjectives will be found in 7.2a.

b When *-ing* is used as an adjective, it usually refers to a characteristic feature of the thing referred to by the noun and not to any specific act. Notice the difference between

89   The speaker was given a standing ovation,

the kind of applause given when all the audience is standing, and

90   I can see several people standing,

ie they are standing now. There could be no question of the *-ing* form coming before the noun in

91   I can see several people standing at the back.

Participle or gerund?
3.23

a The gerund can be preceded by *the* or *a*, as in

92   Every morning, the singing of birds wakes me up.

93   I can hear a singing (= a singing noise) in my ears.

b A gerund can also be preceded by the possessive form of a personal pronoun or of a noun referring to a person, thus:

94   I'll never forget { George's / his } { imitation of / imitating } the headmaster.

We could say

94a   I'll never forget { George / him } imitating the headmaster,

in which case we might say that *imitating* is a participle and could be expanded to *when he is imitating*. However, { George's / His } could not be replaced by { George / Him } (except in substandard English) in an initial position, as in

95   { George's / His } making fun of people got him into serious trouble.

On the other hand, the possessive form would not be used with an impersonal noun or pronoun, as in

96   I'll never forget { the door opening / that happening } just as George began.

c Contrast example [94] with

94b   Mr Turner { found / caught } George imitating the headmaster.

and

97   He { kept us all waiting / had us all laughing }

in which the possessive form could not be used before *-ing*. For verbs that cannot be followed by a possessive form + *-ing*, see 10.4, B9.

-ing as gerund
3.24
The gerund can be:
a the subject of a sentence:
   98 *Swimming* is my favourite sport.
b the complement of subject + BE:
   99 My favourite sport is *swimming*.
c the object:
   100 I like *swimming*.
d the object of a preposition or of a prepositional verb (1.37, 2) I'm fond *of swimming*. Thank you *for calling*. We learn *by listening*. Get on with your work *without talking*. Think, *instead of writing*. I don't *object to dancing*.
   Distinguish between the preposition *to* and the infinitive marker *to* (1.16, 4). *To* is the infinitive marker in *I agree to go with you*; it is a preposition, governing a noun or a gerund, in

101 I agree to $\begin{cases} \text{your proposal that we should share} \\ \text{sharing} \end{cases}$ the profits.

   and in

102 I object to $\begin{cases} \text{such stupid criticisms.} \\ \text{being criticised so stupidly.} \end{cases}$

e replaceable by *it*, as in
   103 A Do you like swimming?
       B I like it very much. I'm very fond of it.

D Infinitive or *-ing* ?
-ing obligatory
3.25

a *-ing* is obligatory when a verb is the object of AVOID, DISLIKE, ENJOY; also KEEP (*ON*) and CARRY ON, which refer to the continuation of an action or state, and PRACTISE, as in *practise swimming*, which refers to activity in progress rather than to a completed act. FINISH and STOP, which refer to the end of activity, as in *stop talking*, fit into this pattern. After DENY, REGRET and other verbs which can refer to past action or lack of action, either *-ing* or *having* + the *-ed* participle may occur. Examples:

104 I $\begin{cases} \text{dislike} \\ \text{enjoy} \end{cases}$ $\begin{cases} \text{driving} \\ \text{being driven} \end{cases}$ along a motorway.

105 George $\begin{cases} \text{denied} \\ \text{regretted} \end{cases}$ $\begin{cases} \text{giving} \\ \text{having given} \end{cases}$ Dick any money.

b *-ing* also occurs after *It's no* $\begin{cases} good \\ use \end{cases}$ and *It's worth (while)*:

106 It's no $\left\{\begin{array}{l}\text{good}\\\text{use}\end{array}\right\}$ worrying. It's worth (while) trying. (informal)

and after *BE better* in an example like

107 You would be better coming with us.

(Contrast [107] with examples [1], [2] and [66]).

c Be careful to distinguish constructions like *stop talking, go on working* from constructions in which an intransitive verb is followed by an infinitive expressing *purpose* as in example [48] and in *He went on to tell us a very interesting story.*

Infinitive or -ing? Either acceptable
3.26

a Some verbs can have either the infinitive or *-ing* as object without change of meaning. They include CAN'T BEAR, BEGIN, CEASE, PREFER and others: see 10.7. Thus:

108 They $\left\{\begin{array}{l}\text{began}\\\text{preferred}\\\text{couldn't bear}\\\text{ceased}\end{array}\right\}$ $\left\{\begin{array}{l}\text{to watch}\\\text{=watching}\end{array}\right\}$ television.

b Only the infinitive is normal in the following cases:

after *would* $\left\{\begin{array}{l}\textit{hate}\\\textit{love}\\\textit{like}\\\textit{prefer}\end{array}\right\}$ referring to a new act in the future:

109 A Would you $\left\{\begin{array}{l}\text{like}\\\text{prefer}\end{array}\right\}$ to dance?

B I would $\left\{\begin{array}{l}\text{hate}\\\text{love}\end{array}\right\}$ to (dance); and

when the second verb is a 'stative' one like SEE and BELIEVE (1.24b, iii & iv) as in

110 We began to $\left\{\begin{array}{l}\text{see what he meant.}\\\text{believe his story.}\end{array}\right.$

However, HAVE may be used in the *-ing* form, as in

111 I prefer $\left\{\begin{array}{l}\text{to have}\\\text{having}\end{array}\right\}$ my own desk.

c The infinitive is preferable, so as to avoid a repetition of *-ing*, when the first verb is in the progressive, as in

112 We are proposing to start at eight.

On the other hand, only *-ing* occurs in *Cease firing!* marking the end of a process, as in 3.25a.

3.27

After all of the verbs in 3.26, we can use the infinitive to refer to a new or completed act, and -*ing* to refer to action in progress, although many speakers would neither see nor make any difference between *We began to work* and *We began working*. A difference becomes clear, however, when we compare example [109], where the infinitive is obligatory, with

113 I wouldn't like lying in a tiny spaceship for four or five days (*ie* I wouldn't like that experience),

where either *lying* or *to lie* would be acceptable.

3.28

The gerund cannot replace the infinitive in *He is* $\left\{ \begin{array}{l} anxious \\ likely \end{array} \right\}$ *to see her* (3.15a & b), where the infinitive refers to 'something that is to come'. But it may replace the infinitive in 3.15c & d. Thus:

59a He is happy seeing her again

or

Seeing her again $\left\{ \begin{array}{l} \text{makes} \\ \text{(has) made} \end{array} \right\}$ him very happy.

62a He is foolish meeting her again

or

It was foolish of him meeting her again.

We can also say *It is expensive running this car*, and *It is better turning the key the other way*. The gerund would not occur after *essential, important, necessary*.

3.29

A few verbs (10.7) can be followed directly by an infinitive or by a preposition + -*ing*, eg

114 They $\left\{ \begin{array}{l} \text{agreed} \\ \text{decided} \end{array} \right\}$ $\left\{ \begin{array}{l} \text{to share} \\ \text{on sharing} \end{array} \right\}$ the profits equally.

There is a similar choice after certain nouns and adjectives:

115 I hope to have $\left\{ \begin{array}{l} \text{a(n)} \\ \text{the} \end{array} \right\}$ $\left\{ \begin{array}{l} \text{chance} \\ \text{opportunity} \end{array} \right\}$ $\left\{ \begin{array}{l} \text{to see} \\ \text{of seeing} \end{array} \right\}$ you.

116 They were quite content $\left\{ \begin{array}{l} \text{to stay} \\ \text{with staying} \end{array} \right\}$ where they were.

Infinitive or -ing? Either possible, but with different meaning
3.30

After certain verbs and adjectives, either the infinitive or -*ing* may be used but with a difference in meaning. The difference is of two main kinds.

1 When two verbs are used together, as in *I remembered to post your letter* and *I remembered posting it*, they refer to two separate events. In *I remembered to post it*, the second event follows the first, thus:

I remembered to post it = I remembered, then I posted it.

In *I remember posting it*, the first event follows the second, thus:
I posted it. Now I remember.
We can make it clear that *posting* refers to a previous event by saying *I remember having posted it*. The same applies to FORGET, other verbs listed in 10.7, and *BE ashamed*, thus:

117a I *remembered to post* your letter: I remembered that I had to: then I posted it.

b I *remember* $\left\{ \begin{array}{l} posting \\ = \text{having posted} \\ = \text{(that) I posted} \end{array} \right\}$ it: I posted it, and remember performing that action.

118a He's too *ashamed to look* at us: as in 3.15a.

b He's *ashamed of* $\left\{ \begin{array}{l} losing \\ = \text{having lost} \end{array} \right\}$
his temper.   ashamed of past action.

2 The second verb can refer to a new act in a chain of events, in which case it is in the infinitive; or it can refer to an activity in general or to a process, in which case it takes the *-ing* form. Here are two examples, others being listed in 10.7:

119a I $\left\{ \begin{array}{l} am \\ would\ be \end{array} \right\}$ very *interested to hear* your news

b I am $\left\{ \begin{array}{l} interested\ in \\ keen\ on \end{array} \right\}$ *collecting* stamps

120a *Try to* write better: or *Try and write better*, the new act being expressed by *and write*

I tried to write better: *to write* not replaceable by *and wrote*

b A I can't unlock the door.
B *Try turning* the key the other way: Make that experiment and see what happens.

E The *-ed* participle
3.31
The past, or *-ed* participle can be used in an active verbal group, as in
121 The guests have arrived,
or a passive verbal group, as in
122 Someone has been injured.

-ed as adjective
3.32
a When it is passive, the *-ed* participle is often used as an adjective:
123 The injured man was taken to hospital.

'Active' participles are rarely used in this way: we could not, for example, use *arrived* as an adjective before *guests*.

b Examples of passive participles used as attributive adjectives (1.43a) are

a broken window   lost property

a closed shop   a murdered man

a defeated army   an organised attempt

a finished article   a recorded talk

an honoured guest   the spoken word

For other examples, see 7.2b.

c The negative PREFIX *un-* (1.59d) is often attached to a passive -*ed* participle, as in

an unbroken record   an unfinished article

Negative adjectives on this pattern are even formed when there is no corresponding positive adjective: *eg*

untold wealth   His conduct was $\left\{ \begin{array}{l} \text{uncalled for} \\ \text{unheard of} \end{array} \right\}$

d An -*ed* participle is often made into a compound with the help of *well*, *badly* or *half*, as in

A $\left\{ \begin{array}{l} \text{well-} \\ \text{badly-} \\ \text{half-} \end{array} \right\}$ finished job.

Such compounds are sometimes used even when the -*ed* participle in its simple form is not used as an adjective. Thus, *built* is not used alone as an adjective, but we can say

124 This is a $\left\{ \begin{array}{l} \text{well-built} \\ \text{badly-built} \end{array} \right\}$ house.

3.33

a Among the few active participles that can be used adjectivally are *escaped*, *faded*, *fallen* and *grown*:

·an escaped prisoner = one who has escaped

a faded flower   = one that has faded

fallen leaves   = those that have fallen

a grown man   = one who has grown to a man's size

b A few active participles can be used adjectivally in compounds although they would not be so used in their simple form. For example, we could not form adjectives on the pattern of *behaved* and *spoken* from such sentences as *Those children are behaving themselves* or *They are speaking*; but we can say

125 They are well-behaved and well-spoken.

3.34

-*ed* can be added to a noun when there is no corresponding verb. We can therefore talk of *a bearded man,* ie a man with a beard. Such *-ed* forms are usually modified, *eg*

> a blue-eyed baby
> a four-engined aircraft
> a long-legged animal
> a ragged,[1] wretched,[1] aged[1] man leaning heavily on a crooked[1] stick, helped along by his good-tempered wife.

3.35

a As with *-ing* when it is used adjectivally (3.22a), only a small number of *-ed* participles can be modified by *very* or *too* or can be compared. These few include *tired, interested, worried,* and others listed in 7.2, *eg*

126   We are $\left\{ \begin{array}{l} \text{very} \\ \text{too} \\ \text{more} \end{array} \right\}$ $\left\{ \begin{array}{l} \text{tired} \\ \text{interested} \\ \text{worried} \end{array} \right\}$.

b We must distinguish the *-ed* adjectives from the *-ing*, as in

127a   This story $\left\{ \begin{array}{l} \text{interests} \\ \text{amuses} \\ \text{fascinates} \end{array} \right\}$ me.

   b   This story is $\left\{ \begin{array}{l} \text{interesting} \\ \text{amusing} \\ \text{fascinating} \end{array} \right\}$

   c   I am $\left\{ \begin{array}{l} \text{interested in} \\ \text{amused by} \\ \text{fascinated by} \end{array} \right\}$ it.

c The *-ed* adjectives are often followed by a prepositional phrase beginning with *by*, as in [127c], so that *I am amused by it* can either provide an example of an adjective describing my state of mind or of a verb in the passive. The difference between *-ed* as adjective and *-ed* as pure passive is seen in these two examples:

128   I am very *worried about* you. (adjective)
129   We were *worried by* mosquitoes all night. (passive)

3.36

Many *-ed* participles which cannot be preceded by *very* can be modified by other intensifiers such as *(very) much, well, badly, completely, greatly, highly*:

130   Her performance was $\left\{ \begin{array}{l} \text{(very) much} \\ \text{greatly} \end{array} \right\}$ admired.

---

[1] The *-ed* is pronounced as an extra syllable in these words: /rægid/, /retʃid/, /eidʒid/, /krukid/. These are exceptions to the rule given in 1.16.3. Similarly, *naked* /neikid/, *sacred* /seikrid/, *wicked* /wikid/.

131 The pedestrian was $\left\{ \begin{array}{c} \text{badly} \\ \text{seriously} \end{array} \right\}$ injured.

132 He is a $\left\{ \begin{array}{c} \text{well} \\ \text{highly} \end{array} \right\}$ qualified engineer.

133 The story was completely forgotten.

For other examples, see 15.28.

3.37

Concerned and *involved* follow the nouns they modify:

134 I would like to see all the students $\left\{ \begin{array}{c} \text{concerned} \\ \text{involved} \end{array} \right\}$.

The students $\left\{ \begin{array}{c} concerned \\ involved \end{array} \right\}$ may be considered as a reduced form of *The students who are concerned*, as we shall see in the next Chapter. (4.19)

3.38

A few old past participles survive as adjectives in a form different from that of the past participle:

PAST PARTICIPLE	ADJECTIVE, ATTRIBUTIVE	ADJECTIVE, PREDICATIVE
—	beloved /biˈlʌvid/	beloved /biˈlʌvd/
bent	bent, bended	bent
blessed /blest/	blessed /blesid/	blest /blest/
bound	bounden	bound
drunk	drunken	drunk
lit	lighted	lit
melted	molten	melted
rotted	rotten	rotten
shaved	shaven	shaved
shrunk	shrunken	shrunk
sunk	sunken	sunk

Examples:

135 Wood that has rotted is rotten (wood).

136 A clean-shaven man is one who has (been) shaved.

Bended is found in the phrase *on bended knees* (=kneeling); otherwise the attributive adjective is *bent*. Note: *my blessed father* but *I'm blest if I know* (=I really don't, informal). *Bounden* occurs in *my bounden duty*. *Lighted* occurs in phrases like a *lighted* $\left\{ \begin{array}{c} match \\ candle \\ torch \end{array} \right\}$. *Molten* occurs in *molten* $\left\{ \begin{array}{c} lava \\ lead \\ steel \end{array} \right\}$; *shaven* in *clean-shaven cheeks*; *sunken* in *a sunken garden*.

Get your hair cut

3.39

The past participle can be the complement of the object of a clause, as in

137 We found the door (to be) locked (it was locked when we came),

or in

138 You must $\left\{ \begin{array}{l} \text{have} \\ \text{get} \end{array} \right\}$ your hair cut.

In [138], the past participle expresses the result of an action, and *to be* could not be inserted here. The following example,

139 I have had my car stolen,

refers to an action that I have suffered, and means *My car has been stolen.*

Chapter Four
Condensing the sentence

4.1

Sentence construction can proceed in three stages. First, we can compose a string of simple sentences, *eg*

1 We are sitting here in the sun. We can see snow-covered hills.

Second, two or more simple sentences can be made into a compound one:

2 We are sitting here in the sun and can see snow-covered hills,

or into a complex one:

3 As we sit here in the sun, we can see snow-covered hills.

Third, we can reduce the number of finite clauses in a compound or a complex sentence in the various ways discussed in this chapter.

A Non-finite clauses

4.2

a Sentences [2] and [3] above can be reduced by converting the first finite clause into a NON-FINITE clause, thus:

4 *Sitting here in the sun*, we can see snow-covered hills.

Sitting here in the sun is a non-finite, *-ing* clause. In other non-finite clauses, the verb can be an *-ed* participle or an infinitive, as in:

4a We could see the distant hills *covered with snow*.

4b We are perfectly content *to sit here in the sun*.

All the examples of the *to*-infinitive, the *-ing* and the *-ed* participles that we had in Chapter Three, except when they were used to premodify nouns, could be regarded as the verbal elements in non-finite clauses. In the present chapter we shall see how non-finite clauses can serve to make sentences more compact.

b *-ing* and infinitive clauses can follow patterns similar to the five main types of clause structure that we had in 1.55, Table 9, though the subject is usually absent. Thus:

TYPE	EXAMPLE	NON-FINITE CLAUSE IN ITALICS
1	We waited.	*While waiting*, we did our homework.
		I have come *to apologise*.
2	He was my friend.	*Being my friend*, he helped me a lot.
		To be successful, you must never give up.

TYPE	EXAMPLE	NON-FINITE CLAUSE IN ITALICS
3	I made a mistake.	*Having made that mistake once*, I shall not make it again.
		I am very happy *to see you again.*
4	I gave him an answer.	*Giving you the answer* would be cheating.
		To tell you the truth, I don't know.
5	I found him a bore.	*Finding him a bore*, I kept out of his way.
		She tries *to make everyone happy.*

-ing clauses

4.3

An *-ing* clause can replace a CO-ORDINATE finite clause (2.1). In

> 5 The spectators $\begin{cases} \text{leapt to their feet and roared approval} \\ \text{roared approval and leapt to their feet} \end{cases}$

the two actions occurred more or less simultaneously; and we can re-word that sentence in the following six ways:

5a The spectators leapt to their feet, roaring approval.

 b Roaring approval, the spectators leapt to their feet.

 c The spectators, roaring approval, leapt to their feet.

 d Leaping to their feet, the spectators roared approval.

 e The spectators roared approval, leaping to their feet.

 f The spectators, leaping to their feet, roared appoval.

But in

> 6 The spectators leapt to their feet and ran out onto the pitch,

one action obviously preceded the other, in which case we have only two possibilities for using an *-ing* clause:

6a Leaping to their feet, the spectators ran out onto the pitch.

 b The spectators, leaping to their feet, ran out onto the pitch.

Leaping indicates progressive aspect in *Leaping over the fence, he caught his hand on a nail* (ie He caught his hand on a nail as he was leaping . . .), but it does not in [5d, e and f], nor in [6a and b], where it refers to a completed act in a combination of events.

4.4

An *-ing* clause can correspond to one of the three main types of SUBORDINATE clause described in Chapter 2: noun, adverbial, relative.

4.5

a Acting as a NOUN, the *-ing* clause, like the gerund (3.24), can be

 i the subject of a verb in another clause:

 7 Sitting here in the sun is very pleasant;

 ii the complement of BE:

8 My greatest pleasure is sitting here in the sun;

iii the object of one of the verbs that can be followed by -ing:

9 I enjoy sitting here in the sun;

iv the object of a preposition:

10 Every year, I look forward to sitting here in the sun.

v replaceable by it:

11 A Do you like sitting in the sun?

   B Yes, I thoroughly enjoy it.

In examples [7–10], it is the speaker who is sitting; but you are sitting in

12 I don't mind $\left\{ \begin{matrix} \text{you} \\ = \text{your} \end{matrix} \right\}$ sitting here in the sun at all.

b Note what happens to there $\left\{ \begin{matrix} is \\ are \end{matrix} \right\}$. There is an index to this book. It is a

great advantage can be reduced to

13 There being an index to this book is a great advantage.

The negative would be:

14 There $\left\{ \begin{matrix} \text{not being an} \\ = \text{being no} \end{matrix} \right\}$ index to that book is a disadvantage.

After a preposition, the there being clause would take the form:

15 I'm surprised $\left\{ \begin{matrix} \text{(that) there isn't an} \\ = \text{at there} \left\{ \begin{matrix} \text{not being an} \\ \text{being no} \end{matrix} \right\} \text{index.} \end{matrix} \right.$

c Note how a that-clause can be replaced by a non-finite clause in:

16 I can't imagine $\left\{ \begin{matrix} \text{that anything will happen} \\ = \text{anything happening} \end{matrix} \right\}$ to him.

17 I was afraid $\left\{ \begin{matrix} \text{that} \left\{ \begin{matrix} \text{John} \\ \text{he} \end{matrix} \right\} \text{might have} \\ = \text{of} \left\{ \begin{matrix} \text{John's} \\ \text{his} \\ \text{him} \end{matrix} \right\} \text{having} \end{matrix} \right\}$ an accident.

Notice how the preposition is restored in [15] and [17]: see 2.9.

4.6

If it corresponds to a finite ADVERBIAL clause, an -ing clause can express
time, as in [4], or time + cause as in

18 Being only a student, I can't afford to get married

   or

19 There being no further business, the meeting was adjourned.

It can express time + contrast, as in

20 Sitting here in the sun, I still feel cold.

Note that the -ing clause in example [4] may correspond to a clause
beginning with As. A finite as-clause is often added to the -ing clause, eg

21 Sitting here in the sun as I am, I feel thoroughly content.

4.7

a A finite adverbial clause of TIME (2.37) can be reduced to an *-ing* clause by retaining the subordinating conjunction but deleting the subject and the auxiliary (if any) – *provided the subject is the same as in the main clause.* Thus:

22 When you are writing a business letter, begin 'Dear Sir',

can be reduced to

22a When writing a business letter, begin 'Dear Sir'.

This device can also be used with clauses introduced by *while, after, before* and *since* (but not with *as, as soon as, till, until*). Thus:

23 While waiting at the dentist's, I read a whole short story.

24 After reading the story, I did a crossword puzzle.

25 Before going to the dentist, I have a cup of tea.

26 Since leaving school, I have never met George again.

b The *-ing* clause in [26] refers only to time: it cannot replace the subordinate clause in

27 I don't need these books now $\left\{ \begin{array}{l} \text{since} \\ =\text{because} \end{array} \right\}$ I've left school.

c *Being* can be used with *after, before* and *since* (time), as in

28 $\left\{ \begin{array}{l} \text{After} \\ \text{Before} \end{array} \right\} \left\{ \begin{array}{l} \text{he was} \\ =\text{being} \end{array} \right\}$ in the army, he was an engineer.

29 Since $\left\{ \begin{array}{l} \text{he was} \\ =\text{being} \end{array} \right\}$ in the army, he has been in much better health.[1]

4.8

An *-ing* clause of time can also be introduced by optional *on* or *in*:

30 $\left\{ \begin{array}{l} \text{When we opened} \\ =\text{(On) opening} \end{array} \right\}$ the cupboard, we found a skeleton inside.

ie we found the skeleton at that point in time. And

31 $\left\{ \begin{array}{l} \text{While I was} \\ =\text{(In)} \end{array} \right\}$ trying to open the door, I broke the key.

ie I broke the key in the process of trying to open the door.

4.9

By + *-ing* introduces a very useful clause of MANNER (2.37)

32 You lock this door by turning the key twice to the left,

ie you lock it in that way. Manner is suggested by *as if* (2.37)

33 He locked the cupboard quickly, as if trying to hide something from us.

4.10

If and *unless* can introduce shortened CONDITIONAL clauses (2.42):

---

[1] Since being in the army can also mean 'Since he has been in the army': see 2.40, [87].

34 $\left\{\begin{array}{l} \text{If} \\ \text{Unless} \end{array}\right\}$ (you are) arriving by coach, please let the secretary know.

Even if (2.46c) and *whether* (2.43b) can also introduce an *-ing* clause.

4.11

(Al)though and *while* can introduce a shortened CONTRAST clause (2.46):

35 $\left\{\begin{array}{l} \text{(Al)though} \\ \text{While} \end{array}\right\}$ impressing the examiners, he nevertheless failed.

Being can occur with *while* in this sense:

36 While $\left\{\begin{array}{l} \text{I am not optimistic} \\ = \text{not being optimistic} \end{array}\right\}$, I have not given up all hope.

4.12

We cannot form *-ing* clauses of reason (2.45) beginning with *as, because* and *since* on the models in 4.7–11; but we can form an *-ing* clause of manner (2.37) beginning with *as if, eg He moved his lips as if (he were) trying to speak.*

4.13

Sitting here in the sun can replace a RELATIVE CLAUSE (2.26) in

37 The people (who are) sitting here in the sun are tourists,
     and
38 These tourists, (who are) sitting here in the sun, arrived this morning.

The *-ing* clause is restrictive in [37], non-restrictive in [38].

4.14

An *-ing* can replace either a simple tense (1.14) or a progressive (1.24); it can replace a stative verb (1.24) as well as an action verb; it can refer to present, perfective and past; but it can only replace a verb in the active voice.

39 Will anyone $\left\{\begin{array}{l} \text{who wants} \\ = \text{wanting} \end{array}\right\}$ a ticket please apply to me.

40 Will the people $\left\{\begin{array}{l} \text{who are sitting} \\ = \text{sitting} \end{array}\right\}$ at the back please move forward.

41 The boys $\left\{\begin{array}{l} \text{who have shouted} \\ \text{who have been shouting} \\ = \text{shouting} \end{array}\right\}$ the loudest are the winners.

42 The boys $\left\{\begin{array}{l} \text{who had shouted} \\ \text{who had been shouting} \\ \text{who shouted} \\ \text{who were shouting} \\ = \text{shouting} \end{array}\right\}$ the loudest were the winners.

Note the sequence of tenses in [41] and [42], and the various interpretations that the *-ing* participle could have in all those examples. We can often make

it clear which interpretation is intended by adding an *as*-clause, as in
example [21]. Thus:
. 43 Wanting a ticket as I do, I shall apply for one at once.
44 Sitting at the back as we are, we can't hear a word.
45 Shouting loudly as they were, the boys got quite hoarse.

4.15
a In adverbial and relative *-ing* clauses, *-ing* is a participle that needs to be
related to a subject. Thus, in example [30], the subject of *opening* is *we*.
The sentence
46 *(On) opening the cupboard, a skeleton fell out,
would suggest that the skeleton opened the cupboard. When the *-ing*
clause precedes the main clause, it is desirable that the subjects of both
clauses should be the same, otherwise the result may be comic, as in [46],
or ambiguous, as in
47 Drinking at the spring, the hunter saw a huge lion.
The ambiguity in [47] would not occur in
48 The hunter saw a huge lion drinking at the spring,
where the *-ing* clause would be interpreted as replacing *It* (= *the lion)
was drinking at the spring*. Or we could say

49 $\begin{cases} \text{While (he was)} \\ = \text{As he was} \end{cases}$ drinking at the spring, the hunter saw a huge
lion,

which makes it clear that *drinking* 'relates' to the huntei.
b *Opening*, in [46], would traditionally be called an UNRELATED PARTICIPLE.
An unrelated participle should be avoided if misunderstanding is likely
to occur. In all of the examples in 4.3, there is no doubt who were roaring
and leaping. Nor would there be any doubt about the subject of *leaping*
in *He caught his hand on a nail leaping over the fence*, though in that
sentence there would be a break in intonation, after *nail*, which would
not occur in [48] after *lion* if it was the lion that was drinking.

Perfective -ing clauses
4.16
We have sat here in the sun for two hours and are very thirsty can be reduced
to
50 Having sat here in the sun for two hours, we are very thirsty.
Note again that the *-ing* participle replaces a verb in the active voice.

-ed clauses
4.17
An *-ed* participle clause is normally a contraction of a clause in which the
verb is in the passive voice. Thus:

51 $\begin{Bmatrix} \text{If} \\ \text{When} \\ \text{Now (that)} \end{Bmatrix}$ this house $\begin{Bmatrix} \text{is} \\ \text{has been} \end{Bmatrix}$ painted white, it looks bigger

can be contracted to

52 Painted white, this house looks bigger; and

53 I like your house $\begin{Bmatrix} \text{if} \\ \text{when} \\ \text{now (that)} \end{Bmatrix}$ it $\begin{Bmatrix} \text{is} \\ \text{has been} \end{Bmatrix}$ painted white

can be contracted to

54 I like your house painted white.

4.18

The *-ed* clauses in [52] and [54] are of the adverbial type. Adverbial *-ed* clauses can be introduced by a subordinating conjunction; but the conjunctions that can be used in this way are not the same set as those introducing *-ing* clauses (4.7a). Note:

55 I will gladly come to your house $\begin{Bmatrix} \text{if} \\ \text{when} \\ \text{whenever} \end{Bmatrix}$ (I am) invited.

56 I won't come $\begin{Bmatrix} \text{until} \\ \text{unless} \end{Bmatrix}$ (I am) invited properly.

57 (Al)though (I was) invited, I didn't go.

58 $\begin{Bmatrix} \text{Even if (I am) invited} \\ \text{Whether (I am) invited or not} \end{Bmatrix}$ I won't go.

59 I am returning your letter, as (I was) requested (to do).

Note also *He fell off his horse as if (he had been) shot.*

After, before, since, on, in and *by* are not used as in [55–59], but they can be used with *being* + *-ed*, as in

60 $\begin{Bmatrix} \text{After} \\ \text{Since} \end{Bmatrix}$ being invited, I have been told the party was cancelled.

61 On being told the party was cancelled, she burst into tears.

On being told in [61] = when she was told.

4.19

An *-ed* clause replaces a relative clause, restrictive, in

62 Cars (which have been) parked illegally will be removed,

or non-restrictive, in

63 The castle, (which was) burnt down in 1485, was never rebuilt.

The participle can be in the progressive form, as in

64 We were delayed by heavy trucks (which were) being loaded onto the ship.

Notice the difference between an *-ed* participle clause, as in

65 Will the students (who are) $\begin{Bmatrix} \text{interested} \\ \text{concerned} \\ \text{involved} \end{Bmatrix}$ please write their names on

this piece of paper,
and an *-ed* participle used as an adjective, as in *The defeated army fled into the hills* (3.32).

4.20
In a noun clause, *-ed* must be preceded by *-ing*. Thus, compared with example [7], we have
66 Being invited to come here is a great honour,
and compared with [9] and [10], we have

67 I $\begin{Bmatrix} \text{appreciate} \\ \text{look forward to} \end{Bmatrix}$ being invited here again.

4.21
Compared with the active perfective in 4.16, we have the passive perfective in

68 $\begin{Bmatrix} \text{I have been invited to speak to you and} \\ \text{Having been invited to speak to you I} \end{Bmatrix}$ must say a few words.

4.22
Like *-ing* (4.15), the *-ed* participle needs to be related to a subject in adverbial and relative clauses, and either a comic effect or ambiguity might be produced by a participle that is not clearly related, as in
69 *Painted white, we liked the house much better.
70 *Being loaded onto the ship, we were delayed by several enormous trucks.
Both [69] and [70] have the effect of suggesting that *we* is the subject of the *-ed* clause; but this effect would not be produced if the *-ed* clause followed the main clause in those examples. Again, an unrelated participle should be avoided if misunderstanding is likely.

Infinitive clauses
4.23
An infinitive clause can be subject, complement or object, as we saw in 3.17. It can replace a *that*-clause in examples such as the following:

71 I hope $\begin{Bmatrix} \text{that I'll be able to come.} \\ =\text{to be able to come.} \end{Bmatrix}$

72 We consider $\begin{Bmatrix} \text{that he is very trustworthy.} \\ =\text{him to be very trustworthy.} \end{Bmatrix}$

73 We thought it wrong $\begin{cases} \text{that he should be punished.} \\ = \text{to punish him.} \end{cases}$

However, an infinitive clause like that in [71] is only possible (a) if the verb in the main clause is one that will fit into the *hope to* pattern (3.5), and if the subject and time reference are the same in both clauses (3.5b). Likewise, an infinitive clause like that in [72] is only possible after a small set of verbs, including BELIEVE and CONSIDER (10.6, D3); and a similar comment applies to [73].

4.24

An infinitive clause can replace a finite adverbial clause of purpose, as in

74 He worked all night $\begin{cases} \text{so that he could} \\ = \text{so as to} \end{cases}$ get the job done in time,

provided that the subject and time reference are the same in both clauses. It can replace a finite clause of result, as in

75 His work was so good $\begin{cases} \text{that it made} \\ = \text{as to make} \end{cases}$ him internationally famous.

76 He was in such bad health $\begin{cases} \text{that he was} \\ = \text{as to be} \end{cases}$ obliged to resign.

4.25

A finite *wh*-clause can be reduced to an infinitive clause in the following types of example:

77 I don't know what $\begin{cases} \text{I should do.} \\ = \text{to do.} \end{cases}$

78 I don't know who(m) $\begin{cases} \text{I should ask.} \\ = \text{to ask.} \end{cases}$

79 Can you tell me where $\begin{cases} \text{I should go?} \\ = \text{to go?} \end{cases}$

80 I wonder when $\begin{cases} \text{I should leave.} \\ = \text{to leave.} \end{cases}$

81 Tell me how $\begin{cases} \text{I can start this car.} \\ = \text{to start this car.} \end{cases}$

82 I haven't decided whether $\begin{cases} \text{I shall sell it or not.} \\ = \text{to sell it or not.} \end{cases}$

83 We must reach a decision (as to) whether $\begin{cases} \text{we should sell.} \\ = \text{to sell.} \end{cases}$

Note that the subject is the same in both clauses, except in [79] and [81]; and that time reference is the same in all those examples. An infinitive clause could not replace the finite *wh*-clause in *I don't know what you should do* or in *I can't remember now whom I had to ask*.

4.26

An infinitive clause can replace relative clauses corresponding to the examples below:

77a The thing { that you should do / = to do } is what everyone else is doing.

78a The person { (whom) you should ask / = to ask } is George Lamb.

79a The place { where you should go / = to go } is Brown's.

80a The time { when you should leave / = to leave } is after they've served coffee.

81a The way { you should start it / = to start it } is to give it a push.

82a The question of whether { we should sell / = to sell } is still undecided.

Why does not fit into the *what to do* pattern; but note:

84 A I don't know why we should do that.
     B The reason for doing it is perfectly clear.

4.27

An infinitive clause can also replace relative clauses in the following types of example:

85 You need someone { who can look after you. / = to look after you. }

Someone to look after you could be replaced by *something to eat, somewhere to sleep*; and we can form similar sentences with *anything to do, nowhere to go* and so on. Then we can have

86 I've brought a book { that I can read. / = to read. }

where the infinitive also expresses purpose; and

87 George is the man { for whom we should vote. / = to vote for. }

88 He was the first man { who flew / = to fly } across the Atlantic.

The infinitive is in the passive voice in

89 There are several people { who have to / = to } be consulted.

90 There are still many obstacles { that must / = to } be overcome.

91 There is a lot of work { that must / = to } be done first.

92 Is he really a man { who can / = to } be trusted?

A further contraction can be made in examples [89–92] by using the active voice with a passive meaning, as in

89a There are several people to consult first.

90a There are still many obstacles to overcome.

91a There is a lot of work to do first.

92a Is he really a man to trust?

4.28

There are a number of fixed infinitive clauses used as disjunct adverbials (1.52). They include:

93 $\left\{\begin{array}{l}\text{To tell you the truth,}\\ \text{To be (quite) honest with you,}\\ \text{To speak frankly,}\\ \text{To cut a long story short,}\end{array}\right\}$ I think you are wrong.

The subject of an infinitive clause
4.29

a In *I hope to go* and *I don't know what to do*, the subject of the infinitive clause is the same as the subject of the main clause. In *I would like you to go* and *Tell me what to do*, the subject of the infinitive clause is *NOT* THE SUBJECT of the main clause. In *There are several people to consult*, we understand that people will be consulted; but who exactly is to consult them? The answer to that question, *ie* the subject of the infinitive clause, can be given by a phrase beginning with *for*; eg

94 There are several people for $\left\{\begin{array}{l}\text{me}\\ \text{us}\\ \text{you}\end{array}\right\}$ to consult.

While *I've brought a book to read* suggests that *I* will read it, the reader will be *you* in

95 Here is a book for you to read.

The *for*-phrase would be unacceptable in

96 Stanley took three weeks to reach the coast,

but would make the meaning clearer in

96a It took three weeks (for Stanley) to reach the coast.

Responsibility is attributed to nobody in particular in

97 To say such a thing is ridiculous.

but it is attributed to the person named by the *for*-phrase in

98 For Roberts to say such a thing is nonsense.

The *for*-phrase is obligatory when the example

99 There is some disagreement between us. I think it is a pity,

is converted into

100 I think it is a pity for there to be any disagreement between us.

b An *of*-phrase is used after adjectives in the pattern
   101 It is foolish (of him) to meet her again (3.15d).
The *of*-phrase is obligatory in this pattern after *good*; *eg*

102 It was $\begin{Bmatrix} \text{kind (of you)} \\ \text{good of you} \end{Bmatrix}$ to write her that letter.

Non-finite clauses in the negative
4.30
All the three types of non-finite clause are negated if the non-finite verb is
preceded by *not* or *never*. Thus:

103 $\begin{Bmatrix} \text{Not} \\ \text{Never} \end{Bmatrix}$ having a telephone can save you a great deal of trouble.

   104 Though never defeated in battle, they finally surrendered.
   105 He stood all night so as not to lose his place in the queue.

B Verbless clauses
4.31
In a clause of the type SUBJECT + BE + $\begin{Bmatrix} \text{NP} \\ \text{ADJECTIVE} \\ \text{ADVERB} \end{Bmatrix}$ (1.55), the subject + BE

can be deleted to form a VERBLESS CLAUSE. Thus:
   106 He was an excellent speaker and was never at a loss for a word,
can be reduced to either
   107a An excellent speaker, he was never at a loss for a word
or to
   107b Never at a loss for a word, he was an excellent speaker.
Similarly,
   108 They were utterly exhausted and fell asleep at once
can become either
   108a Utterly exhausted, they fell asleep at once
or
   108b They fell asleep at once, utterly exhausted.

4.32
When, while, if and *(al)though* can precede a verbless clause:
   109 When (you are) in Rome, do as Rome does.
   110 While (he was) still at school, he wrote his first novel.
   111 If (you are) in doubt, ask me.

112 We shall start at six, if (it is) $\begin{Bmatrix} \text{necessary.} \\ \text{possible.} \end{Bmatrix}$

   113 (Al)though (he was) a lawyer by training, he became a great soldier.
   114 While (we were) never in doubt, we had to have proof of your
      identity.
   115 We shall continue our policy, whatever your objections (may be).

C Replacement of a finite verb by a noun
4.33
A finite clause can be replaced by means of NOMINALISATION of the verb.
Thus:

116 $\left\{ \begin{array}{l} \text{When you arrive at your hotel,} \\ \text{When you have completed the experiment,} \\ \text{While you are absent,} \end{array} \right\}$ please write to me.

can be reduced to

117 $\left\{ \begin{array}{l} \text{On arrival at your hotel,} \\ \text{On completion of the experiment,} \\ \text{During your absence,} \end{array} \right\}$ please write to me.

D Complex prepositional phrases
4.34
What we have in [117] are prepositional phrases beginning with simple
prepositions. Complex prepositions are used in the following examples:

118 The match was postponed $\left\{ \begin{array}{l} \text{because the weather was bad.} \\ = \text{because of bad weather.} \end{array} \right.$

Owing to could replace *because of* in [118]. *Due to* is widely used instead of
owing to, despite the traditional 'rule' that *owing to* + NP replaces an
adverbial clause (as in [118]), while *due to* is adjectival, is related to a noun,
and has the sense of *caused by*, as in

119 The accident was $\left\{ \begin{array}{l} \text{serious.} \\ \text{due to human error.} \end{array} \right.$

The use of *due to* instead of *owing to* or *because of* may lead to ambiguity in
a case like

120 Many children were separated from their parents during the disturbance due to the huge crowd that quickly gathered.

The reader of that sentence might wonder whether the disturbance or the
separation was caused by the huge crowd; *owing to* instead of *due to* would
make it clear that the separation occurred because of the huge crowd.

4.35
Other complex prepositions include: *in spite of*, or the slightly more formal
despite; *notwithstanding*, definitely more formal; *regardless of*; *considering*
and *in view of*; *according to*; *in accordance with*; *as regards* and *with regard
to*, as in

121 We shall continue $\left\{ \begin{array}{l} \text{although you do not wish us to.} \\ \left. \begin{array}{l} \text{in spite of} \\ \text{despite} \\ \text{notwithstanding} \\ \text{regardless of} \end{array} \right\} \text{your wishes.} \end{array} \right.$

122 $\left\{ \begin{array}{l} \text{Considering} \\ \text{In view of} \end{array} \right\}$ his illness, $\left\{ \begin{array}{l} \text{we had to postpone the meeting.} \\ \text{he has done remarkably well.} \end{array} \right.$

Despite the *-ing*, *considering* may be regarded as a preposition, and not as a participle which has to have the same subject as the main clause (4.15). Note also:

123 The meeting has been cancelled $\left\{ \begin{array}{l} \text{– or so John says.} \\ =according\ to\ \text{John.} \end{array} \right.$

124 The meeting was held $\left\{ \begin{array}{l} \text{because Article 16 required it.} \\ =in\ accordance\ with\ \text{Article 16.} \end{array} \right.$

125 *With regard to* your letter of June 22nd, I enclose our most recent catalogue. *As regards* delivery, this normally takes two or three weeks.

As regards usually introduces a new item, not the first, in formal correspondence.

E Pro-forms (1.5c)
Pro-forms for the NP
4.36
No doubt the best-known pro-forms are the personal pronouns *he*, *she*, *it* and *they* (1.10; 6.28).

4.37
One and *ones* can be used as pro-forms, as follows:

126 I'd like a ticket and John would like one (*ie* a ticket) too.

127 A Which coat is yours?
    B The one (*ie* the coat) (hanging) behind the door.

128 That shirt is much smarter than the one (*ie* the shirt) (that) you were wearing yesterday.

129 These apples aren't ripe. Give me $\left\{ \begin{array}{l} \text{some} \\ \text{the} \end{array} \right\}$ ripe ones.

4.38
a *One* and *ones* (6.29) can refer to countable things, including persons. *Those* is preferred to *the ones*, especially in more formal style, in

130 The mountains of Switzerland are much higher than those of Wales.

Those, not *the ones*, would occur in

131 The clothes people wear today do not seem to last as long as those · of my father's day,

since *clothes* is not modified by a numeral (5.23d).

b *That* is used as a pro-form in referring to something shapeless, and certainly in replacing a mass noun:

132 The population of China is much greater than that (= the population) of Japan.

133 There is no˙ pleasure greater than that (*ie* the pleasure) of sailing along in a gentle breeze.

Pro-forms for the VP
4.39
The operator is commonly used as a pro-form for the whole predicate (1.26.6), as in

134 A Have you finished your essay?

B Yes, I have (finished my essay).

Remember that DO is used as an operator when the verb is simple present or simple past tense:

135 Not many people smoke fifty cigarettes a day, but I know a few (people) who do.

The pro-form must always correspond in tense and aspect to the verb for which it stands: *have* in [134] = *have finished*, and *do* in [135] = *smoke*. *I have*, alone, would therefore be regarded by many speakers as unacceptable in a response to

136 A I asked you to lock the door.

But B could respond *I've done so* to A's remark.

4.40
So, either, neither and *nor* can be used in conjunction with the operator, thus:

137 I have finished and $\left\{\begin{array}{l} \text{George has (finished) too.} \\ = \text{so has George.} \end{array}\right.$

138 I haven't finished and $\left\{\begin{array}{l} \text{\_ you haven't (finished) either.} \\ \left.\begin{array}{l} = \text{nor} \\ = \text{neither} \end{array}\right\} \text{ have you.} \end{array}\right.$

4.41
Note the difference between *so has he*, as in [137], meaning 'and he has too', and *so he has*:

139 A George has grown a moustache.

B So he has. (= You're right. He *has* grown one.)

4.42
a *So* stands for a whole *that*-clause after BELIEVE, EXPECT, FEAR, GATHER, PRESUME, HOPE, IMAGINE, SAY, SUPPOSE and THINK, as in

140 A Is there going to be a holiday tomorrow?

B I believe $\left\{\begin{array}{l} \text{(that) there's going to be a holiday.} \\ = \text{(that) there's going to be (one).} \\ = \text{so.} \end{array}\right.$

So can come at the beginning of a short response composed of *So* + subject + BELIEVE, FEAR, GATHER, HEAR, IMAGINE, NOTICE, REALISE, SEE, UNDERSTAND, *hoped* and *thought*, to indicate confirmation of something that has just been said:

141　A There's going to be a holiday tomorrow.

　　　B　So I $\begin{cases} \text{hear.} \\ \text{'ve heard.} \\ \text{heard.} \end{cases}$

In the negative, BELIEVE, EXPECT, SUPPOSE and THINK will fit into the patterns

142　I don't think so.　　　　　　143　I think not.

In [142] *think* is negated, while in [143] what is negated is the *that*-clause left unspoken. HOPE will fit into the pattern of [143] but not of [142], and the same applies to FANCY, FEAR, GATHER, GUESS and TRUST.

b After KNOW there is generally no pro-form for the *that*-clause, though the demonstrative *that* can be used to imply that the speaker is not being told anything new:

144　A There's going to be a holiday tomorrow.

　　　B I know. *or* I know that (already).

4.43

As can be used as a pro-form as follows:

145　He was delighted $\begin{cases} \text{and we were all delighted too.} \\ = \text{and so we all were.} \\ = \text{and so were we all.} \\ = \text{as we all were.} \\ = \text{as were we all.} \end{cases}$

4.44

For *to* standing for a whole infinitive clause, *eg I want to, I want you to,* see 3.8 and 3.9.

F Ellipsis
4.45

a We have seen (2.2) that when the subject of two or more co-ordinate clauses refers to the same person or thing, it need not be repeated, as in *The headmaster did not like us and (he) seldom gave us any praise.* The omission of *he* in that sentence is a case of ELLIPSIS.

b There can be ellipsis of other elements that are common to two or more co-ordinate clauses, *eg* the auxiliary, the whole verb group or subject and verb together.

Examples:
146 Mary was trembling and (was) clutching my hand.
147 I have been to Peking and (have) seen the Great Wall.
148 John won the first race and Jim (won) the second (race).
149 Bob came in first in one race yesterday and (he came in first in) one (race) today.

c Note the ellipsis of *race* in [148] and [149]. The head of a nominal group, consisting of determiner + noun or of adjective + noun, need not always be repeated. But not every determiner can be used alone without a noun: a few determiners, *eg every* and *only*, must be followed either by a noun or by the pro-form *one* (6.2). After an adjective, the noun need not be repeated in
150 You take the red card and I'll take the blue,

or in
151 What is the difference between a direct question and an indirect?
However, as we saw in 4.37, the pro-form *one* is normally used in place of a noun that would otherwise be repeated. If an adjective occurs at the head of a nominal group, without a noun or without *one(s)*, it may have a special function which is discussed in 7.21.

4.46
Ellipsis does not normally occur with BE, HAVE and DO if they are used as auxiliaries in one clause and full verbs in the other:
   152 Mary was terrified and was clutching my hand.
   153 That man has a gun and has threatened to use it.

4.47
a The object cannot be omitted, at the end of a sentence, but it can take the form of a pronoun, as in
154 My father planned all these houses and my elder brother built them.
However, we can omit the object when it would first occur, *eg*
155 My father planned (all these houses) and my brother built all these houses,
though a sentence on that pattern is apt to be clumsy, especially if the object is comparatively short.
b With prepositional verbs, we could ellipt the object when it would first occur; and we could ellipt the first preposition, so long as both prepositions are the same, not if they are different:
156 I have heard (about) and read about your adventures.
157 I have listened to and thought about your story carefully.
[157], too, might be considered clumsy and not so elegant as
158 I have listened to your story and thought about it carefully.

4.48

The subject and verb of a subordinate clause cannot be ellipted:

159 The headmaster was kind to us although he disapproved of the way
we dressed.

160 We have made many friends since we have lived here.

161 Mr Saunders has been away for a week because he has been very ill.

However, there can be ellipsis in a clause beginning with *as* in a sentence of
the following kind:

162 Shakespeare was the author of 'Macbeth', as he was (the author) of
'Julius Caesar'.

Part Two
Chapter Five
The noun phrase (1): Nouns

A Typical noun endings
5.1

Typical noun endings are:

a (NOUNS INDICATING PERSONS)

-ER, as in *driver, employer, examiner,* and in COMPOUNDS, on the pattern of *shopkeeper, wage-earner, music lover.* Stress falls on the base *(emplòyer)* or on the first part of the compound *(shòp-, wàge-, mùsic).* The same spelling rules apply as for the past tense of regular verbs (1.16(3) and 9.4). Thus, *writer, player, occupier, runner, beginner, traveller,* except that MONOSYLLABIC words ending in consonant+*y* may retain the *y, eg flier* or *flyer*;

-OR, instead of -er, as in *actor, collector, editor; protector, sailor, visitor;*
-AR, as in *beggar, liar;*
-ANT, as in *assistant, attendant, servant;*
-IST, as in *chemist, scientist, typist.*

All of the above examples could be paraphrased by means of a verb in the active voice, *eg* an *employer* is someone who employs someone else.[1] A passive verb underlies the suffix *-ee,* as in *employee* (someone who is employed). Other examples are: *examinee, referee* (someone who is referred to), *refugee* (someone who is forced to take refuge). Stress falls on the suffix, *ee.*

b (ABSTRACT NOUNS DERIVED FROM VERBS) (See 4.33 and 10.9)

-AGE, *eg* breakage, drainage, leakage
-AL, *eg* approval, arrival, refusal
-ANCE, *eg* acceptance, appearance, performance
-ERY, *eg* delivery, discovery, recovery
-MENT, *eg* agreement, arrangement, employment
-SION, *eg* collision, decision, division
-TION, *eg* education, organisation, attention, solution
-URE, *eg* departure, failure, closure

c (ABSTRACT NOUNS DERIVED FROM ADJECTIVES)

-ANCE, -ENCE, *eg* importance; absence, presence
-ITY, *eg* ability, activity, equality
-NESS, *eg* darkness, happiness, kindness
-TH, *eg* length, strength, truth

---

[1] *-er* may sometimes indicate the *thing* that performs the action, as in *cooker, dryer, lighter, roller, screwdriver, tape-recorder.* 'A ruler' may refer to a person *or* thing.

5.2

Many words are used either as nouns or as verbs (1.6a), *eg*

aim	fall	lock	result
answer	guess	move	smile
cause	hope	note	stop
change	influence	order	talk
doubt	interest	plan	trouble
dream	joke	play	walk
end	laugh	quarrel	work

5.3

There are pairs of words of which one member is a noun ending in a voiceless consonant, and the other a verb ending in a voiced consonant:

Noun	Verb	Noun	Verb
abuse /s/	abuse /z/	house /s/	house /z/
advice /s/	advise /z/	life /f/	live /v/
belief /f/	believe /v/	proof /f/	prove /v/
breath /θ/	breathe /ð/	relief /f/	relieve /v/
choice /s/	choose /z/	shelf /f/	shelve /v/
cloth /θ/	clothe /ð/	teeth /θ/	teethe /ð/
device /s/	devise /z/	use /s/	use /z/
excuse /s/	excuse /z/	wreath /θ/	wreathe /ð/
half /f/	halve /v/		

Note: *practice* (noun) and *practise* (verb) both end in the voiceless /s/. *Licence,* also spelt *license,* the noun, and *license,* the verb, both end in a voiceless /s/, also.

5.4

a In a number of pairs, the noun is stressed on the first syllable, the verb on the second syllable. Examples of words in frequent use are:

abstract	conflict	desert	essay	object	rebel
accent	conscript	dictate	exploit	perfume	record
addict	contest	digest	export	permit	retail
ally	contract	discount	extract	present	subject
attribute	contrast	discourse	import	produce	survey
combine	converse	entrance	impress	progress	suspect
compress	convert	'envelope (n)	incense	project	torment
concert	convict	en'velop (v)	increase	prospect	transfer
conduct	decrease	escort	insult	protest	transport

eg The 'accent in this noun falls on the first syllable.
We ac'cent this verb on the second syllable.

b Note also the noun ˈrefuse /s/ (stress on 1st syllable), and the verb reˈfuse /z/ (stress on second syllable). Distinguish between the two nouns: ˈrefuse (= rubbish) and reˈfusal (= act of refusing).

c In the noun *estimate*, the final syllable is pronounced /ət/ or /it/, while in the verb *estimate* the same syllable is pronounced /eit/. A similar remark applies to *approximate*, and *separate*, verb /eit/, adjective /ət/ or /it/.

5.5

Effect (noun), *affect* (verb), meaning 'have an effect on'. There is also a verb *effect*, meaning 'produce', as in 'effect a cure'.

B Count nouns and mass nouns (1.9)

5.6

Nouns typically used as count nouns include the class-names of:

a persons, animals, plants, etc: *friend, cat, bird, rose*

b concrete objects having shape: *ball, car, hat, hand, house*

c units of measurement, society, language, etc: *metre, hour, dollar, family, word*

d the individual parts of a mass: *part, element, atom, piece, drop*

e a few abstractions, thought of as separate wholes: *idea, nuisance, sake,[1] scheme.*

5.7

Nouns normally used as mass nouns include the names of:

a solid substances and materials: *earth, bread, rice, cotton, nylon*

b liquids, gases, etc: *water, oil, tea, air, oxygen, steam, smoke*

c languages: *English, French, German, Russian, Chinese, Spanish*

d many abstractions: *equality, honesty, ignorance, peace, safety.* Mass nouns also include

e most -ing forms used as nouns: *camping, cooking, clothing, parking, training.* (Corresponding count nouns would be *a camping site; a kitchen, or a cooker; a garment, or an article of clothing; a parking place; a training* { *course* / *centre* } The following are count nouns: *blessing, helping, wedding.*

f the following words, whose equivalent in other languages might be regarded as count nouns:

accommodation	equipment	leisure	news
advice	fun	lightning	permission
behaviour	furniture	luck	poetry
cash	harm	luggage	progress

[1] *sake* is not modified by *a*, but it occurs in the plural. It is only found in such expressions as *for my sake, for (all) our sakes, for the sake of peace.*

china	influenza	money	rubbish
conduct	information	mud	soap
damage (=harm)	laughter	music	weather

i *Weather*, normally mass (*eg What wonderful weather!*) takes a plural form in the fixed expression *(go) out in all weathers*. Cp climate, count noun (*eg What a beautiful climate!*)

ii *Money*, normally a mass noun, takes a plural form, *moneys*, in legal language, with the meaning 'sums of money'.

5.8

For several mass nouns there are corresponding count nouns, *eg*

Mass	*Count*	*Mass*	*Count*
bread	a loaf	pay	a payment
clothing	a garment	permission	a permit
laughter	a laugh	poetry	a poem
luggage	a suitcase	work	a job
money	a coin		

A play is not an example of play, but a dramatic performance. *Work* is used as a count noun in *a work of art, the works of Shakespeare, road works*.

5.9

Mass nouns are not normally preceded by *a* or *one* and do not have a plural form. One example of a mass can be indicated:

a by *a piece*, or *bit* (informal) of something not liquid; or *a drop* of liquid:
a piece (or bit) of paper, string, advice, information, furniture
an article of clothing, furniture
an item of news (or a news item)
a drop of water, oil, blood
Piece and *bit* are often used as pro-forms.

1 I want a $\left\{\begin{array}{l}\text{piece}\\ =\text{bit}\end{array}\right\}$ of paper. Ah, here's a $\left\{\begin{array}{l}\text{piece}\\ =\text{bit}\end{array}\right\}$

b by referring to a piece of a certain shape, as in:

a ball of string	a heap of earth	a sheet of paper or metal
a bar of chocolate	a loaf of bread	a slice of bread or meat
a blade of grass	a lump of coal	a stick of chalk or dynamite
a block of ice	a roll of cloth	a strip of cloth or land

Ball, bar, etc. can also be used as pro-forms, as in

2 Have some more bread. May I give you another slice?

c by reference to a container, *eg a bag of flour, a bottle of milk, a basket of fruit, a bucket of water, a sack of coal*;

d by reference to a measure, *eg a gallon of oil, a kilo of sugar*;

e More than one example of the mass can then be indicated by
bits of paper, drops of water, items of news, slices of bread, etc.

5.10

Often a word can be used as a mass noun when it refers to a substance, material or phenomenon in general, but as a count noun when it refers to one separate unit composed of that substance or to one occurrence of that phenomenon.

AS MASS NOUN	AS COUNT NOUN
3 All plants need *light*.	Do you have *a light* by your bed?
4 Houses were built of *stone*.	Wait! I have *a stone* in my shoe.
5 I will come with *pleasure*.	It will be *a pleasure* to see you.
6 Have *pity*! Have you no *shame*?	What *a pity*! What *a shame*!
7 This is the age of *science*.	Physics is *a science*.
8 A city without *art* is dead.	Painting is *an art*.
9 *Honour* must be satisfied.	It is *an honour* for me to be here.
10 Most men want *success*.	Your play was *a great success*.
	George was *a great success* in it.

Words that can be used in both those ways include:

bone	noise	fire	duty	activity	injustice
brick	sound	pain	history	agreement	justice
cake	space	war	hope	decision	language
hair	time	worry	thought	kindness	virtue

Dress (mass noun) = clothing, for either sex, usually for a special occasion; *a dress* = a frock for a woman or girl. *A justice* is a man who administers justice. *An injustice* is one example of injustice.

5.11

Other words can be used in both ways, as in 5.10, except that as count nouns they refer only to special objects. Thus, *cloth, glass, iron, paper, wood* are mass nouns when they refer to the substances or materials in general, but count nouns when they have these special meanings:

a cloth = a piece of cloth made to cover a table, or for cleaning;
a glass = a drinking vessel, or a mirror;
an iron = a metal object made for pressing clothes;
a paper = a newspaper, memorandum, or set of examination questions;
a wood = a group of trees.

Similarly, *business, trade* and *traffic* are mass nouns when they refer to those activities in general, but count nouns in the b examples below:

11a Mr Price has gone to London on *business*.

   b He runs *a small business* (*ie* a small shop)

12a Trade (*ie* exchange of goods) between our two countries is flourishing.

  b I think every boy should learn a trade. (*ie* a way of earning his living, especially by manual work)

13a Traffic roars through the city all day long.

  b Mr Price was convicted of conducting an illegal traffic in drugs.

5.12

a Names of substances can be used as count nouns, singular and plural, when they refer to a kind of the substance or to a portion of it, as in

14 This is a very good butter (*ie* a good kind of butter).

15 You've only brought me one butter. I asked for two (butters). (*ie* packets of butter)

Similarly, we can refer to *a coffee, two coffees*, though this, like *two butters*, is very informal.

b On the other hand, a word normally used as a count noun (*eg onion*) can be used as a mass noun when it refers to the substance of which the thing is composed, as in

16 This soup tastes of onion.

5.13

Certain abstract nouns normally used as mass nouns can be preceded by *a* or *an* (usually followed by an adjective) when they refer to a kind, as in example [14]. Examples are *education, importance, knowledge*:

17 In most countries, education is the responsibility of the state.

17a Scott received a very strict education.

  18 I attach importance to regular exercise;

18a but some people attach an exaggerated importance to it.

19 It is said that knowledge is power.

19a A (good) knowledge of English is essential.

Education, importance, knowledge, are not normally preceded by *one*, nor would they occur in the plural.

C Irregular plural of nouns

For regular plurals (1.11). Sections 5.14–5.23 below deal with irregularities and special cases.

Irregular in pronunciation only
5.14

The following are regular in spelling, but in pronunciation a final consonant that is voiceless in the singular becomes voiced in the plural:

a *nouns ending in -th*. In *bath*, the final /θ/ becomes /ð/ in the plural, which is therefore pronounced /bɑːðz/. The same applies to *mouth, oath, path*, *sheath, truth, wreath, youth* (=young man), and can also apply to *berth* and *birth*. It does not apply to nouns ending in -*nth*, *eg months*.

b The voiceless /s/ in *house* becomes /z/ in the plural, /hauziz/.

Irregular in spelling only: nouns ending in -o
5.15

a Examples of the rule given in 1.11.1e are:
echoes, embargoes, heroes, mottoes, Negroes, potatoes, tomatoes torpedoes, vetoes
The *e* is optional in:
buffalo(e)s, cargo(e)s, commando(e)s, grotto(e)s, halo(e)s, mosquito(e)s, tornado(e)s, volcano(e)s.

b The following do not have *e* in the spelling:
  i nouns ending in the singular in *o* preceded by any vowel letter or vowel sound:
     bamboos, embryos, folios, kangaroos, oratorios, radios, zoos
  ii abbreviations, *eg*
     kilos (=kilograms), memos (=memoranda), photos (=photographs)
 iii musical terms of Italian origin:
     concertos, contraltos, pianos, solos, sopranos
  iv proper names, *eg*
     Eskimos, Filipinos
  v dynamos.

Irregular in both pronunciation and spelling
5.16

The following words ending in the singular with the sound /f/, spelt *f* or *fe*, end in the plural with /vz/, spelt -*ves*:
Examples: *loaf, loaves; life, lives*
Like *loaf*:

calf	half	leaf	self	shelf	wharf
elf	hoof	scarf	sheaf	thief	wolf

Like *life*: *knife, wife*
Hoof, scarf and *wharf* also have a plural that is regular in pronunciation and spelling.
Handkerchiefs and *roofs*, regular in spelling, may end in pronunciation with /fs/ or /vz/. Treat all other words ending in *f* as regular, *eg cliffs*.

5.17

These old plural forms have survived in modern English:
a *man/men*; *woman*/wumən/, *women*/wimin/.
  The spelling -*men* occurs in *airman/airmen, fireman/firemen, gentleman/ gentlemen, postman/postmen, workman/workmen*, etc., though in normal

fluent speech the pronunciation of the singular and plural is the same, *ie* the final syllable is pronounced /mən/. The plural is regular in *Germans, Romans,* and *the Bowmans* (5.27);

b *child* /tʃaild/, *children* /tʃildrən/; *ox*/*oxen*;

c *foot*/*feet*; *tooth*/*teeth*; *goose*/*geese*;

d *mouse*/*mice*; *louse*/*lice*;

e *brethren* survives as a plural of *brother* but is only used in a religious context; otherwise, the plural of *brother* is *brothers*;

f *pence* survives as a plural of *penny*, but only to indicate a total amount, as in *The fare is now tenpence. Tenpence* may refer to one silver coin or to ten individual pennies, *ie* coins worth a penny each.

5.18

Pennies might be regarded as a 'separate' plural, *pence* as a collective one. A similar distinction is found in the plural of *fish* and *person*:

Singular	More than one unit, separately	More than one, collectively
Who is that person?	Three separate persons.	Those people are my friends.
This fish is good.	Two separate fishes.	Those fish are bad.

Distinguish between the following two uses of *people*:

20 Most people (=persons) are good at heart.
21 Most peoples (=races) have a country of their own.

5.19

a In addition to the regular plural, certain names of animals, birds and fish can have a collective plural, as in:

22 Hunters shoot $\begin{cases} \text{lion} \\ \text{tiger} \\ \text{elephant} \\ \text{duck} \end{cases}$, which are plentiful here.

23 Fishermen catch $\begin{cases} \text{herring} \\ \text{shark} \end{cases}$, which are plentiful here.

This collective plural can also be applied to trees and to human beings, as in

24 No trees grow at that height except $\begin{cases} \text{pine.} \\ \text{birch.} \end{cases}$

and

25 In the middle ages, the master was responsible for everyone under his roof, for man, woman and child.

b Collective plurals in 5.19a are optional. They are obligatory when wild birds are referred to as *wild-fowl* and when cavalry is referred to as *horse*.

5.20
There is no separate plural form for
a the names of certain animals, birds and fish, namely *deer, grouse, mackerel, plaice, salmon, sheep, trout*.
Thus we can say either *That is a deer, a sheep,* etc., or *Those are deer, sheep,* etc.
b *craft* (but only with the meaning of *boat*) and *aircraft*.

Thus, $\begin{Bmatrix} one \\ fifty \end{Bmatrix}$ *aircraft*; but *arts and crafts*

c nouns, meaning 'a person or people of that nationality', ending in the sound /z/ or /s/, *eg*
a hundred Vietnamese, Chinese, Japanese, Portuguese, Swiss.

5.21
a In definite numbers and measurements, *hundred, thousand, million, dozen, score* (=20), *gross* (=144), *stone* (=14 pounds), *hundredweight, head* (of cattle) have the same form for singular and plural. Thus:
A hundred pages. Two hundred dollars. Three thousand four hundred men.
The normal span of a man's life is three score and ten (years).
The farmer was too fat: he weighed nineteen stone.
He owned a hundred head of cattle.
b The normal plural is found with indefinite numbers, as in
I've told you that dozens of times, hundreds of times.
All that happened thousands of years ago.
But *gross* and *head* (of cattle) do not occur in a separate plural form.
c *Foot*, as a measurement, can occur in the plural as well as the singular,

eg George is six $\begin{Bmatrix} foot \\ feet \end{Bmatrix}$ *tall.*

d Only the singular form is normally used when a measurement comes before the head in a nominal group, as in *a fivepenny piece, a four-foot pole, a two mile walk, a five pound note.*

Latin, Greek and French plurals
5.22
Latin, Greek and French plurals occur in a number of words borrowed from the languages concerned, though there is a strong tendency to make the plural of those words conform to the rule given in 1.11 and to restrict the foreign plural to specialised uses in a scientific context.

Examples:

a singular ending in -*us*, plural is -*i*, pronounced /ai/ or /iː/:
singular: radius, stimulus   *plural:* radii, stimuli
This rule applies to *bacillus, cactus, fungus, nucleus, terminus.* However, *terminuses, cactuses* and *radiuses* are also used, both by people who do not know the foreign plural and by those who purposely avoid it. Regard other words ending in -*us* as regular, *eg genius, geniuses*; except those in 5.22b.

b singular ending in -*us*, plural in -*era* or -*ora*, pronounced /ərə/:
genus, corpus   genera, corpora

c singular ending in -*a*, plural in -*ae*, pronounced /ai/ or /iː/:
amoeba, antenna, formula, nebula   amoebae, antennae, formulae,
                                   nebulae
Formulas is being increasingly adopted, with *formulae* reserved for scientific contexts.

d singular ending in -*um*, plural in -*a*, pronounced /ə/:
curriculum   curricula
Also: *bacterium, desideratum, erratum, medium, memorandum, stratum, symposium.*
The plural ending, -*a*, occurs in *agenda* and *data*, though *agenda* is generally accepted as a count noun, singular, as in
26 Is there an agenda for the meeting?
while *data* is used both as mass noun and as count noun plural:

27 The results of the experiment are still uncertain: there $\left\{ \begin{array}{c} \text{is} \\ =\text{are} \end{array} \right\}$ not
   enough data yet.

e singular ending in -*is*, plural in -*es*, pronounced /iːz/:
analysis   analyses
Also: *axis, basis, crisis, diagnosis, hypothesis, neurosis, oasis, parenthesis, synopsis, thesis.*

f singular ending in -*on*, plural in -*a*, pronounced /ə/:
criterion, phenomenon   criteria, phenomena

g singular ending in -*ex* or -*ix*, plural in -*ices*, pronounced /isiːz/:
appendix, index, matrix   appendices, indices, matrices
However, these foreign plurals are usually reserved for scientific contexts. *Indexes* is used to refer to lists at the end of books, and *matrixes* is used with reference to gramophone records.

h singular ending in -*eau*, pronounced /əu/, plural in -*eaux*, pronounced /əu/ or /əuz/:
bureau   bureaux
Also: *plateau, portmanteau, tableau, trousseau.*

D Nouns ending in -*s*
5.23
The rule given in 1.11 applies to *bus/buses, gas/gases,*[1] with no doubling of the *s* of the base. It also applies to *lens* and *summons,* thus:

$$\left.\begin{array}{l} A \\ This \end{array}\right\} \left\{\begin{array}{l} lens \\ summons \end{array}\right\} has \ldots \qquad \left.\begin{array}{l} These \\ Several \end{array}\right\} \left\{\begin{array}{l} lenses \\ summonses \end{array}\right\} have \ldots$$

But many words ending in *s* do not follow that rule. Examples are:

a *Words used as singular only, with a singular verb:*

28 This is very good news. $\left\{\begin{array}{l} These \\ Several \end{array}\right\} \begin{array}{l} items \ of \ news \\ = news \ items \end{array}$

29 $\left\{\begin{array}{l} Measles \\ Mumps \end{array}\right\}$ is an infectious disease.

This $\left\{\begin{array}{l} kind \\ type \end{array}\right\}$ of $\left\{\begin{array}{l} measles \\ mumps \end{array}\right\}$ is dangerous.

Names of sciences

30 Physics is a science.

31 This $\left\{\begin{array}{l} kind \\ type \end{array}\right\}$ of physics is difficult to understand.

Similarly: *acoustics, linguistics, mathematics, politics, statistics.*

However, when a word of this type is not used to refer directly to a science, it takes a plural verb and can be preceded by *these* as in the following example:

32 $\left\{\begin{array}{l} The \ acoustics \ in \ this \ room \\ These \ statistics \end{array}\right\}$ are unreliable.

The verb may be singular or plural in the following:

33 George's mathematics $\left\{\begin{array}{l} is \\ =are \end{array}\right\}$ not so good as $\left\{\begin{array}{l} it \ was. \\ =they \ were. \end{array}\right\}$

b *Words used as singular with reference to one unit, or as plural with reference to more than one:*

34 We must find a means (= a way) of solving our problem.

35 There are several means (ways) of solving it.

The following can also be used as in [34] and [35]:

barracks	gallows	golf-links	innings	series
bellows	gasworks	headquarters	kennels	species

i. We can say either *a bellows* or *a pair of bellows.*

ii Side by side with *a kennel,* plural *kennels,* we have *a kennels,* ie a collection of kennels where dogs are kept.

iii *The* + *innings, series, species,* referring to one unit only, is used with a singular verb (*eg is*). *The* + any other word in this section may occur with a singular or plural verb, whether it refers to one unit or more.

---

[1] The *s* is doubled in the verb *(gassing, gassed)* and the adjective *gassy,* but not in *gaseous.*

c *Used either with a plural verb and with* these, *or in the construction* a pair of . . .

36a $\left\{ \begin{array}{l} \text{These trousers (\textit{ie} this garment) are} \\ = \text{This pair of trousers \qquad is} \end{array} \right\}$ too tight for me.

   b George has ten pairs of trousers.

A numeral does not occur immediately before words in this group, which includes:

binoculars	knickers	scales	tights
braces (to wear)	pants	scissors	tongs
breeches	pincers	shorts	tweezers
glasses (=	pliers	spectacles (=	
spectacles)	pyjamas	glasses)	

d *Used only in the plural, with a plural verb, not with a numeral:*

the Middle Ages	damages (=	proceeds
(make) amends	compensation)	provisions (= food
annals	dregs	supplies)
the Antipodes	earnings	quarters (= lodgings)
archives	entrails	regards
arms (= weapons)	goods	remains
arrears	looks (= appearance)	resources
ashes (= human	manners (=	riches
remains)	behaviour)	shortcomings
auspices	misgivings	suds
banns	odds	surroundings
belongings	outskirts	thanks
bounds (= boundary)	pains (= trouble)	the tropics
clothes[1]	particulars (= detailed	tidings
congratulations	information)	valuables
credentials	premises (= buildings)	whereabouts

Notice the difference between these pairs of words in bold type:

37a X was found guilty of causing **damage** to Y's property.

   b and was ordered to pay **damages**.

38a May I have a **look** at your magazine?

   b The accident has spoilt my good **looks**.

39a How much do you pay for board and **lodging**?

   b Come round to my **lodgings** and we'll have a party.

40a I didn't like that man's **manner** (= attitude).

   b George has very good **manners** (= ways of behaving).

41a A **minute** is a short official note or memorandum.

   b The official records of a meeting are called the **minutes**.

[1] The noun, pronounced /kləuðz/ in precise speech, can be pronounced /kləuz/ in more fluent speech; but the verb (see 5.3) is only pronounced /kləuðz/.

42a We can make a considerable **saving** (=economy) by selling the car.

   b Then we can use our **savings** (=money saved) to buy some new furniture.

43a In some countries, a minimum **wage** is fixed by law.

   b Mr Turner takes all his **wages** home to his wife.

44a We were all enchanted by his **wit**.

   b The ladies were frightened out of their **wits**.

e In all the words in 5.23, a–d inclusive, the final *s* is pronounced. It is only pronounced in the plural in *chassis* and *corps*, thus:

SINGULAR   PLURAL

chassis/'ʃæsi/, corps /kɔː/   chassis /'ʃæsiz/, corps /kɔːz/

E Collective nouns
5.24

a Using a collective noun (1.12b) in the singular, we can say either
   The committee, crew, staff etc. is . . .
   or
   The committee, crew, staff etc. are . . .
   In the plural, only *The committees* etc *are* . . . is possible.

b Individual members of a group can be referred to as
   members of the committee, crew, staff, etc.
   or
   committee members, crew members, staff members, etc.
   With *crew* and *staff*, we may sometimes hear expressions like *ten crew* (=ten members of the crew), *fifty staff*. *Ten crewmen* is also current.

c A few collective nouns occur only in the singular, but with a singular or plural verb, *eg*

45 The $\begin{Bmatrix} \text{clergy} \\ \text{gentry} \\ \text{youth of today} \end{Bmatrix}$ $\begin{Bmatrix} \text{is} \\ \text{are} \end{Bmatrix}$ trying to adapt $\begin{Bmatrix} \text{itself} \\ \text{themselves} \end{Bmatrix}$ to

   rapidly changing circumstances.

d Other collective nouns occur only in the singular form but with a plural verb, *eg*

46 These cattle are on their way to market.

47 These people are waiting for their passports.

48 Police (=policemen) are controlling the crowds.

49 Vermin are harmful animals or insects.

Reference to individual members of the group is made thus: *a hundred head of cattle; thirty people; fifty police* or *fifty policemen*.

e *Offspring* can refer to one human or animal and take a singular verb; or to more than one, with a plural verb: it has no plural form.

f *Folk*, meaning 'people' occurs mainly in the singular, though also in the plural, but only with a plural verb, *eg Some folk(s) are* . . .

F Compound nouns, singular and plural
5.25
a COMPOUND NOUNS consist of two (or more) words joined together to form a single lexical unit. They are written
a as one word, *eg railway, headache*
b with a HYPHEN, *eg tooth-brush, mouse-trap*
c as two (or more) words, *eg flower shop, police station.*
There are unfortunately no clear rules that can tell us when the compound is written as (a), (b) or (c). A good modern dictionary is the only reliable guide. Generally speaking, a compound tends to be written as one word the more often it is used.

b Note that the first element in a compound normally keeps the singular form. Thus:
A flower shop is a shop where flowers are sold
A bookcase is a case where books are kept
A tooth-brush is a brush for cleaning teeth
This happens with a few of the words ending in *s* (5.23), as in
A trouser leg, a trouser pocket
A spectacle case (=case for holding spectacles)
Pyjama tops (tops of pyjamas)
But, normally, nouns ending in *s* retain the *s* in compounds, as in
newspaper, clothes hanger, means test, goods train, lodgings bureau, savings bank.

5.26
a Compounds whose final element is a mass noun have no plural forms, *eg homework, moonlight, sunshine.* Compounds whose final element is a count noun have a plural ending which normally comes only at the end of the compound, *eg*
railways, bookcases, tooth-brushes, information offices.

b In compounds whose first element is *man* or *woman*, both elements normally become plural: thus
menservants, men students, women students, women drivers, gentlemen farmers.
The first element is always singular in *man-holes, woman-haters,* where emphasis is on *holes* and *haters* rather than on *man* and *woman.*
The first element keeps the singular form in
boy friends, girl friends, lady drivers.

c Compounds consisting of count noun + preposition or prepositional phrase, take the plural on the noun element:
looker-on/lookers-on, passer-by/passers-by,
brother-in-law/brothers-in-law, grant-in-aid/grants-in-aid,
man-of-war/men-of-war.

d Compounds formed by verb or adjective + preposition take the plural inflexion at the end:
close-ups, grown-ups, lay-bys, pullovers.
sit-ins, stand-bys, take-offs.

e nouns ending in *-ful* tend to follow the pattern
bucketfuls, mouthfuls, spoonfuls
though *spoonsful* etc. are also found; and the plural of, *eg a bucket full of water* will always be *buckets full of water*.

f The few compounds, typical of legal English, on the pattern count noun + adjective take the plural inflexion on the noun, as in
attorneys general, courts-martial, notaries public.

G Plural of proper nouns
5.27
Surnames can be used in the plural, as in
50 I see that the Robinsons are having their house repainted.
There, *the Robinsons* = Mr and Mrs Robinson, or the Robinson family. Such plurals are formed only by adding /iz/, /z/ or /s/, as in 1.11, to the pronunciation of the name, and by adding *s* to the spelling. Thus, Mr and Mrs Berry = *the Berrys*, and Mr and Mrs Bowman = *the Bowmans*. However, if the spelling of the name ends in a sibilant, as in *Jones* or *Church*, the plural is spelt with *es, eg the Joneses, the Churches*.

H Nouns as modifiers of other nouns
5.28
Generally speaking, a compound noun (5.25) is a combination of two or more words which has developed a special meaning of its own: for example, we could not give the name *bookcase* to any case or box in which books are placed. A speaker has little or no freedom to invent a new compound that other people will accept. He has much more freedom to use the model *coal mine* in order to make up expressions like *gold mine, silver mine, diamond mine*, or, especially in science, expressions like *body temperature* or *body weight*.

5.29
Constructions on the pattern *noun modifying another noun* are of two main types:
1 Those that have, in pronunciation, a nuclear stress on the first element, as in *school friend* (1.7b ii) and *bathing costume* (3.21b).
Let us take as an example:
ˈgold ˌmine
This construction is commonly used to indicate a subclass: thus 'a gold mine' is a subclass of 'mine', and 'a flower shop' is a subclass of 'shop'.

Similarly, and with the same stress pattern, we have

blood test	bus driver	danger signal
electricity company	fire station	fish market
light rays	market town	music teacher
poison bottle	police station	space ship
sports shirt	sound waves	telephone number
telephone message	traffic lights	water works

2a Those that have, in pronunciation, a nuclear stress on the second
element, as in *a good friend* (1.7b i) or *boiling water* (3.21a), thus:
á ¦gold ˋwatch
ie a watch made of gold. On this stress pattern, we have

cane sugar	a cotton shirt	an iron bar	a lead pencil
a leather belt	rubber gloves	a silk tie	a steel girder

A ˋsports ¦shirt is a shirt used for sports, while a ¦cotton ˋshirt is one made
of cotton. In this construction, *wood* and *wool* are usually replaced by the
adjectives *wooden* and *woollen, eg a wooden stool, a woollen pullover.*
Note the difference between *a ˋwood¦shed* (a shed for storing wood) and
a ¦wooden ˋshed (a shed made of wood). *Golden, leaden* and *silken* are also
found on the pattern of *wooden*, but only in poetic or figurative expressions such as

a golden opportunity	a leaden sky	a silken thread

b The same stress pattern as that in ¦gold ˋwatch occurs in

table drawer	bedroom furniture	bedroom window
city centre	town hall	school clock
government department	summer holidays	mountain roads

These constructions indicate, for example, that the drawer belongs to
the table, or that the holidays take place in the summer.

5.30

a Notice the difference between

a danger signal   (as in 5.29.1) and a dangerous corner
a music teacher   (as in 5.29.1) and a musical instrument
a poison bottle   (as in 5.29.1) and a poisonous snake
a science lesson   (as in 5.29.1) and a scientific experiment
the city centre   (as in 5.29.2) and a civic reception
a mountain road (as in 5.29.2) and a mountainous country

The adjectives *dangerous* etc. DESCRIBE the thing referred to by the head
word. *Danger* does not describe 'signal' but it tells us what the purpose of
the signal is.

b Sometimes an adjective is used instead of a noun to indicate a subclass,
as in 5.29.1. Thus, side by side with *làw¦school* we find *mèdical¦school, ie*
school where medicine is studied. Note the difference in stress between

medical school and *medical history* where *medical* is used as an adjective comparable with *musical*.

I The genitive
5.31

a The GENITIVE FORM WITH APOSTROPHE s is used with personal nouns and personal indefinite pronouns to indicate possession, as in
John's name, *ie* the name that John has
somebody (else)'s opinion
It need not indicate possession: for example, *John's present* can be the present that John received, or will receive, or gave, or will give. *John's mistake* is the mistake that John makes or made.

b The genitive can also be used with the names of animals, though it is more likely to occur with domestic animals or with those that are credited with some intelligence, than with creatures of a lower order. Thus, *a cat's tail, a dog's bark, an elephant's trunk.*

5.32

The boy's cap is an example of GENITIVE SINGULAR, *the boys' school* of GENITIVE PLURAL. The pronunciation of *boys, boy's* and *boys'* is exactly the same. So is the pronunciation of the words in bold type in

GENITIVE SINGULAR	ORDINARY PLURAL	GENITIVE PLURAL
a **lady's** handbag	**ladies**	the **ladies'** room
a **hero's** name	**heroes**	the **heroes'** welcome
Mr **Jones's** cousin	the **Joneses**	the **Joneses'** house

Notice what happens with nouns whose plural is irregular and with compounds like *brother-in-law*:

GENITIVE SINGULAR	ORDINARY PLURAL	GENITIVE PLURAL
a child's toy	children	children's games
a deer's tracks	deer	the deer's tracks
a man's work	men	a men's club
a woman's privilege	women	women's rights
a wife's troubles	wives	old wives' tales
my brother-in-law's car	brothers-in-law	my brothers-in-law's property
the King of Spain's daughter	the Kings of Spain	the daughters of the Kings of Spain

The reader may safely deduce his own rules from those examples.

5.33

The genitive of nouns whose singular ends in *s* is normally regular in spelling:

St James's Palace   St Thomas's Hospital

In pronunciation, it normally follows the rule stated in 1.11.2, *ie* it has an extra syllable, /iz/. But we sometimes find only an apostrophe, with or without the extra syllable, as in *Keats' poetry* (the poetry of Keats) and *Pepys' Diary* (the Diary of John Pepys, /piːps/). An apostrophe with no extra syllable is normal after Greek names, especially if they are long, as in *Archimedes' Law*.

The genitive with inanimate nouns
5.34
The genitive with apostrophe *s* is not normally used with inanimate nouns.[1] Instead, the noun is postmodified by a phrase beginning with *of*, as in

the leg of the chair   the foot of the mountain

That construction can be freely used with inanimate nouns. An alternative is available in cases like the following:

the side of the { road / hill / mountain }   *or*   the { roadside / hillside / mountainside }

the top of the { hill / mountain }   *or*   the { hilltop / mountaintop }

the bank of the river   .   *or*   the riverbank.

Stress in *roadside* etc is on the first element, *roadside*.

Apostrophe s with inanimate nouns
5.35
The genitive with apostrophe *s* is optional with inanimate nouns that refer to a group of people, to places where people live, to human institutions and so on, as in

Africa's future   America's resources
the committee's business   the club's finances
the country's needs   the earth's surface
London's traffic   the nation's affairs

5.36
a Apostrophe *s* is obligatory with nouns that refer to the length of duration of an event, in phrases on the pattern:

a day's rest   an hour (and a half)'s drive
a month (or two)'s time   today's programme
a week's holiday   a year's work

b Apostrophe *s* is also obligatory in a number of fixed expressions, *eg*

the ship's company   the ship's doctor

---

[1] There is a current tendency to use expressions like *the chemical's effect* in oral (*ie* radio) news reporting.

have something at one's fingers' ends   be only a stone's throw away
keep someone at arm's length   be at one's wits' end
keep out of harm's way   be at death's door
do something to one's heart's content   for goodness' sake

Avoidance of genitive with apostrophe s
5.37
The genitive with apostrophe *s* is not normally used with a nominal group when the head is postmodified by a phrase or relative clause. Thus we would find:

The name of the man $\left\{\begin{array}{l}\text{over there}\\ \text{in the corner}\\ \text{who came yesterday}\end{array}\right\}$

The double genitive
5.38
A so-called double genitive occurs in examples like
a friend of my father's   that dog of Robert's
with the meaning 'one of the friends that my father has', 'that dog that Robert has'. This construction is obligatory when the speaker wishes to use more than one of a certain set of modifiers in the same nominal group: see 6.50.

J Male and female
5.39
a The closed set of words denoting 'female' (1.10c) includes:
actress, hostess, lioness, usherette, waitress.
b Other ways of denoting 'female' are:
girl scout, woman student, lady cashier, female patient.
Lady is used out of exaggerated politeness; *female* is used in an official, scientific or clinical context.
c Ways of denoting 'male' are:
boy scout, man student, male nurse.

Chapter Six
The noun phrase (2): Determiners and pronouns

限定词(後面的)才一定/是 noun

A Seven ways of using a determiner

6.1 不是所有的 deter。都有七种用法。

Any can be used in seven ways:
a before a count noun, singular:
    1 Come any day. You can come <u>any day</u> you like.
b before a count noun, plural:
    2 I haven't any books. You can borrow <u>any books</u> you like.
c before a mass noun:
    3 I haven't any bread. Help yourself to any bread you want.
d before *one*, standing for a count noun already mentioned:
    4 May I borrow a book? Borrow any one you want.
e before *ones*, standing for a count noun, plural:
    5 May I borrow some books? Borrow any ones you want.
f as a pronoun, or pro-form (1.5c) for the nominal group, *any* + noun:

    6 I haven't any $\left\{\begin{array}{l}\text{(book)}\\\text{(books)}\\\text{(bread)}\end{array}\right\}$.

g as a PREDETERMINER, *ie* a determiner occurring in the pattern *any of*

of。
construction

    $\left\{\begin{array}{l}\textit{the}\\\textit{those}\\\textit{my}\end{array}\right\}$ *books*:

    7a I haven't read any (one) of these books yet.
    b I haven't read any of this book yet.
    c Help yourself to any of this bread that you want.

6.2

Table 11 gives a list of the determiners and indicates in which of those seven ways each determiner can be used. The determiners, in the first column, and the pro-form (if any) in column *f*, are in italic type. Where the determiner and the pro-form are different, it is the pro-form that acts as the pre-determiner. The sign -* in the last column indicates that the word is not normally used as a predeterminer. Note that *of*, in a case like *a lot of*, is absent in the pro-form. Note also that ZERO, *ie* the absence of a determiner, is included in the list; that the concept of 'zero' is a very old one; and that it serves to fill a gap in the scheme below.

all, half, both, fraction ——— (of) 其他 Det 不可以

Table 11 Determiners

multipliers twice thrice twice four
the amount their 5 times
salaries strength

Determiner	a Count singular	b Count plural	c Mass	d + one	e + ones	f Pro-form and Predeterminer
a	man	—	—	—(6.10) —		*one*/of the men
all	day	men	life	—	—	*all*/(of) the { book / books / bread } +V sg. pl. sg.
a great amount of	—	—	bread	—	—	*a great amount*/of the bread
any	man	men	bread	one	ones	*any*/of the { book / books / bread }
both	—	men	—	—	—	*both*/ { (of) the men / = men }
a certain	man	—	—	one	—	*a certain one*/of the men
certain	—	men	—	—	ones	—
a { good / great } deal of	—	—	bread	—	—	*a { good / great } deal*/of the bread
each	man	—	—	one	—	*each (one)*/of the men + V sg.
either	man	—	—	one	—	*either (one)*/of the men
∆ *enough*	—	men	bread	—	—	*enough*/of the { men / bread }
every	man	—	—	one	—	*every one*/of the men
(a) few	—	men	—	—	—	*(a) few*/of the men
fewer, fewest	—	men	—	—	—	*fewer*/of the men
the first, the second, the last	man	men (6.32)	—	one	ones (6.32)	*the first*/of the men / *the last*/of the bread
half	an (of) hour	the men	the bread	—	—	*half*/(of) the { men / bread }
(the) least	thing	—	bread	—	—	*the least*/of the bread
less	—	—	bread	—	—	*less*/of the bread
(a) little	—	—	bread	—	—	*(a) little*/of the bread
a lot of	—	men	bread	—	—	*a lot*/of the { men / bread }
lots of (informal)	—	men	bread	—	—	*lots*/of { men / bread }
many	—	men	—	—	—	*many*/of the men
a { good / great } many	—	men	—	—	—	*a { good / great } many*/of the men
many a (formal)	man	—	—	one	—	*many a one*:-*
more	—	men	bread	—	—	*more*/of the { men / bread }
most	—	men	bread	—	—	*most*/of the { men / bread }
much	—	—	bread	—	—	*much*/of the bread
my, your, etc.	book	books	bread	—	—	*mine, yours,* etc.:-* (6.30)
neither	man	—	—	one	—	*neither (one)*/of the men
the next	man	men	—	one	ones	*the next*/of the men
no	man	men	bread	one	—	*none*/of the { men / bread }

差不多, 信不多, 多不多, 述不多

fraction

* not 不可省 Det.

1/3 (of) the { building + V sg. / rooms + V pl. / beef + V sg. }

Table 11 Determiners—*continued*

Determiner	a Count singular	b Count plural	ç Mass	d + one	e + ones	f Pro-form and Predeterminer
a (great) number of	—	men	—	—	—	a (great) number/of the men
one	man	—	—	—→	—	one/of the men
the only	man	men	bread	one	ones	the only one/of the men
another (indef.)	man	—	—	one	—	another (one)/of the men
other (indef.)	—	men	bread	—	ones	others or other ones :-*
the other (sing.)	man	—	bread	one	—	the other (one) :-*
the other (plur.)	—	men	—	—	ones	the others or the other ones :-*
plenty of	—	men	bread	—	—	plenty/of the { men / bread
the same	man	men	bread	one	ones	the same { (one) / (ones) } :-*
several	—	men	—	—	—	several/of the men
some (6.42)	—	men	bread	—	—	some/sʌm//of the { men / bread
some (6.43)	man	men	bread	—	—	See 6.47
such a	man	—	—	one	—	—
such	—	men	bread	—	ones	
that	man	—	bread	one	—	that :-*
the	man	men	bread	one	ones	—
these	—	men	—	—	ones	these :-*
this	man	—	bread	one	—	this :-*
those	—	men	—	—	ones	those :-*
the very	man	men	bread	one	ones	the very one(s) :-*
what	man	men	bread	one	—	what :-*
which	man	men	bread	one	ones	which/of the { men / bread
whose	book	books	bread	—	—	whose :-*
zero	man	men	bread	—	—	—

Notes: i. All the determiners are premodifiers, coming before the head in a nominal group, eg *enough money*. Exceptionally, *enough* can follow the head, *eg We'll have time enough to do that later*, but that use of *enough* is usually found only in formal or old-fashioned English. *Enough* modifying an adjective or an adverb, as in *This isn't good enough* is only a postmodifier.

ii. *One*, as in *the only one*, *the same one*, *the very one*, can only replace a count noun. There is no pro-form available for *the only* or *the very*+mass noun, except an expression like *the only kind*. For *the same*+mass noun, we can use *the same* as a pro-form, or say *the same kind*.

6.3
Determiners will be discussed under the headings IDENTIFIERS, INDEFINITE AND DEFINITE and QUANTIFIERS, INDEFINITE AND DEFINITE.

B Indefinite identifiers
The indefinite article
6.4

The indefinite article is *a* or *an* when the head of a nominal group is a singular count noun: *a* is used before a word beginning with a consonant sound, *an* before a vowel sound:

a man	a red apple	a university	a history
an apple	an old man	an uncle	a(n) historical event

6.5

A(n) + noun can refer to a class of thing as a whole (1.6d) *eg: a cat* in

    8 A cat is a small domestic animal,

which is a typical form of DEFINITION. Class is also emphasised in

    9 This is an apple, not a pear,

ie this is an example of that CLASS of thing. On the other hand, the idea of one EXAMPLE of the class is expressed in

    10 May I have an apple, please?

The difference between [9] and [10] becomes apparent in the plural: see examples [23] and [25]. In [10], we refer to an unidentified example of apple, just as we refer to an unidentified example of light in

    11 There is a light on in the house over there. (*cp* example [53])

6.6

A(n) is obligatory when a count noun singular is an indefinite complement of BE, *eg: a small animal* in example [8], and

    12 Mr Cartwright was a famous surgeon.

BE in [12] could be replaced by BECOME: but see example [32].

6.7

A(n) or *the* may be used in this pattern:

    13 These apples $\begin{Bmatrix} \text{are} \\ \text{cost} \end{Bmatrix}$ 20 pence $\begin{Bmatrix} \text{a} \\ \text{the} \end{Bmatrix}$ kilo.

In commercial English, *a* in [13] could be replaced by *per*.

6.8

Ellipsis (4.45) of *a(n)* is common in *a cup and (a) saucer, a knife and (a) fork, a hat and (a) coat, a raincoat and (an) umbrella.* Such ellipsis will only occur when the objects referred to are normally associated with each other, not in an example like *I found a hat and a camera in the car. Are they yours?* A similar ellipsis will occur with other determiners, *eg: the first and (the) second, my mother and (my) father,* and so on.

A(n) or one
6.9
A(n) can be regarded as a weak form of *one*, the strong form, *one*, being
used in the following cases:
a when emphasis is on the number, *one*, as opposed to more than one
   14 I only want one ticket. You've given me two.
b when one person or thing is compared with another:
   15 One man's meat is another man's poison.
c in constructions of the type *One day*, as in

16 One $\left\{ \begin{array}{l} \text{day} \\ \text{morning} \end{array} \right\}$, George came and told me all about it.

d as a pro-form for *a(n)* + noun, or for the noun alone in a group consisting
   of *a(n)* + adjective + noun:
   17 A Have you seen my coat anywhere?
       B Here's one. Is this yours?

   A No, mine is a grey $\left\{ \begin{array}{l} \text{coat} \\ \text{= one} \end{array} \right\}$ (*cp* example [50])
       Isn't there another (one) somewhere?

6.10
A one occurs, exceptionally, in colloquial English, as in
   18 Oh, you are a one! (*ie* an amusing, or daring, person)

6.11
(A) certain is less indefinite than *a(n)*. In
   19 A certain man had three sons,
which might be the beginning of a story, *certain* suggests that the story-
teller has someone definite in mind, but that the man's identity is not yet
known to the audience.

The zero article
6.12
The ZERO ARTICLE, *ie* absence of article, serves as an indefinite identifier. It
occurs before
a A COUNT NOUN PLURAL referring to a class as a whole, *eg* cats, as in
   20 Cats like fish, don't they?
   Example [20] states a CHARACTERISTIC of cats in general. A similar pattern
   can be used for definitions, especially in a case like
   21 Grapes are a kind of fruit,
   ie when we are more likely to think of a number of the objects being
   defined than of one object singly. Zero + plural would be obligatory in

22 I don't like $\left\{ \begin{array}{l} \text{cats} \\ \text{grapes} \end{array} \right\}$.

Note how class is emphasised in

23 These are apples, not pears. (*cp* example [9])

b A COUNT NOUN PLURAL referring not to the class as a whole but to a number of INDEFINITE examples, *eg people* in

24 Don't stand in the doorway. There are $\left\{ \begin{array}{l} \text{(other) people} \\ =\text{others} \end{array} \right\}$ waiting to come in.

We could insert *some* before *people* in [24] (but not before *apples* and *pears* in [23]); and a normal plural of *an apple* in example [10] would be

25 (May I have) some apples (,please)?

c A COUNT NOUN PLURAL, *eg engineers* as in

26 Mr Cartwright's sons were engineers. (*cp* example [12])

6.13

The zero article occurs BEFORE A MASS NOUN referring to the whole class of thing or to an indefinite, unidentified amount, *eg silver*, and *honesty*, as in

27 Silver is a precious metal. (*cp* example [8])

28 Honesty is the best policy.

and

29 This is lead, not silver. (*cp* example [9])

Compared with example [10], we have

30 (Can you change this £5 note?) May I have (some) silver, please?

6.14

The zero article does not normally occur before a count noun singular in a sentence. But the dividing line between count and mass nouns, or between common and proper nouns, is not always easy to draw. It is difficult to say whether *breakfast* is a count or a mass noun. *President* can be a common noun, as in *A republic usually has a president*, or a proper noun, as in [32] below. Whatever classification we may adopt, we find the zero article in the following examples:

31 $\left\{ \begin{array}{l} \text{Breakfast} \\ \text{Dinner} \end{array} \right\}$ tomorrow will be at 8 o'clock.

32 In 1861, Lincoln $\left\{ \begin{array}{l} \text{was} \\ \text{became} \\ \text{was elected} \end{array} \right\}$ President. (*cp* example [12])

33 Mr G. Hall was (the) Director of the National Bank.

34 They elected George captain.

Example [34] follows verb pattern D1 (10.1). However, *a* would occur in *He became a famous President* and *They elected Mr White a director* (= one of the directors) *of the company*.

The dividing line between a common and a proper noun is also vague when the noun refers to an institution which is felt by a community to be the only one of its kind that matters, as in

35 This is a question that only $\left\{\begin{array}{l} \text{parliament} \\ = \text{Parliament} \end{array}\right\}$ can answer.

36 When will $\left\{\begin{array}{l} \text{school} \\ = \text{School} \end{array}\right\}$ begin again?

37 Does (the) $\left\{\begin{array}{l} \text{term} \\ = \text{Term} \end{array}\right\}$ end on the 15th or the 16th?

The vagueness of the dividing line is reflected in an uncertainty whether to begin *parliament, school,* etc. with a capital letter or not. Either would be acceptable in the above examples.

6.15

Other examples of the zero article before a count noun singular are found

a in what is traditionally called the VOCATIVE case, *eg Father, Mother, Doctor, Captain,* in

38 Don't you worry, $\left\{\begin{array}{l} \text{Father} \\ \text{Mother} \end{array}\right\}$. I'll be all right.

Note that $\left\{\begin{array}{l} \text{Father} \\ \text{Mother} \end{array}\right\}$ is not the subject of the imperative in [38]; the subject, stated, is *you* (1.3b).

b optionally, in an NP in apposition to another NP, *eg (the) author* in

39 Mr J. Hall, (the) author of 'Escape', was G. H.'s elder brother,

    and

40 (The) author of 'Escape'(,) Mr J. Hall(,) arrived in New York last night.

The and the commas in [40] are more likely to be absent in American English than in British. Zero would not replace an indefinite article in a case of apposition, *eg Mr Hall, an old friend of mine . . .*

c before *man* (meaning either human beings in general, or *men* as opposed to *women*) and *woman* (meaning women in general):

41 Man is a social animal.

42 Man is a hunter; woman is his game. (Tennyson)

d before two or more nouns referring to a human couple, or to a pair of inanimate objects, or to a larger group:

43 Father and son were both soldiers.

44 They kept the treasure under lock and key, day and night.

e after TURN in the pattern

45 He turned traitor and fought against the King.

f in notes, notices, signs, labels, newspaper headlines; telegrams, etc., *eg*

46 Buy present for E.

47 PRIVATE ROAD

48 PLANE CRASHES ON MOTORWAY

g in numerous prepositional phrases, *eg at school, by bus, on foot,* which are dealt with in 8.9.

C Definite identifiers
The definite article
6.16

The definite article, *the,* can be used before a count noun singular, a count noun plural, or a mass noun. One of its chief functions is to indicate that the speaker is referring to a particular example, or to particular examples, of a class of thing. In using *the,* the speaker assumes that his audience can identify the particular example(s) to which he is referring. The word *the* alone is insufficient to identify the example(s), but it is a signal that identification can be made by

a something already said: reference backwards;
b something about to be said: reference forwards; or
c the context or situation.

REFERENCE BACKWARDS

49 Here is a glass, some water and three coins. Watch! I pour the water into the glass, then drop the coins one by one into the water.

In that example, *the water* (mass), *the glass* (count, singular) and *the coins* (count, plural) refer to *water* etc. just mentioned.

REFERENCE FORWARDS

50 A There are three coats here. Which is yours?

B Mine is the grey $\left\{ \begin{array}{l} \text{coat} \\ =\text{one} \end{array} \right\}$. The grey $\left\{ \begin{array}{l} \text{coat} \\ =\text{one} \end{array} \right\}$ is mine.

(Note that in [50], B's response can follow two different patterns, whereas in [17], only *Mine is a grey one* would be normal.)

51 My office is the room on your right. It's the one on your right. That's the one.

52 The water in this glass has now turned pink.

53 The light is on in the dining-room.

54 The $\left\{ \begin{array}{l} \text{coat} \\ =\text{one} \end{array} \right\}$ you gave me isn't mine after all.

In [50], the coat is identified by *grey,* the speaker assuming that *grey* is sufficient for the hearer to pick out the right coat. In [51], [52] and [53], the room, the water and the light are identified by prepositional phrases, which follow the nouns they modify (1.36d). Compare the form of sentence [53] with that of sentence [11] in 6.5. In [54], the coat is identified by means of a relative clause, *(that) you gave me,* which must follow its antecedent.

Notes:

i In saying *the room* in [51], *the light* in [53], and *the coat* in [54], the speaker assumes there is only one room on the hearer's right, and so on. It is possible to say *a room on your right, a light in the dining-room, a coat you gave me,* to mean 'one of the rooms on your right' etc.

ii Mass nouns, especially abstract nouns, are often modified by a prepositional phrase beginning with *of, eg the history of China;*

iii An adjective, like *grey* in example [50], only attracts *the* if it serves definitely to identify the thing mentioned, *eg coat. The* is not required in nominal groups like *ancient history, Chinese history,* unless, for example,

they are postmodified as in *The* $\begin{Bmatrix} ancient \\ Chinese \end{Bmatrix}$ *history we studied at school was not always true.*

6.17

Reference forward is made by a SUPERLATIVE, by an ORDINAL NUMBER (*first, second, third,* etc: 6.32), by *next* and *same, eg*

55 Tokyo is now the largest city in the world.

56 That's the third time you've trodden on my toe.

57 Woodside Road is the next turning on your right.

58 The same thing happened to me yesterday.

Notes:

i exceptionally, *a(n)* or zero can be used with a superlative or an ordinal number, in examples like *His novel became a best-seller, Best-sellers are not always classics, I have never won a first prize in my life.*

ii *The* does not occur before *last* or *next* in $\begin{Bmatrix} last \\ next \end{Bmatrix}$ - $\begin{Bmatrix} week \\ month, \\ year \end{Bmatrix}$ *ie* the week

etc. before or after the present one.

6.18

The indicates reference to a particular function in

59 Eighty people attended the dinner in honour of Sherlock Holmes last night. (*Cp* [31])

Identification by context
6.19

The + noun frequently occurs when the speaker is referring to some object or person that he assumes the hearer can identify in the environment which they share. Thus:

60 A There's someone at *the door*. Didn't you hear *the bell*?

B Perhaps it's *the milkman*. No, it's *the postman*.

61 Mr Turner is in *the garden*, watering *the flowers*.

62 I'll meet you at *the post office*, or at *the bank*.

63 The President will fly round *the world* next year.

64 Have you ever seen *the sun, the moon* and *the stars* in *the sky* together?

6.20

The is also used as a signal that the speaker is distinguishing one part of his environment from another. He speaks of living in *the town* as distinct from *the country*; of *the land* as distinct from *the sea*, of *the left* as distinct from *the right*. The seasons can be mentioned with the zero article, *eg If Winter comes, can Spring be far behind?* But *the* can be used in distinguishing one season from another, *eg*

65 Birds fly north in (the) summer and south in (the) winter.

Reference to one class as distinct from another
6.21

Like *a(n)* (in example [8]) and zero (in [20] and [27]), *the* can be used in referring to the class as a whole, and especially in distinguishing one class from another:

66 The housewife has a harder life than the office-worker.

We could replace *the housewife* by *a housewife* or by *housewives* in that sentence, making other changes that would then be necessary; but [66], as it stands, follows a pattern commonly used when a GENERALISATION is made about a whole class, whether of people, animals, plants or inanimate objects. Thus:

67 The cat has been a domestic pet for thousands of years.
68 The olive grows only in warm climates.
69 The aeroplane has revolutionised travel.

6.22

a *The + adjective*, with a plural verb, refers to a whole class in

70 The English like to be with their families at Christmas.

Individual members of the class are referred to in *Two Englishmen were on the plane when it crashed.* A similar distinction would be made between *the British* and *two Britons*, *the Welsh* and *two Welshmen*, *the Irish* and *two Irishmen*, *the Scottish/Scots* and *two Scotsmen*, *the French* and *two Frenchmen*, *the Dutch* and *two Dutchmen*. No such difference is made in other cases, *eg*

the Americans, the Russians – two Americans, two Russians

the Chinese, the Japanese – two Chinese, two Japanese (*Cp* 5.20c).

b For *the blind* etc., see 7.21.

The more the merrier
6.23

Note the use of *the* in fixed expressions on the pattern *The more the merrier. The sooner the better*, and the comparison on the pattern

71 The quicker you are, the more likely you are to make mistakes.

The articles with proper nouns
6.24
Normally, a proper noun, being the name of someone or something imagined as unique (1.6d), needs no determiner. Exceptionally, a proper noun can be modified by *the* in the following circumstances:
a when we use a family name in the plural, as in *the Robinsons* (5.27);
b when there are two or more people or places of the same name and the speaker wishes to specify which one he is referring to, *eg*
72 That's not the George Lamb I knew;
c in referring to a place as it was in a certain period:
73 The London of 1665 was far smaller than the London of today;
d when the speaker wishes to emphasise that one person or place named is the very one that everybody knows:
74 You say Shakespeare lived here. Do you mean *the* Shakespeare or somebody else?
(*The* in that example is strongly stressed and pronounced /ði:/: normally in fluent speech *the* is pronounced /ðə/ before a consonant sound and /ði/ before a vowel sound.)

6.25
A(n) + proper noun can be used to mean 'someone having characteristics of the person named', as in
75 George will never be a Napoleon in any walk of life.
A + proper noun can also be used to mean 'a certain person named' as in *There is a Mr James Hall to see you.*

The as part of a name
6.26
The is part of the name of a country in
The Argentine (*or* Argentina)   The Netherlands
The Philippine Islands (*or* The Philippines)
The Soviet Union   The United States (of America)
However, *the* would generally be omitted from those names on maps, name plates, etc.

6.27
The is also used with:
a SEAS AND OCEANS:
The Black Sea •	The Atlantic (Ocean)
The Red Sea	The Pacific (Ocean)
The Indian Ocean	The Mediterranean (Sea)
The Baltic (Sea)	

Ocean or *Sea* is commonly omitted in the last four cases; but not in the first three.

b RIVERS:

The $\left\{ \begin{array}{l} \text{River} \\ =\text{river} \end{array} \right\}$ Nile   The $\left\{ \begin{array}{l} \text{River} \\ =\text{river} \end{array} \right\}$ Amazon   *or*

The Nile   The Amazon

But *the* is not normally used with the names of *lakes*, eg *Lake Baikal*.

c MOUNTAIN RANGES:

The Alps		The Andes
The Himalaya Mountains	*or*	The Himalayas
The Rocky Mountains	*or*	The Rockies

The is not usually used with names of *mountains*, eg *Snowdon, Mount Everest*.[1]

d SHIPS:

The *Queen Elizabeth*   The *Orleans*

e HOTELS:

The Grand (Hotel)   The (Hotel) Cecil

f NEWSPAPERS:

The Times   *The Daily News*

g ORGANISATIONS: when the name follows the pattern *the University of Oxford*. If the place name is put first, it is normal to omit *the*, eg: *Oxford University*. With other patterns, usage varies. We find

The United Nations	The British Museum	The British Council
British Rail	(the) High Street	
`Oxford ,Street	the 'Oxford `Road (5.29)	

There is no way of telling which pattern is adopted in examples such as these, except by noting actual usage in each case.

It, he, she
6.28

a *It* stands for 'the thing, activity or situation mentioned or indicated', the thing being either abstract, or concrete and inanimate, or animate but not considered as male or female:

76 Love ceases to be a pleasure when it (=love) ceases to be a secret.

It stands for a person, in *Who is it? It's* $\left\{ \begin{array}{l} \textit{George.} \\ \textit{Jane.} \end{array} \right.$

77 Silver is a precious metal. It (=silver) has been used as currency for centuries.

78 The elephant is intelligent. It never forgets.

79 John and Mary are engaged. Who would have thought it?

It can stand for an *-ing* clause (4.5a).

b *He* stands for 'the person or animal mentioned or indicated, and considered as a male', or 'someone', as in [81] below:

[1] Exceptions include *The Peak, the Matterhorn.*

80 A It's a policeman.
    B Who is he? ⁻
81 A There's someone at the door.
    B What does he want?
82 Be careful of Danny (our male dog). He's very fierce.

c *She* stands for 'the person or animal mentioned or indicated and considered as female'. It is also used, optionally, with reference to a ship, or boat, or a machine, especially one in which the speaker takes a personal pride:

83 A Miss Bowling is waiting to speak to you.
    B What does she want?

84 Look at my $\left\{\begin{array}{l}\text{boat}\\\text{sports car}\end{array}\right\}$. Isn't she a beauty?

d *They* stands for 'the persons or animals or things mentioned' whether male or female or neuter.

The demonstratives
6.29

a *This* and *these* (referring to an object or objects, animate or inanimate, near the speaker), and *that* and *those* (referring to (an) object(s) farther away), are sufficient by themselves to make a definite identification:

85 I'd like $\left\{\begin{array}{l}\text{this}\\\text{that}\end{array}\right\}$ book. I'd like $\left\{\begin{array}{l}\text{this}\\\text{that}\end{array}\right\}$ (one).

86 I'd prefer $\left\{\begin{array}{l}\text{this}\\\text{that}\end{array}\right\}$ bread. I'd prefer $\left\{\begin{array}{l}\text{this}\\\text{that}\end{array}\right\}$ kind.

87 I'll take $\left\{\begin{array}{l}\text{these}\\\text{those}\end{array}\right\}$ books. I'll take $\left\{\begin{array}{l}\text{these}\\\text{those}\end{array}\right\}$.

Ones is possible after *these* and *those*, but less usual than *one* is after *this* and *that*.

b In a text, either *this* or *that* can have backward reference (6.16), though only *this* has forward reference:

88 I heard Friday's meeting has been cancelled. If $\left\{\begin{array}{l}\text{this}\\\text{=that}\end{array}\right\}$ is so, I shall protest very strongly.

89 Listen to this! They've cancelled Friday's meeting.

c Only *that* and *those*, not *this*, *these*, will occur in the following examples:

90a The population of China is much greater than that (=the population) of the United States.

   b The mountains of Greece are less thickly wooded than those (=the mountains) of my own country.

91 Those (=those people) who would like to leave early are kindly asked to sit near the exit.

Possessives
6.30

The possessives (1.8a, ii) are also sufficient to make a definite identification. Each of the possessives can be followed immediately by *own*. The pro-forms for the possessive + noun are listed below. The pro-form for *my own book* is *my own*. There is normally no pro-form for *its* alone; but *its own* can be used as a pro-form. Thus:

This is my book.	It's *mine*.	It's my own.
This is your book.	It's *yours*.	It's your own.
This is John's/his book.	It's *his*.	It's his own.
This is Mary's/her book.	It's *hers*.	It's her own.
That's the cat's/its basket.	—	It's its own.
This is our house.	It's *ours*.	It's our own.
This is their room.	It's *theirs*.	It's their own.

6.31

A noun with apostrophe *s* can act as a premodifier or as a pro-form, as in
    92 That's George's camera. It's George's (own).
The pro-form is often used when *house* or *shop* etc. could be supplied as the head of the nominal group:
    93 A I'm just going round to George's (house).
        B We've been invited to the Taylors' (house).
    94 You can buy that at the $\left\{\begin{array}{l}\text{grocer's}\\\text{baker's}\\\text{stationer's}\end{array}\right\}$ (shop).
    95 Your sister is at the dentist's.

Ordinal numbers
6.32

a FORM. After *first, second* and *third,* the ORDINAL NUMBERS are formed regularly by adding the sound /θ/ to the CARDINAL NUMBER. This ending is always spelt *th*; but note the spelling of *twentieth, thirtieth* etc. and the irregular spelling of
    fifth   eighth   ninth   twelfth
b Normally, an ordinal number will occur only before a count noun singular, *eg*
    96 George is the $\left\{\begin{array}{l}\text{first}\\\text{second}\\\text{third}\end{array}\right\}$ boy on the left. Dick is the $\left\{\begin{array}{l}\text{third}\\\text{fourth}\\\text{fifth}\end{array}\right\}$.
But note:
    97 The first three questions (*ie* the first, second and third) are easy.
    98 The last three boys (*ie* the last, last but one and last but two) must run again.

99 The three last boys (*ie* those who came in last together, or the three
who each finished his race last) were obviously not trying.
100 This is the first bread I've eaten this week. (*ie* the first time I've eaten
bread)
101 We've finished the last of the bread. (*ie* all that remains of it)

D Definite quantifiers
Cardinal numbers
6.33
These are *one* before a count noun singular, *two, three, four*, etc. before a
count noun plural. Note how certain numbers are pronounced and written:
100 = a (*or* one) hundred
200, 300, etc. = two hundred, three hundred, etc.
101–199, 201–299, etc. = a (*or* one) hundred and one, etc.
1,000 = a (*or* one) thousand
2,000, 3,000, etc. = two thousand, etc.
1,001 etc. = a (*or* one) thousand and one, etc.
1,201 etc. = a (*or* one) thousand two hundred and one, etc.
1,000,000 = a (*or* one) million

6.34
With mass nouns, definite quantities can be indicated in one of the following
ways:

twenty pieces of paper   six $\left\{ \begin{array}{l} \text{slices} \\ \text{loaves} \end{array} \right\}$ of bread

twelve bottles of milk   two kilos of rice

seven articles of furniture   and so on.

E Indefinite quantifiers
6.35
Some of these are used only with count nouns plural, some only with mass
nouns, some with either count or mass, as shown in Table 12.

Table 12
INDEFINITE QUANTIFIERS

With count nouns	*With mass*	*With either*
	a bit of	
(a) few	(a) little	all
fewer	less	plenty of
(the) fewest	(the) least	a lot of, lots of
a (great) number of	a great $\left\{ \begin{array}{l} \text{deal} \\ =\text{amount} \end{array} \right\}$ of	enough
many	much	more, most
several		some, any

Note: Regard *a bit of, lots* as informal; *a great number, a great amount* as more formal. *Large* could replace *great* before *amount* and *number*.

A few, a little
6.36
A few suggests a small, positive number – more than none; *few* suggests a small, negative number, almost none:

102 We have a few moments to spare. There's no need to hurry.

103 He's a man of few words. He rarely says anything.

Similarly, *a little* suggests a small, positive amount, more than none; *little* = almost none.

104 There's no need to hurry. We still have a little time left.

105 He said very little, practically nothing in fact.

Few and *little* are often modified by *very*, as in [105]. The difference between *a few, a little* and *few, little*, could be illustrated thus:

$$\text{None} \begin{array}{l} \nearrow \text{a few, a little} \\ \searrow \text{few, little} \end{array}$$

Fewer, fewest; less, least
6.37
Examples:

106 There were fewer people today than yesterday.

107 Harry made the fewest mistakes.

108 Please make less noise.

109 George gives me the least trouble.

Despite example [106], there is a growing tendency to put *less* before a count noun plural. *Less* would be normal in *That cost less than five pounds*. *Least* may occur before a count noun singular, as in *He faints at the least* (= smallest) *sign of blood*.

Many, much
6.38
Examples:

110a I haven't made many mistakes.

  b How many (mistakes) have you made?

  c Robert has made too many.

111a I haven't much money in the bank.

  b How much (money) have you (got)?

  c Walter has (got) too much.

Notice that in these examples *many* and *much* (without a modifier) are used only in negative and interrogative sentences (1.4).

In informal English, *many* in [110c] would have to be modified by *so, too,* or *a great*; and *much* in [111c] would have to be modified by *so* or *too*. Otherwise, *many* and *much* could be replaced by *plenty* or *a lot*; or, more informally, by *lots*. In formal English, *many* and *much* are more freely used without a modifier in affirmative sentences, as in

112   We have $\begin{Bmatrix} \text{much (work) to do} \\ \text{many obstacles to overcome} \end{Bmatrix}$ before we can claim that
real progress has been achieved.

Exceptionally, *much* may occur before a count noun singular, as in *There's not much point in going on.* Note also: *He's not much of a* $\begin{Bmatrix} success \\ gentleman \end{Bmatrix}$.

More, most, the most
6.39

Note the following examples:

113   George did more $\begin{Bmatrix} \text{work} \\ \text{exercises} \end{Bmatrix}$ than anyone else.

So he did the most $\begin{Bmatrix} \text{(work)} \\ \text{(exercises)} \end{Bmatrix}$.

114   The most work is often done by the quietest worker. (*ie* he does more than anyone else)

115   George did most of the $\begin{Bmatrix} \text{work} \\ \text{exercises} \end{Bmatrix}$; he didn't do $\begin{Bmatrix} \text{it} \\ \text{them} \end{Bmatrix}$ all.

116   Most people (*ie* not all) want a peaceful life.

F Determiners which are either identifiers or quantifiers
6.40

All, both, some, any, no, every, each, either and *neither* can answer either the question *Which one(s)?* or *How many?* Thus:

117   A $\begin{Bmatrix} \text{Which} \\ \text{How many} \end{Bmatrix}$ doors are open?
      B   All of them.

Some of this group of determiners refer to more than two units, some to two only, as in Table 13.

Table 13

More than two	Only two
the whole number = *all*	the two = *both*
all the units = *every*	
all, singly = *each*	both, singly = *each*
one, or one set, of all = *any*	one of both = *either*
not one of all = *no*	not one of both = *neither*

As indicated in Table 11, *all, some, any* and *no* can also refer to an amount and be used with mass nouns.

All and both
6.41
a *All* and *both* are most frequently used as predeterminers with *of* optional:

118 $\left\{\begin{array}{l}\text{All}\\\text{Both}\end{array}\right\}$ (of) the windows were broken.

After *both*, both *the* and *of the* are optional, thus:

119 Both of the windows were broken. Both the windows . . . *or* Both windows . . .

All can also be used with a count noun singular and a mass noun, as in

120 You haven't eaten all (of) the $\left\{\begin{array}{l}\text{loaf}\\\text{bread}\end{array}\right\}$, have you?

Cp all the loaf with *the whole loaf* = *the entire loaf*.
Before *day* and *night*, *of the* is normally absent, as in

121 I haven't seen George all $\left\{\begin{array}{l}\text{day}\\\text{night}\end{array}\right\}$.

The pattern in [121] is found with *week, month, year, summer, winter*, etc., specially in American English.
Notes:
  i *Half* occurs in the pattern *half (of) the* $\left\{\begin{array}{l}\text{book}\\\text{men}\\\text{bread}\end{array}\right\}$, and in the patterns *half an hour, a half hour*.
  ii *Twice* occurs in the patterns *twice sixteen, twice that number*.
b *All* and *both* can be used in two special constructions. The first is *they* $\left\{\begin{array}{l}\textit{all}\\\textit{both}\end{array}\right\}$ (as subject of a clause) or *them* $\left\{\begin{array}{l}\textit{all}\\\textit{both}\end{array}\right\}$ (as object), which is a pattern not available to any of the other determiners:

122 A Were $\left\{\begin{array}{l}\text{all}\\\text{both}\end{array}\right\}$ of the windows broken?

  B Yes, $\left\{\begin{array}{l}\text{all}\\\text{both}\end{array}\right\}$ of them were. *They* $\left\{\begin{array}{l}\textit{all}\\\textit{both}\end{array}\right\}$ were.

123 A Did he break $\left\{\begin{array}{l}\text{all}\\\text{both}\end{array}\right\}$ the windows?

  B Yes, he broke $\left\{\begin{array}{l}\text{all}\\\text{both}\end{array}\right\}$ of them. He broke *them* $\left\{\begin{array}{l}\textit{all}\\\textit{both}\end{array}\right\}$.

It could replace the noun in example [120]. Therefore
120a A You haven't eaten all of it, have you?
    B Yes, I've eaten *it all*.
c The second construction available to *all, both* and *each*, but not to other determiners, is found in:

124 They were $\left\{\begin{array}{l}\text{all}\\\text{both}\end{array}\right\}$ waiting for the headmaster.

Note that in *They* $\left\{\begin{array}{l}\textit{all}\\\textit{both}\end{array}\right\}$ *came* and *They were* $\left\{\begin{array}{l}\textit{both}\\\textit{all}\end{array}\right\}$ *waiting*, *all* and *both* occupy the same positions as simple adverbs of frequency (1.50).

d *All* is generally used as a predeterminer, but also occurs immediately before a count noun, plural, or a mass noun, thus:

125 All men are born equal.

126 All life is sacred.

Some and any
6.42

a *Some* and *any* are most frequently used as quantifiers, with *some* normal in affirmative contexts, and *any* in negative ones (1.4). *Any* is usual in questions if the answer is completely open. However, *some* may occur in questions, if the speaker has a certain quantity in mind, or if he is expecting an affirmative answer. Examples:

127 There are some /səm/ letters for you. (*Any* not acceptable here)

128 There aren't any letters for me. (*Some* not acceptable here)

129 Are there any letters for me? Any at all?

130 Are there some /səm/ letters for me? I was expecting some /sʌm/.

Note the difference between *Have you any apples?* (I can't see any) and *Could I have some of those apples?* (which I can see).

b The negative element can be transferred from a main clause to a subordinate clause, finite or non-finite; *eg*

129a I don't think there are any letters.

b He denied $\begin{cases} \text{that there were any letters.} \\ \text{finding any letters.} \end{cases}$

The negative element may also be contained in a preposition, as in *I can answer your question without any hesitation.*

c The basic difference between examples [127] and [128] is not that the *verb* is affirmative in the one and negative in the other, but that [127] is concerned with a certain (though unspecified) quantity while [128] is concerned with a completely indefinite quantity. Thus in

131 Some /sʌm/ boys haven't done their homework.

the verb is negative but the number of boys is fixed (though unspecified). [131] could be re-stated: *There are some boys who haven't....* On the other hand, in the conditional sentence,

132 Let me know if you need any help.

both verbs are affirmative, but the question of whether help is needed is completely open, or else the amount of help the speaker is offering is unlimited. *Any* could not replace *some* in [131]; but *some* could replace *any* in [132] if the speaker had certain help in mind, or if he is expecting a positive response.

6.43

a The distinction between a certain (but unspecified) unit and a completely indefinite range is made when *some* and *any* are used as identifiers, answering the question *which?* Thus:

133 A Please come and see us.
     B Which day would be convenient?
     A Oh, come any day. (completely indefinite)
     B Then I'll 'phone you some day next week, perhaps on Wednesday.

Note the difference between *Some boy knows the answer. Who is it?* and *Any child can answer that, ie* There isn't any child who can't.

b The quantifier *any* cannot be used alone in a short response, though *some* and *none* can be, as in

A Have we any eggs?

B $\left\{ \begin{array}{l} \text{Some} \\ \text{None} \\ \text{*Any} \end{array} \right\}$

However, the *identifier any* can be used in that way, as in

A Which of these books may I borrow?
B Oh, any. (= any one you like, it doesn't matter which)

Every and each
6.44

a Either *every* or *each* can be used in an example like:

134 $\left\{ \begin{array}{l} \text{Every} \\ \text{=Each} \end{array} \right\}$ man knows $\left\{ \begin{array}{l} \text{what he has to do.} \\ \text{his job.} \end{array} \right\}$

and

135 On $\left\{ \begin{array}{l} \text{every} \\ \text{=each} \end{array} \right\}$ side of the square there were soldiers.

But only *each* is usable in the following five examples:

136 On each side of the street (which has two sides), . . .
137 Each has two coats. (see Table 11)
138 The men have two coats each.
139 They each have two coats. (*cp* 6.41c)
140 They have each told me the same story. (6.41c)

b *Every* and *each* are normally followed by a singular verb, as in example [134]. But only a plural verb is used in examples on the patterns of [138], [139] and [140].

c *Every* and *each* are also normally associated with *he, him, his,* as in [134]. But in

141 When every man had assembled, the master paid them their wages, *them* and *their* would be regarded as more sensible than *him* and *his*.

d Example [141] illustrates a difference in meaning between *every* and *each* indicated in Table 13. It would make sense if every man – all, together – assembled, but it would be impossible for each to assemble separately.

e Exceptionally, *every* may occur before a mass noun, as in: He gave us

$$\text{every} \left\{ \begin{array}{l} \textit{assistance} \\ \textit{encouragement} \end{array} \right\} (= \text{He} \left\{ \begin{array}{l} \textit{assisted} \\ \textit{encouraged} \end{array} \right\} \text{us in every way})$$

No, none
6.45

$$I\ haven't\ any \left\{ \begin{array}{l} book \\ books \\ bread \end{array} \right\} \text{could be re-worded } I\ have\ no \left\{ \begin{array}{l} book \\ books \\ bread \end{array} \right\} ; \text{and } I$$

haven't any = I have none. The verb with *no, none* may be singular or plural, as in

142 There $\left\{ \begin{array}{l} \text{is no book} \\ \text{are no books} \end{array} \right\}$ here.

143 None of them $\left\{ \begin{array}{l} \text{is} \\ \text{are} \end{array} \right\}$ in my cupboard,

though 'careful' speakers and writers tend to prefer *none of them is.*
Contrast *Any child can answer that* (6.43) with *No child can answer it,*
ie There isn't any child who can answer it.

Either, neither
6.46
Either (of two) corresponds to *any* (of more than two), and *neither* corresponds to *no, none.*
    144 A Have you seen George and Harry?
          B I haven't seen either (of them).
              I've seen neither (of them).
              Either (George or Harry) is usually here.
              Neither $\left\{ \begin{array}{l} \text{seems} \\ = \text{seem} \end{array} \right\}$ to be here now.

Again, 'careful' speech would prefer *neither seems.*

G Indefinite pronouns, formed from *some, any, every, no*
6.47
a *Some* and *any* (as identifiers 6.43), also *every* and *no* can all be combined
    with *one* (or *body*) and with *thing*, so that
    some person *becomes* someone *or* somebody
    some thing *becomes* something
    all things   *becomes* everything
    All of the compounds so formed are stressed on the first element
    (*someone, somebody, everything*); and all except *no one* are written as one
    word. *Nothing* is pronounced /nʌθiŋ/. Note the difference between
    everyone and *every one*, which has nuclear stress on *one*:

145 Everyone (*or* everybody[1]) in the room stood up,
ie all the people in the room.

146 I have three $\left\{ \begin{array}{l} \text{sisters} \\ \text{pictures} \end{array} \right\}$. Every one of them is beautiful.

There is a similar difference between *anyone* and *any one*, as in *Give me any of those books – any one will do.*

b All of the compounds formed with *some, any, every* and *no + one, body* or *thing* can be postmodified by *else*, so that, for example,
some other person *becomes* somebody else.

c The personal indefinite pronouns, alone or with *else*, can have a possessive form with apostrophe *s*:

147 This is $\left\{ \begin{array}{l} \text{someone's} \\ \text{someone else's} \end{array} \right\}$ (coat).

148 Everyone's business is nobody's business. (*proverb*)

d *Some, any, no* and *every* can also be combined with *where*, and the resulting compound can be modified by *else*, to form adverbials *somewhere (else)* etc. *Some* can also enter into the compounds *somehow, sometime, sometimes* and *somewhat*. *Any* can enter into *anyhow, anyway*.

e The compounds of *some* and *any* are affected by affirmation and by negation in the same way as *some* and *any* by themselves are (6.42). *Cp* [127] and [128], with

149 There is something for you.

150 There isn't anything for you.

6.48

You and *they*, in informal English, and *one*, usually in more formal style, can be used as indefinite pronouns referring to people, thus:

151 If you want to see the ruins, you must go on foot.

There, *you* could either refer to the person(s) addressed, or to anyone, including you and me, whereas in

152 If you want to see the ruins, they will tell you that you must have a guide,

they means 'certain people, excluding you and me,' and could be replaced by *people*. In

153 If you want to see the ruins, they won't let you in before nine o'clock,

they means 'the authorities responsible'. *One* could replace *you* as in

154 One must buy a ticket at the office.

But the repetition of *one*, as in

155 If one wants to see the ruins, one must find one's own guide,

[1] Only *everyone*, not *everybody*, will occur in *everyone of* $\left\{ \begin{array}{l} \textit{them.} \\ \textit{us.} \\ \textit{you.} \end{array} \right\}$

is awkward. American English in that sentence would replace the second *one* by *he* and *one's* by *his*.

H Negation of determiners
6.49

The old proverb *All is not gold that glitters* could be re-worded thus in modern English:

156 Not everything that glitters is gold.

Not everything is implies that some things are but others are not. See 6.51(1).

I Combinations of determiners
6.50

a The determiners in italics are mutually exclusive, *ie* only one of them can be used as a premodifier in the same nominal group:

$$\left\{ \begin{array}{l} a \quad the \quad this \quad that \quad these \\ those \quad my \quad your \quad John's \\ \text{etc.} \end{array} \right\} \quad + \text{friend(s)}$$

However, we can combine *a, this, that, these* or *those* with a possessive (5.38) by using the double genitive:

a friend of mine   this great country of ours

That new dress of Susan's must have been terribly expensive.

What shall I do with all $\left\{ \begin{array}{l} these \\ those \end{array} \right\}$ old books of yours?

Note that *the* cannot begin a double genitive construction.

b The determiners in italics can combine with *more* as in *Have you any more stamps?*

$$\left\{ \begin{array}{l} any \quad (a) \, few \quad (a) \, little \\ a \, lot \quad much \quad many \\ no \quad plenty \quad several \\ some \quad any \\ any \, cardinal \, number \end{array} \right\} \quad + more$$

c Those on the left can precede those on the right.

$$a \, few \quad the \, first \, \text{etc} \quad several \quad + \left\{ \begin{array}{l} dozen \quad score \quad hundred \\ thousand \quad million \end{array} \right\}$$

Note that *some hundred* = about a hundred.

d *Another* can precede any cardinal number, as well as *dozen* and *score*, to mean '(that number) more':

another   +*six   dozen   twenty* etc

e *Few* and *many* can be modified by *the, these, those, my* or any other possessive, thus:

157 His many friends all came to support him.

158 The few friends (that) he possessed deserted him one by one.

f *Only* and *other* can combine with other determiners, thus:

159   I have four brothers. Two are married. $\left\{ \begin{array}{l} \text{The} \\ \text{My} \end{array} \right\}$ other two brothers
want to remain single.

160   I have only two suits. $\left\{ \begin{array}{l} \text{The} \\ \text{My} \end{array} \right\}$ only other suit is at the dry cleaner's.

g *The first three, the three first*: see 6.32.

J Modifiers of determiners
6.51
The modifiers on the left can be used with the determiners indicated.
An asterisk refers to the notes below:

a *a good* $+\left\{ \begin{array}{l} few \quad = \text{more than a few} \\ many = \text{very many} \end{array} \right\}$

b *a great* $+amount$ *deal*   *many*   *number*
  a large $+amount$ *number*

c *about* $+\left\{ \begin{array}{l} a\ (week) \quad all \quad enough \\ the\ first\ etc. \quad half \quad the\ least \\ the\ only \quad the\ same \\ any\ cardinal\ number \end{array} \right\}$

d *almost* $+\left\{ \begin{array}{l} a\ (week) \quad all \quad any^* \\ enough \quad every \quad the\ first\ etc. \\ half \quad no \quad none \quad the\ only \\ the\ same \end{array} \right\}$

e *fewer than* $+half$ *any number*

f *hardly* $+\left\{ \begin{array}{l} a\ (week) \quad any^* \quad enough \\ any\ number \end{array} \right\}$

g *less than* $+a\ (week)$ *half*   *any number*

h *more than* $+\left\{ \begin{array}{l} a\ (week) \quad enough \quad half \\ any\ number \end{array} \right\}$

i *nearly* $+\left\{ \begin{array}{l} a\ (week) \quad all \quad enough \\ every \quad half \quad a\ hundred \\ a\ thousand \end{array} \right\}$

j *no fewer than* $+half$ *any number*

k $\left\{ \begin{array}{l} no \\ not \end{array} \right\} \left\{ \begin{array}{l} less \\ more \end{array} \right\}$ than $+$ *a (week)*   *half*   *any number*

l *not* (6.49) $+\left\{ \begin{array}{l} all \quad enough \quad every \quad a\ few \\ half \quad the\ least \quad a\ little \\ many \quad more \quad much \quad one \\ the\ only \quad another \quad the\ same \end{array} \right\}$

m *not nearly* $+enough$

n *not quite* $+all$ *the same*   *enough*

o *over* $+a\ week$ *half*   *any number*

p *quite* $+\begin{cases} a\ (time) \quad enough \quad a\ few \\ a\ lot \end{cases}$

q *scarcely* $+\begin{cases} (a)\ week \quad any^* \quad enough \\ half \quad any\ number \end{cases}$

r $\begin{cases} so \\ too \\ very \end{cases}$ $+few \quad little \quad many \quad much$

s *far too* $+few \quad little \quad many \quad much$

t *much too* $+few \quad little \quad much$

u *some* (=*about*) $+(any\ number)$

Notes:

i *Come almost any day – not Friday.*

ii *We have* $\begin{cases} hardly \\ scarcely \end{cases}$ *any bread left – it has almost all gone.*

iii In informal style, *ever so* (=very) is commonly used before *many* and *much*, and *ever such* before *a lot*.

Chapter Seven
Adjectives

A Form
7.1

-ABLE: *eg comfortable, drinkable, eatable*; a space-ship is *steerable* if it can be steered, it is *unsteerable* when it cannot be. Note the spelling of *(re'gret) re'grettable, (forget) unfor'gettable* (but *'preferable*[1]), *(rely) reliable, (deny) undeniable, (note) notable, (love) lovable*; but, when the base ends in *-ee*, *-ce* or *-ge – agreeable, manageable, noticeable*;

-AL: *cultural, medical, musical*;

-IBLE: *legible, sensible, visible*;

-IC: *atomic, heroic, scientific*;

-ISH: *childish, foolish, selfish*. The suffix *-ish* is often added, especially to adjectives of colour, *eg brownish, whitish, reddish*, to convey the meaning 'not definitely brown but approaching that condition or quality'.

-IVE: *attractive, expensive, productive*;

-FUL: *careful, useful*. Note the spelling when the base ends in consonant $+y$, *eg beautiful* but *playful*, and when the base ends in *-ll*, *eg skilful, wilful*;

-LESS: *careless, helpless, useless*;

-LY: *brotherly, deadly, elderly, fatherly, friendly, goodly, likely, lively, lonely, lovely, lowly, motherly, poorly*;

-OUS: *dangerous, poisonous*. The *e* is retained after *g (courage, courageous)* but changes to *i* after *c (space, spacious)*. Final *our* in the base changes to *or (vigour, vigorous)*. Note *gaseous, piteous*;

-Y: *dirty, dusty, sleepy*. Many adjectives are formed on this model, especially when the base is a monosyllabic mass noun. The spelling of *funny, muddy, woody*, etc. follows the rule given in 1.16 (3f). Exceptionally, *woolly* has LL: *cp woollen*. For the spelling of *icy, stony* etc. *cp* 1.16 (5).

Other typical adjective endings are found in *suburbAN, elegANT, circulAR, woodEN, dependENT, martIAL, economicAL, pretentIOUS*.

Participles used adjectivally (3.22, 3.32)
7.2

-ing and *-ed* participles which can be used both as attributive and as predicative adjectives (1.43) and which can be modified by *very*, include:

a alarming   daring   fascinating   retiring

---

[1] See the rule in 1.16(3f). The *t* is doubled in *regrettable* and *unforgettable*, because the syllable before *-able* is stressed; but that syllable is not stressed in *preferable*.

amazing	deafening	frightening	rewarding
amusing	disturbing	heartening	satisfying
astonishing	embarrassing	humiliating	shocking
boring	encouraging	insulting	striking
charming	enterprising	interesting	surprising
comforting	entertaining	lasting	thrilling
confusing	exacting	pleasing	tiring
damaging	exciting	promising	worrying
b alarmed	conceited	embarrassed	reserved
amazed	contented	excited	satisfied
amused	well-defined	fascinated	shocked
balanced	disappointed	frightened	surprised
badly-behaved	distinguished	interested	tired
well-behaved	divided	limited	unexpected
bored	well-dressed	pleased	unsettled
well-built	well-educated	relaxed	worried

Note: *Alarmed, amazed* and *amused* will usually modify a noun like *look* or *expression* (on one's face). *Beloved* can be pronounced /bi'lʌvd/ or /bi'lʌvid/: other parts of the old verb BELOVE will rarely, if ever, occur in modern English.

B Comparison (1.44)

7.3

With gradable adjectives, we can make three types of comparison:

a →, to a higher degree;
b =, the same degree;
c ←, to a lower degree.

A higher degree

7.4

In comparing one thing or set of things with another thing or set, the COMPARATIVE degree is indicated by the inflexion *-er* or the premodifier *more*. In comparing one thing or set with two or more other things or sets, the SUPERLATIVE degree is indicated by the inflexion *-est* or the premodifier *most*. Thus:

1 This watch is $\begin{Bmatrix} \text{cheaper} \\ \text{more expensive} \end{Bmatrix}$ than that one.

2 The one over there is $\begin{Bmatrix} \text{the cheapest of the three} \\ \text{the most expensive of them all} \end{Bmatrix}$.

Note the preposition *than* in example [1], and the conjunction *than* in 2.44; and the use of *the* in example [2]. *The* can be used with the comparative, as in

3 Look at these two watches. Which is the cheaper (of the two)?

However, *Which is the cheapest?* is frequently heard in informal speech, even when only two things are being compared.

7.5

a Comparison with *-er, -est* is normal with monosyllabic words, *eg*

| cheap | cheaper | cheapest |

b The spelling rules given in 1.16 apply, as in

big	bigger	biggest
fat	fatter	fattest
late	later	latest
dry	drier	driest

Note also:

| cruel | crueller | cruellest |

c In *longer, longest, stronger, strongest and younger, youngest*, a /g/ sound is added to the /ŋ/ of the base to produce

| /lɔŋ/ | /lɔŋgə/ | /lɔŋgist/ |
| /strɔŋ/ | /strɔŋgə/ | /strɔŋgist/ |

(Note that this extra /g/ sound is not added in the present participle *longing* /ˈbŋiŋ/, or in a noun ending in *-er, eg singer* /siŋə/.

d *Dear* and *near* have no final /r/ sound in Southern British English; but the r is pronounced when followed by a vowel, as in *dearer, dearest* and *nearer, nearest*.

e The comparative is repeated, as in *This tree is getting bigger and bigger every day*, to suggest a continuous process.

7.6

Seven monosyllabic adjectives do not follow the rule given in 7.5a. They are

	COMPARATIVE	SUPERLATIVE
good	better	best
{ bad ill }	worse	worst
far	{ farther further }	{ farthest furthest }
like	more like	most like (8.8)
real	more real	most real
tired	more tired	most tired

Either *farther, farthest* or *further, furthest* can be used with reference to distance, though *farther, farthest* is preferred as an adjective in that sense in traditional grammar, *eg*

4 We live on the farther side of the town.

Further, as an adjective, is preferred in the sense of *another*:

5 Here is a further example.

For *farther, further* as adverbs (15.6).

7.7

Old follows the rule in 7.5a when it is used predicatively:

  6 My brother John is three years older (than I am).

The comparative *elder* and superlative *eldest* are optional replacements for *older* and *oldest*, but are only used (a) attributively, and (b) with reference to membership of a human family or social group:

  7a John is my elder brother.
   b He is the elder (brother).
  8a He is the eldest (child).
   b He is the eldest (child) in the family.

Note the expression *an elder statesman*.

7.8

a Comparison with *-er, -est* is normal for two-syllable adjectives ending in the suffix *-y* (see 7.1), and is optional with such adjectives when they have the addition of the prefix *un-*:

Normal	happy	happier	happiest
	tidy	tidier	tidiest
Optional	unhappy	unhappier	unhappiest
	untidy	untidier	untidiest

b Comparison with *-er, -est* occurs optionally with certain two-syllable adjectives stressed on the first syllable, eg

able	abler	ablest
clever	cleverer	cleverest
common	commoner	commonest
feeble˙	feebler	feeblest
gentle	gentler	gentlest
narrow	narrower	narrowest
shallow	shallower	shallowest
simple	simpler	simplest

c In *able, feeble, gentle, simple,* the *-le* is pronounced /l/, at the back of the mouth, as a separate syllable. In *abler, ablest,* etc., the *-ler, -lest* are pronounced /lə/, /list/, with a front l sound.

d *Little* is not usually compared. The opposite of *big, bigger, biggest* would therefore be

$$\left\{ \begin{array}{l} \text{little} \\ \text{small} \end{array} \right\} \qquad \text{smaller} \qquad \text{smallest}$$

e Comparison with *-er* and *-est* is also optional in a few other two-syllable adjectives, *eg pleasant, polite* and *solid*. It would not occur with the following two-syllable adjectives:

careful	careless	certain	complex	fertile
foolish	frequent.	normal	public	private

7.9

Gradable adjectives not compared with *-er, -est*, follow the pattern:

This book is more $\left\{ \begin{matrix} \text{expensive} \\ \text{interesting} \end{matrix} \right\}$ than that one.

The one I just showed you is the most $\left\{ \begin{matrix} \text{expensive} \\ \text{interesting} \end{matrix} \right\}$ of them all.

Which is the more $\left\{ \begin{matrix} \text{expensive} \\ \text{interesting} \end{matrix} \right\}$ of the two?

The comparative with *more* can be repeated (see 7.5e) as in
Food is getting more and more expensive every week.

7.10

While longer adjectives, such as *comfortable, comforting, expensive, interested* are not compared with *-er, -est*, any adjective can optionally be compared with *more* and *most* when emphasis is not on the comparison but on the idea expressed by the adjective itself, as in

    9 Little by little, the farmer became more rich (He was not rich before)

or when two adjectives are co-ordinated, the first being a long one, as in

   10   Trains have become more comfortable and $\left\{ \begin{matrix} \text{safer} \\ =\text{more safe} \end{matrix} \right\}$.

      Cp

   10a Trains have become safer and more comfortable.

The same degree
7.11

The same degree is indicated by the construction *as* + adjective + *as, eg*

   11 This watch is as $\left\{ \begin{matrix} \text{cheap} \\ \text{expensive} \end{matrix} \right\}$ as that one.

Example [11] can be negated in the normal way (1.26, 1) to produce

   11a This watch is not as $\left\{ \begin{matrix} \text{cheap} \\ \text{expensive} \end{matrix} \right\}$ as that one,

which means that the price of one watch is not equal to that of the other.

A lower degree
7.12

Comparison to a lower degree can be indicated in two ways:

The lowest degree	*Lower than standard*	*Standard*
a —	not $\left\{ \begin{matrix} \text{as} \\ =\text{so} \end{matrix} \right\}$ dear as	dear
b the least expensive	less expensive than	expensive

Example:

   12 This watch is $\left\{ \begin{matrix} \text{not} \left\{ \begin{matrix} \text{so} \\ =\text{as} \end{matrix} \right\} \text{dear as} \\ \text{less expensive than} \end{matrix} \right\}$ that one.

The main points of difference between *a* and *b* are as follows:

i *not* $\left\{ \begin{array}{c} as \\ =so \end{array} \right\}$ *dear as* is freely used in informal style in the predicate, after BE, as in example [12];

ii *less expensive* in the predicate, as in [12], would be rather more formal;

iii *less expensive* would, in either style, be normal in an attributive position, as in

13 I would prefer the less expensive one

though in informal style *not so expensive*, too, would occur attributively, as in

13a I'd prefer the not so expensive one.

iv only *b* (*the least expensive*) is available for the superlative.

c Continuous process (7.5e and 7.9) can be expressed by *less and less* as in *children become less and less dependent on their parents*.

7.13

The complications discussed in 7.12 could always be avoided by re-wording an example like [12] as follows:

12a This watch is cheaper than that one.

However, there is a slight difference in meaning between [12] and [12a]. In [12], the impression is given that both watches are expensive but that one is less so than the other. In [12a], the impression is given that both watches are cheap.

C Adjectives in the noun phrase
Adjectives used attributively
7.14

All the adjectives in 7.1 can be used both in the noun phrase, *ie* attributively (1.43), and predicatively. We shall now consider three types of adjective which can be used only attributively, or which are used attributively with special meanings:

a THOSE THAT FUNCTION RATHER AS DETERMINERS answering, more or less definitely, the question *which?* For example, *certain*, listed as a determiner in Chapter Six, could also be classified as an attributive adjective in

14 A certain man had three sons.

Certain is used differently in

14a Now this man was certain (that he was right).

Particular, in the sense of 'special', is used only attributively:

15 We had a particular reason for abandoning the project.

Cp He's very particular (=fussy) *about his clothes.* But *chief, main, principal* are not used predicatively at all:

16 Our $\left\{ \begin{array}{c} \text{chief} \\ \text{main} \\ \text{principal} \end{array} \right\}$ reason for abandoning the project was financial.

b THOSE THAT FUNCTION RATHER LIKE INTENSIFIERS (1.51). The intensifier *very* can be used before an adjective, and we can say *Jane is very young.* We cannot use *very* to modify a noun like *child.* Instead, we can say
17 Jane is a mere child.
Similarly, instead of *This expenditure was very wasteful* we can say
18 This expenditure was a sheer waste of money.
Note the difference between *mere* and *sheer*:

MINIMUM   MAXIMUM
a mere child ⟵

⟶ a sheer waste.

Another adjective of the type of *mere* and *sheer* is *utter.* Thus, *That man is extremely foolish* could be re-worded
19 That man is an utter fool.
Mere, sheer and *utter* are used only attributively. *Utter*, in [19], could be replaced by *complete* or *perfect*, which can also be used predicatively, but with different meanings, as in

20 Your work is now $\begin{cases} \text{complete.} \\ \text{perfect.} \end{cases}$

c THOSE THAT OCCUR IN A NOMINAL GROUP THAT COULD BE REPLACED BY VERB + ADVERBIAL, or verb + relative clause:

21 He $\begin{cases} \text{is } \textit{a heavy smoker.} \text{ (nominal group)} \\ = \textit{smokes heavily.} \text{ (verb + adverbial)} \end{cases}$

Similarly,

22 He $\begin{cases} \text{is a hard worker.} \\ = \text{works hard.} \end{cases}$

23 Mr Turner is the $\begin{cases} \text{present Chairman.} \\ = \text{Chairman at present.} \end{cases}$

24 George Lamb $\begin{cases} \text{is an old friend.} \\ = \text{has been a friend for many years.} \end{cases}$

25 These are $\begin{cases} \text{new students.} \\ = \text{students who have newly arrived.} \end{cases}$

Order of modifiers in a nominal group
7.15
In any nominal group, if there are both determiners and attributive adjectives, the determiners come first. Thus

Nominal group

DETERMINERS	ADJECTIVES ETC.	HEAD
26 several thousand	fresh white	loaves
27 the only other	green Chinese	carpet

Combinations and modifiers of determiners have been discussed in 6.50 and 6.51.

7.16

After the determiner(s), if any, adjectives and other modifiers will normally come IN THE FOLLOWING ORDER, starting from the left in writing:

1 EPITHETS, *ie* adjectives that describe or express some characteristic of the thing referred to by the head; *eg tall, handsome*. Epithets include participial adjectives (7.2), *eg daring, well-dressed*. If two or more epithets are used in the same group, they may be separated by co-ordinators (1.53) or by a comma:

    28 a handsome and daring hero
        or
    29 a tall, well-dressed man

Adjectives indicating size will usually precede those indicating shape, as in

    30 a small round table

One or more of the epithets can be modified:

    31 a rather tall and very handsome man
    32 a tall but very graceful woman

Notice the difference between

    33 a pretty intelligent girl

in which *pretty intelligent* (informal style) = rather intelligent, and

    34 a pretty, intelligent girl

ie one who is both pretty and intelligent.

2 ADJECTIVES INDICATING COMPARATIVE AGE, *eg*

    35 a handsome young man
    36 a very courageous old lady

3 ADJECTIVES OF COLOUR:

    37 the deep blue sea
    38 a dirty old brown coat

If two or more adjectives of colour are used, they will be separated by co-ordination:

    39 a blue and white flag
    40 a red, white and blue flag

4 ADJECTIVES INDICATING NATIONALITY, place of origin or situation:

    41 a beautiful green Chinese carpet
    42 those tall young London policemen

5 NOUNS OR ADJECTIVES INDICATING THE SUBSTANCE of which something is made, *eg silk, iron, wooden* (5.29) in

    43 a blue and white silk tie

    44 a large $\left\{ \begin{array}{l} \text{iron} \\ \text{wooden} \end{array} \right\}$ box

6 either a gerund, as in 3.21b, or a noun or adjective of the type *law, medical*, as in 5.30b (it is hardly likely that both of them would occur in the same group). Thus

    45 a valuable old French writing desk

46 a famous German $\begin{Bmatrix} law \\ medical \end{Bmatrix}$ school

We might consider *writing desk* as one inseparable lexical unit, and the same would apply to *law school* and *medical school*. Note that, while in examples [26] to [44] all the modifiers that come after the determiners are stressed and nuclear stress falls on the head, in examples [45] and [46] nuclear stress falls on *writing* (as in 3.21b) and $\begin{Bmatrix} law \\ medical \end{Bmatrix}$ (as in 5.30b).

We could sum all this up in the following table:

Table 14
ORDER OF ADJECTIVES BEFORE A NOUN

Epithet	Size	Shape	Age	Colour	Origin	Sub-stance	Gerund etc.	
a daring			young					man
a	small	round				oak		table
a dirty			old	brown				coat
a charming					French		writing	desk
a	large			green	Chinese			carpet
a famous					German		medical	school

Notice that not all of the spaces on each horizontal line are filled. A nominal group in which all of the spaces were filled would be rare – and cumbersome.

D Adjectives used predicatively
7.17
a Adjectives used predicatively and not attributively tend to refer to a temporary condition rather than a permanent characteristic. This is noticeable with adjectives referring to health:
47 A How is your mother today?

B She is $\begin{Bmatrix} ill \\ unwell \\ well \end{Bmatrix}$. She's feeling $\begin{Bmatrix} faint. \\ poorly. \end{Bmatrix}$

Comparable attributive adjectives would be *healthy* or *sick*, both of which suggest a more permanent state in

48 He's a very $\begin{Bmatrix} healthy \\ sick \end{Bmatrix}$ man.

Faint can be used attributively, but not with the meaning it has in [47]; for example
49 There's a very faint hope of finding him alive.
b There is a group of adjectives beginning with *a-* that are used only predicatively. Note their attributive counterparts:
50 That child is afraid.   It's a frightened child.

51 These two men are alike.   —
52 These problems are alike.   They're similar problems.
53 Thank goodness! He's alive.   —
54 This tree is alive.   It's a living tree.
55 The old lady lives alone.   She's a lonely old lady.
56 I am ashamed.   —
57 The dog is asleep.   Let sleeping dogs lie.
58 Now it's awake.

Note, for example, that *alone* can refer to a temporary state, whereas *lonely* expresses a more permanent characteristic. Other predicative adjectives of this type are *ablaze, adrift, afire, afloat, aghast, alight*. On the other hand, a number of words beginning with *a-* are only used adverbially: see 15.1e.

c Another predicative adjective beginning with *a-* is *aware*; but note that *aware* must have a complement, *eg*

59 Are you aware $\begin{cases} \text{of the danger?} \\ \text{that we are in serious danger?} \end{cases}$

Adjectives with complementation
7.18

Many adjectives used predicatively can, and some must, have complementation. In 7.20 we shall find an alphabetical list of frequently-used adjectives, with indications of the kind of complementations that they can or must have. The list is not intended to be exhaustive. If the complementation can be omitted, provided it is understood, it will be shown after an oblique stroke in the list, like this:

60 Are you afraid / of the danger?

If it cannot be omitted, it will be shown without an oblique stroke:

[59] Are you aware of the danger?

Adjectival complementation is of three main types:

a PREPOSITIONAL PHRASES, prep + NP, or prep + *-ing*:

61 Most cats are fond of fish.
62 I am interested in collecting stamps.

b AN INFINITIVE (3.15)

Section 3.15 gave six types of adjective complementation:

63a He is anxious to see her
  b He is likely to see her
  c He is happy to see her
  d He is foolish to see her
  e He is quick to understand
  f He is easy to teach

These six types will be referred to in the list in 7.20 by the letters *a, b, c, d*, etc.

c a *that*-clause. There are three types of *that*-clause following an adjective;
eg
64 I am glad (that) you came.
This type will be indicated in the list by *glad / that*.
65 I am sorry (that) you (*should*) feel offended.
This will be indicated by *sorry / that . . . (should)*.
66 I am determined that there should be no delay,
indicated by *determined that . . . should*.

It is important $\begin{cases} \textbf{to} \dots \\ \textbf{·that} \dots \end{cases}$

7.19

There *appears* to be adjective complementation in *It is important to remember this* (3.15g); but that sentence can be seen as a re-wording of *To remember this is important*. A similar comment applies to *It is clear that he lost his head*. When an adjective (*eg important, clear*) is commonly used with anticipatory *it*, the list in 7.20 will give one of the following indications:
IMPORTANT: it . . . to (= *It is important to* + infinitive)
CLEAR: it . . . that (= *It is clear that* + verb in any tense or + any modal)
STRANGE: it . . . that . . . (should) (= *It is strange that they (should) feel so angry*)
ESSENTIAL: it . . . that . . . should (= *It is essential that he should apologise*).

ADJECTIVES FOLLOWED BY PREPOSITIONS . . .

7.20

stg = something   sby = somebody
Stg (*eg* a house) is ABLAZE / with
  lights
ABLE / to go (*a*)
ABSENT / from school
ACCUSTOMED to stg; to going
AFRAID / of stg *or* sby; to go (*a*), *or*
  of going (10.7); that
sby is AGREEABLE to go (*a*), to
  teach (*f*); it...to
AHEAD / of sby
AMAZED / at stg; to find (*c*)
AMUSED / at sby; with a toy; that...
  (should)
AMUSING / to teach (*f*); it...that...
  (should)

ANGRY / with sby; about stg; to
  hear (*c*); about having to go
ANNOYED / with sby; about stg
ANSWERABLE to sby, for stg
ANXIOUS / about sby *or* stg; to go
  (*a*); that...should
APT to go (*a*)
ASHAMED / of sby, of oneself *or*
  one's actions; to go (*a*) *or* of
  going (10.7); that...(should)
ASTONISHED / at sby *or* at sby's
  action; to see (*c*) *or* at seeing;
  that...(should)
ASTONISHING / it...that
ATTENTIVE / to sby *or* stg

AVERSE to stg; to going
AWARE of stg; of being; that
BAD (=unsuccessful) at stg; at
   reading; bad (=harmful) for
   sby
BLIND to other's faults
BOUND for a destination; to go (a)
BRAVE / to do stg (d)
BRILLIANT / (=very successful) at
   mathematics; at solving
   problems
BUSY / with stg
CAPABLE / of doing stg; of
   improvement
CAREFUL (=watchful) / of stg or
   sby; (=taking trouble) with
   stg; to see (e); about answering
   letters
CARELESS of danger; careless / with
   eg tools; careless / in what one
   does, in answering letters
CERTAIN of stg or sby (=have
   confidence in); certain / about
   stg or sby (=have no doubt);
   to go (b); of going (10.7); that
CLEAR / about a subject; of an
   obstacle; it...that
CLEVER / at stg, at doing stg; with
   one's hands; to do stg (d)
CLOSE / to or by stg or sby; to
   winning
CONCERNED / (=worried) about
   sby or stg; about getting the
   work done; (=engaged) in or
   with an enterprise; (=worried)
   that...should
CONFIDENT / of success; of
   succeeding; in the hope of
   success; that...will
CONSCIOUS of stg; of being a
   failure; that
CONTENT(ED) with stg; to go
   (a & c); with going; that...should

CONTRARY to my advice
CONVENIENT / (=suitable) for sby;
   (=well-placed) for stg, for
   parking; (=suitable) it...to;
   it...that...(should)
CRAZY about sby or stg; to go
   (a & d)
CRITICAL / of stg or sby
CRUEL / to sby; to do stg (d); it...to
CURIOUS / (=anxious to know)
   about stg; to know (a);
   (=strange) it...to; it...that
DEAF to eg an appeal
DEAR / to sby (=loved by sby)
DELIGHTED / with a present; at
   hearing good news; to do (a), to
   see (c); that
DEPENDENT on sby or stg; on being
DESIRABLE / it...to; it...that...
   should
DETERMINED / on a course of
   action: to go (a) or on going
   (10.7); that...should
DIFFERENT / from stg or sby
DISAPPOINTED / with stg; with or
   in sby; at not finding; that
DISGUSTED / with stg; that
DOUBTFUL / about stg or sby,
   about going
DUE to stg or sby (=caused by);
   (=ready) for stg; (=planned)
   to arrive (a)
EAGER for stg; to go (a)
EASY (=not worried) about stg;
   (=not applying strain) on sby
   or stg; to teach (f)
ENVIOUS / of sby
EQUAL / to stg; sby is equal to a
   task
ESSENTIAL / to a purpose; it...to;
   it...that...should
EVIDENT / to sby; it...that
EXCITED / about stg; about or at

going; to see (c); that
EXPERIENCED / in stg; in doing stg
EXPERT / at a skill; at doing stg
FAITHFUL / to sby
Sby is FAMILIAR with sby *or* stg;
  stg is f... to sby
FAMOUS / for his achievements;
  for telling stories
FIT (= suitable) for sby, stg is fit to
  eat; for eating; sby is fit
  (= ready) for work, to work (a)
FOND of sby *or* stg; of swimming
sby is FORTUNATE / to go (c); in
  having; it...(for sby) that
FREE / for a purpose; to go (a)
FULL / of stg
FURIOUS / with sby; about stg; that
GAME (= ready) for anything
GENEROUS / to sby; with money;
  to go (d)
GENTLE / with sby
GLAD / (= happy to know) about
  stg; glad of stg (= happy to
  have it); to see (c); that
GOOD / (= successful) at stg, at
  solving problems; (= kind) to
  sby; (= beneficial) for sby or
  stg; (= kind) to do that (d);
  it...that
GRATEFUL / to sby, for stg; to have
  (c); that
GUILTY / of a crime, of stealing
HAPPY / about stg, about going;
  to go (c); that
HARD / (= difficult) for sby;
  (= applying strain) on sby *or*
  stg; to teach (f)
HARMFUL / to *or* for sby *or* stg
HESITANT / to go (a & e); about
  going
HONEST / about stg
HONOURED / to have (c)
HOPEFUL / about the future; of

success; about winning; that...
  will
HOPELESS / (= not at all successful)
  at games; at acting
HUNGRY for knowledge
IGNORANT of the facts
IMPORTANT / for sby *or* for one's
  work; it...to; it...that...should
IMPOSSIBLE; it...to; it...that
INCLINED to go (a)
INDEPENDENT / of sby
INFERIOR / to stg *or* sby
INTENT on going; on one's work
INTERESTED / in stg *or* sby; to see
  (c) or in seeing (10.7); would be
  interested to see (a); that...
  should
JEALOUS / of sby
KEEN / on stg *or* sby; to go (a) *or*
  on going (10.7); that...should
KIND / to sby; to do that (d)
LATE / for work
LEVEL / with stg *or* sby
LIKELY to go (b); it...that...will.
  Stg is likely, *ie* it may happen
LOYAL / to sby
sby is LUCKY / to go (c); it...(for
  you) that
MAD (= very keen) about *or* on stg
  or sby; about dancing; (= very
  keen) to go (a) *or* on going;
  (= very angry) at *or* with sby,
  about stg; (= very foolish) to go
  (d); (= very angry) that
MARRIED / to sby
MISTAKEN / (= wrong) about stg;
  in one's actions; in thinking stg
NECESSARY / for sby *or* stg; it...to;
  it...that...should
NEW (= previously unknown) to
  sby; to stg (= unfamiliar with it)
NICE to go (d); to teach (f); it...
  that

OBEDIENT / to sby
OBVIOUS / to sby; it...that
PATIENT / with sby; in suffering
PECULIAR (= belonging exclusively)
   to stg; it... / (= strange) that
PLEASANT to teach (*f*)
PLEASED / with stg *or* sby; to be
   here (*c*); that
POLITE / to do stg (*d*)
POSITIVE / of *or* about stg
POSSIBLE / it...to; it...that
PREJUDICED / against stg *or* sby
PREPARED / for stg; to go (*a*)
PROBABLE / it...that
PROMPT / to answer (*e*), at
   answering
PROUD of stg *or* sby; of having;
   to say (*c*); that
PUZZLED / about *or* by stg
QUALIFIED / for a task; to say (*a*)
QUICK / to see (*e*): at doing stg
READY / for work; to go (*a*)
REASONABLE to go (*d*); it...that...
   should
RELIEVED / to hear (*c*) *or* at
   hearing; that
RIGHT / to say that (*d*); it...to; it...
   that...should
RIPE for mischief
RUDE / to sby; to do that (*d*)
SACRED / to the memory
SAD / about stg *or* sby; about
   going; to see (*c*); it...that
SAFE / from danger; it...to say that
SATISFIED / with stg; with being;
   that
SELFISH / about stg; to go (*d*)
SENSIBLE / (= reasonable) about
   stg; about dieting; to go (*d*)
SENSITIVE / to something that can
   be felt; about one's deficiencies
SEPARATE / from stg
SERIOUS / about stg *or* sby

SEVERE / on sby
SHOCKED / at sby; at *or* by the
   news; to hear (*c*); at hearing;
   that
SICK of stg *or* sby; of hearing stg
SILLY / about stg; to go (*d*)
SIMILAR / to stg
SINCERE / about stg
SKILFUL / at stg
SLOW / to react (*e*) *or* in reacting;
   at one's work
SORRY / for sby (= sympathetic);
   about sby *or* stg (= to hear
   about); to hear (*c*); (= regretful)
   for a mistake; that; that...
   (should)
STRONG in languages
STUPID / about stg; to go (*d*)
SUFFICIENT / for one's needs; it...to
SUITABLE / for sby *or* some purpose
SUPERIOR / to stg *or* sby
SURE of stg *or* sby (= have
   confidence in); sure / about stg
   or sby (= have no doubt); to
   win (*b*), of winning (10.7)
SURPRISED / at sby *or* stg; to see (*c*)
   or at seeing; that; that...
   (should)
SUSPICIOUS / of sby (= suspect
   him); about stg (= have doubts)
THANKFUL / to sby for stg; to be
   here (*c*); that
THRILLED / about stg, about going;
   to be here (*c*); that
TIRED of stg, of waiting
TRUE to a friend, to one's word;
   it...that
UNCERTAIN /: as for CERTAIN
UNEASY / about stg
USED to sby *or* stg; to going
USEFUL / for sby, for some purpose
WEAK in languages; to give up (*d*)
WELL: it...to (3.15.g)

WICKED / to say that (*d*); it...to

WIDE of the mark

WISE / to go (*d*); it...to

WORRIED / about sby *or* stg; about going, that

Stg *or* sby is WORTH knowing

WORTHY of stg *or* sby; of having; to go (*a*)

WRONG / about stg; to go (*d*); it... that...should

E Adjectives as head of a nominal group
7.21
If the noun at the head of a nominal group is not repeated it is frequently replaced by *one* or *ones*, thus:

26a Several thousand fresh white $\left\{\begin{array}{l}\text{loaves} \\ \text{ones}\end{array}\right\}$

27a The only other green Chinese $\left\{\begin{array}{l}\text{carpet} \\ \text{one}\end{array}\right\}$

However, an adjective can be the head of a nominal group in the following cases:

a with a small set of adjectives, eg *blind, brave, dead, deaf, disabled, elderly, homeless, injured, living, poor, rich, sick, unemployed, wealthy, young,* but only with the meaning 'the class of people who are blind, brave, dead, etc. eg

67 We are collecting money for the $\left\{\begin{array}{l}\text{blind.} \\ \text{injured.} \\ \text{sick.}\end{array}\right\}$

68 The poor are always with us.

When such a nominal group is subject, it takes only a plural verb.

b with a few adjectives, including participials, referring to abstractions:

69 Overcome evil (=what is evil) with good.

70 The $\left\{\begin{array}{l}\text{unexpected} \\ \text{unknown}\end{array}\right\}$ (=what is $\left\{\begin{array}{l}\text{unexpected} \\ \text{unknown}\end{array}\right\}$) is $\left\{\begin{array}{l}\text{bound to happen.} \\ \text{usually feared.}\end{array}\right\}$

c with *the English, the French*, etc. as in 6.22.

7.22
In addition to the examples in 7.21, there are cases of ellipsis of a particular noun, especially in informal English. For example:

71 I'm having my medical (examination) tomorrow.

72 John is a possible (candidate).

73 Have you got a spare (tyre)?

Chapter Eight

Prepositional phrases and adverb particles

A Prepositions and adverb particles expressing relationships in space

8.1

See 1.35–1.38. The following are examples of prepositions and adverb particles referring to movement or position in space:

a IN RELATION TO A POINT, OR DIMENSION UNSPECIFIED

	Preposition	Corresponding adverb particle, if any
———→ X	Go *to* X	—
⊠	Stay *at* X	—
◄——— X	Go *away from* X	Come / Go } *away*
Y ◄——— X	Go *from* X *to* Y	—
Y ◄———	Go *back to* Y	Come / Go } *back*
o X	Stay *away from* X	Stay *away*

b ANALYSIS OF GOING TO X

o – – – → X	We are leaving *for* X	—
– o – – → X	We are walking *toward(s)* X	—
– – o → X	We are { coming / getting } *to* X	—
– – – → ⊠	We have arrived *at* X	—

c IN RELATION TO A LINE, ONE DIMENSION

	Drive *onto* the motorway	Drive *on*
	We are *on* the motorway	We are *on*
	Drive *off* the motorway	Drive *off*
	We are *off* the motorway	We are *off*

d IN RELATION TO A SURFACE, TWO DIMENSIONS

	Go *on(to)* the platform	Go *on*
	Stay *on* the platform	Stay *on*

| | Get *off* the platform | Get *off* |
| | Stay *off* the platform | Stay *off* |

e IN RELATION TO A SPACE, THREE DIMENSIONS

	Come *in(to)* my office	Come *in*
	Come *inside* my office	Come *inside*
	Stay *in* your room	Stay *in*
	Stay *inside* your room	Stay *inside*
	Go *out of* my office	Go *out*
	Go *outside (of)* my office	Go *outside*
	Stay *out of* my office	Stay *out*
	Stay *outside (of)* my office	Stay *outside*

f IN RELATION TO A POINT AGAIN

	Go *as* far *as* X	Go *so far*
	Go *through* X	Go *through*
	We passed *by* X	We passed *by*
	We stood *by* X	Stand *by*! (=wait for orders)
	We have gone *past* X	We have gone *past*
	We have gone *beyond* X	We have gone *beyond*
	We are *past* X	—
	We are *beyond* X	—

g IN RELATION TO A LINE AGAIN

	We are driving *along* the road	We are driving *along*
	They live *along* the road	I'll be *along* soon
	We are driving *along* the river	—
	We are going *across* the road	We are going *across*
	We are safely *across* the road	We are safely *across*
	They live *across* the road	—

h IN RELATION TO A SURFACE AGAIN

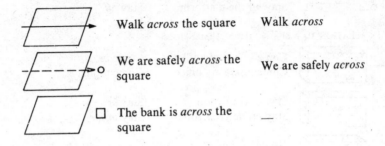

Walk *across* the square	Walk *across*
We are safely *across* the square	We are safely *across*
The bank is *across* the square	—

i IN RELATION TO AN AREA AGAIN

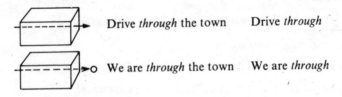

Drive *through* the town	Drive *through*
We are *through* the town	We are *through*

j TO AND AT HIGHER OR LOWER LEVELS

Go *up* the hill	Go *up*
We are *up* the hill	We are *up*
Go *down* the hill	Go *down*
We are *down* the hill	We are *down*
Jump *over* X	Jump *over*
The plane is flying *over* X	It is flying *over*
It is *over* X	—
Now we are *over* X	We are safely *over*
Crawl *under* X	Crawl *under*
Stay *under* X	Stay *under*
We are flying *above* the water	—
We are *above* the water	—

He is swimming
$\begin{Bmatrix} below \\ beneath \\ underneath \end{Bmatrix}$ the surface   Go *below*

The stone is $\begin{Bmatrix} below \\ beneath \\ underneath \end{Bmatrix}$ It is $\begin{Bmatrix} below \\ underneath \end{Bmatrix}$

the surface

k AT THE FRONT, AT THE BACK, AT THE SIDE, OR FACING

X is running *in front of* Y	X is running *in front*
X is *in front of* Y	X is *in front*
X is running *behind* Y	X is running *behind*
X is *behind* Y	X is *behind*
X is running *beside* Y	—
X is *beside* Y	—
X is *opposite* Y	X is *opposite* Y is *opposite*

l ON MORE THAN ONE SIDE

We are going *(a)round* the circle   We are going *(a)round*

We have gone *all (a)round* the circle   We have gone *all (a)round*

My belt is *(a)round* my waist   —

m HAVING OTHER THINGS ON TWO OR MORE SIDES

X ↓ Y   We are going *between* X and Y   We are going *between*

X Y Z   Y is *between* X and Z   —

Don't worry – you are *among(st)* friends   —

n ACCOMPANYING, OR NOT ACCOMPANYING

X is walking *with* Y   —

Y is walking *with* X   —

X is *with* Y, Y is *with* X   —

X is proceeding *without* Y   —

X is fighting $\left\{ \begin{matrix} against \\ = with \end{matrix} \right\}$ Y   —

There's a ladder *against*
the wall   —

o AT A SHORT OR LONG DISTANCE FROM

I am sitting *next to* you   —

Are we going
$\left\{ \begin{matrix} near \\ far\,(away)\,from \end{matrix} \right\}$ X?

We are coming *nearer*
Are we going *far away*?   (8.2b)

We are
$\left\{ \begin{matrix} near \\ far\,(away)\,from \end{matrix} \right\}$ X

Stay *near*
We are *far away*

Notes on the prepositions in 8.1
8.2

a GENERAL. In deciding whether to use, for example, *at, on* or *in* in the pattern—*X*, we must first answer the question: Is X a point, a line, a surface, or an area? The question is answered SUBJECTIVELY, not OBJECTIVELY: that is to say, the answer depends on what the speaker IMAGINES X to be at the time of speaking, not on how X can be measured mathematically. Thus, we can say *stay in Tokyo* if we are thinking of Tokyo as an area; but we can say *The plane will land at Tokyo to refuel* if we are thinking of Tokyo as a point on the map. Similarly, a car can be *on the road*, ie on the line or surface, or *in the road*, ie in the space before us. Notice, however, the difference between the following pairs:
$\left\{ \begin{matrix} \end{matrix} \right.$ *I am on my way to X (on the motorway)*, as in 8.1c;
You are in my way, ie in the space I want to occupy.
$\left\{ \begin{matrix} \end{matrix} \right.$ *Throw the ball to John*, as in 8.1a, ie in his direction
Throw the ball at John, so as to hit him, as in 8.1b.
$\left\{ \begin{matrix} \end{matrix} \right.$ *Point to the stars*, in that direction
Never point a gun at anybody, as if aiming at a target.

b INDIVIDUAL PREPOSITIONS EXPRESSING RELATIONSHIPS IN SPACE
ABOVE emphasises the idea of 'at a higher level than';
'AMONG (or AMONGST) friends' suggests having more than two friends with or around one. See BETWEEN;
AS FAR AS X = to X and no farther;
AT is used when X is a destination or target, as in *aim at, laugh at, point at*;

BELOW emphasises the idea of 'at a lower level than';

BENEATH is less common and more literary than *below*, and is not replaceable by BELOW in metaphorical expressions such as *beneath one's dignity, beneath contempt*;

BESIDE = at the side of: *cp* BESIDES, as in *Who was there besides you? ie* in addition to you;

BETWEEN occurs in *We* $\begin{Bmatrix} swam \\ were \end{Bmatrix}$ *between one point and another* (*ie* two points). We would normally find BETWEEN in *Divide this money between you two*, while AMONG is usually preferred in *Divide this among you four* (*ie* more than two). However, BETWEEN often replaces AMONG in that last example; and BETWEEN, not AMONG, would be used in both of the following sentences:

1 The Rhine flows between France and Germany.

2 Switzerland is between France, Germany, Austria and Italy.

BEYOND, *ie* farther than, is less common and more literary than PAST, but is usual in metaphorical expressions such as *It is beyond my comprehension*;

FAR (AWAY) FROM would normally be replaced BY A LONG WAY FROM in short affirmative sentences in informal English, *eg We are a long way from X*, compared with *Are we far (away) from X? No, we're not far from X.* FAR can be compared, and modified by *so, too* and *very, eg We are* $\begin{Bmatrix} too\ far \\ farther \end{Bmatrix}$ *(away) from X*; and in this case there is no restriction as far as short affirmative sentences are concerned.

FOR indicates destination, as in *The train for Paris*.

FROM is often reinforced by AWAY, as in the examples given in 8.1a, but not in the pattern *from X to Y*.

IN, INTO. *In* can indicate movement in an example like *Put this in your pocket*; but INTO is obligatory in the following cases:

a To make the distinction between (i) going to and then being inside, as in

    Run into the house,

and (ii) moving when already inside, as in

    Don't run (when you are) in the house.

b in metaphorical expressions, such as

    Run into difficulties

    Get into trouble.

INSIDE stresses the idea of sheltering or being enclosed in a space;

NEAR can be compared, and modified by, *so, too* and *very, eg Come nearer (to) the fire. Come nearer. Who is nearest the door? Don't come* $\begin{Bmatrix} so \\ too \\ very \end{Bmatrix}$ *near.*

NEXT to = occupying the adjoining space;
ON, ONTO can both indicate movement ending on a surface, ONTO often emphasising the effort of making that movement. ONTO can also be spelt ON TO, but needs to be distinguished from adverb particle + preposition as in *We went on* (continued our journey) *to Rome.*
OUTSIDE stresses the idea of being excluded from a space;
OVER suggests the idea of 'covering', as in *Hold the umbrella over your head.* Note the use of OVER in the following examples:

3 Ants are running all over me.
4 There is mud all over your coat.

THROUGH: note the use of the particle in

5 We were soaked through. (*ie* the water had gone right through our clothes)
6 We were soaked through and through;

THROUGHOUT suggests movement into every part of an area, as in

7 The news spread throughout the land;

TOWARD(S) = in the direction of. TOWARDS is more usual in British English, TOWARD in American;
UNDER suggests 'covered by': *cp* OVER;
UNDERNEATH = completely covered by;
WITHIN suggests restriction to an area, as in

8 Over a thousand civilians were crowded together within the fortress

or it can be used metaphorically as in

9 It is sometimes difficult to live within one's income.

Notes on the adverb particles in 8.1
Movement
8.3

a All the particles in 8.1 except *opposite*, can be used freely with COME, GO (*eg come in, come out, come up,* etc); and all can be used, in informal English, with GET, which usually expresses abruptness, as in *get away, get back.* *Get up,* besides carrying the general meaning of 'rise', has the special meaning 'get out of bed'. *About* can be used with GO and GET as in *Don't go about spreading rumours, George has hurt his leg and can't get about easily.*

b BRING, PULL, PUSH, TAKE, and the more informal GET, can be freely used with *across, along, away, back, down, in(side), out(side), over, round, through, under, up* in the pattern
Bring that book back.   Bring it back.
Monosyllabic particles are also used with the same set of verbs in the pattern
Bring back that book.

The pattern $\left\{ \begin{array}{c} Ask \\ = Invite \end{array} \right\}$ *someone in* (*ie* into one's house) can be used with *across, along, back, down, in(side), out, over, round, up.*

Position
c KEEP, meaning 'stay', and STAY itself, are freely used with *away, back, behind, down, in(side) in front, out(side)*, as in

$\left. \begin{array}{c} \text{Keep} \\ = \text{Stay} \end{array} \right\}$ away.

BE is used with the same particles, but generally with special meanings: *be away* = be absent, or be on holiday; *he is back* = he has returned; *be in* = be in one's house or office; *be out* = not be in one's house etc.; *be up* = be out of bed.

d KEEP can be used in the pattern

Keep your head $\left\{ \begin{array}{l} \text{away, back,} \\ \text{in, out} \\ \text{down, up} \end{array} \right\}$

Over and through
e *We are safely over* = we have come safely over a certain obstacle. *We have got our examinations over* = we have finished them, have left them behind us. *Our examinations are over* = they have ended. *Repeat something over and over (again)* = repeat it many times.

f *We are through* = we have passed through certain obstacles. *See something* (*ie* a difficult experience) *through* = give one's attention to it until it has ended. *Through and through* = thoroughly.

Prepositions and particles referring to movement or position, but with functions different from those indicated in 8.[1]
8.4
OFF = away (from a starting point) as in
   10 He was quick off the mark. (*ie* the starting point)
   11 They're off! (= They've started)
   12 We $\left\{ \begin{array}{c} \text{set} \\ = \text{started} \end{array} \right\}$ off at six o'clock.
   13 The firework went off. (See *go off*, 12.3)
ON = forward, as in *carry on* (= continue), *come on, go on, keep on, play on, read on, work on.*
OUT = away from a centre, as in
   14 We $\left\{ \begin{array}{c} \text{set} \\ = \text{started} \end{array} \right\}$ out at six o'clock.
   15 Don't keep together – spread out.

Combinations of adverb particle + preposition
8.5

Combination	Examples
across to:	16 Go across (the road) to the baker's.
along to:	17 Go along (the road) to the post office.
away from:	18 Go, or stay, away from home.
away to:	19 Go away (from one's home) to the seaside.
back to:	20 Go back to your place.
down to:	21 Go down to the basement.
off for:	22 Set off for the capital.
off to:	23 Go off to school.
on to:	24 Go on to the end of-the road.
out onto:	25 They ran out onto the pitch.
over to:	26 Go over (the road) to the bank.
round to:	27 Come round (the corner) to my house.
up at:	28 Look up at the light.

Modifiers of prepositions and particles
8.6

Prepositions and particles indicating movement can be modified by *straight*, to suggest that the movement is direct; and those indicating target or position can be modified by *right*:

29 I'm very tired. I think I'll go straight to bed.

30 Go straight along this road and you'll find number 86 right at the end.

31 Stand back. Keep right away from the edge.

Other modifiers of prepositions are *almost* and *nearly*:

32 We walked $\left\{ \begin{array}{l} \text{almost} \\ = \text{nearly} \end{array} \right\}$ as far as York.

B Prepositions expressing relationships in time
8.7

AFTER = later than, as in

33 Come (at) any time after six o'clock.

AT is used with *a point of time* (cp 8.1a):

34 I'll meet you at six o'clock, at midday, at midnight, at dinner, at sunrise, at sunset.

35 At that moment, there was a loud crash.

36 We have a holiday at New Year, at Christmas, at Easter.

Note:

37 We always lock the doors at night.

BEFORE = earlier than, as in

38 Don't come before six o'clock.

BY = not later than, as in

39 Be ready by the time I get back.

40 We must leave by six o'clock, or we shall not arrive in time.

Note: the verb in [40] can only refer to activity taking place at a *point* of time, or have the meaning *have finished -ing*, *eg* Can you read this by Tuesday? *Cp* UNTIL.

DURING $\begin{Bmatrix} \textit{the night} \\ \textit{the concert} \end{Bmatrix}$, *ie* while that period of time, or that event, is in progress, as in

41 I woke up three times $\begin{Bmatrix} \text{during} \\ \text{in} \end{Bmatrix}$ the night.

42 The doors will remain shut during the concert.

FOR marks the length of time during which an action or state continues:

43 I walk (for) two hours every day.   .

44 We have been here (for) six weeks.

45 We shall stay (for) another fortnight.

46 For a year we waited to hear what had happened to him.

47 The train will not arrive for two hours.

Note that *for* is optional in [43], [44] and [45], but is required in [46] and [47].

FROM marks the beginning of a period, as in

48 The bank will be open from eight o'clock (onwards).

49 It will be open from eight $\begin{Bmatrix} \text{until} \\ = \text{to} \end{Bmatrix}$ four.

IN is used with *periods* of time, except those associated with ON:

50 I do most of my work in $\begin{Bmatrix} \text{the morning, the afternoon,} \\ \text{the evening, January,} \\ \text{(the) winter, (the) summer.} \end{Bmatrix}$

51 They reached America in $\begin{Bmatrix} \text{March} \\ \text{1968} \end{Bmatrix}$.

Note the use of *in* in example [41].

IN is required in

52 We shall meet in May next

    and

53 We met in June last

but is omitted in

54 We shall meet next May

    and

55 We met last June

IN marks the end of a period of time in

56 I'll call again in five minutes. (*ie* after an interval of five minutes)

The word *time* is often added to emphasise the extent of the period of time starting now.

57 I can't give you an answer yet. Come back in three months' time.

    (*ie* in three months from now)

IN also marks the length of time within which an action is completed:

58 G. ran a mile $\begin{cases} \text{in} \\ \text{in under} \\ \text{in less than} \end{cases}$ four minutes.

ON is used before days of the week, and dates:

59 We'll meet again (on) Friday (next).

60 My birthday is on March 28th.

61 They landed on $\begin{cases} \text{the morning of May 1st.} \\ \text{the afternoon of July 4th.} \\ \text{an evening in October.} \end{cases}$

No preposition is used in

62 We'll meet again next Thursday.

63 We met last Friday.

PAST is used before a specific hour of the day, or before the words *time* or *age*:

64 It is past six o'clock, a quarter past six to be precise.

65 It is (long) past $\begin{cases} \text{my bedtime.} \\ =\text{the time I usually go to bed.} \end{cases}$

66 You are free to marry; you are past the age of consent.

(A)ROUND = about, as in

67 I'll see you (a)round six o'clock.

THROUGH(OUT) = from the beginning to the end of a period:

68 Dancing went on $\begin{cases} \text{(all) through} \\ =\text{throughout} \end{cases}$ the night.

TILL: see UNTIL

TO marks the end of a period, but is only used in this way in conjunction with FROM, as in

69 The exhibition will be open from May 1st $\begin{cases} \text{until} \\ \text{to} \end{cases}$ June 30th.

UNTIL (always replaceable by TILL), marks the end of a period as in example [69], and in

70 We waited until eight o'clock.

71 We did not leave until eight o'clock.

Note: the verb in [70] can only refer to an action or state of inaction, or a series of actions, that can last for a period of time. *Cp* [40]. UNTIL could not replace BY in [40], nor could BY replace UNTIL in [70]. The meaning of [71] is 'our state of not-leaving lasted till eight o'clock (and then we left)'. We could replace UNTIL by BY in [71], but then the meaning would be 'our departure did not take place at a point of time before or at eight o'clock (perhaps it took place later)'.

WITHIN suggests that the performance of an action is restricted to a certain period, as in

72 You must be back $\begin{cases} \text{in} \\ \text{within} \end{cases}$ fifteen minutes.

C Prepositions with other meanings
8.8

As well as expressing relationships in space and time, prepositions can refer to agency, instrument, means, purpose, topic, etc. as follows:

ABOUT relates to the *subject* of thought, speech, writing, etc. as in

73 I would like to $\left\{\begin{array}{l}\text{think}\\ \text{talk (to you)}\\ \text{write (to you)}\end{array}\right\}$ about your proposal.

74 What is this book (all) about? It's (all) about ghosts.

75 I dreamt about you last night.

76 Your parents are very $\left\{\begin{array}{l}\text{anxious}\\ \text{concerned}\\ \text{worried}\end{array}\right\}$ about you.

ACCORDING TO = to quote as an authority: see 4.35, [123].

AGAINST = not in favour of:

77 Are you for the motion, or against it?

APART FROM = with the exception of, as in

78 We had no trouble on the journey $\left\{\begin{array}{l}\text{apart from}\\ =\text{except for}\end{array}\right\}$ a flat tyre.

Or it can mean 'in addition to' as in

79 Apart from a flat tyre, we had faulty brakes.

AS = in the role of, as in

80 As your doctor, I advise you to eat less.

AS FOR = speaking of, with reference to, as in

81 I don't blame George. As for John, he has behaved very badly.

AS REGARDS: see 4.35 [125].

AS TO = on the subject of, as in

82 No agreement was reached $\left\{\begin{array}{l}\text{as to}\\ =\text{concerning}\end{array}\right\}$ $\left\{\begin{array}{l}\text{rent.}\\ \text{how much we should}\\ \text{pay.}\end{array}\right.$

AS WELL AS = in addition to, *eg You can go, as well as George.*

AT relates to price or rate, as in *Two kilos of rice at so much a kilo. We were only driving at fifty miles an hour.*

BECAUSE OF: see 4.34.

BESIDES = in *addition* to

83 Who was in the room besides you and John?

BUT = except, as in

84 No one but a fool would go out in such a storm.

BUT FOR contains the idea 'if something had not $\left\{\begin{array}{l}\text{been so}\\ \text{happened}\end{array}\right\}$ ':

85 But for that flat tyre (see [78]) we would have got here twenty minutes ago.

BUT could not replace BUT FOR at the beginning of a clause.

BY expresses *agency*, as in [86], or *instrument* as in [87], or means of transport, as in [88], or means of despatch, as in [89].

86 'War and Peace' was written by Leo Tolstoy. It is a book by Tolstoy.

87 Quick! George has been knocked down by a car.

88 We travelled by $\begin{Bmatrix} \text{bus} \\ \text{plane} \\ \text{train} \end{Bmatrix}$

89 The message was sent by $\begin{Bmatrix} \text{mail} \\ \text{radio} \\ \text{telegram} \end{Bmatrix}$

BY MEANS OF = by making use of (see 4.9):

90 You can only unlock this door by means of one special key.

CONCERNING = on the *subject* of: see example [82].

CONSIDERING = in view of, as in [91], or in spite of, as in [92]:

91 Considering the (bad) weather, we had better postpone the match.

92 Considering the (bad) weather, the match was a great success (*ie* it was a success, although the weather was bad).

DESPITE: see 4.35 [121].

EXCEPT = excluding, as in

93 You can all go except (for) George.

EXCEPT FOR, as in [78], and

94 Except for George, you can all go.

EXCEPT could not replace EXCEPT FOR at the beginning of a clause.

FOR relates to (i) *purpose*, or (ii) *exchange*, or means IN FAVOUR OF:

95 This report is for your information only.

96 A How much did you $\begin{Bmatrix} \text{give} \\ \text{pay} \end{Bmatrix}$ for that picture?

B I bought it for two hundred pounds.

97 Are you for the motion ? (*cp* [77]).

Note also: *He is tall for a boy of his age* = He is taller than most boys of his age.

FROM indicates *origin* when one thing is converted into another, as in:

98 This pair of shoes was made from an old rubber tyre.

IN relates to a *medium of expression*, as in

99 How do you say that in English?

100 Please write your name in ink.

See also 8.9d.

IN ACCORDANCE WITH: see 4.35 [124]

IN SPITE OF: see 4.35 [121]

IN VIEW OF: see 4.35 [122]

INSTEAD OF = in place of

101 Let me go instead of you. Let me go instead.

LIKE = of the same nature, appearance, or quality, as, or in the same way as:

102 George $\begin{Bmatrix} \text{is} \\ \text{walks} \end{Bmatrix}$ like his father.

LIKE is gradable. Thus we·can say

103 George is $\begin{cases} \begin{Bmatrix} \text{quite} \\ \text{very much} \end{Bmatrix} \text{like his father.} \\ \text{more like his father than his mother.} \\ \text{most like his father.} \end{cases}$

NOTWITHSTANDING: see 4.35 [121]

OF serves various purposes, *eg* it relates to

i the *substance* of which something is composed:

104 These shoes are made of rubber (*cp* [98]).

ii *membership* of a (larger) body, as in

105 Holland is a part of Europe.

iii the *subject* towards which thought, speech or writing, etc., is directed.
as in

106 I $\begin{Bmatrix} \text{think} \\ \text{talk} \\ \text{dream} \end{Bmatrix}$ of you often.

107 I would never dream of leaving you.

Cp think about you, which suggests that my thoughts are directed towards you and are then concentrated around you.

iv a *connection* between something and an action in which it is involved:

108 The arrival of the train: the train arrives. (*cp* 4.33)

The derailment of the train: the train is derailed.

ON relates to the *subject* of speech and writing, but suggests more systematic treatment than *about*:

109 $\begin{Bmatrix} \text{Professor X is speaking} \\ \text{He has written a book} \end{Bmatrix}$ on the temples of the Upper Nile.

See also 8.9d.

OUT OF = lacking, as in

110 I'm out of $\begin{Bmatrix} \text{breath} \\ \text{practice} \end{Bmatrix}$

OVER relates to the subject of argument, as in

111 They are $\begin{Bmatrix} \text{arguing} \\ \text{quarrelling} \end{Bmatrix}$ $\begin{Bmatrix} \text{about} \\ \text{over} \end{Bmatrix}$ their share of the property.

OWING TO: see 4.34

RATHER THAN = in preference to, *eg Rather than that, I'd sooner die.*

REGARDLESS OF: see 4.35 [121]

THAN: see 7.4

THROUGH relates to means or cause:

112 He achieved fame $\begin{Bmatrix} \text{through} \\ \text{= by} \end{Bmatrix}$ sheer hard work.

113 We lost the game simply $\left\{\begin{array}{l}\text{through}\\\text{= because of}\end{array}\right\}$ a moment's lack of con-

centration.

UNLIKE = not like, as in

114 George is (quite) unlike any of my other friends.

UPON sometimes replaces ON in formal style and fixed expressions, *eg upon my word.*

UP TO indicates responsibility for future action, as in

115 It's up to you to put things right. (informal)

or it indicates fitness for (a task), *eg*

116 I $\left\{\begin{array}{l}\text{am not}\\\text{do not feel}\end{array}\right\}$ up to this job;

also 'engaged in' (something wrong):

117 Tom's up to mischief (= doing something mischievous).

WITH expresses *instrument*:

118 Do you write with a pen or (with a) pencil?

WITH also stands for 'having', as in

119 Did you see a man $\left\{\begin{array}{l}\text{with}\\\text{= who had}\end{array}\right\}$ a black cat?

WITH REGARD TO: see 4.35 [125].

WITHOUT = not having:

120a I mean the .nan without a hat.

   b You can't succeed without trying = You can't succeed unless you try.

Fixed expressions
8.9

There are numerous fixed prepositional phrases on the pattern *at school, by bus.* Some of these phrases can be grouped together:

a those relating to places or institutions which one goes to or attends for a specific purpose indicated in brackets below:

$\left\{\begin{array}{l}\text{go}\\\text{come}\end{array}\right\}$ to bed   (to rest)

$\left\{\begin{array}{l}\text{be}\\\text{stay}\end{array}\right\}$ in bed   (for rest)

 get out of bed

$\left\{\begin{array}{l}\text{go}\\\text{come}\end{array}\right\}$ to school   (to study)

be at $\left\{\begin{array}{l}\text{breakfast}\\\text{dinner etc.}\\\text{table}\end{array}\right\}$ (having a meal)

be in class   (giving or having a lesson)

go to church   (for worship)

be at church
be at home[1]   (in one's own house)
go (in)to hospital   (for medical treatment)
be in hospital   (for medical treatment)
be in office   (holding an official position)
be out of office   (ceasing to hold that position)
go to prison   (as a punishment)
be in prison   (as a punishment)
go to university   (for study)
be at university   (for study)

For *at the post office*, etc., see 6.19.

b those relating to means of transport:

$\left\{\begin{array}{l}\text{travel}\\\text{send goods}\end{array}\right\}$ $\left\{\begin{array}{l}\text{by air, by bus, by car, by land,}\\\text{by plane, by sea, by ship}\end{array}\right.$

c those relating to means of despatch:

send a message $\left\{\begin{array}{l}\text{by cable, by hand, by letter,}\\\text{by post, by radio, by telegram}\end{array}\right.$

d miscellaneous:

i
at ease	at first	at hand
at heart	at last	at least
at length	at short notice	at once
at peace	at play	at present
at rest	at sight	at sea
at war	at work	

ii
by accident	by chance	by day
by design	by degrees	by good fortune
by heart	by mistake	by name
by oneself	by rights	by sight
by surprise		

iii
in brief	in case (see 2.43e)	in common
in danger	in debt	in difficulties
in due course	in fact	in half
in general	in love	in name
in need	in order	in particular
in pieces	in private	in public
in reply	(with)in reach	in secret
in short	in sight	in stock
in tears	in time	in turn

iv
on business	on duty (off duty)	on fire
on foot	on guard	on holiday
on horseback	on purpose	on sale
on time		

No preposition is used in the expression *go home*, ie go to one's own house.

Note the difference between We arrived on time (= punctually) *and*
We arrived in time to see the procession begin.

v	out of control	out of danger	out of date
	out of doors	out of hearing	out of order
	out of place	out of reach	out of sight
	out of stock	out of turn	out of work
vi	under control	up to date	
vii	within hearing	within reach	within sight

8.10

Each of the prepositional phrases in 8.9 has the following three features:

a it has no modifier, even when the phrase contains a count noun;
b the speaker is not free to use any preposition except the one given;
c the meaning (as indicated in 8.9a) is fixed.

The fixed expression cannot normally be used:

a if a modifier is added. *Cp*

   121 We went by bus

      and

   122 We went by the 2.15 bus.

b if a different preposition is used. *Cp*

   123 He went to bed

      and

   124 He went towards the bed.

c if a different meaning is intended. *Cp*

   125 We travelled by sea

      and

   126 We had a little house by the sea.

Prepositions associated with adjectives (7.20)

Prepositions associated with verbs (10.8)

Prepositions associated with nouns
8.11

a In general a noun is followed by the same preposition as an adjective or verb associated with it. Thus:

{ We cannot be certain of success.
{ There is no certainty of success.
{ He was keenly interested in chess.
{ He took a keen interest in chess.
{ May I congratulate you on your appointment.
{ Please accept my congratulations on your appointment.
{ We cannot complain about the food here.
{ We have no complaints about the food.

b In some cases the preposition is different, or the noun requires a preposition when a corresponding verb does not. Examples:

Answer a question.	Find an answer to it.
I dislike that.	– my dislike of it.
We fear it.	– our fear of it.
We hope for peace.	Is there any hope of peace?
He influenced us.	He had an influence $\left\{ \begin{array}{l} \text{on} \\ \text{over} \end{array} \right\}$ us.
I like that.	– my liking for it.
He was proud of his work.	– his pride in his work.
Solve a problem.	Find a solution to it.
We sympathise with you.	Our sympathy for you.

Chapter Nine

The verb phrase (1): Form

A Typical verb endings
Suffixes
9.1
Typical verb suffixes are:
-ATE, pronounced /eit/, as in *approximate, calculate, educate, estimate, separate.* Cp the adjectives *approximate, separate,* in which *-ate* is pronounced /ət/ or /it/.
-EN, added mainly to monosyllabic adjectives or nouns:

ADJECTIVE			VERB		
black	fat	wide	blacken	fatten	widen

NOUN					
height	length	strength	heighten	lengthen	strengthen

Spelling rules as for the present participle (1.16.5)
-IFY, pronounced /ifai/, as in *certify, identify, simplify*
-ISE, pronounced /aiz/, also spelt *-ize* (preferred thus in American English), as in *modernise, publicise, recognise.*

Inflexions
9.2
See 1.20, Table 2.

Spelling of present participle
9.3
See 1.16. 5
a *Note* die, dying; lie, lying.
b The *e* is retained in the spelling in
age, ageing; agree, agreeing; dye, dyeing; hoe, hoeing; singe, singeing; swinge, swingeing. *Cp: die, dying; sing, singing; swing, swinging.*
c In accordance with the rule given in 1.16.5, the final consonant is doubled in
be'gin, be'ginning   com'mit, com'mitting   com'pel, com'pelling
in'cur, in'curring   oc'cur, oc'curring   o'mit, o'mitting
per'mit, per'mitting   pre'fer, pre'ferring[1]   re'fer, re'ferring[1]
re'gret, re'gretting   sub'mit, sub'mitting   trans'fer, trans'ferring[1]
but it is not doubled in
focus, focusing   offer, offering   suffer, suffering   visit, visiting.

---

[1] But *preference, reference, transference,* which have stress on the first syllable.

d In British English, but not American, final *l* or *p* is doubled in the following words in which the last syllable of the base is unstressed:
handicap, handicapping   label, labelling   libel, libelling
quarrel, quarrelling,   rival, rivalling   signal, signalling
travel, travelling   worship, worshipping
The final *p* is not doubled before *-ing* in
developing   enveloping   galloping   gossiping

e Verbs ending in *-ic* have an *-ing* form ending in *-icking*:
frolic, frolicking   panic, panicking   picnic, picnicking
traffic, trafficking

Spelling of past tense and -ed participle
9.4

a In accordance with the rule given in 1.16.3, we find:
acquitted, committed, compelled, incurred, occurred, omitted
permitted, preferred, referred, regretted, submitted, transferred
but *focused, offered, suffered, visited.*

b As in 9.3d, in British English, not American, we find
handicapped, labelled, libelled, quarrelled, rivalled, signalled, travelled, worshipped
but *developed, enveloped, galloped, gossiped.*

c Verbs in *-ic*: *frolicked, panicked, picnicked, trafficked.*

B Irregular verbs
9.5

The irregular verbs are arranged below in three groups, corresponding to the three types referred to in 1.19.

9.6

TYPE 1: Verbs like PUT, with all three main parts the same, are:

BET[1]	FORECAST	QUIT[1]	SPLIT
BID[2]	HIT	RID	SPREAD /spred/
BROADCAST	HURT	SET	THRUST
BURST	KNIT[1]	SHED	UPSET
CAST	LET	SHUT	WED[1]
COST[1]	PUT	SPIT	WET[1]

Note: 1 These verbs also have regular forms. COST is irregular, as above, in an example like *This book cost two pounds*, but regular in an example like *We costed the project* (=estimated the cost of it).
2 In the sense of 'make an offer to buy something'; see BID in Type 3.

9.7

TYPE 2: Verbs like HEAR, with past tense and past participle the same as each other but different from the base.

Base	Past		
ABIDE	abode	LOSE /luːz/	lost
BEHOLD (→HOLD)		MAKE	made
BEND	bent	MEAN	meant /ment/
BEREAVE[1]	bereft[1]	MEET	met
BESEECH	besought	MISLEAD (→LEAD)	
	/biˈsɔːt/	MISUNDERSTAND (→STAND)	
BIND /baind/	bound	PAY	paid
BLEED	bled	READ	read /red/
BREED	bred	REND	rent
BRING	brought /brɔːt/	SAY	said /sed/
BUILD /bild/	built /bilt/	SEEK	sought /sɔːt/
BURN[1]	burnt	SELL	sold
BUY /bai/	bought /bɔːt/	SEND	sent
CATCH	caught /kɔːt/	SHINE	shone /ʃɔn/
CLING	clung	SHOOT	shot
CREEP	crept	SIT	sat
DEAL	dealt /delt/	SLEEP	slept
DIG	dug	SLIDE	slid
DREAM[1]	dreamt /dremt/	SLING	slung
DWELL[1]	dwelt	SLINK	slunk
FEED	fed	SMELL[1]	smelt
FEEL	felt	SPEED	sped
FIGHT	fought /fɔːt/	SPELL[1]	spelt
FIND /faind/	found	SPEND	spent
FLEE	fled	SPILL[1]	spilt
FLING	flung	SPIN	spun
GET	got	SPIT	spat
GRIND /graind/	ground	SPOIL[1]	spoilt
HANG	hung	STAND[3]	stood
HAVE /hæv/	had	STICK	stuck
HEAR	heard /həːd/	STING	stung
HOLD	held	STRIKE	struck
KEEP	kept	SWEEP	swept
KNEEL[1]	knelt	SWING	swung
LAY	laid	TEACH	taught /tɔːt/
LEAD	led	TELL[4]	told
LEAN[1]	leant /lent/	THINK	thought /θɔːt/
LEAP[1]	leapt /lept/	UNDERSTAND (→STAND)	
LEARN[1] /ləːn/	learnt /ləːnt/	WEEP	wept
LEAVE	left	WIN	won /wʌn/
LEND	lent	WIND[5] /waind/	wound[5]
LIGHT	lit (→3.38)		/waund/
		WRING	wrung

Notes: 1. These verbs also have regular forms. Use *bereaved* in an example
like *A widow is bereaved when her husband has just died*; and
bereft in an example like *She was bereft of her senses*.
2. HANG, meaning 'put to death by hanging' is regular.
3. Similarly, UNDERSTAND, WITHSTAND.
4. Similarly, FORETELL.
5. WIND /wind/ is regular; so is WOUND /wuːnd/.

9.8

TYPE 3: Verbs like WRITE of which the past tense and past participle are
different from each other.

Base	*Past*	*Past participle*
(A)RISE	(a)rose	(a)risen /ə rizn/
(A)WAKE	(a)woke	(a)woken
BE (see 1.16)	was /wɔz/ were /wəː/	been
BEAR /bɛə/	bore	borne[1]
BEAT	beat	beaten
BECOME /biˈkʌm/	became	become /biˈkʌm/
BEFALL (→FALL)		
BEGIN	began	begun
BID[2]	bade /bæd/	bidden
BITE	bit	bitten
BLOW /bləu/	blew	blown /bləun/
BREAK /breik/	broke	broken
CHOOSE /tʃuːz/	chose /tʃəuz/	chosen /tʃəuzn/
COME /kʌm/	came	come /kʌm/
DO /duː/	did	done /dʌn/
DRAW	drew	drawn
DRINK	drank	drunk
DRIVE	drove	driven /drivn/
EAT	ate /et/	eaten
FALL /fɔːl/	fell	fallen
FLY	flew	flown /fləun/
FORBID	forbad(e)	forbidden
FORGET	forgot	forgotten
FORGIVE /-giv/	forgave	forgiven /-givn/
FORSAKE	forsook	forsaken
FREEZE	froze	frozen
GIVE /giv/	gave	given /givn/

Base	Past	Past Participle
GO	went	gone /gɒn/
GROW	grew	grown /grəun/
HEW	hewed	hewn[3]
HIDE	hid	hidden
KNOW /nəu/	knew /njuː/	known /nəun/
LIE[4] /lai/	lay	lain
MISTAKE (→TAKE)		
MOW	mowed	mown[3]
RIDE	rode	ridden
RING	rang	rung
RISE /raiz/	rose	risen /rizn/
RUN	ran	run
SAW	sawed	sawn[3]
SEE[5]	saw	seen
SEW /səu/	sewed /səud/	sewn[3] /səun/
SHAKE	shook	shaken
SHEAR	sheared	shorn[3]
SHOW[6] /ʃəu/	showed[6] /ʃəud/	shown[6] /ʃəun/
SHRINK	shrank	shrunk
SING	sang	sung
SINK	sank	sunk
SLAY	slew	slain
SMITE	smote	smitten
SOW /səu/	sowed	sown[3]
SPEAK	spoke	spoken
SPRING	sprang	sprung
STEAL	stole	stolen
STINK	stank	stunk
STREW	strewed	strewn[3]
STRIDE	strode	stridden
SWEAR[7] /swɛə/	swore	sworn
SWELL	swelled	swollen[3]
SWIM	swam	swum
TAKE	took /tuk/	taken
TEAR /tɛə/	tore	torn
THRIVE	throve[8]	thrived
THROW /θrəu/	threw	thrown /θrəun/
TREAD /tred/	trod	trodden
UNDERTAKE (→TAKE)		
WAKE	woke	woken
WEAR /wɛə/	wore	worn

Base	Past	Past Participle
WEAVE	wove	woven
WITHDRAW (→DRAW)		
WRITE	wrote	written

Notes: 1. But *I was born in 1946*
2. as in *bid farewell, bid someone go*; see BID in Type 1
3. Past participle also *hewed, mowed, sawed, sewed* /səud/, *sheared, sowed, strewed, swelled*
4. LIE, meaning 'tell a lie', is regular
5. Similarly FORESEE
6. Also spelt *shew, shewed, shewn*, with the same pronunciation as *show, showed, shown*. Past participle may also be *showed*
7. Similarly FORSWEAR
8. *Thrived* is also found as a past tense form

Chapter Ten

The verb phrase (2): Verb patterns

A Verb patterns
10.1

Corresponding to the five main sentence types in English (1.55), there are five main types of verb patterns:

Type O has no complement or object: the verb is intransitive (Vi);

Type A consists of BE (or another copula) + complement;

Type B consists of a transitive verb (Vt) + direct object;

Type C consists of Vt + indirect object + direct object;

Type D consists of Vt + direct object + complement.

Each of those five main types can be subdivided as in the Tables below. Each subdivision is an example of a sentence pattern. Certain verbs fit into one or more patterns but not into others, as we see in 10.8.

TYPE O

Verb

Pattern	Example	Structure and notes
1	The sun disappeared	Vi only
a	George sat down	Vi usually with adjunct
	The storm lasted two days	
2	A bell rang	Vi, but the same verb can be used as Vt: see B1
a	It weighed two kilos	
3	You never $\left\{ \begin{array}{l} \text{forget} \\ \text{listen} \end{array} \right\}$	Vi, but an object is understood: see B1 and B2

Variation 1: There are four seasons (1.57)

Variation 2: Here comes the bus
   Up go the prices (1.57)

TYPE A

A			
	1	George was my friend	BE + NP
	2	He was intelligent	BE + adjective
	3	We are in the same class	BE + adverb of place or time
		That was twenty years ago	

Variation 1: Here is an example (1.57)
   Here you are
Variation 2: There is a man at the door (1.57)

TYPE B
Verb

Pattern	Example	Structure and notes
B 1	I rang the bell	Vt + direct object
a	I put the key in the lock	Adjunct obligatory
b	I had two keys	Vt, but no passive
2	I am listening to the news	Prepositional verb
3	I want to go home	Vt + infinitive with *to*
4	I want you to come tóo	Vt + NP + infinitive
5a	I will arrange for you to come	Vt + *for* + NP + infinitive
b	We rely on George to help us	Prepositional verb + object + infinitive
6a	I enjoy listening to the radio	Vt + *-ing*
b	Your shoes want mending	= *need to be mended*
7	I remember $\left\{\begin{array}{l}\text{you}\\=\text{your}\end{array}\right\}$ saying that	Possessive optional
8	I heard the bell ring	Vt + object + bare infinitive
9	I found him standing on the doorstep	Vt + object + *-ing*
10a	We found the door locked	Vt + object + *-ed*
b	I have had my hair cut	Vt + object + *-ed*
11	I believe (that) you have	Vt + *that*-clause
a	I will see (to it) (that) nothing happens to you	Vt + (*to it*) + *that*-clause
b	We all shouted, 'Stop'	Vt + direct speech
12a	We recommend (that) he (should) go	*Should* or subjunctive
b	I regret (that) he $\left\{\begin{array}{l}\text{should feel}\\=\text{feels}\end{array}\right\}$ that way	*Should feel* or *feels*
13	I asked $\left\{\begin{array}{l}\text{if}\\=\text{whether}\end{array}\right\}$ he had gone	Indirect *Yes/No* question
14	I wonder what $\left\{\begin{array}{l}\text{they said}\\\text{to do}\end{array}\right\}$	Vt + *wh*-clause

TYPE C

C 1	I showed you the way	Vt + indirect + direct object
a	I showed you	Vt + indirect object only
b	He gave $\left\{\begin{array}{l}\text{George}\\\text{the door}\end{array}\right\}$ a push	= He pushed $\left\{\begin{array}{l}\text{George}\\\text{the door}\end{array}\right\}$

Verb

Pattern	*Example*	*Structure and notes*
2a	He gave a book to George	Vt + direct object + *to*
b	He provided books for George	Vt + direct object + *for*
3	He told us about the fire	The prep phrase is closely linked with the verb (*told*)
4	He took great care of his wife	The prep phrase is closely linked with the object (*care*)
5a	He convinced us (that) he could do it.	Vt + object + *that*-clause
b	He showed (us) (that) he could	Vt (+ object) + *that*-clause
6a	Tell me $\begin{cases} \text{if} \\ = \text{whether} \end{cases}$ they have gone	Indirect *Yes/No* question
b	I asked (you) $\begin{cases} \text{if} \\ = \text{whether} \end{cases}$ they have gone	
7a	He told us where $\begin{cases} \text{he had gone} \\ \text{to go} \end{cases}$	Vt + object + *wh*-clause
b	He asked (me) $\begin{cases} \text{where I had been} \\ \text{where to go} \end{cases}$	Vt (+ object) + *wh*-clause
8a	He explained (to us) that he was on a diet	Vt (*to* + NP) + *that*-clause
b	He explained (to us) what had happened	Vt (*to* + NP) + *wh*-clause

TYPE D

D 1a	They elected him captain	Two passives possible: see 11.6
b	They made him captain	One passive possible: see 11.6
2a	We found the house $\begin{cases} \text{a ruin} \\ \text{empty} \\ \text{in ruins} \end{cases}$	= It was empty etc. when we found it
b	We painted the wall blue	= It became blue as a result
c	We broke the door open	Or *we broke open the door*
3	We consider him (to be) $\begin{cases} \text{a fool} \\ \text{foolish} \end{cases}$	*To be* optional

Verb		
Pattern	*Example*	*Structure and notes*
4	We know him to be	*To be* obligatory

4   We know him to be   *To be* obligatory
$\left\{ \begin{array}{l} \text{reliable} \\ \text{a good worker} \end{array} \right\}$

5   We regard him as $\left\{ \begin{array}{l} \text{a genius} \\ \text{brilliant} \end{array} \right\}$ *as* + NP or adjective

6   They took him for an   *for* + NP
    American

7a We considered it
    $\left\{ \begin{array}{l} \text{a pity} \\ \text{strange} \end{array} \right\} \left\{ \begin{array}{l} to + \text{verb} \\ that\text{-clause} \end{array} \right\}$

 b We considered it foolish
    ˙(of him) *to* + verb

8   We leave it to
    $\left\{ \begin{array}{l} \text{you} \\ \text{your discretion} \end{array} \right\}$ to decide

All the statements formed on the above patterns can be qualified by a verb like SEEM, as in TYPE E.

TYPE E

1   It seems (to me) (that) somebody $\left\{ \begin{array}{l} \text{wants} \\ \text{is calling} \end{array} \right\}$ you

2   Somebody seems (to me etc.) to $\left\{ \begin{array}{l} \text{want} \\ \text{be calling} \end{array} \right\}$ you

3   It seems (that) somebody $\left\{ \begin{array}{l} \text{wants} \\ \text{is calling} \end{array} \right\}$ you

4   Somebody seems to $\left\{ \begin{array}{l} \text{want} \\ \text{be calling} \end{array} \right\}$ you

5   It seems (to me etc.) as $\left\{ \begin{array}{l} \text{if} \\ \text{though} \end{array} \right\}$ somebody $\left\{ \begin{array}{l} \text{wants} \\ \text{is calling} \end{array} \right\}$ you

The following verbs can replace SEEM:
In E1 and 2: APPEAR
            E3: APPEAR, HAPPEN: and *chanced*, in which case the verb in
                the *that*-clause would be in the past tense
            E4: APPEAR, HAPPEN
            E5: APPEAR, LOOK, SOUND

Verbs that fit into Type O patterns
10.2
O1. Verbs used only as Vi include ACHE, COME, GO, APPEAR (in the

sense of 'come into sight': *cp* A2), DISAPPEAR, FALL, RISE and
ARISE, as in

1 A light appeared, then disappeared at once.
2 The sun rises in the east.
3 A difficult problem arose.

Compare the irregular verbs RISE, ARISE and FALL with the regular
verbs RAISE and FELL, which fit into B1.

O1a. Intransitive verbs usually requiring an adjunct include LIE (down)
and LIVE $\begin{cases} \text{in a certain place} \\ \text{at a certain time} \end{cases}$, as in

4 Don't lie on the wet ground. I lay still and listened.

5 He lived $\begin{cases} \text{in London} \\ \text{in the nineteenth century.} \end{cases}$

Compare the irregular LIE with the irregular LAY, which fits into B1.
Phrasal verbs of Type 2 (1.39c) fit into this verb pattern (*eg Don't give up*).
MOVE, COME, GO, WALK, RUN, FALL, RISE, TRAVEL can take an
adjunct which has the form of an NP, as in the following examples:

6 We have come a long way.

7 They $\begin{cases} \text{walked} \\ \text{ran} \\ \text{travelled} \end{cases}$ the distance in record time.

8 The aircraft $\begin{cases} \text{rose} \\ \text{fell} \end{cases}$ a thousand feet in a second.

For is optional after LAST (a period of time), and after verbs like WALK,
RUN, DRIVE, TRAVEL, ADVANCE, when they refer only to distance
(and not to distance + time as in example [7]):

9 They $\begin{cases} \text{walked} \\ \text{ran} \\ \text{drove} \\ \text{travelled} \end{cases}$ (for) ten miles and then rested.

WALK, RUN, etc. require *for* if the adjunct refers to time only, *eg*

10 They walked etc. for three hours;

and *for* is usual after EXTEND, STRETCH (*out*), as in

11 The desert $\begin{cases} \text{stretched (out) for} \\ \text{extended for} \end{cases}$ miles and miles.

O2. Verbs used both as Vi, with no object stated or understood, and as
Vt with an object, include BREAK, BURN, OPEN, as in

O2	B1
12 Glass breaks easily.	Who broke that window?
13 Paper burns quickly.	We burn all our waste paper.
14 The door opened quietly.	Someone opened the door.

Other verbs used in these two ways include

burst close drop feed fly grow hang hurt keep melt move ring roll   set   shake   shut   stop   turn

In B1, the form and meaning of the verb are both active, while in O2 the form is active but the meaning is often passive. A passive meaning is noticeable in the following examples:

15 Mary photographs well. (= One can take good photographs of her)

16 The book sold rapidly. (= It was sold rapidly)

17 These shirts wash very easily. (= They are very easily washed)

18 This pen writes smoothly. (= One can write smoothly with it)

Complementation is required after WEIGH, MEASURE, COST, as in

19 Our luggage weighed exactly twenty kilos.

20 This table measures two metres by eighty centimetres.

21 It cost eighty dollars.

Compare those last three examples, which cannot be put into the passive, with

19a They have weighed our luggage. It has been weighed.

20a I measured the table. It was measured carefully.

21a We have costed the project. The project has been costed.

In [19a] etc. WEIGH, MEASURE, etc. are transitive: see B1.

O3. Examples of verbs that fit into O3 and either B1 or B2:

O3	BI or B2
22 Elephants never forget.	Elephants never forget a friend (B1)
23 Some people never listen.	They never listen to advice (B2).

In some cases, as in *I haven't eaten today*, it may not be necessary to state the object at all: we know that *I haven't eaten* means *I haven't eaten any food*. In other cases, as in *I accept* or *Let me explain*, the object may be unstated, but it is necessary for the hearer or reader to know exactly what is accepted or what is to be explained. An object may occur, but is not necessary, after READ and WRITE. It may be omitted, but would have to be understood, after ASK and ANSWER.

Verbs in Type A

10.3

The verbs that can be used in Type A refer either to A STATE OF AFFAIRS THAT REMAINS UNCHANGED (*eg* BE, SEEM, etc.) or to A CHANGE OF STATE (*eg* BECOME, GROW).

A1. In the pattern COPULA + NP, the verb can be BE, FEEL, LOOK, PROVE, REMAIN, RESEMBLE, SEEM, SOUND, STAY (unchanged state), or BECOME, GROW, TURN, TURN INTO (change of state). Thus:

24 George was a student. He $\left\{ \begin{array}{l} \text{stayed} \\ = \text{remained} \end{array} \right\}$ a student all his life.

25 His cousin $\left\{ \begin{array}{l} \text{felt} \\ \text{seemed (to be)} \end{array} \right\}$ a fool.

26 Jack was a soldier and then became a famous actor.

TURN + NP, in the sense of BECOME, only occurs in a sentence like

27 The knight turned traitor and fought against the King.

TURN INTO in the same sense is used as follows:

28 At 0 degrees Centigrade, water $\left\{ \begin{array}{l} \text{becomes} \\ = \text{turns into} \end{array} \right\}$ ice.

A2. In the pattern COPULA + ADJECTIVE, verbs referring to an unchanged state are BE, SEEM, APPEAR, FEEL, LOOK, SOUND, TASTE, KEEP, STAY, REMAIN, and occasionally LIE, REST and STAND. Thus:

29 George $\left\{ \begin{array}{l} \text{is} \\ \text{seems (to be)} \\ \text{appears (to be)} \end{array} \right\}$ intelligent.

30 I feel tired.

31 This box feels strong. (= It seems strong when one feels it)

32 You $\left\{ \begin{array}{l} \text{seem (to be)} \\ \text{look} \\ \text{sound} \end{array} \right\}$ rather sad today.

33 This fruit $\left\{ \begin{array}{l} \text{seems (to be)} \\ \text{looks} \\ \text{tastes} \end{array} \right\}$ ripe.

34 You must $\left\{ \begin{array}{l} \text{keep} \\ \text{stay} \end{array} \right\}$ quiet for a few days.

35 The situation remains unchanged.

36 Broken glass lay scattered all over the road.

37 You may rest assured that there will be no danger.

38 You are quite right and I stand corrected.

Verbs referring to a change of state are GET and BECOME; also COME, FALL, GO, GROW, RUN and TURN, which usually occur in certain fixed idiomatic expressions. GET is normal with imperatives (*eg Get ready*) and before adjectives referring to a temporary personal condition, as in

Don't get $\left\{ \begin{array}{l} angry. \\ excited. \\ wet. \end{array} \right\}$ BECOME is normal with more abstract characteristics, *eg He became ambitious.* Otherwise, GET is typical of informal speech, BECOME of more formal style. Thus:

39 Get dry quickly or you'll get cold.

40 It gets dark early these days, doesn't it?

41 The weather gradually became colder and colder. (more formal)

42 Within a few years, George became quite famous.

Idiomatic expressions, with COME, FALL, etc., include:

COME

43 The handle has $\left\{ \begin{array}{l} \text{got} \\ = \text{come} \end{array} \right\}$ loose, and the label has $\left\{ \begin{array}{l} \text{got} \\ = \text{come} \end{array} \right\}$ unstuck.

FALL

44   The child fell $\begin{Bmatrix} \text{asleep.} \\ \text{sick.} \\ \text{ill.} \end{Bmatrix}$

45   The $\begin{Bmatrix} \text{post} \\ \text{job} \end{Bmatrix}$ $\begin{Bmatrix} \text{became} \\ = \text{fell} \end{Bmatrix}$ vacant.

GO

46   The poor man went $\begin{Bmatrix} \text{pale.} \\ \text{bald.} \\ \text{mad.} \end{Bmatrix}$

47   $\begin{Bmatrix} \text{Meat goes bad.} \\ \text{Milk goes sour.} \\ \text{Iron goes rusty.} \end{Bmatrix}$

GROW

48   He grew $\begin{Bmatrix} \text{thin and grey.} \\ \text{old and wise.} \\ \text{older and wiser.} \end{Bmatrix}$

RUN

49   The river ran dry, supplies ran low, the crops ran wild.

TURN

50   The milk $\begin{Bmatrix} \text{went} \\ = \text{turned} \end{Bmatrix}$ sour.

51   The weather $\begin{Bmatrix} \text{got} \\ = \text{became} \\ = \text{turned} \end{Bmatrix}$ $\begin{matrix} \text{warm.} \\ \text{warmer.} \end{matrix}$

52   In autumn, the leaves turn yellow.

A3. In the pattern COPULA + ADVERB OF PLACE, the verb can be BE, KEEP; also SEEM and APPEAR when the verb is used in a figurative sense:

53   We $\begin{Bmatrix} \text{were in} \\ \text{kept out of} \end{Bmatrix}$ the way.

54   Everything $\begin{Bmatrix} \text{seems} \\ \text{appears} \end{Bmatrix}$ (to be) in a muddle.

GET is frequently used, especially in conversational style, to refer to a change of position; and FALL can be used figuratively as in [56]:

55   We got $\begin{Bmatrix} \text{up, down, in, out} \\ \text{into bed, to our place, into the car, into a muddle.} \end{Bmatrix}$

56   The young man fell in love.

Verbs in Type B
10.4

B1. Verbs occurring in this pattern are very numerous. A good dictionary will indicate whether or not a verb is transitive and therefore can normally take an object.

B1a. The following require an adjunct after the object: PUT, PLACE and STAND, as in

57 They $\begin{Bmatrix} \text{put} \\ \text{placed} \\ \text{stood} \end{Bmatrix}$ the ladder against the wall.

LAY also requires this pattern in an example like

58 $\begin{Bmatrix} \text{Lay} \\ \text{They laid} \end{Bmatrix}$ the injured man on the stretcher (*cp* LIE, O1a),

but not in *The chicken has laid an egg.* SET requires pattern B1a, too, in an example like

59 They set the knives and forks on the table

but not in *They set the table* (=set knives, forks, etc. on it).

B1b. HAVE does not normally take the passive; nor does LACK. But see 11.6 (B1).

B2. Verbs that fit into O3 as well as B2 include ASK *(for)*, LOOK *(at)*, LOOK *(for)*, WORRY *(about)*. Those that do not fit into O3 include LONG *for*, LOOK *after*, PART *with*, TASTE *of*. Thus we can say

60 I'm looking. I'm looking $\begin{Bmatrix} \text{at} \\ \text{for} \end{Bmatrix}$ my watch.

61 Don't worry. Don't worry about it;

but the prepositional phrase cannot be omitted in

62 Mary is looking after the neighbour's cat.

63 We're longing for the holidays.

64 This soup tastes of disinfectant.

For other examples, see the alphabetical list in 10.8.

B3. On the pattern *We want to go home* are

afford[1]	consent	hasten	pretend
agree	continue[2]	hate[2,5]	promise
aim	contract	hesitate	propose[2]
appear[3]	contrive	hope	refuse
apply	dare	intend[2]	remember[2,4]
arrange	decide	learn	seek
ask	decline	like[2,5]	seem[3]
attempt	demand	long	start[2]
bear[1,2]	deserve[2,4]	love[2,5]	swear
beg	desire	manage	tend
begin[2]*	determine	mean (=intend)	threaten
care[1]	endeavour	need	try[2,4]
cease[2]	expect	offer	undertake
chance[3]	fail	omit[2]	venture
choose	forget[2,4]	plan	want
claim	happen[3]	prefer[2,5]	wish

Notes: 1 AFFORD and BEAR are generally used with CAN, and both verbs, as well as CARE, usually occur in either the interrogative or the negative, *eg I can't afford to run a car. I can't bear to watch that. Would you care to dance?*

2 These verbs can also be followed by *-ing.*

3 For APPEAR, chanced, HAPPEN and SEEM + infinitive, see Type E

4 See 10.7. 5 See 3.5e.

B4. On the pattern of *I expect you to come* are

advise	dare	invite	remind
allow	direct	lead	request
appoint	drive	like (x)	require
ask	enable	love (x)	sentence
assist	encourage	mean	teach
beg	entitle	need	tell
beseech (x)	expect	oblige	tempt
bribe	forbid	order	train
cause (x)	force	permit	trouble (x)
challenge	get (x)	persuade	trust
charge	would hate (x)	prefer	urge
command	help	press	want (x)
compel	instruct	promise[2] (x)	warn[3]
condemn	intend	recommend	wish (x)

Notes: 1 All the verbs in this list can be used in the passive pattern *You are expected to come*, except those marked (x). (See footnote.)

2 In *I expect you to come, I* expect but *you* are to come. Exceptionally, in *I promise you to come, I* give my promise to you that *I* will come.

3 WARN is often followed in this pattern by the negative, as in *I warned you not to go.*

4 Note: *I don't want there to be any trouble.*

B5a. ARRANGE can be replaced by ASK, LONG, PREPARE, PROVIDE, VOTE, WAIT and WISH in this pattern. Note that in B5a we ask somebody for somebody else to come.

B5b. RELY replaceable by COUNT and DEPEND.

B6a. Verbs that fit into the pattern *I enjoy listening* are

admit[1]	appreciate	begin[2]	continue[2]
advise	avoid	cease[2]	delay
anticipate	bear[2, 3]	consider	deny[1]

---

* In the structure *Vt + you to come, you* can be considered as the object of all the verbs in this list except CAUSE, EXPECT, GET, HATE, INTEND, LIKE, LOVE, MEAN, NEED, PREFER, PROMISE, RECOMMEND, WANT and WISH. In saying *I persuaded her to come,* I persuaded her; whereas *I would love her to come* need not imply that I would love her: it means simply that I would be delighted if she came. *I would love her* is not the same as *I would love her to:* see 3.9d.

detest	hate[2]	omit[2]	remember[1, 2, 4]
dislike[1]	can't help[1]	postpone	resent[1]
enjoy	imagine[1]	practise	resist
escape	intend[2]	prefer[2]	risk
face[3]	keep (on)	propose[2]	start[2]
fancy	like[2]	recollect[1]	stop
favour	love[2]	recommend	suggest
finish	mind[3]	regret[1, 2]	try[2, 4]
forget[1, 2, 4]	miss		

Notes: 1 These verbs fit into the pattern *admit seeing* or *admit having seen.*
     2 These also occur in pattern B3.
     3 BEAR and FACE are generally used with CAN in the interrogative or negative, *eg I can't* $\begin{Bmatrix} bear \\ face \end{Bmatrix}$ *going there again.* MIND is used with the interrogative and negative, as in *Would you mind closing the window?*
     4 See 10.7.

Note: Only the *-ing* form, not the infinitive, follows a preposition or a prepositional verb. Hence: *I don't approve of swearing. Certain people object to dancing. Don't think about doing that now.*
B6b. WANT is replaceable by BEAR, NEED and REQUIRE in this pattern.
B7. Parallel with *I want to go* and *I want you to go*, we have *I remember saying that* (*I* said it) and *I remember* $\begin{Bmatrix} you \\ =your \end{Bmatrix}$ *saying that* (*You* said it).
The verbs that fit into B6a can also fit into B7, if a sensible context allows it.
Thus: *I don't mind* $\begin{Bmatrix} you \\ =your \end{Bmatrix}$ *saying that. I don't approve of* $\begin{Bmatrix} you \\ =your \end{Bmatrix}$
staying out late. The option of using either the objective form (*me, you, him*) or the possessive (*my, your, his*) is only open if the subjects of the two verbs are different (*I* don't mind; *you* say that). If the two subjects are the same, then only the possessive is used, *eg I remember (my) saying that. (You) stop (your) laughing.*
B8. HEAR is replaceable by BID, FEEL, HAVE, HELP, KNOW, LET, MAKE, NOTICE, SEE, WATCH: see 3.2 and 3.3.
B9. FIND is replaceable by CATCH, DISCOVER, FEEL, GET, HAVE, HEAR, KEEP, LEAVE, LISTEN TO, NOTICE, OBSERVE, SEE, SET, SMELL, START, STOP, WATCH, WANT, as in
    65 We saw the car stopping (3.3)
    66 Hurry up and get those people moving.
    67 George had us all laughing (10.7)
    68 Please don't keep me waiting.

69 Can you $\left\{\begin{array}{l}\text{set}\\ =\text{start}\end{array}\right\}$ this engine going?

70 I want you (to be) sitting there.

B10a. FIND is replaceable by LIKE, PREFER and WANT, and all four verbs could fit into the pattern

71 We found the door (to be) locked

B10b. HAVE is replaceable by FEEL, GET, HEAR, KEEP and SEE, as in

72 We saw the door safely locked,

in which case *to be* could not be inserted.

MAKE also fits into this pattern in an example like

73 Some people can always make their presence felt.

B11. The following are frequently-used verbs that take a *that*-clause as object:

acknowledge	confess (")	guess	repeat (")
add (")	confirm (")	hear	reply (")
admit (")	consider	hope	report (")
agree	decide (")	imagine	say (")
announce (")	declare (")	insist (")	see
answer (")	deny	know	shout out (")
argue (")	doubt	learn	show
arrange	dream	maintain (")	suppose
assert (")	expect	mention	suspect
assume	explain (")	note (")	swear
bear in mind	fancy	notice	state (")
believe	fear	observe (")	think (")
bet	feel	pretend	trust (")
boast (")	find	realise	understand
comment (")	find out	remark (")	wish
complain (")	forget	remember	write (")
conclude (")	gather		

See B11b.

B11a. DEPEND, INSIST and SWEAR can fit into this pattern, as follows:

74 You may depend (up)on it that I shall support you.

75 I must insist ((up)on it) that everyone leaves the room.

76 I $\left\{\begin{array}{l}\text{saw}\\ \text{can swear}\end{array}\right\}$ (to it) that he never left my sight.

(Up)on it is obligatory in [74]; but *(up)on it* and *to it* are optional in [75] and [76]. *It* is obligatory in *I take it (that) you all agree.*

B11b. Verbs marked thus (") in the list for B11 are commonly used before direct speech, as are CRY, EXCLAIM, SHOUT and WHISPER, which would not normally occur before a *that*-clause.

B12a. RECOMMEND replaceable by AGREE, ARRANGE, ASK,

COMMAND, CONSIDER, DECIDE, DESIRE, DISAGREE, INSIST, INTEND, PROPOSE, REQUEST, SUGGEST, URGE.

B12b. *I regret* replaceable by another construction, such as *I am sorry* or *It is a pity.*

B13. ASK replaceable by DECIDE, DOUBT, ENQUIRE, FIND OUT, FORGET, NOT KNOW, NOT SAY, WONDER.

B14. WONDER replaceable by ASK, CONSIDER, DECIDE, EX-PLAIN, FIND OUT, FORGET, KNOW, REALISE, REMEMBER, UNDERSTAND; also AGREE and DISAGREE, which may be followed

by *about, as to* and *on,* as in *They* $\begin{Bmatrix} agreed \\ disagreed \end{Bmatrix} \begin{Bmatrix} about \\ as\ to \\ on \end{Bmatrix}$ *where to go next.*

Verbs in Type C

10.5

C1. There are three kinds of verb that will fit into pattern C1:

1 those that can also be used in C2a, *ie* with *to*;

2 those that can also be used in C2b, *ie* with *for*;

3 those that occur in C1 but not normally in C2 at all.

Verbs in the first category will be indicated in the list below by (*to*); those in the second category by (*for*); those in the third by (–):

accord (to)	change (for)	hand (to)	recommend (to)
advance (to)	charge (–)	keep (for)	refuse (to)
afford (–)	choose (for)	leave (to, for)	reserve (for)
allow (to)	cook (for)	lend (to)	save (for)
ask (of)	cost (–)	mean (to)	sell (to)
assign (to)	cut (for)	offer (to)	send (to)
bet (–)	deal (to)	order (for)	serve (to)
bid (to)	deny (to)	owe (to)	show (to)
book (for)	do (to, for)	pass (to)	sing (to, for)
bring (to, for)	fetch (to, for)	pay (to)	spare (for)
build (for)	find (for)	play (to)	take (to)
buy (for)	fix (for)	post (to)	teach (to)
cable (to)	forgive (–)	prepare (for)	telephone (to)
call (for)	get (to, for)	promise (to)	tell (to)
cash (for)	give (to)	quote (to)	throw (to)
catch (for)	grant (to)	reach (for)	wish (to)
cause (to)	guarantee (–)	read (to)	write (to)

Notes: The indirect object in pattern C1 is normally personal: see C1b. Examples: *accord me an interview*; *advance me some money*; *allow me a discount*; *ask me a question*; *book me a room*; *cash me a cheque*; *cause me a lot of trouble*; *charge me two pounds*; *cost me a pound*; *deal me a blow*; *do somebody harm*; *do me a favour*; *forgive me (for) my sins*; *guarantee me satisfaction*; *play me a tune*; *sing me a song*; *throw me the ball*; *wish me good luck*.

  i *Throw me the ball* = throw it *to* me.

  ii MEAN will only occur in this pattern in an example like *He meant me no harm*.

  iii ASK can occur in C2a with *of* (*eg May I ask a favour of you*).

  iv PLAY can also occur in C2a with *with* (*eg I'll play a game of chess with you*).

C1a. The direct object may be omitted, when it is understood, after ALLOW, ASK, BET, CABLE, FORGIVE, GRANT, OWE, PAY, PROMISE, SEND, SHOW, TEACH, TELEPHONE, TELL, WRITE as ir

  77 A When can I know the answer?

    B I'll $\left\{ \begin{array}{l} \text{tell} \\ \text{write} \end{array} \right\}$ you tomorrow.

GRANT can be used as in

  78 This is rather difficult, I grant you.

C1b. The indirect object can refer to something inanimate in C1b, where PUSH could be replaced by PULL, WASH, RUB, POLISH, used as a noun or as a verb.

C2a. All the verbs followed by (*to*) in the list for C1 will also fit into C2a. Pattern C1 is normally preferred if the indirect object is shorter than the direct, *eg Give me that bundle of papers*. C2 is preferred if the indirect object is longer, as in *Give those papers to the girl at the door*. However, the shorter group could come second for the sake of emphasis, as in *Give that bundle of papers to ME, not to HIM*. A number of commonly-used verbs will fit into C2a but not into C1. They include: ANNOUNCE, CONFESS, DEMONSTRATE, DESCRIBE, ENTRUST, EXPLAIN, MENTION, POINT OUT, PROPOSE, REPORT, SAY, STATE and SUGGEST.

C3. In this pattern, TELL can be replaced by ASK, CABLE, INFORM, TELEPHONE. Note also *CONGRATULATE someone (on something)*; *THANK someone (for something)*, and many other constructions on this pattern: see alphabetical list in 10.8.

C4. Other constructions on this pattern include:

TAKE $\left\{ \begin{array}{l} \text{advantage of} \\ \text{note of} \end{array} \right\}$ MAKE $\left\{ \begin{array}{l} \text{fun of} \\ \text{a fuss about} \\ \text{use of} \end{array} \right\}$ LOSE $\left\{ \begin{array}{l} \text{sight of} \\ \text{touch with} \end{array} \right\}$

CATCH sight of	GIVE way to	KEEP pace with
PAY attention to	PUT a stop to	SET fire to
GET rid of		

C5a. CONVINCE replaceable by ASSURE, INFORM, PERSUADE, REMIND, SATISFY, TEACH, TELL.

C5b. SHOW replaceable by BET, PROMISE, WARN

C6a. TELL replaceable by INFORM, REMIND.

C6b. ASK alone in this pattern.

C7a. TELL replaceable by ADVISE, ASK, INFORM, REMIND, SHOW, TEACH.

C7b. ASK replaceable by SHOW.

C8a and b. ANNOUNCE and other verbs that fit into C2a will take pattern C8 when the object is a *that*-clause or *wh*-clause.

Verbs in Type D

10.6

D1a. Also used in this pattern: APPOINT, BAPTISE, CHRISTEN, CROWN, LABEL, NAME, NOMINATE. With CHRISTEN, note these examples: *They christened John last week. They christened their son John.*

D1b. Also CALL, DECLARE, LEAVE, NICKNAME, PROCLAIM, PRONOUNCE, VOTE.

D2a. On the same pattern: *Please HAVE everything ready. We HOLD you responsible. I don't LIKE my bread fresh. I WANT all these windows clean. He'll WISH himself dead.*

D2b. Examples on the same pattern: *The sun will BURN our skin black. It will DRIVE us mad. KEEP yourself warm. Don't GET your feet wet. Please LEAVE the door open. MAKE yourself comfortable. OPEN the window wide. This will RENDER it safe. The shock may TURN his hair white. WASH the plate clean. WIPE the windscreen clear.*

D2c. In the examples *We broke the door open* and *We broke open the door*, BREAK can be replaced by BURST, FLING, FORCE. Note also *We* $\left\{ \begin{array}{l} pulled \\ pushed \end{array} \right\}$ *the door open* and *We* $\left\{ \begin{array}{l} cut \\ slit \end{array} \right\}$ *the packet open.*

D3. With *to be* optional, CONSIDER can be replaced by DECLARE, FIND, PROVE, THINK. However, the infinitive is required after these verbs in examples like *We consider him to have been foolish*, *ie* We consider that he acted foolishly.

D4. With *to be* obligatory, KNOW can be replaced by ACKNOWLEDGE, BELIEVE, DISCOVER, FEEL, IMAGINE, JUDGE, REPORT, SUPPOSE.

D5. REGARD replaceable in this pattern by ACCEPT, ACKNOWLEDGE, CLAIM, CONDEMN, CONSIDER, COUNT, DESCRIBE, LOOK ON, RECOGNISE, SEE, TREAT.

D6. TAKE replaceable in this pattern by MISTAKE.

D7a and b. CONSIDER replaceable in this pattern by BELIEVE, COUNT, THINK. Thus:

79 We $\left\{ \begin{array}{l} believe \\ consider \\ think \end{array} \right\}$ it $\left\{ \begin{array}{l} a\ pity \\ strange \end{array} \right\}$ $\left\{ \begin{array}{l} (for\ him)\ to\ say\ a\ thing\ like\ that. \\ that\ he\ never\ answered\ your\ letter. \end{array} \right\}$

B Infinitive or -*ing*: either possible but with different meanings
10.7

a For a general survey of the problems of whether to use the infinitive or the -*ing* form, see Chapters Three and Four.

b For verbs which can be followed by the infinitive, see 10.4 (B3, B4, B5 and B8).

c For verbs which can be followed by -*ing*, see 10.4 (B6, B7 and B9).

d Either the infinitive or a preposition + -*ing* can follow the verbs *AGREE (on)*, *AIM (at)* and *DECIDE (on)*, the nouns *attempt, pleasure, honour, chance, opportunity*, and the adjective *content*, and *determined*, without any difference in meaning:

80 We $\left\{\begin{array}{l}\text{agreed}\\\text{decided}\end{array}\right\}$ $\left\{\begin{array}{l}\text{to share}\\\text{= on sharing}\end{array}\right\}$ the profits with you.

81 They $\left\{\begin{array}{l}\text{made another attempt}\\\text{aimed}\end{array}\right\}$ $\left\{\begin{array}{l}\text{to cross}\\\text{= at crossing}\end{array}\right\}$ the river next day.

82 It was a great $\left\{\begin{array}{l}\text{pleasure}\\\text{honour}\end{array}\right\}$ $\left\{\begin{array}{l}\text{to be}\\\text{= being}\end{array}\right\}$ with you this evening.

83 I hope to have $\left\{\begin{array}{l}\text{a(n)}\\\text{the}\end{array}\right\}$ $\left\{\begin{array}{l}\text{chance}\\\text{opportunity}\end{array}\right\}$ $\left\{\begin{array}{l}\text{to see}\\\text{= of seeing}\end{array}\right\}$ him.

84 They were quite content $\left\{\begin{array}{l}\text{to stay}\\\text{= with staying}\end{array}\right\}$ where they were.

85 They were determined $\left\{\begin{array}{l}\text{to maintain}\\\text{= on maintaining}\end{array}\right\}$ peace.

e After certain verbs and adjectives, either the infinitive or the -*ing* form may be used with a difference in meaning: Examples:

86a Mary is afraid to drive a car
: as in 3.15a

b She's afraid of having an accident
: afraid that might happen

87a He's too ashamed to look at us
: as in 3.15a

b He's ashamed of $\left\{\begin{array}{l}\text{losing}\\\text{= having lost}\end{array}\right\}$ his temper
: ashamed of past action

88a George is $\left\{\begin{array}{l}\text{certain}\\\text{sure}\end{array}\right\}$ to pass his exam
: the speaker is certain (3.15b)

b George is $\left\{\begin{array}{l}\text{certain}\\\text{sure}\end{array}\right\}$ of passing his exam
: George himself is certain

89a George deserves to succeed
: as in 3.5

b They deserve shooting for that
: they deserve to be shot

90a I forgot to post the letter
: I forgot I had to, and didn't do it

b I shall never forget climbing Mount Fujiyama
: I had that experience and shall never forget it

c I forgot about posting it : I forgot that I had to

91a He had us empty our pockets : He gave instructions and we carried them out.

b He had us all singing : He acted in such a way that we were all singing

92a I $\begin{Bmatrix} \text{am} \\ \text{would be} \end{Bmatrix}$ very interested to hear your news : as in either 3.15a or 3.15c

b I am $\begin{Bmatrix} \text{interested in} \\ \text{keen on} \end{Bmatrix}$ collecting stamps : interested in that hobby

93a I meant to tell you . . . : I intended to tell you

b This illness will mean (your) going to hospital : it will require that treatment

94a I regret to tell you . . . : I regret, but will now tell you

b I regret $\begin{Bmatrix} \text{telling} \\ = \text{having told} \\ = \text{(that) I told} \end{Bmatrix}$ you : I told you and now regret it

95a I remembered to post your letter : I remembered that I had to: then I posted it

b I remembered $\begin{Bmatrix} \text{posting} \\ = \text{having posted} \\ = \text{(that) I posted} \end{Bmatrix}$ it : I posted it, and remembered

96a We stand to lose everything : we run that risk

b I can't stand losing anything : I can't bear it

97a My father taught me to read : He taught me. Then I could read

b He taught me reading[1] : He taught me that subject[1]

98a I'll thank you to leave me alone : Impolite request for future action

b Thank you for $\begin{Bmatrix} \text{being} \\ = \text{having been} \end{Bmatrix}$ so kind : Gratitude for past action

99a I never thought to invite him : I didn't think of it, so I didn't invite him

b I never think about getting married : The idea never occurs to me

---

[1] This pattern can only be used with a few verbs, eg *reading, writing, drawing, painting, singing, swimming, riding,* and then only when the gerund is used alone: it is not used, for example, to replace *He taught me to read* $\begin{Bmatrix} \textit{French.} \\ \textit{fast.} \end{Bmatrix}$

100a Try to write better : or *Try and write better*, the new act being expressed by *and write*

I tried to write better : *to write* not replaceable by *and wrote*

b A I can't unlock the door
B Try turning the key the other way : Make that experiment and see what happens

.101a I $\begin{Bmatrix} \text{want} \\ \text{need} \end{Bmatrix}$ to have a haircut : as in 3.5

b My hair $\begin{Bmatrix} \text{wants} \\ \text{needs} \end{Bmatrix}$ cutting : it needs to be cut

C Alphabetical list of selected verbs, with the patterns in which they occur
10.8
The following is a list of frequently-used verbs with indications of the patterns in which they often occur: the list is not meant to be exhaustive. Verbs whose patterning is not likely to cause difficulty are not included. Particular attention is paid to verbs associated with certain prepositions. When a verb can enter into a variety of patterns (see GET in the list below), Type O patterns are given first, then Type A, then B, C and D. References (*eg* B11) are made to the verb patterns at the beginning of this chapter.

ABBREVIATIONS AND CONVENTIONS USED
a... stands for the verb, beginning with *a*, that is being treated.
ACCOUNT FOR *stg*, P: P indicates that ACCOUNT FOR occurs in the passive, to produce *Stg was accounted for*.
ACT; a semicolon immediately after an entry means that the verb can be used intransitively and without an adjunct.
APPEAL *(to sby) (for stg)*: the parentheses indicate 'optional'. Thus we can say *I appeal* or *I appeal to you* or *I appeal for mercy* or *I appeal to you for mercy*.
I before an entry: the verb usually has a human subject.
It before an entry: the verb usually has an inanimate subject.
sby (=somebody): human subject or object.
stg (=something): inanimate subject or object.
that indicates that a *that*-clause can follow, as in B11.
that...should: a *that*-clause with *should* can follow, as in B12a.
wh indicates that a *wh*-clause can follow, as in B14.
, " indicates that direct speech can follow, as in B11b.

I ABANDON sby (to his fate); a... a place, an idea
I ABIDE by a decision, P
I ABSOLVE sby (from blame)
Stg ABSORBS a liquid; I a... knowledge
I ABSTAIN from alcohol, from smoking
I ACCEPT (an invitation); a... a present or a newcomer; a... (the fact) that;
a...sby as (a) leader; a... stg as final
I ACCORD (=give) sby stg, C1; stg a...s (=agrees) with stg else
I ACCOUNT for stg, P (to sby); it a...s for (=explains) stg
I ACCUSE sby (of a misdeed, of doing something wrong)
My tooth ACHES; *I a... all over.*
I ACKNOWLEDGE sby or stg, *eg* a fact or message; a... that; a... sby to be
superior; a... sby as a genius; *a... stg as a fact*
I ACQUAINT sby with a fact
I ACT; act (a part); act the fool; act on advice, on instructions, P; a chemical
acts on stg; sby acts as (a) leader, as (the) Chairman; stg acts as a drug
I ADAPT stg (to stg else); a... myself to circumstances
I ADD (numbers); add two and two; add stg (to stg else), P; This adds to our
difficulties; I a... that; a..., ", B11b
I ADDRESS a letter (to sby); a... meeting; a... myself to a task; How do we
a... him? A... him as Doctor
Stg ADHERES to stg solid; I a... to a decision, P *when used in abstract sense*
I ADMIRE sby (for doing good); a... stg, *eg* a view
I ADMIT sby (to or into a place); a... a fault; a... (to) going or (to) having
gone; a... that
I ADOPT a child, a method
I ADVANCE (on the enemy); a... two miles; a... an argument; a... sby money
I ADVISE sby (on or about stg); a... a course of action; a... sby to wait; a...
(your) waiting
I can AFFORD stg; a... £5 (for stg); a... to go; stg a...s sby a pleasure, C1
I AGREE (with sby); X and Y a...; people a... (with one another); a... a figure
in a calculation; a... (with sby) (about or on a subject); my answer a...s with
yours; I a... on or to a plan or price, P; a... to go or on going; a... to your
going; a... that; a... that...should (B12a); a... (as to) wh... B14
I AIM (stg) (at a target), P; a... at going or to go
I ALLOW money or time (for some purpose); a... a claim; stg or sby a...s for
stg, *ie* makes provision for it, P; a... sby to go; I a... sby stg, C1
It AMOUNTS to a total
I AMUSE sby; It a...s sby; I a... myself (by) doing stg
I ANNOUNCE news; a... sby; a... (to sby) that
I ANSWER; a... you; a... your question; a... a call, the telephone; a... for stg
or sby, *ie* take responsibility for it or him, P; sby or stg a...s to a description;
I a:.. that; a..., ".

Sby or stg ANTICIPATES an event; I a... (your) going

I APOLOGISE (to sby) (for an action or for doing stg)

I APPEAL (to sby), P, (for money, for mercy), P; a... against a decision, P; sby or stg a...s to (=attracts) sby

Sby or stg APPEARS, O1; sby or stg a...s strong, A2, a...s (to be) in order, A3; it a...s, 10.1,E

Does this APPLY? (=Is it relevant?) I a... stg (to stg else) (=put it against it); a... myself to a task; a... (to sby) (for permission, for a job) P

I APPOINT sby (to a post); a... sby to go; a... sby Chairman, D1

I APPRECIATE your kindness; a... being asked

I APPROVE accounts; a... (of stg or sby), P; a... of (your) going

I ARGUE (with sby), P, (about a subject), P; a... sby out of going; a... that; a..., "

Stg or sby ARISES, O1; stg a...s from or out of stg else

I ARRANGE stg; a... to go; a... for stg, P; a... for sby to go, for stg to be done; a... that...should, B12a

I ARREST a criminal or a process; stg a...s a process

Sby or stg ARRIVES (a... at a destination, on a surface, in an area)

I ASK (sby) (a question, the time, the way); a... (sby) (for stg) (=make a request for it, P); a... (sby) about a subject; a... for sby (=make a request to see or speak to him, P); a... after sby('s health); a... to go; a... sby to go; a... (sby) for sby (else) to go; a... that...should, B12a; a... if, B13; a... wh, B14; a... sby a favour, C1; a... a favour of sby, C2a; a... (sby) if, C6b; a... (sby) wh, C7b

I ASSENT (to a proposal)

I ASSIGN sby to do stg; a... sby (to) a place, a task

I ASSUME (=adopt) a name, an attitude; I a... (=suppose) that

I ASSURE sby (of a fact); a... sby that, C5a

I ATTACH stg (to stg else); a... sby to an organisation; a... importance to stg

I ATTEMPT a task; a... to go

I ATTEND (a meeting, or meeting-place); a... a patient; a... (to sby, eg a teacher); a... to a matter, P; a... to sby, ie deal with him, P

I AVAIL myself of an opportunity

I AVERT (=turn away) my eyes (from stg); a... (=prevent) an accident

I AVOID stg or sby; a... going

I AWAIT sby or stg; cp WAIT

I AWAKE at six; a... sby; cp WAKE

I BAPTISE sby (John)

I BARGAIN (with sby) (for stg); b... for stg (ie be prepared for it) P

I BASE stg on stg concrete, or (up)on stg abstract; stg is based (up)on stg else

I BATH, ie have a bath; b... a baby

I BATHE (in a river or the sea); b... my eyes

BE: *see* 10.1,O, variation 1; A1, 2 and 3, and variations
A tree BEARS fruit, a woman b...s a child, this matter cannot b... scrutiny;
it b...s on (= relates to) stg else; I can't b... to go or going; b... stg in mind;
b... in mind (that)...
Sby or stg BECOMES + complement, 10.3 (A1–2)
I BEG (for money or food); b... stg, *eg* a meal or one's pardon; b... stg of
sby; b... to differ; b... sby to go; b... (of sby) that
Sby or stg BEGINS; b... stg; b... to go, or going; b... (the lesson) (with a song)
I BEHAVE (well); b... badly (towards sby); b... myself
I BELIEVE stg or sby; b... in (*ie* have faith in) stg or sby, P; b... that, b... so,
b... not; b... sby or stg to be..., P
This BELONGS here (*ie* this is its place). It b...s to sby
Stg or sby BENDS, O2; sby b...s down, forward, back; b... stg; b... it straight,
back, D2b
I BENEFIT (from stg)
I BESEECH sby (to do stg)
I BET; b... money; b... on a horse; b... sby money, C1; b... (sby) (money)
that, C5b
You BEWARE! b... (of the dog). You must or should b... (of danger)
I BID (9.6) (money) (for stg) (against sby else); b... on a project (*ie* state a
price for undertaking it); b... (9.8) sby go, b... (sby) farewell, C1
Sby or stg BINDS stg or sby; b... two things together; I b... myself to an
agreement
I BLAME sby (for stg or for doing stg); b... my tools; b... my mistakes on(to)
sby else; Who is to ...?, 3.18
I BLESS sby (for a good deed, for doing 'stg); *for* blessed, blest, *see* 3.38
Stg or sby BLINDS sby; stg b...s sby to the truth
I BOAST (about stg); b... (of) stg (= be proud to have it); b... that
Water BOILS; I b... water
I BOOK (a room, a passage); b... (a seat) for a theatre; I b... sby a seat, C1
I BORROW (money) (from sby)
Don't BOTHER (yourself); sby or stg b...s me; b... about stg or sby
I BRIBE sby (to do stg); b... sby into doing stg
Sby or stg BRINGS stg or sby; b... sby stg, C1, C2a and b
I BUILD (a house); b... sby a house, C1 and C2b
Stg BURSTS, O2; stg or sby b... stg, *eg* a balloon; I b... out laughing
I BUY (stg); b... sby stg, C1; C2b

I CALCULATE (stg *eg* expense); c... that; c... how much, B14
I CALL; c... sby; c... on (= visit, sby); c... sby stg, C1, C2b; c... sby or stg a
name, D1b
I CARE (about stg); Would you c... to go? I don't c... about going; c... for
sby or stg, P; I don't c... wh, B14

I CATCH stg or sby; c... sby doing stg, B9; c... sby a fish, C1, C2b

Sby or stg CAUSES stg (eg an accident); c... stg to happen, sby to go; c... sby trouble, C1

I CAUTION sby (not to do stg); c... sby against danger

Stg CEASES: I c... stg; c... to go or c... going; c... firing!

I CHALLENGE sby (to do stg); c... sby to a fight

Stg or sby CHANGES, O2; I c... (my clothes); This c...s (=alters) the situation; I c... stg (for stg else); c... stg into stg else; c... sby some money, C1, C2b

I CHARGE (the enemy); c... a battery; c... (=order) sby to go; c... sby with a duty; c... (sby) some money (for stg bought), C1; c... these goods to sby, to sby's account; c... sby (with a crime, with doing stg wrong)

I CHEAT; c... sby (out of stg)

I CHOOSE (wisely); c... stg; c... between two things; c... to go; c... sby stg, C1, C2b; c... sby as leader, D5

I CLAIM (stg) (from sby); c... (stg) on my insurance; c... to be sby, to have done stg; c... sby as my brother, D5

Stg CLEARS, O2; c... stg, eg a windscreen, a space; c... sby's name; c... sby of suspicion

Stg CLOSES, O2; I c... my eyes, a door; c... with sby (=agree on a deal)

X and Y COMBINE; sby or stg c...s stg with stg else

Sby or stg COMES, O1; c... a long way, O1a; c... to know, 3.4; c... dancing

I COMMAND an army, obedience, respect, sympathy; the house c...s a splendid view; I c... sby to go

Stg or sby COMMENCES; c... stg; c... to work, or c... working

I COMMENT (on stg) P; c... that

I COM'MIT a crime; c... suicide; c... sby for trial; c... stg to memory

I COMMUNICATE (with sby); two rooms c... with each other; I c... stg to sby

I COMPARE two things; c... stg with or to stg else; How does X c... with Y?

I COM'PEL sby to go; stg c...s me to say

I COMPETE (with or against others) (in a competition) (for a prize), P

I COMPLAIN (about sby or stg) P; c... of a pain; c... that; c..., "

Two things or people COMPLEMENT each other

I COMPLIMENT sby (on his success, on achieving stg)

I COMPLY (with a request or order), P

I CONCENTRATE; c... my resources; c... (attention) (on stg)

Stg CONCERNS sby or stg; I c... myself with sby else's problems

Stg or sby CONCLUDES stg; I c... that; c..., "

I CONDEMN sby (to a punishment) (for a crime); c... sby to die; c... stg as unsuitable

I CONFESS (a fault) (to sby); c... a weakness; c... to a liking for stg; c... that; c..., "

I CONFIDE in a friend; c... my troubles to sby else; c... sby to sby else's care

I CONFINE stg (with)in a small space; c... sby to his room; c... my remarks to

stg; c... myself to saying stg
Stg or sby CONFIRMS a report: I c... an appointment, a decision; c... that
X and Y CONFLICT; stg c...s with stg else
I CONFORM (to rules) P
Stg or sby CONFUSES sby; 1 c... two things; c... sby or stg with sby or stg else
I CONGRATULATE sby (on his success, on doing stg)
X and Y CONNECT; I c... two things; c... stg with stg else; c... (=physically
join) stg to stg else
I CONNIVE at stg wrong
I CONSENT (to a plan); c... to go; c... to (your) going
I CONSIDER sby; c... a plan; c... going; c... that, c... wh; c... sby or stg (to be),
D3; c... sby or stg as, D5; c... it a pity, foolish to go, or that, D7a and b
I CONSIGN stg to an address; c... goods by air
Stg concrete CONSISTS of its elements; stg abstract c...s in stg, *eg* prudence
c...s in knowing when to be silent
I CONSULT sby (about or on stg); c... a dictionary
Stg CONTAINS (=holds) stg; stg or sby c...s stg (=holds it back); I (cannot)
c... myself (for joy)
Stg or sby CONTINUES; c...s stg, *eg* a story; c...s to go or going; I c..., "
Stg CONTRACTS; I c... an illness; c... to do stg
X and Y CONTRAST with (each other); I c... stg with stg else
I CONTRIVE (=invent) stg; c... to do stg
I CONVERT sby (to a belief); sby or stg c...s stg into stg else
Stg or sby CONVEYS stg; I c... information to sby
I CONVICT sby (of a crime)
Sby or stg convinces sby (of stg); I c... sby that
Food COOKS; I c... (food)
I CO-OPERATE (with sby) (in an enterprise, in doing stg); we c... (with one
another)
I COPE (with a problem, with a situation) P
I CORRESPOND (with sby), *ie* write letters (to him); the numbers 3.20 c...
(=refer) to a section of this book
Stg COSTS money, O2a; c... sby money, effort; *see* 9.6
Stg COUNTS, *ie* is important; I c... (up to 20); c... things or people; c... on sby;
c... on (your) seeing him; c... myself fortunate, D2a; c... sby as a friend, D5
Stg COVERS (=is on top of) stg or sby; sby c...s (=puts stg over) stg or sby;
I c... stg or sby with stg; this book is c...ed with dust
I CREDIT an account; c... (=believe) a story; c... sby with common sense,
with acting sensibly
I CRITICISE (sby or sby's work); c... sby for (doing) stg
I CROWN stg with stg else; c... sby King, D1
I CRY; cry out, O1a; c... (out) for help; c... with pain; c..., "
Stg or sby CURES a wound, an illness; c...s sby (of an illness, of bad habits)

Stg CUTS; stg or sby c...s stg (in(to)) pieces) (with stg else)

I DANCE (with sby); d... (for joy)
I DARE (Modal, 14.29). *Full verb*: I d... to go; d... sby to go
I DEAL cards; d... with sby or with a problem; P; d... (sby) a blow, C1; d...
cards to sby, C2a
We DEBATE (with one another); I d... (about or on) a subject (with sby)
Sby or stg DECEIVES sby; I d... myself (into thinking stg)
Sby or stg DECIDES (a matter); I d... (about a matter); d... on a matter, P; d...
in favour of, or against, (doing) stg; d... to go; that d...d me to go; d... that;
d... that...should, 12a; d... if, B13; d... wh, B14
I DECLARE stg, *eg* results, war, dutiable goods; d... that; d..., "; d... sby the
winner, D1b; d... sby bankrupt, D3
Strength DECLINES; I d... (an offer); d... to go
I DEFEND sby or a position (against attack, from danger)
Stg or sby DELAYS stg or sby; d... (your) going
Stg or sby DELIGHTS sby; I d... in doing stg
I DELIVER stg, *eg* a message (to sby); d... sby (from danger); a doctor d... a
baby; I d... a lecture
Sby or stg DEMANDS stg (of sby); I d... to go; d... that...should, B12a; d... if,
B13; d... wh, B14
I DENY an accusation (= say it is not true); d... saying or having said stg; d...
that...; d... myself or sby else stg (= not let myself or him have it)
That DEPENDS (on circumstances); sby or stg d... on sby or stg else (for stg);
d... on sby to do stg; it d...s (on) wh, B14. For passive, see 11.6, B5b
I DESCRIBE stg or sby (to sby); d... (to you) what I saw; d... stg or sby as, D5
I DESERVE a prize or punishment (for stg, for doing stg); d... to succeed; d...
to be punished, d... shooting: *see* 10.7
I DESIRE stg; d... to go; d... that...should, B12a
I DESPAIR (of success, of succeeding)
I DETEST sby or stg; d... going
People, animals, plants DIE (of disease); people, animals d... from injuries;
people d... for a cause
Things and people DIFFER (from one another) (in appearance etc.)
I DIRECT an operation, an organisation; d... sby (to a place); d... sby to go
I DISCOVER stg or sby; d... sby to be..., D4
I DISCUSS a subject (with sby)
I DISLIKE sby or stg; going; d... your going
I DISMISS sby (from a post); d... sby or stg as (being) unsuitable
I DISPENSE with stg, with sby('s services) P
I DISTINGUISH stg or sby; d... X from Y; d... between X and Y
I DIVIDE 6 by 2; d... 2 into 6; d... stg into parts; d... stg between or among
you; stg or sby d...s (= separates) X from Y

People or things DO stg, *ie* perform an action; I d... sby harm, a favour, C1, C2a and b. *For other examples, see 10.9*
I DOUBT a statement; I don't d... that... B11; I d... if *or* whether... B13
Stg or sby DRAWS (= comes) nearer, O1a; d... (a picture); d... stg, *eg* a chair, nearer, B1a; d... money (from or out of the bank); d... (up)on my resources
I DREAM (about stg or sby); d... that; I wouldn't d... of going

I ECONOMISE (on stg)
I ELECT sby stg, D1a
1 EMBARK; e... (up)on an enterprise
Stg or sby EMERGES (from, or out of, stg)
Stg or sby ENCOURAGES sby (to do stg)
I ENGAGE sby (to do stg); e... in an activity
I ENJOY stg; e... myself; e... going
I ENQUIRE about stg or sby; e... (of sby) if, B13; e... (of sby) wh... B14
I ENTER (a place); e... into an agreement, into negotiations, P
Stg ENTITLES sby to do stg
I ESCAPE (from one place) (to another); e... drowning
I EXCHANGE (X for Y)
I EXCLAIM, ", B11b
Sby or stg EXCUSES sby (for doing or having done stg); e... sby (from doing stg), *ie* say that he need not do it; e... your interruption, your interrupting
I EXEMPT sby (from stg); e... stg from tax
I EXPECT sby or stg; e... sby to go; e... that; e... so
I EXPERIMENT with stg P; e... on sby or on an animal P
I EXPLAIN (stg); e... stg to sby; e... (to sby) that... or wh...
I EXPRESS stg, *eg* a thought; e... myself well
I EXTEND stg; stg e...s for miles, O1a; I e... (= offer) a hand, a welcome, to sby

I FACE stg, *eg* a problem; a problem f...s sby; I f... sby with a problem; I can't f... going
Sby or stg FAILS; I won't f... you; I f... (in) an examination; f... to go
Sby or stg FALLS; f...s (down), f...s (over), O1a; f... a long way; f... ill
I FANCY stg; I don't f... going; f... that
I FAVOUR sby; f... going
I FEAR stg; f... that
—People or animals FEED (on stg); I f... sby (on stg)
I FEEL, A1 and 2; stg f...s strong (10.3, 31); f... stg; f... like going; f... for sby (= sympathise); f... for stg (= try to touch it); f... stg move or moving, B8 and 9; f... that
People or animals FIGHT; I f... (with or against) sby (for stg)
Stg FILLS, O2; I f... stg (with stg else)

I FIND sby or stg; f... sby going, B8; f... the door locked; f... (out) that, B11;
f... (out) if, B13; f... (out) wh, B14; f... sby, stg, C1; f... the house empty
Stg FINISHES; I f... (stg); f... doing stg
This FITS (me) *no passive*; f...s into a pattern
Stg FOLLOWS; I f... (sby or stg); it f...s (from stg) that, B11
I FORBID a course of action; f... sby to go
Stg or sby FORCES stg, *eg* a lock; f... sby to go; f... the door open, D2c
I FORGET (stg); f... to go or f... going, 10.7; f... that
I FORGIVE (sby); f... sby for (doing) stg; f... sby stg, C1
Stg or sby FREES stg or sby; f... sby from stg
Stg or sby FRIGHTENS sby (into doing stg); f...s sby away *or* off
I FURNISH a room; I f... (=supply) stg; f... sby with stg; f... a place with stg

I GAIN (stg) (by or from doing stg)
Crowds GATHER (together); I g... things or people (together); g... that
I GET up, down, in, out, etc., O1a; sby or stg g...s+*adj*, A2; g...s+*adv*, A3;
I g... stg, B1; g... stg up, etc.; g... stg+-*ed*, B10a; g... sby stg, C1, C2a and
b; g... stg+*adj*, D2b and c. *For other examples, see 10.9*
Stg GIVES (=collapses); I g... stg; g... sby stg, C1, C2a. *See also 10.9*
I GLANCE at sby or stg
Stg or sby GOES, O1; g... away, O1a; g... a long way, O1a I g... fishing
Stg or sby goes on (=continues); I g... on talking
I GRANT stg; g... sby stg, C1, C2a; g... that
Stg or sby GROWS (=becomes bigger); I g... up (=become adult); stg or sby
g...s+*adj*, A2; I g... stg (*eg* corn)
I GUESS (stg, *eg* an answer); g... that

I HAND sby stg, C1, C2a
Stg HANGS (on or from stg else); I h... stg (on or from stg...)
Stg HAPPENS (to sby). *See 10.1, E*
I HASTEN (to a place); h... to go
I HATE stg or sby; h... to go or going; h... sby to go or going
I HAVE stg; h... sby go, B8; h... sby laughing. B9; *see 10.7*; h... stg done,
B10b; h... stg ready, D2a and b
Wounds HEAL; h... a wound; h... sby (of his wounds)
I HEAR (with my ears); h... of or about stg or sby; h... stg or sby go or going,
(3.3); h... that
Stg or sby HELPS (sby or a process); I h... sby (with a task); h... (sby) (to)
carry stg; h... sby to food; h... myself; can't h... laughing
I HESITATE; h... to say
I HIDE; h... (from sby); h... stg (from sby)
Stg or sby HINDERS sby (from doing stg)
I HONOUR sby (for stg, for doing stg)

I HOPE (for stg); h... to do stg; h... that; h... so, h... not
Don't HURRY; H... (up), O1a; Don't h... me; h... sby up

I IMAGINE (stg); i... going; i... you *or* your going, B7; i... that; i... so
I IMPOSE (on sby) P; i... stg (on sby) P
I INCLUDE stg (in, or with, stg else)
A number INCREASES; I i... stg (to stg else)
I INDULGE my appetite; i... (=satisfy) sby; i... in a habit
I INFORM sby; i... sby of or about stg; i... sby that... or wh, C5a, C7a
I INQUIRE: See ENQUIRE
I INSIST (on going); i... that; i... that...should, B12a
I INSTRUCT sby (in a subject); i... sby how to do stg
I INSURE stg or sby (for money) (against accidents)
I INTEND to go or going; i... sby to go; i... that...should, B12a
Stg or sby INTERESTS sby (in stg)
Stg or sby INTERFERES (with sby or stg) P
I INTRODUCE sby or stg; i... sby to sby else
I INVEST money (in stg)
I INVITE sby (to a party); i... sby to come
I INVOLVE sby or stg (in stg else); this situation i...s (=will result in) (your) going

X and Y JOIN (each other); I j... a club; j... in an activity; j... stg to stg else
I JOKE about stg
I JUDGE sby or stg; j... by or from stg; j... that; j... sby to be..., D4
I JUMP, O1; j... up or down; j... (over) a wall; j... to conclusions

Eggs don't KEEP, O2; I k... quiet, A2; k... down, A3; k... stg, B1; k... stg up;
k... (on) going; k... sby waiting, B9; k... sby stg, C1, C2b; k... stg warm,
k... (=prevent) sby or stg from falling
I KNOW stg; k... of or about stg; k... sby do stg, see 3.2d; k... that; k... if,
B13; k... wh, B14; k... sby to be, D4; k... sby as, D5

Stg is LACKING; I l... stg *no passive*
Will this LAST? The storm l...ed (for) two days, O1a; This suit will l... me
(for) seven years
I LAUGH (at sby), P; l... about stg
A bird LAYS an egg; I l... stg somewhere B1a
Sby LEADS; sby or stg l...s sby (to a place); This road l...s to X
Sby or stg LEANS DOWN; l... on stg or sby (for support)
I LEARN (stg); l... to do stg; l... that; l... if or whether, B13; l... wh, B14
I LEAVE (a place); l... stg; l... sby stg, *eg* money, C1, C2a and b; l... sby a
widow; l... the door open

I LEND (stg): l... sby stg, C1, C2a
I LET a house; l... sby go
I LIE down, O1a (*see 9.8, 10.2, O1* and *10.3, A2*)
I LIE (=tell an untruth) (to sby) (about stg)
I LIKE sby or stg; l... to go or going; would l... to go; l... sby to go or going;
I don't l... you (or your) going, B7
I LIMIT stg (to stg else); l... myself to saying stg
I LISTEN (to sby or stg), P
I LIVE somewhere or sometime, O1a; l... a good life; l... on fish; l... by fishing
I LONG for stg or sby: l... to go; l... for stg to happen, for sby to go
I LOOK, A1, A2; l... (at stg or sby), P; l... (=search) (for stg or sby); l... after
(=care for) sby or stg, P; l... as if, E5
I LOVE sby or stg; l... to go or going; l... sby to go

Sby or stg MAKES stg; m...s sby or stg go; I m... sby stg, C1, C2b; I m... sby
stg, D1b; m... stg ready, D2b. *For other examples, see 10.9*
I MANAGE stg or sby; m... to go
I MARRY; m... sby (=take sby as wife or husband) (no passive); m... sby
(=perform the marriage ceremony) passive as in 11.6, B1
Sby or stg MEANS stg; I m... (=intend) to go; m... sby to go; This m...s
(=will result in) (your) going; I m... (=my meaning is) that
Stg MEASURES 2 metres, O2a; I m... stg, B1
I MENTION stg or sby (to sby); I m... (to sby) that or wh
You MIND! (=be careful); m... the step; m... the baby; Would you m...
(my) going? I don't m... (your going)
Stg or sby MISSES (=does not hit) (stg); I m... stg or sby (=regret not having
stg or regret sby's absence); m... (=not catch) a train; m... seeing stg
(=fail to see it)
I MISTAKE your meaning; m... sby or stg for sby or stg else
X and Y MIX; m... X and (or with) Y
Things MULTIPLY (=increase in number); I m... one number by another

I NAME a child; n... sby stg, D1a
I NEED (Modal, 14.27). Full verb: n... stg or sby; n... to go; n... sby to go;
this n...s mending, you n... looking after, B6b
I NEGLECT sby or stg (for sby or stg else)
I NOMINATE sby; m... sby stg, D1a
I NOTE stg; n... that; n... if, B13; n... wh, B14
I NOTICE stg; n... stg move or moving; n... that; n... if; n... wh

I OBEY (sby); o... (an order)
I OBJECT (to stg); o... to (your) going; o... that

I OBLIGE (=do a favour to) (sby); o... sby by doing stg; o... (=force) sby
to go
I OBSERVE stg or sby; o... that
I OFFEND sby; o... against a law
I OFFER stg; o... to go; o... sby stg, C1, C2a
I OMIT stg or sby; o... to go or o... going
Sby or stg OPERATES (on sby or stg, P); o...s a machine
I ORDER stg, *eg* a meal; o... sby to go; o... sby stg, C1, C2b
I OWE money (for stg); o... sby stg, C1, C2a
I OWN (=possess) stg; o... (=confess) a fault; o... up (to having done stg
-wrong)

I PAINT (a picture); p... sby a picture, C1, C2b
I PARDON sby (for doing stg); p... sby's faults
We must PART (=leave each other); p... with stg
Sby or stg PASSES; p... stg; I p... sby stg, C1, C2a
I PAY a bill; p... (sby) (for stg); p... for stg, P; p... (sby) (money), C1a, C2a
I PERMIT stg; p... sby to go
Stg (*eg* bad weather) PERSISTS; I p... (in doing stg)
I PERSUADE sby (to do stg); p... sby that, C5a
I PICK (and choose); p... flowers; p... stg up (from the ground)
I PITY sby (for stg)
I PLACE stg somewhere, B1a
I PLAN stg; p... to go
I PLAY; p... games; p... with or against sby; p... (sby) a record; p... (sby)
a game of tennis; p... sby at chess; p... music to sby; p... a game with sby
Sby or stg POINTS (at sby or stg, as if aiming P); p...s (to stg, *ie* in that
direction)
I POST a letter; p... sby a letter, C1, C2a
I POSTPONE stg, *eg* a meeting; p... going
I PRACTISE (an activity); p... diving
I PRAISE sby (for doing stg)
I PREFER sby or stg; p... to go or going; p... sby to go; p... that you go or
went, *as in* 2.16
I PREPARE stg; p... (stg or sby) for an event; p... to go
I PRESENT stg (to sby); p... sby with stg
Sby or stg PRESERVES stg (from danger)
Sby or stg PRESSES; p...es (against) stg or sby; I p... sby to do stg
I PRETEND (to go); p... that
Sby or stg PREVENTS stg; p...s sby (from) doing stg
I PROCLAIM stg; p... that; p... sby stg, D1b
I PROFIT by (doing) stg
I PROHIBIT stg; p... sby from doing stg

I PROMISE (stg); p... (sby) (to do stg); p... (sby) that; p... sby stg, C1, C2a
I PRONOUNCE stg; p... you man and wife, D1b ·
I PROPOSE a plan; p... to go; p... going; p... that...should, B12a
Stg or sby PROTECTS sby or stg (from sby or stg else)
Stg or sby PROVES a statement; p...s (to be) right; p... (to me) that
Stg or sby PROVIDES stg (for sby); p... sby with stg
I PUNISH sby (for stg, for doing stg)
I PUT stg somewhere, B1a; p... stg (eg a garment, a record) on

I QUALIFY (for stg); This q... sby for stg
People QUARREL; I q... (with sby) (about stg)
I QUESTION sby (about or on stg); q... stg (=express doubt about it)

Sby or stg RAISES stg
Sby or stg RANKS with sby or stg
I REACH a goal, an agreement; r... for stg (=try to r... it); stg r...s to (= as
far as) stg
Stg or sby REACTS (to a stimulus), P; I r... against stg unfavourable, P; stg
(eg a chemical) r...s (=has an effect) on sby or stg else
I READ (stg); r... about it; r... that; r... sby stg, C1, C2a
I REALISE stg; r... that
I REASON with sby P
I RECOGNISE sby or stg; r... sby as (being) stg, D5
I RECOMMEND stg or sby; r... sby to go; r... going; r... that...should, B12a
Stg or sby REDUCES stg (to stg lower)
I REFER to stg or sby P; r... sby to stg or sby P else
Stg REFLECTS light; I r... (=meditate) on stg; r... that
I REFUSE (stg or sby); sby or stg r...s (to go); I r... (to give) sby stg, C1, C2a
I REGARD sby or stg with suspicion; r... sby or stg as, D5
I REGRET (stg); r... to say; r... going or having gone; r... that; r... that...
(should) B12b
I RELATE stg (to stg else); r... (= report) stg; r... that
Stg or sby RELIEVES pain, tension; r...s sby (of stg, eg a burden, a responsi-
bility)
I RELY (up)on sby or stg; r... (up)on sby to do stg, B5b; see 11.6, B5b
Stg or sby REMAINS; A1, A2 and A3; That r...s to be seen; the fact r...s that
I REMARK on stg; r... (to sby) that; r..., "
I REMEMBER (an event or fact); r... a place or person; r... to go, r... going
(10.7); r... that
I REMIND sby (to do stg); stg or sby r...s sby (of stg); r...s sby that..., C5a
I RENDER an account; r... stg safe
I REPEAT stg, eg a statement (to sby); r... that
Stg or sby REPLACES stg or sby (by stg or sby else)

I REPLY (to sby); r... that; r..., "
I REPORT an event; r... sby (to sby else); r... on sby or stg P; r... (to sby) that; r... (to sby) wh
I REQUEST stg; r... sby to go; r... that...should B12a
Sby or stg RESCUES sby or stg (from sby or stg else, from *eg* drowning)
I RESENT stg; r... having to go; r... your saying stg
I RESERVE stg; r... sby stg, C1, C2b
I RESIGN (from a post), or r... (a post); r... myself to fate
Sby or stg RESISTS (sby or stg); I can't r... going
I RESPECT sby or stg; r... sby for (doing) stg
I RESPOND (to a question, to a stimulus, to treatment)
I REST; r... assured, A2
Stg RESULTS (in success)
I RETIRE (from work) (to somewhere else)
Sby or stg RETURNS (from X) (to Y); r...s stg (to sby), C2a
I REVENGE stg, *eg* an insult; r... myself on sby
I REWARD sby (for stg) (for doing stg)
Sby or stg RIDS a place or sby of stg; I r... myself of stg
Sby or stg RISES (up); r... from, or out of, a place
I RISK stg; r... going
I ROAR (with laughter, with pain)
I ROB sby (of stg); rob a bank
I RUN (a mile); r... for a mile; r... for an hour; r... a mile in four minutes, O1a

I SACRIFICE stg or sby (for stg or sby else)
Stg or sby will SATISFY sby; s... sby that..., C5a
Stg or sby SAVES sby or stg (from danger); s... sby stg, C1, C2b
I SAY stg (to sby); s... (to sby) that; s... (to sby), "; s... (to sby) that...should. B12a; s... (to sby) wh
I SCOLD sby (for doing stg)
I SCORN stg; s... sby (for doing stg)
I SEARCH (for stg); s... sby or stg
I SEE (stg or sby); s... stg or sby go or going; s... stg -ed, B10a; s... that; s... to it that; s... if; s... wh
Stg or sby SEEMS, A1, 2 and 3; *see 10.1, E*
Stg SELLS, O2; I s... (stg) (at a price, at the price asked); s... stg for a price, the price received; s... sby stg, C1, C2a
I SEND stg; s... sby stg, C1, C2a; s... stg or sby to a place, C2a
I SENTENCE sby (to a punishment) (for a crime)
Stg or sby SEPARATES X and Y; s...s X from Y
I SERVE (sby or stg); stg s... as stg else; I s... sby stg, C1, C2a
Stg SETS, O2; I s... stg; I s... stg somewhere, B1a
I SHARE (stg) (with sby, between or among you); s... in an enterprise

Stg or sby SHELTERS (sby or stg) (from a danger)
Stg or sby SHIELDS stg or sby (from stg or sby else)
A light SHINES, O2; I s... a light; s... (a light) on stg
I SHOOT (a gun) (at a target); s... sby
Stg SHOWS = is seen, O2; 1 s... stg; s... sby to the door; s... sby stg C1,
C1a, C2a; s... (sby) that... C5b; s... (sby) wh, C7b
Flowers SMELL; stg s...s good, A2; I s... stg; stg s...s of stg. *See 13.2c*
I SMILE (at sby or stg)
Sby or stg SOUNDS good, A2; I s... the alarm; That s... like stg or sby.
See 10.1, E5
I SPARE stg; s... sby's life; s.., sby stg, C1, C2b; s... (=not tell) sby details,
C1 only
I SPEAK (to sby) (about or of a subject); s..., = lecture (on a subject); s... a
language
I SPEND money (on stg)
Sby or stg STANDS (up), O1, O1a; I can't s... (=bear) stg or sby; I can't s... -*ing*
I STARE (at sby or stg); stg s...s you in the face (=is obvious)
Sby or stg STARTS, O2; s...s stg; s... to go or going; s... stg going, B9
I STATE stg; s... that; s..., "; s... if; s... wh
Sby or stg STAYS, A1; s... still (=does not move); s... at a place, on a surface,
in an area
I STEAL (stg) (from sby)
I STEER (a car, a ship, a course); s... towards a point
I STEP this way, O1a; s... on sby's toe, onto a surface, into an area
Stg or sby STICKS (on or to stg); I s... to sby (=remain close to him); I s... to
the point
Stg or sby STOPS, O2; s...s stg or sby; I s... talking; stg or sby s...s sby (from)
doing stg
Stg STRETCHES a long way, for miles, O1a; stg or sby s...., O2; s...s stg, B1
The clock STRIKES; workmen s...; I s... stg or sby (a blow); stg s...s me as
strange
I STRUGGLE (with or against stg or sby)
I SUBMIT (to stg or sby); s... stg or sby or myself to a test
I SUCCEED (in doing stg, in an enterprise)
I SUFFER (pain); s... from an illness
I SUGGEST a plan; s... (your) going; s... (=think) that; s... (=propose)
that...should, B12a; s... wh, B14
I SUPPLY stg (to sby); s... sby (with stg)
I SUPPOSE that, B11; s... so; s... sby to be... D4
I SURRENDER; s... stg or sby to sby else
A fence SURROUNDS stg; I s... stg (with stg else)
I SUSPECT sby (of a crime, of doing wrong)
I SWEAR (an oath); s... (at sby); s... to be loyal; s... that; s... sby to secrecy

I SYMPATHISE (with sby); s... with sby in his troubles

Sby or stg TAKES stg or sby (from, off, out of, to, onto, into, a place); t... stg away, off, etc.; it took (me) six weeks to get there; t... sby stg, C1, C2a; t... (=mistake) sby P for sby else
I TALK (a language); t... (to sby) (about or of a subject); t... = lecture (on a subject); t... about or of doing stg
Stg TASTES good, A2; t... of onion; I t... stg. *See 13.2c*
I TEACH (sby) (stg), C1, C1a, C2a; t... sby how to do stg, C7a
I TELEPHONE (sby) (a message), C1, C2a
I TELL the truth, the time; t... sby to go; t... sby stg, C1, C1a, C2a; t... sby that; t... if; t... sby wh
I TEMPT sby (to do stg)
Stg or sby TENDS to do stg
I THANK sby (for stg) (for doing stg); I'll t... you not to do that: *see 10.7*
I THINK; t... about or of stg or sby; t... that; t... so, t... not; t... that...should B12a; I can't t... wh; t... sby foolish, D3; t... it a pity, strange, D7a and b
I THREATEN sby; t... to do stg
I THROW (stg); t... sby stg, C1, C2a; t... stg at sby (to hit him); t... stg to sby (in his direction)
Stg or sby TIRES me; I t... of stg; t... sby
I TRADE (with sby) (in certain goods)
I TRAIN sby (to do stg)
I TRANSLATE stg (from one language) (into another)
I TRAP sby (into doing stg)
I TRAVEL (about) the world; t... (from X) (to Y)
I TREAT sby well, badly, like a child; t... a patient; t... sby as..., D5; t... sby as if he were... (2.37)
I TRICK sby (into doing stg)
Stg or sby TROUBLES sby; I t... sby (to do stg); sby about stg
I TRUST sby (to do stg); t... that
I TRY (=attempt); t... stg; t... sby (*ie* a criminal); t... to go; t... turning, 10.7
Stg or sby TURNS, O2; t... traitor, A1; t... into stg, A1; t... sour, A2; t... a handle, a corner, B1; t... stg into stg else; t... sby against sby else

I UNDERSTAND (stg or sby); u... that; u... if; u... wh
X and Y UNITE; stg or sby u...s X and Y; people u... (with one another)
I URGE patience; u... sby to go; u... that; u... that...should, B12a
Sby or stg USES stg (as stg else) (for a purpose)

I VOTE (for or against sby or stg); v... on a proposal; v... that... B12a; D1b

Sby or stg WAITS (for stg or sby)

I WAKE up, O1a; w... sby; w... sby up
I WALK; w... (for) six miles, w... for six hours; w... four miles in an hour, O1a
I WANT stg; w... to go; w... you to go; w... mending, B6b; w... sby working,
B9; w... the door locked, B10; w... my tea hot, D2a
I WARN sby (of or against danger); w... sby not to do stg; w... (sby) that
I WASH; These clothes w... well, O2; I w... stg or sby; w... stg clean, D2b
I WATCH; w... sby or stg (go or going: 3.3)
Stg or sby WEIGHS ten kilos; I w... a parcel
I WELCOME sby or stg; w... sby to or into one's house
I WHISPER; w... stg (to sby); w..., "
Sby or stg WIPES stg; I w... stg clean, D2b
I WISH stg; w... to go; w... you to go; w... that (2.16); w... myself dead, D2b
I WONDER; w... (= be surprised) that, B11; w... (= ask myself) if or wh
I WORRY (about stg or sby); w... sby (about stg)
I WRITE (stg); w... about stg; w... that; w... sby stg, C1, C2a

C Collocations with simple verbs
10.9
We *do* right or *make* trouble, *put* a question or *give* an answer. Note the
following commonly-used COLLOCATIONS:
CATCH
  a cold, or some other infection; CATCH a bus
COME to
  an agreement   a conclusion   a decision
DO
  business (with sby)   one's best   damage (to stg)   one's duty
  an experiment   (sby) a favour   good   one's hair   (sby or stg) harm
  (sby) an injury   (stg or sby) justice   (sby) a kindness   a lesson
  right   (sby) a service   a translation   the washing-up   wonders
  work, homework   wrong
EARN
  a living   money   a salary   a reputation   wages
FIND
  an answer (to a question)   a solution (to a problem)   time (for stg)
FOLLOW
  sby's example   a procedure   advice
GAIN
  an advantage (over sby)   a grip on stg   a hold on stg
GET AND KEEP WILL OCCUR FREQUENTLY IN THE FOLLOWING PATTERNS:
  GET the tickets   KEEP the change
  GET me a newspaper   KEEP me a seat

GET your books out KEEP your head down
GET ready KEEP warm
GET your room ready KEEP your room tidy

GIVE (sby)
  (some) advice an answer a blow a definition (of stg)
  a description (of stg) encouragement an excuse an explanation
  (some) help a kick a kiss permission (to do stg) a pinch
  a punch a push a reply support trouble a welcome

GIVE stg
  a brush a polish a rub a trial a wash a wipe

GO for
  a drive a run a swim a walk

GRANT (sby)
  admission an interview permission a request

HAVE
  an argument (with sby) a bath a bathe a dance $\left\{ \begin{array}{c} a \\ no \end{array} \right\}$ desire for stg

  a drink (of water) an effect (on sby or stg) a fight (with sby)

  a game an influence ($\left\{ \begin{array}{c} on \\ over \end{array} \right\}$ sby) a look (at stg) a rest a sleep

  a talk (with sby) a swim a wash

KEEP
  an eye on stg stg under control one's temper (see also GET)

LOSE
  the advantage control of stg one's temper

MAKE
  an accusation (against sby) an agreement (with sby) an attack on sby
  an attempt a bargain (with sby) a bed certain (of stg)
  a calculation a choice a comment a contribution (to stg)
  a copy (of stg) a correction a criticism a decision a difference
  a discovery an escape an excuse friends a fortune
  fun of stg or sby a good job of stg haste an inquiry (into stg)
  an improvement (on stg) an investigation (into stg) a journey
  love (to sby) a mark a mistake money a move a noise
  a note (of stg) an observation (sby) an offer peace progress
  a proposal a recommendation a reduction (in stg)
  a reference (to stg) a report on stg a request (to sby, for stg)
  a reservation room for sby sense of stg sure (of stg) a suggestion
  time for stg trouble (for sby) use of stg or sby war on people
  a will

OFFER (sby)
  an apology one's congratulations an explanation one's resignation
  a suggestion

PAY
    attention to stg or sby   a call on sby   a visit to sby
PUT
    emphasis on stg a question to sby   stg on record
REACH
    an agreement   a conclusion   a decision
SUBMIT
    an application   one's resignation
TAKE
    a breath   care of   hold of   an interest in   measurements of stg
    a note of   notice of   a photograph   pity on sby
    trouble over sby or stg

Notes:

i The pattern *give a push* is frequently used to refer to one performance of an action, *eg* PUSH.

ii The pattern *find a solution* enables the speaker to replace a verb, *eg* SOLVE, in a case like the following:

102 We cannot solve this problem in such a way that everyone will be satisfied.

102a We cannot find a solution $\begin{Bmatrix} \text{that will} \\ \text{to} \end{Bmatrix}$ satisfy everybody.

Chapter Eleven
The verb phrase (3): The passive

11.1
The passive often occurs in a sentence which could be converted into one containing an active transitive verb + object. Thus:
   1 George and I were placed in the same class
= 2 Someone placed George and me in the same class.
The subject in [1] thus becomes the object in [2]. However, a passive is often produced directly, without there being any suggestion of an active counterpart, as in
   3 People are killed on the roads every day
     or
   4 This book was first published in 1975.
We can only make [3] and [4] 'active' by imagining a subject, *eg*
   5 Cars kill people on the roads every day
     or
   6 Someone first published this book in 1975.

11.2
The subject of the corresponding active sentence can be represented in the passive sentence by means of a prepositional phrase beginning with *by*. Thus, *Shakespeare wrote* 'Hamlet' becomes
   7 'Hamlet' was written by Shakespeare.
This *by*-phrase is only required when the speaker or writer needs to mention the AGENT, *ie* who or what caused something to happen to someone or something else. It is not necessary to mention the agent in examples [1], [3] and [4] above.

11.3
-ed participles used as adjectives (3.35c) may sometimes be followed by prepositions other than *by*. Note the difference between

-ed as adjective	and	*-ed as part of a passive construction*
I am very annoyed with him.		I was annoyed by mosquitoes all night.
I am very interested in chess.		I was interested by what you told me.
I am very surprised at you.		I was surprised by a knock at the door.

Note that *very* cannot modify the *-ed* participle in the right-hand column.

11.4
Sometimes, it may be difficult to tell the difference between an *-ed* form

referring to a state and one referring to an event. For example, *John and Mary were married last year* may mean either (a) that they were not single last year, or (b) that their wedding took place last year. In that example, we can use GET, in spoken English at least, to form the passive: only meaning (b) is expressed by

8 John and Mary got married last year.

However, not every *-ed* participle is used after GET, which emphasises the RESULT of an action that is done to someone or something. Verbs that are so used include *broken, burnt, caught, drowned, engaged* (to be married), *found out, hurt, killed, stuck.*

11.5

In producing a sentence with a verb in the passive, we must take care that the whole NP which would form the object of the active verb is placed before the passive verb. Thus *He told everyone in the class* would become

9 Everyone in the class was told.

Notice the difference between

10 The man with a scar on his face was found yesterday,

which suggests that it was known, before he was found, that the scar was there, and

11 The man was found yesterday with a scar on his face,

which suggests that, when he was found, he had a scar that was not there before. In [10], *with a scar on his face* is a postmodifier (1.7) following the head in an NP; in [11], the same group of words is an adjunct phrase (1.47).

11.6

Let us now see which of the verb patterns in Chapter Ten can occur in the passive. A dash means that no corresponding passive sentence is likely to occur:

Type O
O1 --

O1a Normally, no passive. Exceptionally:

Someone has sat on my hat.   My hat has been sat on.
George hasn't slept in his bed.   His bed hasn't been slept in.

The distance has never been $\left\{ \begin{array}{l} \text{walked} \\ \text{run} \end{array} \right\}$ in under five minutes before.

Come to and *arrive at* may occur in the passive, but only in a figurative sense, *eg*

No conclusion was $\left\{ \begin{array}{l} \text{come to.} \\ \text{arrived at.} \end{array} \right\}$

Another example is:

I had a little room which got the morning sun, so that I could sit in my bath and be shone upon (E. M. Forster),

· but that might be regarded as an amusing deviation from the normal.
O2 and 3 —

Type A
A1, 2 and 3 —

Type B

B1   Almost all the verbs that fit into B1 can be put into the passive, *eg*

My finger. $\left\{ \begin{array}{l} \text{was} \\ \text{got} \end{array} \right\}$ badly burnt.

MARRY is only used in the passive as follows:

The Consul married John and Mary. (*ie* he performed the marriage ceremony)

John and Mary were married by the Consul.

$\left. \begin{array}{l} \text{John} \\ \text{Mary} \end{array} \right\}$ was married to $\left\{ \begin{array}{l} \text{Mary.} \\ \text{John.} \end{array} \right.$

B1a   All the verbs in this group can be put into the passive; *eg*
The car was put in the garage.
Which is the garage (that) my car was put in?

B1b   HAVE, meaning 'hold' or 'possess' (1.29) does not occur in the passive; but HAVE meaning something else may be found in the passive in an example like
A good time was had by all.
LACK (= not have), as *We lack support*, has no passive.

B2   Many prepositional verbs occur in the passive. See the alphabetical list in 10.8; *eg*

    All the expenditure has now been accounted for.
    Have these goods been paid for?
    He is a man who is always listened to.
Note the passive participle in the non-finite clause
    Looked at in this way, the affair is not so serious.

B3   The infinitive can freely be put into the passive, *eg*

I $\left\{ \begin{array}{l} \text{hope} \\ \text{want} \\ \text{would like} \end{array} \right\}$ to be asked.

B4   Most verbs in this group occur in the passive: see 10.4, B4. *eg*
    You are expected to come tomorrow.
Note *You are supposed to come tomorrow*, which has no active equivalent. The infinitive can be put into the passive, too, as in *I want you to be asked.*

B5a   Note this form of the passive:

We $\begin{Bmatrix} \text{asked} \\ \text{arranged} \\ \text{longed} \\ \text{waited} \end{Bmatrix}$ for that to be done.

  b   A passive is possible with *can* or *could*, as in
      He can be relied on to help us.

B6a   The *-ing* form can freely be put into the passive, *eg I appreciate being asked*. The whole pattern is sometimes put into the passive as in
      Re-heating $\begin{Bmatrix} \text{is suggested.} \\ \text{should be avoided.} \end{Bmatrix}$

B7   In formal style, we find examples like *Your telling him that is regretted.*

B8   The passive is used with all the verbs that fit into B8 except HAVE, NOTICE and WATCH; but it requires the infinitive with *to*:
      The car was seen to stop.
      We were made to empty all our suitcases.
      He has never been known to behave like that before.
      Exceptionally, when a monosyllabic verb follows *let*, we can say, for example, *The prisoners were let go*; but with a longer phrase we must replace LET by ALLOW or PERMIT in using the passive, thus:

$\begin{Bmatrix} \text{They did not let us} \\ \text{We were not} \begin{Bmatrix} \text{allowed} \\ \text{permitted} \end{Bmatrix} \text{to} \end{Bmatrix} \begin{Bmatrix} \text{go on board.} \\ \text{take any photographs.} \end{Bmatrix}$

B9   The passive can be used with CATCH, DISCOVER, FIND, HEAR, KEEP, LEAVE, OBSERVE, SEE, SET, as in
      We were kept waiting.
      The car was seen backing into a garage.
      He was found smoking.

B10a The passive occurs with FIND, KEEP and THINK, as in
      The door was found (to be) locked.

  b   The passive occurs in
      The door was seen to be locked.
      in which *to be* would usually be inserted.

B11   There are two passive constructions for this pattern:
      A It is believed that he is ill   *or*   B He is believed to be ill
         It is believed that he is coming   He is believed to be coming
         It is believed that he $\begin{Bmatrix} \text{has come} \\ \text{came} \end{Bmatrix}$ He is believed to have come.

      Construction A can be used with most of the verbs that fit into pattern B11. Construction B is frequently used with ASSUME, BELIEVE, CONSIDER, DECLARE, EXPECT (future reference), FEEL, KNOW, REPORT, SAY, SEE, SUPPOSE, THINK, UNDERSTAND.

  a —

  b —

B12a One passive construction:

   It is recommended that he should go.

  (*He was recommended to go* would be a passive equivalent of *Someone recommended him to go,* B4.) The passive occurs with all the verbs that fit into B12a, except DESIRE, DISAGREE, INSIST.

  b One passive construction:

   It is regretted that he should feel that way about it.

B13 It was not known $\left\{\begin{array}{l}\text{if} \\ \text{whether}\end{array}\right\}$ he would ask.

B14 A passive may occur in the following form:

   What happened to him was never explained.

  Explained replaceable by *asked, found out, forgotten, known, remembered, understood.*

Type C

C1 A passive construction can be formed with all verbs which fit into this pattern except CALL, COST, CUT, FIX, GET, MEAN, REACH, WISH:

   He was shown the way.

  a The passive is possible with all verbs in this group except GRANT and OWE, *eg*

   You were $\left\{\begin{array}{l}\text{asked} \\ \text{shown} \\ \text{told}\end{array}\right.$

  b One passive construction only:

   $\left\{\begin{array}{l}\text{George} \\ \text{The car}\end{array}\right\}$ was given a push.

C2a and b The passive can be used with all verbs in C1, C2a and b, except COST, REACH, WISH on the following model:

   A book was given to George.

   Nothing was said to me about it.

   Books were provided for George.

C3 Passive freely used:

   We were $\left\{\begin{array}{l}\text{informed} \\ \text{told}\end{array}\right\}$ about the fire.

   He was accused of the murder.

   They were congratulated on their success.

C4 Two passive constructions are possible:

   (1) Great care was taken of his books.

   (2) His books were taken great care of.

  (1) is more likely to occur in formal style than (2).

C5a and b One passive possibility:

We were $\left\{\begin{array}{l}\text{convinced}\\\text{shown}\\\text{warned}\end{array}\right\}$ (that) he could do it.

C6a and b One passive construction:

I was not $\left\{\begin{array}{l}\text{told}\\\text{asked}\end{array}\right\}$ $\left\{\begin{array}{l}\text{if}\\\text{whether}\end{array}\right\}$ anyone had telephoned.

C7a and b One passive construction:

I was $\left\{\begin{array}{l}\text{told}\\\text{asked}\end{array}\right\}$ when the accident had happened.

C8a A passive is possible with all verbs in this group except COMPLAIN and REMARK, on the following pattern:

It was reported to us that he had had an accident.

b Passive possible with EXPLAIN on the model

It was explained to us how the accident had happened.

Type D

D1a Two passive constructions possible for all verbs in this group, *eg*

He was elected.   He was elected captain.

b Only one passive possible:

He was made captain.

D2a, b and c Passive possible, except with HAVE, WISH, *eg*

The house was found (to   We were nearly driven mad.
be) empty.   Our rooms were got ready.
The walls were painted blue.   The glasses were wiped clean.
The door was broken open.

D3, 4, 5 and 6 Passive used with all verbs in these groups.

He is considered (to be) $\left\{\begin{array}{l}\text{a fool}\\\text{foolish}\end{array}\right\}$.

He is known to be $\left\{\begin{array}{l}\text{reliable}\\\text{a good worker}\end{array}\right\}$.

He is $\left\{\begin{array}{l}\text{acknowledged}\\\text{regarded}\\\text{looked (up)on}\end{array}\right\}$ as $\left\{\begin{array}{l}\text{a genius}\\\text{brilliant}\end{array}\right\}$.

He was taken for an American.

D7a and b Passive used with CONSIDER and THINK, *eg*

It was $\left\{\begin{array}{l}\text{considered}\\\text{thought}\end{array}\right\}$ $\left\{\begin{array}{l}\text{a pity}\\\text{strange}\\\text{foolish}\end{array}\right\}$ etc.

D8 Passive can be used, *eg*

It is left to $\left\{\begin{array}{l}\text{you}\\\text{your discretion}\end{array}\right\}$ to decide.

Chapter Twelve
The verb phrase (4): Phrasal verbs

12.1

The present chapter gives examples of the four types of phrasal verbs summarised in 1.42. It will not include expressions like *Come in. Take off your coat. Keep away from the fire*, whose meaning and use can be assumed from a study of Chapter 8. Nor will it include prepositional verbs, *eg belong to, listen to, look for*, listed in 10.8. In the lists below, *inf* indicates that the phrasal verb concerned is typical of informal style, though generally speaking any phrasal verb, *eg break down*, is more likely to occur in informal style than a comparable verb, *eg collapse,* or *analyse*, which would be more formal. Note, from the examples given, the kind of context in which the phrasal verbs occur.

Type 1

VERB + PREPOSITION + NP: prepositions are unstressed, unless otherwise indicated (as in *a'cross*), passive frequently used where an example of it is given.

12.2

BE ABOUT (IT) = *be doing it*: Please get me some stamps, and post these letters while you're about it.

BREAK INTO = *enter (by force or for robbery)*: Thieves broke into our house last night. The house was broken into.

CLOSE WITH, (i) = *approach so as to hold*: Two policemen closed with the hijacker and held him by the arms; (ii) = *conclude a business deal*: I've sold my house. I closed with a buyer yesterday.

COME A'CROSS = (i) *find*, or (ii) *meet, by chance*: (i) If you should come across my slippers, put them in the cupboard, will you? (ii) I came across a very strange old man in the village today.

DO WITH'OUT = *manage otherwise*: If there's no bread, we must do without it, that's all.

GET AT, *inf* = (i) *mean*, (ii) *criticise*: (i) What exactly are you getting at? (ii) Are you getting at me? Am I being got at?

GET 'OVER, *inf* = *recover from*: You've only got a slight cold. You'll get over it in a day or two.

GO FOR, *inf* = *attack*: Your dog suddenly went for me!

GO 'INTO, *inf* = *investigate*: The auditors have gone into our accounts and have found a few serious mistakes. These must be gone into immediately.

JUMP AT, *inf* = *accept immediately*: It's an offer that you won't get again, so I should jump at it if I were you.

LOOK 'INTO = *investigate*: I'm sorry you were not satisfied with our service, madam. I will look into your complaint at once. It will be looked into.

MAKE FOR = *go towards*: The ship was making straight for the rocks.

RUN INTO, *inf* = *meet (an acquaintance) accidentally*: I ran into George Lamb when I was in town this morning.

SEE ABOUT, *inf* = *give some thought or attention to*: I haven't done anything about your complaint yet, but I'll see about it tomorrow.

SEE TO, *inf* = *put right*: This lock wasn't working this morning. Has anyone seen to it? Has it been seen to?

STAND BY (*by* stressed) = *support*: I'm your friend. I'll always stand by you.

STAND FOR = *represent*: The sign + stands for 'plus'.

TAKE 'AFTER, *inf* = *resemble*: George takes after his father.

TAKE TO = *come to like*: The new headmaster took to George immediately.

TURN ON, *inf* = *become aggressive towards*: What's the matter with Martha? She suddenly turned on me and told me to get out.

Type 2
VERB + ADVERB PARTICLE; particle always stressed; no passive

12.3
ANSWER BACK = *argue after receiving an order or rebuke*: Do what I tell you and don't answer back.

BACK DOWN, *inf* = *become less aggressive*: Bullies often back down when you stand up to them. (see 12.5)

BACK OUT, *inf* = *withdraw*, as in *back out of*, 12.5.

BEAR UP, *inf* = *not give in to fatigue, sorrow, etc*: In spite of her $\begin{Bmatrix} \text{tiredness} \\ \text{grief} \end{Bmatrix}$, she bore up bravely throughout the ceremony.

BREAK DOWN, (i) = *collapse*: She broke down when they told her the sad news; (ii) = *come to a premature end*: The negotiations have broken down.

BREAK IN, *inf* = *interrupt (a discussion)*: I must break in at this point and remind you that coffee is being served in the next room.

BREAK OFF = *stop (eg a meeting, a speech)*: I suggest we break off now and meet again at three o'clock.

BREAK OUT = *start*: An epidemic of influenza has broken out.

BREAK UP = *come to the end, eg of a meeting*: School has broken up for the summer holidays. The meeting broke up in disorder.

CARRY ON = *continue*: Don't stop. Carry on (working).

CATCH ON, *inf* = *understand*: I didn't understand anything at first, but now I'm beginning to catch on.

CATCH UP = *reduce the distance between oneself and those in front*: George is running fourth in the race, but he's beginning to catch up (with the leaders).

CLEAR OUT, *very inf* = *go away*: I see I'm in your way. I'll clear out and leave you alone.

CLEAR UP = *improve*: The clouds are drifting away and the weather is clearing up.

COME ABOUT = *happen*: What happened? How did this all come about?

COME TO = *regain consciousness*: She fainted, and it was half an hour before she came to again.

DO WITHOUT: see 12.2

DRAW BACK = *step back*: Seeing the snake, he drew back in horror.

DRAW UP = *approach and stop*: A car drew up beside me and a man with a strange accent asked me the way.

DROP IN, *inf* = *call on sby*: Why don't you drop in and see me some time?

DROP OUT = *withdraw*: John has dropped out (of the race). See 12.5.

FALL BACK = *retreat*: The defeated army fell back (on its last lines of defence).

FALL BEHIND, *opposite of catch up, above*: George was catching up, but he's now falling behind again.

FALL IN = *get into ranks, on parade*: At the sound of the bugle, the troops fell in and waited for the next word of command.

FALL OFF = *decrease*: Attendance at classes has fallen off considerably since the bad weather started.

FALL OUT, (i) *opposite of fall in, above*: The troops fell out and walked slowly to their tents; (ii) = *quarrel*: I hear that George and Mary have fallen out (with each other).

FALL THROUGH, *inf* = *come to nothing*: I'm afraid our plans have fallen through. We'll have to think again.

FIND OUT, *inf* = *discover the truth*. If you've told a lie someone is bound to find out sooner or later.

GET ON, (i) = *make progress*: Good. You're getting on. Your work is much better; (ii) = *agree (with each other)*: Do you and Mary get on?

GIVE IN = *stop, acknowledging weakness*: You're not beaten yet. Don't give in (to your opponent) so easily.

GIVE OUT, *inf* = *announce*: The enemy have given out that they want a truce.

GIVE UP = *stop, acknowledging oneself beaten*: You're too strong for me, *or* I can't solve the problem. I give up.

GO OFF = *explode*: The bomb went off with a deafening crash.

GO ROUND = *be sufficient for everybody*: Are there enough books to go round or shall I get some more?

HANG $\left\{ \begin{matrix} \text{ABOUT, } inf \\ = \text{AROUND, } inf \end{matrix} \right\}$ = *wait, doing nothing*: I can't wait any longer. I've

been hanging $\left\{ \begin{matrix} \text{about} \\ = \text{around} \end{matrix} \right\}$ too long already.

HOLD OFF = *delay making an approach*: The storm has held off so far. Let's hope it will move away.

HOLD ON = *maintain one's position*: Our troops held on desperately, refusing to yield an inch.

HOLD ON, *inf* = *wait*: George has gone out of the room for a moment. Hold on, I'll call him.

HOLD OUT = *not give in*: Don't give in yet. You can hold out a little longer.

KEEP UP = *maintain one's place*: George has joined the leaders, and is keeping up (with them) well.

KNOCK OFF, *inf* = *stop work*: I'm tired. Let's knock off and have a rest.

LEAVE OFF, *inf* = *stop*: Can't you leave off? You're annoying me.

LIVE IN = *sleep in the place where one works*: At some universities, most of the students live in. (*ie* have a bedroom on the university premises.)

LOOK OUT!, *inf* = *pay attention, be careful*: Look out! There's a heavy truck coming very fast behind us.

LOOK UP, *inf* = *appear to be improving*: The situation is getting better. Things are looking up.

MAKE OUT, *inf*, (i) = *manage*: I can look after myself, thank you. I'll make out somehow; (ii) = *pretend*: That man isn't nearly as ill as he makes out.

MAKE UP = *use cosmetics, powder or paint on one's face*: Actors usually make up before they go on to the stage.

PULL THROUGH, *inf* = *recover*: Don't worry about your operation. You'll pull through all right.

PULL UP = *come to a stop*: The car in front pulled up suddenly at the traffic lights and we ran into the back of it.

RING OFF, *inf.* = *end a telephone conversation*: I must ring off now. Someone else is waiting to use the 'phone.

RING UP, *inf* = *telephone*: George rang up to say he'd be late.

SET IN = *start*: We start our central heating as soon as the cold weather sets in.

SETTLE UP = *pay one's bill*: I owe you some money. I'd like to settle up before I forget.

SHUT UP, *inf* and rather vulgar = *be quiet*: Shut up and leave me alone.

STAND BY = *wait*: Stand by for further orders!

TAKE OFF = *begin to fly*: Your 'plane takes off at 1800 hours.

TURN OUT, (i) = *assemble, usually in the open air*: The whole town turned out to welcome the winning team; (ii) *inf* = *happen*: All went well. Everything turned out perfectly.

TURN UP, *inf* = *come, usually to a meeting*: The meeting was postponed, as only half a dozen people turned up.

WIND UP, *inf* = *end (a speech)*: The speaker wound up by making us all laugh.

Type 3

VERB + OBJECT + PARTICIPLE *or* VERB + PARTICLE + OBJECT: particle stressed when it follows the object; passive freely used, as in the first three examples. All the phrasal verbs in this section are freely used in the two patterns *put your coat on, put on your coat*, except those marked by an asterisk (*); in these cases note the examples given. Remember that when the object is a personal pronoun it must come between the verb and the particle: *back me up*.

12.4

ANSWER BACK,* *as in 12.3*: Don't answer your parents back. Parents don't like being answered back.

BACK UP = *support*: Always back up your friends. They like being backed up.

BEAR OUT = *confirm*. The results of the experiment bear out your theory. It has been borne out by statistics.

BREAK DOWN, (i) = *overcome*: Resistance was finally broken down; (ii) = *analyse*: Can you break down these figures (*ie* a financial statement) and let me have the details?

BREAK UP = *cause to end*: I don't want to break up the party, but I'm afraid I must go.

BRING ABOUT = *cause to happen*: It was Jane who brought about a reconciliation between George and Mary.

BRING ROUND = *persuade*: We finally brought them round to our point of view.

BRING TO* = *cause to come to*: see *come to*, 12.3.

BRING UP = *educate*: James was brought up by his two old aunts.

CALL OFF = *cancel*: The meeting has been called off as neither side is prepared to negotiate.

CALL UP = *mobilise*: The Government is calling up men for the army.

CARRY ON = *continue*: Let us carry on the good work.

CARRY OUT = *fulfil*: Let us carry out our original plan.

CATCH UP, *as in 12.3*: George is catching the leaders up.

CLEAR OUT, *inf* = *empty, so as to clean*: These cupboards are full of rubbish We must clear them out.

CLEAR UP = *put in order*: Your room is very untidy. You must clear it up.

CUT OFF, (i) = *stop (supplies)*: They will cut the electricity off if you don't pay the bill; (ii) = *separate; or prevent progress*: The tanks advanced rapidly, cutting us off (from our base).

DO OVER, *inf* = *wash, paint, etc., again*: I'll re-paint the walls, and do over the woodwork while I'm about it.

DO UP, *inf* = *repair, redecorate*: Your car looks very smart. Has it been done up?

DRAW UP = *compile*: Would you like to draw up a list of people that I could invite to meet you?

FIND OUT, (i) = *discover*: We must find out the truth; (ii) *inf* = *discover someone to be at fault*: If you've told a lie, someone will soon find you out.

GET OFF,* *inf* = *send away*: Please get that telegram off at once.

GET OVER,* *inf* = *finish*: Can we get this meeting over quickly? I have to leave early. *Cp get over* in 12.2

GET UP, *inf* = *organise*: We're getting up a dance. Can you come?

GIVE AWAY, (i) = *make known*: That's a secret. Don't give it away; (ii) *betray*: Don't tell anyone I wrote that article. Don't give me away.

GIVE UP, (i) = *surrender*: I want your gun. Give it up; (ii) = *stop*: Why don't you give up smoking?

HOLD UP = *stop, delay*: Police held up the traffic while they searched for the escaped prisoners.

KNOCK OUT, (i) = *eliminate from a contest*: Our local football team were knocked out in the semi-final; (ii) = *make unconscious*: The ceiling fell on me and knocked me out.

KEEP UNDER* = *suppress*: A gentleman learns to keep his feelings under.

KNOCK UP = *knock at a door to wake sby up*: Knock me up at six.

LAY IN = *store*: People in cold climates lay in supplies (of food and fuel) for the winter.

LAY OUT, (i) = *spread in an orderly way*: A printed page is easy to read if you lay it out clearly; (ii) *inf* = *knock down, perhaps unconscious*: Bob, who knew how to box, laid out his attacker with a quick blow to the chin.

LAY UP = *take out of service*: Ships are laid up, from time to time, for repairs. People are laid up when they are ill.

LEAVE OUT, *inf* = *omit*: Have you got everyone down (on your list), or have you left anyone out?

LET DOWN, *inf* = *opposite of back up*: You promised to stand by me. You won't let me down, will you?

LET OFF, (i) = *not punish*: I'll let you off this time, but I'll punish you if you do it again; (ii) = *cause to explode*: Two boys let a firework off under my chair; (iii)* = *allow to escape*. The engine let off steam with a loud hiss.

LOOK UP = *look in a dictionary, catalogue, etc, for*: Look that word up (in the dictionary).

MAKE OUT, *inf* = *understand*: I can't make out what you've written. You are a strange man. I can't make you out at all.

MAKE ONESELF OUT TO BE* = *pretend*: An impostor is a person who makes himself out to be someone more important than he is.

MAKE UP, (i) *inf* = *invent*: Is that story true, or did you make it up? (ii) = *end a quarrel*: We've settled our little quarrel. We've made it up, I'm glad to say.

PAY BACK, *inf*, (i) = *re-pay a debt*: I owe you some money. Let me pay you back now; (ii) *have revenge*: He has insulted me. I'll pay him back.

PULL UP, *inf* = *stop*. If you drive too fast, the police will pull you up.

PUT ACROSS,* *inf* = *communicate*: A good speaker knows how to put his message across (to his audience).

PUT OFF, *inf* = *postpone*: Don't put off till tomorrow what you can do today.

RING UP, *inf* = *telephone*: Ring up my wife and say I'll be late.

RUB UP, *inf* = *restore to a former state*. You must rub up your grammar. It's not as good as it was.

RUN DOWN, *inf* = *criticise adversely*: If you run down everyone you disagree with, everyone will run *you* down.

RUN IN = *use a new engine carefully*: Don't drive this car too fast yet. It hasn't been run in properly.

RUN OVER, (i) = *knock down (by traffic)*: Hundreds of pedestrians are run over in the streets every year; (ii) *run over* or *run through, inf = read quickly, rehearse*: Can we run $\left\{ \begin{array}{l} \text{over} \\ \text{through} \end{array} \right\}$ the last scene (of the play) again and see if we can get it perfect?

RUN UP *(a bill), inf = cause to get big(ger)*: Don't run up big bills if you haven't the money to pay them.

SEE OFF, *inf = be with sby to say goodbye*: He was all alone when he left. No one was there to see him off.

STEP UP = *increase*: Production is slowing down. We must step it up.

TAKE IN = *deceive*: His story took everybody in. They all believed it, though he had made it all up.

TAKE OFF, (i) = *deduct*: I'll take 10 pence off (the price); (ii) = *give oneself a holiday*: I'll take Friday afternoon off; (iii) = *imitate somebody*: George took off the headmaster perfectly.

TAKE ON = *undertake*: If you haven't time to do a job properly, it's better not to take it on at all.

TAKE OVER = *take responsibility for*: If you think you can do my job better than I can, you are welcome to take it over.

TAKE UP (i) = *occupy*: This work takes up too much time; (ii) = *start (an occupation or hobby)*: You need exercise. Why don't you take up tennis?

THROW UP = *abandon (an occupation)*: Morgan began studying medicine, but threw it up after seeing his first operation.

TRY ON, (i) = *see if clothes fit*: I think this coat is your size, sir. Would you like to try it on? (ii) *inf = attempt to deceive*: I know exactly what your plan is. Don't try it on.

TRY OUT = *test*: Before you buy any sort of machine, it's best to try it out first.

TURN DOWN, *inf = refuse*: I applied for the job but my application was turned down. They said I was too young.

TURN OUT = *empty*: The Customs made us turn out every one of our suitcases.

WIND UP = *bring to an end*: The Company has gone bankrupt and will now be wound up.

Type 4

VERB + PARTICLE + PREPOSITION + NP: particle stressed.

12.5

BACK OUT OF, *inf* = *withdraw from*: You've signed an agreement and you can't back out of it now.

BE FED UP WITH, *inf* = *have had enough of*: I'm fed up with your nonsense. Please stop it.

BE UP TO, *inf* = *be doing something wrong*: What are those boys doing? Are they up to mischief? *(Cp* 8.8).

BREAK IN ON, *inf* = *interrupt*: I'm sorry, did I break in on a private conversation?

CATCH UP WITH, *as in 12.3*: He's catching up with the leaders.

CUT DOWN ON, *inf* = *reduce consumption of*: You're smoking too much. You must cut down on cigarettes.

DROP IN ON, *inf* = *visit, see drop in, 12.3*: Drop in on me some time.

DROP OUT OF, *inf* = *withdraw from*: John has hurt his leg and has had to drop out of the race.

FACE UP TO, *inf* = *be realistic*: You're too old. Why don't you face up to it?

FALL BACK ON = *retreat to, see fall back, 12.3*: The army fell back on the river. Take some travellers cheques, so you have have something to fall back on.

FALL IN WITH, *inf* = *agree to*: You can rely on me. I'll fall in with anything you suggest.

GET AWAY WITH, *inf* = *escape the penalty of*: Someone will find you out *(see 12.4)*. You won't be able to get away with it.

GET ON WITH, *inf,* (i) = *make progress with*: John is getting on with his mathematics nicely; (ii) = *agree with (12.3)*: They get on with each other very well.

GIVE IN TO = *surrender to, see 12.3*: Don't give in to him so easily.

GO BACK ON, *inf* = *break a promise*: You promised to let me have that. You can't go back on your word now.

GO IN FOR, *inf* = *start an occupation or subject*: You need something to do. Why don't you go in for teaching English?

GO THROUGH WITH, *inf* = *finish something begun*: We've started this job. I know it's difficult, but we ought to go through with it now.

KEEP UP WITH = *see 12.3*: He's keeping up with them well.

LOOK OUT FOR, *inf* = *watch carefully for, see 12.3*: Look out for that truck.

MAKE UP FOR = *compensate for*: Hurry. We must make up for lost time.

PUT UP WITH, *inf* = *bear, tolerate*: I don't like this noise, but I suppose we must put up with it.

RUN OUT OF, *inf* = *have no more supplies of*: We have run out of bread. Will you buy a couple of loaves while you're out?

RUN UP AGAINST, *inf = meet (an obstacle)*: You'll find that job difficult. You'll run up against some very tricky problems.

STAND UP FOR = *support*: Will no one stand up for me, or will you all let me down?

STAND UP TO = *not refuse to fight*: Don't let him bully you. Stand up to him and he'll soon back down (*see 12.3*).

Nouns formed from phrasal verbs
12.6

a There are a number of nouns, *eg outcome, output, input*, formed from the construction *come out, put something* $\left\{ \begin{array}{c} out \\ in \end{array} \right\}$

b Nouns formed from phrasal verbs include:

(Type 2)	breakdown	break-up	outbreak
	drawback	dropout	turnout
(Type 3)	breakdown	break-up	upbringing
	call-up	clear-out	hold-up
	knockout	takeover	try-out

Chapter Thirteen
The verb phrase (5): Tense and aspect

A Present and past tense, progressive and perfective aspect
13.1
There are two main tenses in English – present and past. Each tense can have a simple form; and each can be combined with either progressive aspect or with perfective aspect, or with both, thus: 正在進行中

	PRESENT 動作已完成	PAST
a simple:	I play	I played
b progressive:	I am playing	I was playing
c perfect:	I have played	I had played
d perfect-progressive:	I have been playing	I had been playing

Those are the forms for the active voice (1.25). The forms for the passive are:

a	I am asked	I was asked
b	I am being asked	I was being asked
c	I have been asked	I had been asked

d (The perfect-progressive is rarely used in the passive (1.25).)
Ways of referring to the future are dealt with in 13.25–36.

Stative verbs 不能在 progressive aspect 內
13.2
Stative verbs are normally found only in the non-progressive forms. Stative verbs include

a BE and HAVE, as in
   1 Go away. We are busy. We have a lot of work to do.
   But BE meaning 'act (in a certain way)', and HAVE meaning something other than 'possess', can be used in the progressive, eg:
   2 Wait for me. You are being impatient. (=acting impatiently) I am still having my breakfast.

b verbs which contain the idea of being or having, eg

APPLY TO	meaning 'be true of' or 'have reference to'
BELONG TO	meaning 'be the property of'
COMPARE	meaning 'be like' or 'be as good as'
CONCERN	meaning 'be of importance to'
CONTAIN	meaning 'have' or 'hold'
COST	meaning 'be equal in value to'
DEPEND ON	meaning 'be dependent on'
DESERVE	meaning 'be worthy of'

DIFFER FROM	meaning 'be different from'
EXIST	meaning 'be'
HOLD	meaning 'have'
INTEREST	meaning 'be interesting for'
MATTER	meaning 'be of importance'
MEASURE	meaning 'be of a certain length etc.
OWN	meaning 'have'
POSSESS	meaning 'have'
RESEMBLE	meaning 'be like'
STAND FOR	meaning 'be a substitute for'
WEIGH	meaning 'be of a certain weight'

Examples:
3 This rule applies to everyone.
4 This camera belongs to me.
5 My roses do not compare with yours.
6 This matter concerns you, I think.
7 How much does this book cost?
8 Whether the meeting will be held or not depends on you.
9 I hope you win. You certainly deserve to.
10 My answer differs from yours in every detail.
11 Mammoths do not exist in the modern world.
12 How many people does this hall hold?
13 Archaeology interests me very much.
14 It doesn't matter to me whether you like it or not.
15 This room measures five metres by four.
16 Many people in this country own the houses they live in.
17 I owe such qualities as I possess to my parents.
18 George resembles his father in the way he walks.
19 The sign + stands for 'plus'.
20 I weigh sixty-five kilos. How much do you (weigh)?

Some of the verbs in examples [3–20] can also refer to activity, in which case they can freely be used in the progressive, eg
21 I am applying (=making application) to you for assistance.
22 I am applying this ointment to the wound to ease the pain.
23 In this book, the author is comparing X with Y.
24 We are depending (=relying) on you to help us.
25 Hold your arm out – I'm just measuring your sleeve.
26 You're not holding your arm out straight.
27 In the disaster area, people are existing (=keeping themselves alive) on what scraps of food they can find.

c verbs referring to an involuntary reaction of the senses:
feel hear see smell taste 五官之意
HEAR and SEE refer to involuntary reactions which correspond to the

deliberate acts of listening and looking. FEEL, SMELL and TASTE can refer to both the involuntary reaction and to the voluntary, deliberate act. Thus:

VOLUNTARY	INVOLUNTARY
I'm listening to you	I hear you
I'm looking at you	I see you
I'm feeling this cushion	I feel a pin in it somewhere
I'm smelling this flower	I smell gas. It smells awful
I'm tasting this soup	I taste pepper in it. It tastes hot.

CAN often occurs before the five verbs in the right-hand column, *eg I can hear, see, feel, smell, taste something.* FEEL can occur freely in the simple tense or in the progressive when it refers to one's own physical condition, as in

$$28 \quad I \begin{Bmatrix} \text{don't feel} \\ \text{'m not feeling} \end{Bmatrix} \text{very} \begin{Bmatrix} \text{hungry} \\ \text{tired} \\ \text{well} \end{Bmatrix}.$$

d verbs referring to mental or emotional states:

assume	fear	know	regret
believe	feel (=think)	like	remember
care	find (=consider)	love	suggest
consider	forget	mean	suppose
detest	hate	mind	think
envy	hope	notice	understand
expect	imagine	prefer	want, wish

Notice the difference between the following pairs:

29a We consider (=believe) him to be very loyal.

b We are considering (=studying) your application.

30a I expect (=suppose) you're rather tired.

b I am expecting (=waiting for) a visitor.

31a I feel (=think) you're right.

b I'm feeling very hungry.

32a Does anyone mind (=object) if I open the window?

b Is anyone minding (=looking after) the baby while you're out?

33a I think (=believe) he's crazy.

b Be quiet. I'm thinking (=giving thought to a problem).

13.3

Note that stative verbs do not *normally* occur in the progressive. But it is possible for any of them to be used in the progressive provided the speaker is emphasising the idea of an uncompleted involuntary act, or incomplete physical or mental state, as in

34 Something is wrong with my eyes. I'm seeing double.

35 I'm forgetting (=beginning to forget) my French.

36 Now we're understanding (=beginning to understand) this a little better.

13.4

All the examples in 13.2 and 3 are in the present tense. The same verbs could equally well be used in the past, or in the present and past perfect, *eg This watch belonged to my father. This farm has always belonged to our family.*

Action verbs
13.5

Action verbs can freely occur in the progressive as well as in the non-progressive forms. They include verbs referring to

a ACTIVITY HAVING DURATION, *eg* WRITE (a letter to someone), READ, WORK, PLAY, WALK, RUN, etc.:

37 Please be quiet. I'm writing an important letter.

There the progressive refers to writing that is in progress.

b A CHANGE OF STATE OR POSITION. A verb in this group might be one of the copulas (10.3) referring to a change of state, *eg* GET, BECOME, GROW, TURN, as in

38 We are all $\left\{\begin{array}{l}\text{becoming}\\\text{growing}\end{array}\right\}$ older;

or it might be a verb like ARRIVE, DROWN, DIE. Note that

39 They are $\left\{\begin{array}{l}\text{arriving}\\\text{drowning}\\\text{dying}\end{array}\right\}$

means 'They are beginning to arrive, etc.': it does not necessarily imply that the arriving, drowning, dying are accomplished.

c A MOMENTARY ACT, *eg* WRITE (the letter *e*), OPEN or CLOSE (a book or a door), PUT (something on the table), HIT, JUMP, BARK, and so on. Note that *I am opening the door* would only make sense if it were a commentary made during very slow motion, or if the speaker were opening (and shutting) the door repeatedly (or if he were referring to the future, as in 13.34); and note that *I am jumping*, when it refers to the present, means 'I am giving a series of jumps'. The idea of a series of momentary acts is conveyed in

40 Hurry up. The caretaker is closing all the doors.

Progressive aspect
13.6

The progressive therefore conveys the idea of ACTIVITY WHICH HAS BEGUN BUT IS NOT COMPLETED. This incomplete activity can be continuous, as in [37], [38] and [39], or it may consist of an uncompleted series of acts, as in [40]. Whether, in actual fact, the activity or series is completed or not, is irrelevant: WHAT IS IMPORTANT IS THAT, IN USING THE PROGRESSIVE, THE SPEAKER IS CONCERNED WITH THE UNCOMPLETED PART OF IT, OR THE TEMPORARY DURATION OF IT.

Simple present
13.7
The simple present is used with stative verbs, and with action verbs if the special emphasis described in 13.6 is not intended, when the speaker is referring to the following aspects of time:

a ALL OR ANY TIME not separated from the present:
    41 Paint contains a certain amount of lead.
    42 The Rhine flows between Germany and France;
b THE PRESENT PERIOD as distinct from the past. In this case, the speaker may be thinking either of an activity that continues throughout the period, as in [43], or of a whole series of acts performed throughout the period, as in [44]:
    43 I live in the country.
    44 We all speak English at home;
c THE PRESENT MOMENT, as in [45]:
    45 This tape-recorder is easy to work. Watch what I do. I switch it on, press this button and it starts.
    Switch, press and *starts* in [45] refer to momentary acts (13.5c) considered as completed at the moment of speaking. In [45], they are examples of a MOMENTARY PRESENT, whereas in
    46 I (always) switch off all the lights before I go to bed,
    switch and *go*, like *speak* in [44], are examples of the HABITUAL PRESENT. The habitual present is often reinforced by an adverb of frequency, *eg always*, though such adverbs can also be used with the progressive, as we shall see below (13.8);
d THE PRESENT MOMENT, as in [47–50]:
    47 I declare the meeting open. (formal remark by the Chairman)
    48 I pronounce you man and wife. (at a wedding ceremony)
    49 We gladly accept your offer. (declaration of acceptance)
    50 I wish you all a very happy New Year.
    Those are examples of DECLARATIONS. The following are among the verbs that can be similarly used:

admire	confess	forbid	offer
agree	confirm	guess	promise
apologise	congratulate	maintain	propose
approve	excuse	note	suggest
calculate	express	object	sympathise

However, all those verbs can be freely used in the progressive if the emphasis described in 13.6 is intended. Thus, we can compare

51 I admire your courage

with

52 Wait for me. I'm admiring this wonderful view;

e FUTURE TIME, in temporal and conditional clauses (2.38 and 2.42):

53 Mr X will telephone you as soon as he returns.

54 The police will take your car away if you park it there.

55 The meeting will be held out of doors unless it rains;

f PAST TIME, in newspaper headlines, sometimes in narrative and usually in the synopsis of a novel or play:

56 EARTHQUAKE ROCKS NICARAGUA.

57 Tom stands up on the coach and looks back at his father's figure.

58 That night Romeo sees Juliet alone on her balcony.

The newspaper article under the headline [56] would report the incident in the past tense; example [57] illustrates the use of the so-called HISTORIC PRESENT; and in a synopsis [58] each new development in the story is usually recorded in the simple present tense.

Present progressive
13.8

The speaker can emphasise the idea of activity in progress, or of activity uncompleted, by using an action verb referring to

a ALL OR ANY TIME

59 The Rhine is $\begin{Bmatrix} \text{always} \\ \text{constantly} \\ \text{for ever} \end{Bmatrix}$ pouring its waters into the sea.

There, the idea is that the activity is uncompleted because it never stops, and this idea is reinforced by an obligatory adverbial, *eg always, constantly, for ever*;

b THE PRESENT PERIOD. The speaker may be thinking of an activity that continues throughout the period, as in [60], or a series of acts throughout the period as in [61]:

60 A Where $\begin{Bmatrix} \text{do you live} \\ \text{are you living} \end{Bmatrix}$?

B I $\begin{Bmatrix} \text{live} \\ \text{am living} \end{Bmatrix}$ in the country.

61 George $\begin{Bmatrix} \text{goes} \\ \text{is going} \end{Bmatrix}$ to the university now.

Note that either the simple present or the progressive is acceptable in [60] and [61]. However, in [60] the progressive suggests that the activity is temporary, while in [61] it suggests that the 'going' is something that has just begun. [61] means that George is now a university student: it does not mean that he is now on his way to the university or that he is just about to go there. The idea of a temporary series of acts, as distinct from a regular habit, is emphasised in

62 George is getting up at five o'clock every day this week to prepare for his examination.

The idea of an annoying habit that goes on and on, is emphasised in

63 The postman is always putting your letters in my letter box.

Again, as in [59], an adverbial such as *always* is obligatory.

c THE PRESENT MOMENT, as in

64 George is $\begin{Bmatrix} \text{going} \\ = \text{on his way} \end{Bmatrix}$ to the university at this moment.

There, *is going* could *not* be replaced by *goes*. The progressive rather than the simple present would also be obligatory in

65 A Where are you, Fred?

　　B I'm in the garden. I'm watering the roses.

66 (The frying pan is on the stove.) It's getting really hot this time.

We can refer to two activities in progress in one sentence, as in

67 While I am cooking this omelette, Mary is making a salad.

There, we emphasise the uncompleted nature of both activities. But note the following from a radio commentary:

68 As I stand here, the procession is entering the hall.

In that example, both the standing and the entering are incomplete when the speaker makes his statement; but he is free not to highlight his 'standing', and to focus attention instead on the gradual progress of the procession. Note, too, the contrast between the constant flowing of the river in [59], and the temporary, partial picture of it in

69 The Rhine is flowing unusually fast today.

d FUTURE TIME in temporal or conditional clauses, as in

70 I'll telephone you this afternoon while I'm waiting.

71 The police won't take your car away if you're sitting in it.

e IMMEDIATE PAST TIME, as in

72 A That cheque. What did you do with it?

　　B What are you talking about? What cheque?

　　or

73 A I don't believe what you've just said.

　　B You do believe it. You know I'm telling the truth.

f PAST TIME, when the speaker refers to activity that is the background to a new development in a narrative, as in

57a While Tom is standing up on the coach looking back at his father, the horses suddenly break into a gallop.

Present perfect
13.9
The present perfect is used, with action and stative verbs, when the speaker is referring to an activity or a state which

either begins in the past and continues up to the moment of speaking,

or occurs at some unspecified time within the pre-present period.
WE CANNOT USE THE PRESENT PERFECT WITH ANY ADVERBIAL OF PAST TIME
(*eg an hour ago, yesterday*) to suggest that the period within which the
activity occurred is separated from the present. Thus:

a ACTIVITY CONTINUING UNTIL NOW

74 I have lived in London $\begin{cases} \text{since 1970} \\ \text{for the last six years} \end{cases}$

75 We have taken our holidays in August so far.

76 Man has always been a fighter.

In those three examples there is an obligatory adverbial – *since 1970, for
the last six years, so far, always* – which implies that the statement is true
of a period EXTENDING UP TO THE MOMENT OF SPEAKING. Other adverbials
that could be used in this way are *until* (or *till* or *up to*) *now*, or the rather
more formal *up to the present (time)* or the definitely formal *hitherto*. In
[74], the adverbial contributes to the meaning that my living in London
has continued until now, and you may assume that I am living there still.
In [75], *so far* indicates that our habit of taking our holidays in August
has not yet been broken; and in [76] *always* suggests that man is still
pugnacious.

b ACTIVITY IN A PERIOD CONTINUING UNTIL NOW

Study the next set of examples and the notes below them:

77 I have lived in China.

78 A Have you ever been to Peking?

  B Yes, I've been there $\begin{cases} \text{once.} \\ \text{often.} \end{cases}$

  C I've been there twice already.

  D I haven't been there yet.

79 A police inspector has been here. He has now gone next door.

80 This is the first time $\begin{cases} \text{I've} \\ \text{he's} \end{cases}$ been here.

81a Have you been to the bank already? (It appears that you have)

  b Have you been to the bank yet? (I really don't know)

82 There has just been an accident.

Notes:

  i All the affirmative statements in [77–82] refer to 'some time before
  now', without SPECIFYING the time in any way. The negative statement
  in [78D] refers to 'any time before now'; and 'at any time before
  now' is the meaning of *ever* in [78A].

  ii You may assume from [77] that I am *not* living in China now. A natural
  response to [77] would be *Oh, when was that?*

  iii In [78 A and B], *been (somewhere)* is normally used instead of *gone
  there and left*. In [79], *been here* = come here and gone away. Note
  been in the first part of [79] and *gone* in the second. In [80], *he's been* =

either 'he's come' or 'he's come and gone away'; but *I've been* in [80] only means 'I've come'. Note the construction 'the first time' + present perfect.

iv *Already* is used in an affirmative statement [78C] or in an affirmatively-orientated question [81a], *yet* in a negative statement [78D] or in a completely open question [81b].

v *Yet* frequently occurs with the present perfect, as in [78D]. It can also occur in the past perfect (13.21) and in the present (*eg I can't see it yet*) but is not acceptable with the simple past tense.

vi *Just*, in the sense of 'in the very recent past', often occurs with the present perfect, but is unacceptable with the simple past tense.[1]

13.10

The link between the present perfect and the present moment often results in an example such as

83 A telegram has arrived for you. Here it is,

The presence of the telegram is justification for saying 'it has arrived'. However, the essential factor in the present perfect is explained in 13.9. The present perfect is often used when there is *no* 'present evidence' (see example [77]). On the other hand, we have present evidence and simple past tense in, *eg The burglar came in through this window. Here are his footmarks.*.

13.11

We saw in the example *I have lived in China* that the time was unspecified. In conversation and in narrative, this type of example is often followed by statements or questions in which the speaker or writer moves back into past tense, thus:

77a A I have lived in China (at some time in the past).

    B When did you live there (at that time in the past)?

84 I've been to Peking. It was fantastic (at that time).

This move back into the past will even occur within one sentence:

85 I have been in countries where it was so hot that you could fry an egg on the sun-baked rock.

13.12

Note the use of the present perfect in temporal and conditional clauses, as in

86 I will return your book on Monday $\left\{ \begin{array}{l} \text{when} \\ \text{if} \end{array} \right\}$ I've read it.

See 2.38 ([78]) and 2.42 ([98]).

---

[1] This applies to British English, at least. *I just ran* is acceptable, but only with the meaning 'I simply ran and did nothing else'.

Present perfect progressive

13.13

a The present perfect progressive is used, with action verbs, when the speaker is emphasising the idea of activity in progress in the pre-present period, as in 13.9. The activity may have ended in the recent past, as in

87 It has been raining, but it has stopped now;

or may have continued up till the moment of speaking, as in

88 I've been working for six hours and now I'll stop;

or may be continuing into the present period, as in

89 We've been learning this language for ten years (and are still learning it).

b As the present perfect progressive refers to activity continuing until now (or until recently, as in [87]), we can replace [74] and [75] by

74a I have been living in London $\left\{ \begin{array}{l} \text{since 1970} \\ \text{for the last six years}^1 \end{array} \right\}$

and

75a· We have been taking our holidays in August so far.

However, [75a], especially, contains the idea of a temporary arrangement which may be changed; and that idea is certainly conveyed in

90 I've been staying in a hostel so far, but I'm just about to take a furnished apartment.

c There may be no difference in meaning between *I've been living here since 1970* and *I've lived here since 1970*. But with certain verbs there *would* be a difference in meaning between the two forms. Note:

91 I've been reading your book (but I haven't finished it yet).

92 I've read your book: I finished it last night.

93 I've been learning Russian since we last met and have made some progress in it.

94 I've learnt all the irregular verbs since we last met (and now I know them all).

d The progressive rather than the non-progressive would occur in

95 (The streets are flooded.) It's been raining hard.

and

96 (Your eyes are red.) You've been crying, haven't you?

But either form would be acceptable in

97 It has $\left\{ \begin{array}{l} \text{rained} \\ \text{been raining} \end{array} \right\}$ every day this week.

13.14

There is a tone of complaint in some examples of the present perfect progressive, *eg*

---

¹ Note that *I am living in London for six years* is only acceptable if it is intended to mean 'I am going to live in London for that period', as in 13.34.

98 Someone has been using my typewriter and has torn the ribbon.

13.15

A normal passive counterpart of an example like *They have been building a lot of houses recently* would be *A lot of houses have been built recently*, though *have been being built* is a possible construction.

Simple past
13.16

a We have seen, in 13.11, that when the speaker thinks of an activity or state occurring at a specific time in the past, he uses past tense. Time past can be specified by an adverbial – (single adverb), (adverb phrase, (adverb clause, *eg yesterday)(an hour ago)(last night)(in 1972,(when I was at school –)* or (by the context.) A phrase containing *ago*, which means 'back from now', will always be associated with the simple past or the past progressive. Examples:

99 I telephoned George Lamb $\begin{cases} \text{an hour ago.} \\ \text{last night.} \end{cases}$

100 We went to school together when we were boys, so

101 we saw (*ie* met) each other every day. (Past time specified by the context.

b The simple past can be used to refer to a single act, as in [99], or to past habit, as in [100].

13.17

There is no adverbial of past time in the question in

102 $\begin{cases} \text{When} \\ \text{Where} \end{cases}$ were you born? I was born in $\begin{cases} \text{such-and-such a year.} \\ \text{such-and-such a place.} \end{cases}$

or

103 Rome was not built in a day.

But obviously one's birth and the building of an old city occurred at a time that the speaker can only think of as past.

13.18

Past tense is used to indicate present or future non-fact, as in

104 $\begin{cases} \text{I wish} \\ \text{I'd rather} \\ \text{It's time} \end{cases}$ you were here (2.16).

105 If you parked your car there, ... (2.42 [103])

Present perfect or simple past
13.19

a The present perfect, not the simple past, can be used with certain adverbials, while the simple past, not the present perfect can be used with others, *eg*

PRESENT PERFECT
till now, by now, up to the
present, in the last few years,
since 1972, so far, yet

SIMPLE PAST
a moment ago, an hour ago,
yesterday, last night,
when we were at school, in 1965

b Either the present perfect or the simple past could occur in

106 I $\begin{Bmatrix} \text{have seen} \\ \text{saw} \end{Bmatrix}$ George Lamb $\begin{Bmatrix} \text{today.} \\ \text{this morning.} \\ \text{this afternoon.} \end{Bmatrix}$

But the present perfect is not acceptable with *this morning* if the morning has passed, nor with *this afternoon* if it is afternoon no longer.

c We often find sentences, with no adverbial, in which either the present perfect or the simple past can be used. Thus:

107 Who $\begin{Bmatrix} \text{broke} \\ \text{has broken} \end{Bmatrix}$ the window?

108 $\begin{Bmatrix} \text{Did you have} \\ \text{Have you had} \end{Bmatrix}$ a good time? *the day after / at the end of a party*

109 I $\begin{Bmatrix} \text{spoke} \\ \text{have spoken} \end{Bmatrix}$ to George about his problems.

Have you had . . . [108] would be a reasonable question to ask at the end of a party, while *Did you have* . . .would be the right question to ask the day after.

Past progressive
13.20
a This is simply an application of progressive aspect, as described in 13.6, to past tense. Thus:

60a I $\begin{Bmatrix} \text{lived} \\ \text{was living} \end{Bmatrix}$ in the country in 1972.

62a George was getting up at five o'clock every day that week.
63a The postman was always putting your letters in my letter-box.
67a While I was cooking an omelette, Mary was making a salad.
69a. The Rhine was flowing unusually fast that day.
99a I was telephoning George Lamb only an hour ago.
Note that *We were seeing (ie meeting) each other every day* is acceptable, but only to emphasise the temporary nature of a series of events, not to express the idea of a fixed habit.
b The past progressive is frequently used in narrative to supply a background to a new event in the story:

57b While Tom was standing up on the coach looking back at his father,
the horses suddenly broke into a gallop.

For the past progressive with *while*, see also 2.41.

c The past progressive can be used to indicate non-fact, as in

104a $\left\{\begin{array}{l}\text{I wish}\\\text{I'd rather}\\\text{It's time}\end{array}\right\}$ we were going home.

Past perfect
13.21

The past perfect is used to make it clear which event or state in a sequence
preceded which. It can be regarded as a transference either (a) of the present
perfect to the past, or (b) of the past to a previous past:

a We have present perfect in

110 Hallo George. I haven't met your sister $\left\{\begin{array}{l}\text{yet, until now.}\\\text{since May.}\\\text{for two days.}\end{array}\right.$

Transferred to the past, that could become

111 I saw George on Friday. (I told him) I hadn't met his sister
$\left\{\begin{array}{l}\text{yet, until then}\\\text{since May, for two days}\end{array}\right\}.$

The past perfect, in the second sentence of [111], is obligatory; and just
as a past time adverbial could not occur with *I haven't met*, so it could not
occur with *I hadn't met* there.

b We have two occurrences of simple past tense in

112 I opened my eyes again. The snake disappeared.

By putting those two sentences in that order, we convey the meaning that
opening my eyes preceded the snake's departure. We would not use the
past perfect in that case. But by saying

113 I opened my eyes again. The snake had disappeared,

we can make it clear that the snake had vanished before I opened my eyes;
and, if that is the meaning, then the past perfect is obligatory in the second
part of [113]. However, in

114 We arrived at the station after the train (had) left,

the past perfect is optional, since *after* makes it clear that the departure
of the train preceded our arrival at the station. On the other hand, the
past perfect would be obligatory in

115 We arrived at the station to find that the train had left;

and note that, in such a case, we *can* use an adverbial of past time, *eg*

115a We arrived to find that the train had left $\left\{\begin{array}{l}\text{two minutes before.}\\\text{at 10.25.}\end{array}\right.$

We could not use *ago* instead of *before* in [115a], since *ago* means 'back
from now'.

13.22

In indirect speech, the past perfect is obligatory in a transference of the present perfect, as in

116 'The bridge has collapsed.' I told you the bridge had collapsed.

but optional in a transference of the simple past, as in

117 'The floods weakened it in the autumn of 1972.' I told you that the floods (had) weakened it in the autumn. . . .

13.23

Distinguish between the past perfect of HAVE *something*, and the past perfect of HAVE *something -ed*:

118 My typewriter was broken. I had had it since 1970.

119 Later, it was working well. $\begin{cases} \text{I had had it mended (by someone).} \\ \text{I had mended it myself.} \end{cases}$

Past perfect progressive

13.24

The past perfect progressive is an application of progressive aspect to the past perfect. Thus:

120 'It has been raining.' I told you it had been raining.

121 'I've been driving for three hours and I'm tired.' I told you I had been driving for three hours and was tired.

B Future

13.25

a Here are five ways of referring to the future:

1 George will leave tomorrow
2 George is going to leave tomorrow
3 George is to leave tomorrow
4 George is leaving tomorrow
5 George leaves tomorrow

b Since 'tense' can be defined as 'form taken by the verb to indicate the time of an action',[1] there is no reason for not giving the name 'tense' to each of those five ways of referring to the future. What we cannot do is to speak of 'the future tense' as if there were only one form taken by the verb to indicate future time.

13.26

Each of the 'tenses' in 13.25 could fill the gap in the sentence *George . . . tomorrow*. But they are far from being always interchangeable. For example:

a *Will* + infinitive and *be going to* + infinitive can have either an animate or an inanimate subject, and may refer to an action or state that is or is not subject to human control. Thus:

---

[1] Concise Oxford Dictionary.

122 $\left\{ \begin{array}{l} \text{George} \\ \text{It} \end{array} \right\}$ will $\left\{ \begin{array}{l} \text{leave} \\ \text{rain} \end{array} \right\}$ tomorrow.

123 $\left\{ \begin{array}{l} \text{He} \\ \text{It} \end{array} \right\}$ is going to $\left\{ \begin{array}{l} \text{stay at home} \\ \text{be very cold} \end{array} \right\}$ tomorrow.

The other three 'tenses' are normally used only when they refer to an event or state that is subject to human control[1] *eg*

$\left\{ \begin{array}{l} \text{They are widening our road next year.} \\ \text{Our road is being widened (by human agency) next year.} \\ \text{That tree is to come down } (\approx \text{to be cut down) next winter.} \end{array} \right.$

b The emphasis in *will* + infinitive is on the future event or state. With the other four 'tenses' the emphasis is more on the present indications – signs, intentions, plans, etc. – that point to a future event.

c *Be going to* is typical of informal, conversational style. *Will* would be preferred to *be going to* in the following cases:

　i in more formal style;

　ii often in writing, and certainly in advertising, since *will* obviously occupies less space than *be going to.*;

　iii in accurate reporting, since *be going to* can have a variety of meanings, as we shall see later (13.32);

　iv in a continuous text, where a repetition of *going to* would become monotonous, as in this weather forecast:

124 Tomorrow is going to be another hot day. Temperatures will be around 30 degrees by mid-morning and there will be very little wind.

Will + infinitive
13.27

a We must distinguish between the TEMPORAL AUXILIARY *will*, which helps to make a plain statement about the future, and the MODAL AUXILIARY *will*, which expresses some personal attitude towards the future and will be dealt with in the next chapter.

b The temporal *will* + infinitive can, like the present and past tenses, have a simple form, or be combined with either progressive aspect or perfective aspect, or both (13.29). Thus:

ACTIVE	PASSIVE
a I will learn	It will be learnt
b I will be learning	—
c I will have learnt	It will have been learnt
d I will have been learning	—

---

[1] Examples may be found of future natural events being predicted according to a man-made timetable thus:

　　The tide $\left\{ \begin{array}{l} \textit{is reaching} \\ \textit{reaches} \end{array} \right\}$ *its highest level at 11.47 tonight.*

It is essential to remember that those forms can have modal meanings (dealt with in Chapter Fourteen), as well as temporal ones.

c The temporal *will* can be used with all persons as subject – first, second, third, singular and plural. But it can be replaced, optionally, by *shall* when the subject is *I* or *we*, as in

125 $\left. \begin{array}{c} I \\ We \end{array} \right\}$ $\left\{ \begin{array}{c} will \\ = shall \end{array} \right\}$ be here tomorrow.

$\left. \begin{array}{c} I \\ We \end{array} \right\}$ $\cdot \left\{ \begin{array}{c} will\ not\ (won't) \\ = shall\ not\ (shan't) \end{array} \right\}$ be away.

Since the speaker or writer can choose between *will* and *shall* when the subject is *I* or *we*, it may be that he will select *shall* simply to avoid repeating *will* in a sentence like

126 The telephone will never ring and I shall never have to answer it.

d *Shall* does not normally occur in modern English when the subject is a phrase like *You and I* or *Both of us*. Thus:

127 $\left. \begin{array}{c} You\ and\ I \\ Both\ of\ us \end{array} \right\}$ will be here tomorrow.

e *Will* is frequently reduced to *'ll* /l/, and *will not* to *won't*, in informal, especially conversational, style. But there are certain positions in the clause in which *'ll* cannot occur: see 1.31, Note *a*.

f Whether *'ll* stands for *shall*, as well as *will*, only becomes a real question when one is trying to put something like *I'll arrive at six o'clock* into more formal style, or when one is producing a tag question to complete an utterance like *We'll not be here tomorrow, – – ?* In those circumstances, for a plain statement or question about the future either *will* or *shall* would be acceptable.

g The temporal *will, shall, 'll, won't* and *shan't* do not normally occur in a temporal or a conditional clause, as we saw in 2.38 2.42 and 2.43. However, they *could* occur in such a clause. Notice the difference between

128 If the lava (from the volcano) comes down as far as this, it will be too late to evacuate these houses,
   and

129 If the lava will (= is likely to) come down as far as this, we must evacuate these houses immediately.

h *Will now* refers to the immediate future in

130 The concert will now begin;

but *will now* means 'will, according to information now available', in

131 The concert will now begin at 8.30.

i *Just* in *will just* means 'only', *eg*

132 There will just be the two of us – no more.

Will be -ing
13.28
a We have a clear example of future progressive in
133 (The procession is leaving the Town Hall now.) It *will be passing* our
house in about five minutes,
and
134 It *will be raining* on Thursday. (It always rains on Thursdays.)
b *Will be -ing* can also be used when the usual meaning of progressive aspect
is not intended. In an example like
135 I'll be writing to you about that soon,
the speaker may be making a plain statement about the future, without
wishing to emphasise the idea of action in progress and without wishing to
make the particular modal emphasis that would be contained in *I'll
write* (14.2). Or he may be adding an expression of his present intentions
to his statement about the future. *Will be -ing* is most likely to be used in
this way either with a human subject or with reference to an action that
is subject to human control, as in

136 $\left\{\begin{matrix} \text{We shall} \\ \text{The ship will} \end{matrix}\right\}$ be sailing at midnight.

Will have -ed, will have been -ing
13.29
We have examples of future perfect and future perfect progressive in
137 I haven't learnt those verbs yet but *I'll have learnt* them before the
next lesson; *and*
138 By the end of this month, we *shall have been learning* this language for
ten years.

BE going to
13.30
a *BE going to* can replace *will* with a human subject, when emphasis is on
the speaker's present intention or preparations, as in
139 I'm going to play tennis this afternoon,
or when there are signs or symptoms of what may happen in the future,
as in
140 I feel dizzy. I think I'm going to faint,
or
141 George is putting on weight. He's going to be quite fat.
or
142 Be careful. You're going to break that chair.
BE going to can also be used freely with an inanimate subject when there
are perceptible signs of what may happen in the future, as in
143 Look at those clouds. There's going to be a storm.

b *Just* in *just going to* can mean either 'only' (as in 13.27i) or 'in the immediate future':

144 I'm just going to post your letter. $\left\{\begin{array}{l}\text{I'll do only that}\\\text{I'll do it right away}\end{array}\right\}$.

c In using *be going to*, we can refer separately to (a) the present indications of what the future may bring, and (b) the future event or state itself. Notice the difference between

145 If you're going to play tennis this afternoon (if those are your intentions) you'd better get your shoes cleaned,
   and
146 If you play tennis this afternoon (=if that event takes place), keep your service under control.

There is, as in [145], no restriction against using *be going to* in a conditional clause, if emphasis is on the present indications or intentions and not on the future event. Note that only the intentions or plans have the focus in *were going to* in

147 A You were going to play tennis yesterday afternoon.

   B I *did* play. *or*, *eg* I couldn't play after all.

With *have been going to*, not only are the intentions emphasised but the meaning is conveyed that the intentions have not been fulfilled:

148 You've been going to play tennis with me for months, but you've never played with me *yet*.

I was going to . . . tomorrow is also possible:

149 I was going to play tennis with you tomorrow (=those were my intentions till recently), but I won't be able to now.

BE going to or will
13.31

Will is preferred to *BE going to* in an *if*-sentence which *assumes* that conditions are provided when they do not, in fact, exist:

150 If you play tennis this afternoon (that may not happen), you'll be too tired to go out with me this evening.

On the other hand, *be going to* is preferred to *will* in

   [139] I'm going to play tennis this afternoon.

ie when what the speaker really means is not *I will* (or *shall*) *play tennis* but something like *I've arranged to play*.

Vagueness of BE going to
13.32

What was said at the end of 13.31 illustrates the fact that the meaning of *be going to* is often imprecise. In precisely written English, *be going to* may need to be replaced by words that make the writer's meaning clearer. See how this clarification may be necessary.

151 I $\begin{Bmatrix} \text{am going to} \\ \text{intend to} \\ \text{have planned to} \end{Bmatrix}$ emigrate.

152 The Municipality $\begin{Bmatrix} \text{is going to} \\ \text{proposes to} \\ \text{has agreed to} \end{Bmatrix}$ widen this road.

Intend, have planned, propose and *have agreed* could all be replaced by the vague *be going*; but obviously they do not all mean the same thing.

BE to
13.33

a *BE to* + infinitive is often used in newspapers and radio to report an official plan or decision:

153 The Prime Minister is to speak on television tonight.

That example would be reduced, in headlines, to

153a PRIME MINISTER TO SPEAK ON TV TONIGHT.

b The same construction serves to report orders or prohibitions, as in

154 You are (not) to stand here. Do you understand?

Only the situation or the context could tell us whether a sentence like the following refers to an official plan or to an instruction:

155 This gate is not to be opened today.

According to the context, that could mean either (a) plans to have an opening ceremony have been cancelled or postponed, or (b) people are forbidden to open it. On the other hand,

156 The poor old lady is not to be comforted

means that she is inconsolable.

c As *BE to* is one of the expressions of futurity that are used only to refer to actions or states subject to human control, we could delete *going* in [139] (*I'm going to play tennis*) if we mean that those are my plans or instructions, but we could not delete *going* in [140] (*I'm going to faint*), [141] (*He's going to be fat*), [142] (*You're going to break that chair*) or [143] (*There's going to be a storm*).

d *BE to* can freely be used in a conditional clause if the emphasis is on the present plan etc, eg *If the Prime Minister is to speak . . . , I suppose that means there's another crisis.*

BE -ing
13.34

a *BE -ing* + an adverbial of future time can also be used to express the idea that a course of action has been arranged, without giving the impression that the arrangement is due to an official plan or decision or instructions or prohibitions. Thus *I'm going to play tennis this afternoon* could be replaced by

139a I'm playing tennis this afternoon,
which would be preferable on grounds of economy of expression,
especially if the speaker meant that preparations for the event were
already in train. There are obvious reasons for changing *going to go* and
going to come to the simpler *going* and *coming* respectively.

b On the other hand, for the reasons given in 13.33c, we could not replace
going to faint [140], *going to be fat* [141], *going to break* [142], *going to be a
storm* [143], by *fainting, being fat, breaking, being a storm.*

c *BE -ing* can be used without an adverbial of future time to suggest action
in the immediate future, as in
157 Hurry up. The train's starting,
which could mean either that the train will start very soon or that it has
already begun to move. Without an adverbial of future time, therefore,
this 'future tense' can be ambiguous. The idea of immediate future would
be slightly stronger in
157a ... The train's just starting,
though even that could be interpreted to mean 'the train has just begun to
move'.

d *BE -ing* can be freely used in a conditional clause if emphasis is on the
present arrangement, as in *If the train is starting in two minutes, you'll have
to run and get the tickets.*

He leaves tomorrow

13.35

a This 'tense' can refer to a future action that the speaker considers as
certain to take place in accordance with a firm decision or a fixed timetable. In

158 $\begin{Bmatrix} \text{George} \\ \text{The ship} \end{Bmatrix}$ $\begin{Bmatrix} \text{is leaving} \\ \text{leaves} \end{Bmatrix}$ at six o'clock tomorrow morning,

is leaving and *leaves* are both acceptable, but *leaves* gives the impression
of a firmer arrangement or a firmer decision on the part of the speaker or
of whoever may have made the plan.

b The idea of firm plans may be contained in a predicative adjective:

159 I'm $\begin{Bmatrix} \text{busy} \\ \text{engaged} \end{Bmatrix}$ all day tomorrow.

I am being could not replace *I am* before *busy* in that case. *Busy* in [159]
could not be replaced by, *eg happy, ill, tired*, since being happy etc. is not
something that can be planned.

c This 'future tense' can be used in a conditional clause if emphasis is on the
present plan. Notice the difference between
160 If you leave (*ie* are due to leave) at six tomorrow morning you'd
      better go to bed now,
      and

160a If you leave at six tomorrow morning (*ie* if your departure actually takes place then), you will be in Dublin by twelve.

About to leave
13.36
BE about to can be used, with animate or inanimate subjects, to refer to imminent future. It requires no adverbial of future time:

161 The President is about to make an important announcement.

162 I feel (that) something terrible is about to happen.

BE on the point of -ing could replace *BE about to* with an animate subject, as in

163 I can't see you now. I'm just on the point of leaving.

C Future in the past
13.37
a A future-as-seen-from-the-past can be expressed by *would*, or optional *should* after *I* or *we*, or by $\left\{ \begin{array}{l} was \\ were \end{array} \right\}$ *going to* in indirect speech (see the example in 2.14c), or in the continuous context of a narrative:

164 The climbers were moving steadily up the final slope. Soon they $\left\{ \begin{array}{l} would \\ =were\ going\ to \end{array} \right\}$ see the summit

b $\left\{ \begin{array}{l} Was \\ Were \end{array} \right\}$ *going to* can be the past equivalent of examples [139–145]:

139b I was going to play tennis that afternoon,

140a I felt dizzy. I thought I was going to faint,

and so on. In such cases, the imagined future event may or may not have taken place.

c Similarly, $\left\{ \begin{array}{l} was \\ were \end{array} \right\}$ *leaving* could be used as a past equivalent of $\left\{ \begin{array}{l} am,\ is \\ are \end{array} \right\}$ *leaving*, with a similar risk of ambiguity, *eg*

139c I was playing tennis that afternoon.

As that could easily be mistaken for an example of the past progressive, *I was going to play* . . . would be preferable if the meaning of future in the past was intended. On the other hand, in *The train was leaving in two minutes* the meaning is clearly 'was going to leave.'

d It would be possible to say

165 As George left on Friday at six in the morning, he went to bed early on Thursday evening,

with the meaning of 'As he was due to leave'; but the risk of confusion with the simple past tense would be considerable in such a case.

e *I was to leave next day* can be safely used when the meaning is 'my plans or instructions were that I should leave then': my departure may or may not have occurred. But *I was to have left next day* means 'my plans or instructions were that I should leave but they were not carried out'.

f *I felt (that) something terrible was about to happen* would be the past equivalent of example [162].

13.38

Will be -ing (13.28) and *will have -ed* (13.29) will become *would be -ing* and *would have -ed* in past reported speech, as in *I told you the procession would be passing* . . . and *I told you I would have learnt, would have been learning* . . .

D Sequence of tenses ; *shift in tense*

13.39

a In a continuous text, it is usually considered desirable to retain the same tense, present or past, for each new step in the narrative, description or argument. This involves using one or the other of two combinations:

  i SIMPLE PRESENT, PRESENT PROGRESSIVE, PRESENT PERFECT AND ONE OF THE 'FUTURE TENSES', as in

  166 We live in Maple Street. They are building a swimming pool near our house. We have been here for ten years and will probably stay here for the rest of our lives.

  ii SIMPLE PAST, PAST PROGRESSIVE, PAST PERFECT AND FUTURE IN THE PAST:

  167 We lived in Maple Street. They were building houses all around us then. We had been there for ten years and imagined we would stay there for the rest of our lives.

b However, any combination of tenses is possible if each tense is used appropriately to express the speaker's exact meaning. Thus:

  168 We live in Maple Street. This is where my father always wanted to live. He moved here from Burton Road in 1962.

  In any case, a past tense is obligatory with an adverbial of past time, as in that last sentence. *necessary*

c For tenses in reported statements, see 2.11–13;

  For tenses in reported questions,　see 2.20;

  For tenses in temporal clauses,　　see 2.38–41;

  For tenses in conditional clauses,　see 2.42–43.

Chapter Fourteen
The verb phrase (6): The modals

14.1

a The modals express a variety of moods or attitudes towards a possible state or action. They will be discussed in this chapter under the headings A PRIMARY USES, and B SECONDARY USES. The difference between A and B can be illustrated by MUST:

    A   B

    1a We must be very careful.   1b John must be very careless.

In normal human situations, *must* in [1a] could be paraphrased by *have to*, and the past tense would be *had to*. On the other hand, [1b] could be re-phrased

$$\left.\begin{cases} \text{Undoubtedly} \\ \text{I am quite sure (that)} \end{cases}\right\} \text{John is very careless.}$$

Undoubtedly is a disjunct adverb (1.52) expressing the speaker's attitude towards the statement he is making, and *must* in [1b] serves the same purpose. The past of [1b] would be *John must have been very careless*.

b All the ten modals, except *shall*, can be used in those two ways, though in some of them there is a general theme running through the uses of each one. *Must*, for example, contains the idea of 'a course that is unavoidable'. We have an unavoidable obligation to be careful; and the fact of John's carelessness is inescapable – there is no other explanation of his actions.

A Primary uses
Will
14.2

a The general theme in both the primary and secondary uses of the modal *will* is the same as the theme of the temporal *will*, namely *futurity*. In its primary uses, the modal *will* adds to the idea of futurity an expression either of volition or of confident certainty that a future event will take place. The speaker may be expressing his own volition about his own or other people's actions, or he may be attributing volition to a third party. Naturally, volition is only likely to be expressed about an action or state that is subject to human control, whether the verb is in the active voice (*Someone will do that*) or the passive (*That will be done*). We are therefore more likely to find volition expressed in an action verb than in a stative verb referring to involuntary activity.

b In the examples below, where italic type is used it indicates that *will* is always strongly stressed and is not reducible to *'ll*. Otherwise, *will* is reducible to *'ll*, except in the circumstances described in 1.31, Note *a*.

Shall could not replace *will* in the following examples without change of meaning: see 14.4. *Will* expresses:

c DETERMINATION ON THE PART OF THE SPEAKER OR OF A THIRD PARTY:

2 $\begin{Bmatrix} \text{I} \\ \text{He} \end{Bmatrix}$ *will* have $\begin{Bmatrix} \text{my} \\ \text{his} \end{Bmatrix}$ own way, *ie* $\begin{Bmatrix} \text{I am} \\ \text{He is} \end{Bmatrix}$ determined to have it.

3 $\begin{Bmatrix} \text{I} \\ \text{He} \end{Bmatrix}$ *will not* (*or won't*) be bullied. (= $\begin{Bmatrix} \text{I'm} \\ \text{He's} \end{Bmatrix}$ determined not to be.)

d PERSISTENT HABIT ON THE PART OF THE PERSON REFERRED TO BY THE SUBJECT:

4 $\begin{Bmatrix} \text{I} \\ \text{You} \\ \text{He} \end{Bmatrix}$ *will* leave that door open. $\begin{Bmatrix} \text{You} \\ \text{He} \end{Bmatrix}$ *won't* leave me alone.

There, *will leave* is replaceable by *keep (on) leaving*, and *won't leave* by *refuse(s) to leave*. *Will leave* could be replaced by *insist on leaving* in

5 If you *will* leave that door open, what can you expect?

In that sense, *will* can freely occur in a conditional clause.

e A CHARACTERISTIC HABIT:

6 Danny will sit and look at the sea for hours. (He has often done so in the past and I'm sure he'll go on doing it.)

f A PROMISE:

7 You'll have your money tomorrow, I promise you. (See 14.4b)

g AN ORDER:

8 You will wait here till I return.

9 All staff will leave the building at once.

h WILLINGNESS ON THE PART OF THE PERSON REFERRED TO BY THE SUBJECT:

10 George will help you. I'll answer the phone.

11 If you'll help me, we can finish this in no time.

Again, *will* can freely occur in a conditional clause.

14.3

The modal *will* is used in questions:

a IN MAKING AN OFFER:

12 $\begin{Bmatrix} \text{Will} \\ \text{Won't} \end{Bmatrix}$ you have a piece of cake?

13 Have a piece of cake, $\begin{Bmatrix} \text{will} \\ \text{won't} \end{Bmatrix}$ you?

14 Who will have some coffee?

b IN ISSUING AN INVITATION:

15 $\begin{Bmatrix} \text{Will} \\ \text{Won't} \end{Bmatrix}$ you come inside? (rising intonation)

16 Come inside, $\begin{Bmatrix} \text{will} \\ \text{won't} \end{Bmatrix}$ you? (rising intonation)

c IN MAKING A REQUEST:
  17 Will you lend me your pen for a moment?
  The speaker takes compliance for granted in
  18 Lend me your pen for a moment, will you?
d IN GIVING A COMMAND:
  19 Will you sit down! (falling intonation)
  20 Sit down, will you. (falling intonation)

Shall
14.4
Again, we must distinguish between the temporal auxiliary *shall* (13.27c) and the modal. The basic theme in both is 'futurity'. *Shall* can express:
a AN OBSTINATE ATTITUDE ON THE PART OF THE SPEAKER with regard to his own actions:
  21 A Please don't go.
    B I shall go if I want to.
Shall is there replaceable by *will* (*'ll*), though the tone of obstinacy would then be weakened;
b DECISION OR DETERMINATION ON THE PART OF THE SPEAKER with regard to the future of someone else:
  22 You shall have whatever you want.
  You shall replaceable by *I promise (that) you will* (See 14.2f)
  23 The enemy shall not pass,
  ie we are determined not to let them pass;
  24 We $\begin{cases} \text{propose} \\ \text{agree} \\ \text{have decided} \end{cases}$ that each member of the club shall be asked to pay a subscription of £10 a year.
  Shall be is there replaceable by *should be*, or simply by *be*, as in 2.17, [31c].

14.5
The modal *shall* occurs in questions:
  25 $\begin{cases} \text{Shall I call for you this evening?} \\ \text{I'll call for you this evening, shall I?} \end{cases}$
  Shall I replaceable by *Would you like me to.*
  26 $\begin{cases} \text{Shall we have coffee outside?} \\ \text{Let's have coffee outside, shall we?} \end{cases}$
  Shall we there replaceable by *I suggest.*

Would
Reducible to *'d* unless strongly stressed and subject to the restrictions mentioned in 1.31, Note *a*.
14.6
Apart from its use in forming a future-in-the-past (13.37a), *would* occurs:

a in sentences containing a conditional clause: see 2.42, examples [103–4], [106–7], [112–4];

b in transferring most of the examples in 14.2–3 into the past, as in the list below. Italic type indicates strong stress, with *would* not reducible to *'d*. Otherwise, *would* can be reduced to *'d* except in the circumstances described in 1.31, Note *a*. *Should* could not replace *would* in these examples without change of meaning: see 14.8–9.

[2] $\begin{Bmatrix} I \\ He \end{Bmatrix}$ *will* have $\begin{Bmatrix} my \\ his \end{Bmatrix}$ own way. $\begin{Bmatrix} I \\ He \end{Bmatrix}$ *would* have $\begin{Bmatrix} my \\ his \end{Bmatrix}$ own way.

[3] $\begin{Bmatrix} I \\ He \end{Bmatrix}$ *won't* be bullied. $\begin{Bmatrix} I \\ He \end{Bmatrix}$ *wouldn't* be bullied.

[4] $\begin{Bmatrix} I \\ You \\ He \end{Bmatrix}$ *will* leave that door $\begin{Bmatrix} I \\ You \\ He \end{Bmatrix}$ *would* leave it open.

[5] If you *will* leave it open,   If you *would* leave it open,

[6] Danny will sit here . . .   Danny would sit here . . .

[7] You'll have your money.   I promised you'd have your money.

[8] You will wait here . . .   You were to wait here . . .
                                   I told you to wait here . . .

[9] All staff will leave . . .   All staff were to leave . . .
                                   I told all staff to leave . . .

[10] George will help you.   George was willing to help you
                               He said he would help you.

    I'll answer the phone.   I offered to answer the phone.
                               I said I would answer the phone.

[11] If you'll help me, . . .   If you had been willing to help me,
                                  we could have finished the job.
                                  I said if you'd help me we could
                                  finish the job.

[12] Will you have some cake?   I offered you some cake.
                                  I asked if you'd have some cake.

[15] Will you come inside?   I invited you (to come) inside.
                               I asked if you'd come inside.

[17] Will you lend me your pen?   I asked if you'd lend me your pen.

[19] Will you sit down!   I told you to sit down.

14.7

a *Would* also serves as a milder, more hesitant replacement for *will* in 14.3:
15a Would you come inside now?

b *Would* is not replaceable by *will* in:

27 Would you $\left\{\begin{array}{l}\text{like to go}\\\text{prefer to go}\\\text{mind going}\\\text{be interested in going}\end{array}\right\}$ instead of me?

28 A What's the matter with George? Has he gone mad?

B I would say so, from the way he's behaving.

c *Would*, strongly stressed, indicates typical behaviour and is not replaceable by either *will* or *should*, in

29 You've lost a button off your coat. You *would* do that, just as we're going out.

Should

Not reducible except to /ʃəd/.

14.8

a *Should* can optionally replace *would* after *I* or *we* in sentences containing conditional clauses, *eg*

30 If you did that, $\left\{\begin{array}{l}\text{I}\\\text{we}\end{array}\right\}$ $\left\{\begin{array}{l}\text{would}\\\text{=should}\end{array}\right\}$ be very sorry.

b *Should*, not replaceable by *would*, occurs when the examples in 14.5 are put into past reported speech:

25a I asked if I should call for you.

26a Who suggested (that) we should have coffee outside?

c *Should* can replace *would* after *I* or *we* in the examples in 14.7b :

27a $\left\{\begin{array}{l}\text{I}\\\text{We}\end{array}\right\}$ $\left\{\begin{array}{l}\text{would}\\\text{=should}\end{array}\right\}$ $\left\{\begin{array}{l}\text{like}\\\text{prefer}\end{array}\right\}$ to go.

28a $\left\{\begin{array}{l}\text{I}\\\text{We}\end{array}\right\}$ $\left\{\begin{array}{l}\text{would}\\\text{=should}\end{array}\right\}$ think so.

14.9

Should, not replaceable by *would*, expresses escapable obligation or duty, or what is advisable, as in

31 Mr X should go. It is $\left\{\begin{array}{l}\text{his duty}\\\text{advisable}\end{array}\right\}$.

Notice the difference between

32 We think that Mr X should go,

ie we think that it is his duty or it is advisable, and

33 We $\left\{\begin{array}{l}\text{propose}\\\text{recommend}\end{array}\right\}$ that he $\left\{\begin{array}{l}\text{should go}\\\text{=goes}\\\text{=go}\end{array}\right\}$.

Example [31] could be put into the past as

31a Mr X had to go.

and [32] and [33] as

32a We thought that Mr X should go
     and

33a We $\left\{ \begin{array}{l} \text{proposed} \\ \text{etc} \end{array} \right\}$ that Mr X $\left\{ \begin{array}{l} \text{should go} \\ \text{went} \end{array} \right\}$

Would have, should have + past participle
14.10

Would have (or *should have* after *I* or *we*) + past participle may occur in the main clause on which a conditional clause depends, as in 2.42, [108], or in the future perfect (13.29) transferred to the past:

34 (He will have been there by this time next year.)
     I told you he would have been there.

It can suggest non-fact in the past, *eg*

35 I $\left\{ \begin{array}{l} \text{would} \\ \text{=should} \end{array} \right\}$ have $\left\{ \begin{array}{l} \text{liked} \\ \text{preferred} \end{array} \right\}$ to go yesterday, but I didn't have
     the chance (See 3.5e),

or present non-fact, as in

36 A Has he gone mad? [28]
     B Anyone would have thought so,

where B's reply is less definite than *Anyone would think so.*

14.11

Should have + past participle refers to obligation unfulfilled in:

37 Mr X should have gone. Why $\left\{ \begin{array}{l} \text{hasn't he gone} \\ \text{didn't he go} \end{array} \right\}$?

Should not have etc. refers to action taken despite obligation not to take it, as in

38 He should not have refused. Why $\left\{ \begin{array}{l} \text{has he refused} \\ \text{did he refuse} \end{array} \right\}$?

Note that *should have gone* replaces either the present perfect (*He hasn't gone*) or the simple past (*He didn't go*).

Ought to, ought to have gone
14.12

Ought to, expressing obligation, can replace *should* in examples [31], [32], [32a], [37] and [38], but not [33] or [33a].

14.13

In the six operations described in 1.26, *ought to* is used as follows:

1 He $\left\{ \begin{array}{l} \text{ought not} \\ \text{oughtn't} \end{array} \right\}$ to $\left\{ \begin{array}{l} \text{refuse} \\ \text{have refused} \end{array} \right\}$.
2 Ought we to go?
3 $\left\{ \begin{array}{l} \text{Ought we not} \\ \text{Oughtn't we} \end{array} \right\}$ to go?

4 We ought to go, $\begin{Bmatrix} \text{ought we not} \\ \text{oughtn't we} \\ \text{should we not} \\ \text{shouldn't we} \end{Bmatrix}$?

5 We *ought* to go.

6 We ought to go and so $\begin{Bmatrix} \text{ought} \\ \text{should} \end{Bmatrix}$ you,

Ought we not is decidedly formal; and the substitution of *should* for *ought* in operations 4 and 6 would be quite usual.

Can
14.14
The basic theme in *can* is 'what the speaker assumes to be freedom to act'. *Can* is, as it were, a green light signalling that a certain road is open. Our 'freedom to act' may be the result of our ability, or of the permission that someone else has given us, or of the opportunities that circumstances provide. Thus:

a *I can* = I am able to = I have the ability to, in

39 I can use a typewriter perfectly now.

Note that an adverb of manner (1.48), eg *perfectly*, is usable with *can* in this sense, and that *can* often precedes *see, hear* etc. as in 13.2c.

b *I can* = I am able to = I have the chance to, in

40 We can sit at home and watch football matches in comfort, thanks to television.

c *I can* = I am able to = I am free to, in

41 Come when you like. I can see you at any time.

d *I can* = I am able to = I am allowed to, in

42 Permission has been granted. We can go now.

e *Can I . . . ?* asks for permission, in

43 Can I borrow your pen for a moment?

where *Can I borrow* is replaceable by *Will you lend me* as in [17]. An affirmative answer to [43] would be *Yes, you can*; a negative, *No, (I'm afraid) you can't.*

14.15
Can in [39] refers to my present ability. To refer to future ability, we should have to say

39a I'll be able to use a typewriter perfectly after a few more lessons.

In the other examples in 14.14, *can* is usable with future as well as present reference. Thus:

40a We can sit at home tomorrow and watch the match in comfort.

41a I can see you tomorrow afternoon.

42a Permission is granted. We can go next week,

though in examples [40a], [41a] and [42a] we would reinforce the future reference by replacing *can* by *'ll be able to, 'll be free to, 'll be allowed to* respectively.

Could
14.16
'We had the freedom to act' (in the past) can be expressed by *we could* – or, if we wish to be more precise, *we were able to, we were free to, we were allowed to*: and *could* is used as the past for *can* in indirect speech. Thus, [39] can be turned into the past as

39b $\begin{cases} \text{I could use a typewriter perfectly then.} \\ \text{I told you I could use a typewriter.} \end{cases}$

However, *we could* does not mean that we made successful use of the freedom to act. For example,

44 I could pass the examination

does not mean that I succeeded in passing it. To indicate 'freedom to act + achievement' we could say

45 I $\begin{cases} \text{was able to pass} \\ \text{managed to pass} \\ \text{succeeded in passing} \end{cases}$ it, *ie* I actually passed.

On the other hand,

46 I couldn't pass the examination,

means that I did not have the capacity and therefore did not try or did not succeed; while

47 I could have passed it

means that I had the capacity and $\begin{cases} \text{have not used} \\ \text{did not use} \end{cases}$ it, and either did not take the examination, or took it and failed. Note the difference between:

48 The President was always available. We could see him at any time.
   (*ie* we were always free to see him)
   and

49 You never came to see me. Why not? You could have seen me at any time (but you didn't).

14.17
Could also serves as a milder, more hesitant alternative for *can* in examples [41], [42] and [43], *eg*

50 Come when you like. I could see you at any time.
51 You could go now if you like(d).
52 Could I borrow your pen?

These examples could have future as well as present reference, *eg I could see you tomorrow* etc.

May
14.18

May, in its primary use, refers to permission, as in

53 A May I borrow your pen for a moment?

  B Yes, you may, *or* No, you may not (see 1.31, Note b)

For some speakers *may* throws emphasis on permission rather than on freedom to act. None the less, *Can I borrow your pen? Yes, you can. No, you can't*, is widely accepted.

14.19

May can have future reference as well as present:

54 You may take next Friday afternoon off.

The past equivalent in indirect speech would be *might*:

55 You said I might borrow your pen.

But *might* is not used as a past for *may* in *direct* speech. Thus the past of [54] would be

56 You $\left\{ \begin{array}{l} \text{could} \\ =\text{were allowed to} \end{array} \right\}$ take every Friday off last year.

  or

57 You could have taken last Friday afternoon off. Why didn't you take it?

Might
14.20

Might, besides its use as in [55], suggests more uncertainty than *may* in

58 Might I borrow your pen?

where the speaker does not assume that permission will be granted. If the answer to [58] were *Yes, you might*, the enquirer would still not be sure that permission had been freely given. *No, you might not* would be a discouraging refusal.

Must, have to
14.21

a Inescapable obligation is expressed in

59 We must all keep together.

Must can be replaced by *have to* and, in informal style, *have got to*. Thus

60 We $\left\{ \begin{array}{l} \text{all have to} \\ =\text{'ve all got to} \end{array} \right\}$ keep together.

Have (got) to suggests that the obligation is prescribed by someone (*eg* a leader) or by a rule, though that meaning may be absent in the past, *had to*.

b The future of [59] and [60] would be the same as the present, though future reference can be made stronger, as in

61 We'll all have to keep together.

c The past, in direct speech, would be

62 We all had to keep together,

though in indirect speech *must* can remain:

63 The officer reminded us (that) we $\left\{ \begin{array}{l} \text{must all} \\ = \text{all had to} \end{array} \right\}$ keep together.

14.22

The negative of [59] would be

64 We $\left\{ \begin{array}{l} \text{don't have to} \\ = \text{haven't got to} \\ = \text{don't need to} \\ = \text{needn't} \end{array} \right\}$ keep together.

ie There is no obligation to do so. On the other hand, prohibition is expressed in

65 You $\left\{ \begin{array}{l} \text{must not} \\ = \text{are not to} \end{array} \right\}$ get separated from the group.

Notice the difference between [66] and [67]:

66 $\left\{ \begin{array}{l} \text{Must we} \\ \text{Do we have to} \\ \text{Have we (got) to}^1 \\ \text{Need we} \end{array} \right\}$ keep together? $\left\{ \begin{array}{l} \text{Yes you} \left\{ \begin{array}{l} \text{must} \\ \text{have to} \\ \text{'ve got to} \end{array} \right\} \\ \text{No, you} \left\{ \begin{array}{l} \text{don't have to} \\ \text{haven't got to} \\ \text{don't need to} \\ \text{needn't} \end{array} \right\} \end{array} \right.$

67 $\left\{ \begin{array}{l} \text{Can} \\ \text{May} \end{array} \right\}$ we go separately? $\left\{ \begin{array}{l} \text{Yes, you} \left\{ \begin{array}{l} \text{can} \\ \text{may} \end{array} \right\} \\ \text{No, you} \left\{ \begin{array}{l} \text{may not} \\ \text{can't} \\ \text{'re not to} \\ \text{mustn't} \end{array} \right\} \end{array} \right.$

In [67], *may not, can't, 're not to, mustn't* are arranged in increasing order of severity, *mustn't* being an absolute prohibition.

Compensating for the defectiveness of the modals
14.23

The modals are DEFECTIVE in that they lack the forms found in every full verb (1.17). We can make up for that defectiveness by replacing

can *and* could   *by*   be $\left\{ \begin{array}{l} \text{able} \\ \text{free} \\ \text{allowed} \end{array} \right\}$ to

may *and* might (as in [55])   *by*   be allowed to

---

[1] *Have we to,* formal; *Have we got to,* informal.

should, ought to, must	*by*	have to
must not	*by*	not be allowed to
		or be forbidden to

Note how such replacements are used in the following sentences to provide an infinitive (in [68]), a present participle (in [69]), a present perfect (in [70]), and so on:

	REPLACING	BY
68	can	You must *be able* to answer in English.
69	can	*Not being able to* speak Chinese, I couldn't make myself understood.
70	can	At last I *have been able to* translate this sentence.
71	must	You may *have to* wait a long time.
72	must	*Having to* wait for the train, I spent the time trying to telephone Mary.
73	must	The doctor *has had to* operate.
74	may	You ought *to be allowed to* sit down.

B Secondary uses
14.24
In their secondary uses, nine modals (excluding *shall*) can be arranged according to the degrees of certainty or uncertainty that the speaker feels. *Might* can be considered as the most uncertain, *must* as the most certain. A scale (which might vary in detail from one speaker to another) would be

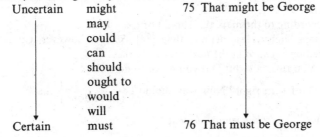

Uncertain   might   75 That might be George
           may
           could
           can
           should
           ought to
           would
           will
Certain   must   76 That must be George

14.25
The past of all the modals as they are used in section B of this chapter is formed by retaining the modal and adding *have* + past participle. Thus

77 That $\left\{\begin{array}{l}\text{might}\\\text{must}\end{array}\right\}$ have been George.

Note that *He must have gone* = either *I'm sure he has gone* or *I'm sure he went*. The negative is formed on the pattern of

78 That $\left\{\begin{array}{l}\text{might not be}\\\text{might not have been}\end{array}\right\}$ George,

with every one of the nine modals, except *must*, for which the negative
equivalent is an emphatic *can't*:

CERTAIN POSITIVE   CERTAIN NEGATIVE

79a That $\begin{Bmatrix} \text{must be} \\ \text{must have been} \end{Bmatrix}$ George.   79b That $\begin{Bmatrix} \text{can't be} \\ \text{can't have been} \end{Bmatrix}$ George.

Examples of the secondary uses
14.26
a MUST: see examples [1b], [76], [77].
b WILL:
  80 That will be George at the door, I expect,
  ie I assume (that) it will prove to be him.
  81 You will all have heard the news,
  ie I assume (that) you have heard it, or that you heard it.
  82 You will all have heard the news last night,
  can only be *I assume you heard it* (13.16).
c WOULD:
  83 This seat would be mine, would it?
  – *would* making more hesitant assumption than *will*.
d OUGHT TO:
  84 According to the map, this ought to be the way,
  ie this is what the map tells me is the way.
e SHOULD:
  85 According to the map, this should be the way
  – perhaps slightly less definite than [84]. *Should*, however, cannot be
  replaced by *ought to* in the next four examples:
  86 A You turned right. Did you mean to do so?

   B Did I turn right? Now why should I $\begin{Bmatrix} \text{do} \\ \text{have done} \end{Bmatrix}$ that?

ie Why $\begin{Bmatrix} \text{do} \\ \text{did} \end{Bmatrix}$ I (happen to) do that?

  87 I was sitting in the park when who should walk by (= who happened
  to walk by) but Mary.

  88 We $\begin{Bmatrix} \text{regret} \\ \text{are sorry} \end{Bmatrix}$ that you $\begin{Bmatrix} \text{should feel} \\ \text{should have felt} \end{Bmatrix}$ obliged to resign,

ie that you $\begin{Bmatrix} \text{do} \\ \text{did} \end{Bmatrix}$ feel obliged.

  89 It is $\begin{Bmatrix} \text{essential} \\ \text{right} \end{Bmatrix}$ that he $\begin{Bmatrix} \text{should be} \\ \text{should have been} \end{Bmatrix}$ punished.

ie that he $\begin{Bmatrix} \text{is} \\ \text{was} \end{Bmatrix}$ punished.

f CAN:

90 John can be very annoying, I agree,

ie it is possible that he is.

91 Where's Dick? Where can he have gone?

ie where is it possible that he $\begin{cases} \text{has gone.} \\ \text{went.} \end{cases}$

g COULD:

92 You'll like John. He could be a little annoying, I believe, but I think you'll get on well with him

ie it is just possible that he is or will be,

h MAY: Uncertainty becomes much stronger with *may*, which suggests that at least two (or more) courses are possible, and often leaves us in a situation of *it may be this* or *it may not*. Thus:

93 Don't go near that snake. It may be dangerous (=perhaps it is).

94 It may have been dangerous (=perhaps it was), but it soon disappeared.

95 Don't wait for me this evening. I may be late home (=perhaps I will be).

96 Such qualities as I $\begin{cases} \text{may have} \\ \text{may have had} \end{cases}$, I owe(d) to my parents and

teachers, (Perhaps I $\begin{cases} \text{have} \\ \text{had} \end{cases}$ some, perhaps not.)

May in this sense will not occur in the interrogative. To convert *You may be late home* (=that is possible) into a *Yes/No* question, one would have to say something like *Are you likely to be late home?*

i MIGHT could replace *may* in all the last four examples, adding to the degree of uncertainty. Note how this uncertainty varies in the next four examples.

97 I wonder where John is. He might be in Switzerland by now. (=It is possible that he is.)

98 What wonderful scenery! We might be in Switzerland. (It looks like it, but we're not.)

99 Those rocks are very dangerous. You might $\begin{cases} \text{be} \\ \text{have been} \end{cases}$ killed. (I hope you won't be. I'm relieved you weren't.)

100 What really happened? You might $\begin{cases} \text{tell} \\ \text{have told} \end{cases}$ me. (I wish you would tell me. I wish you had told me.)

C Other modals
Need
14.27
NEED as a modal can be used with any of the negators (1.59). Thus:

101   I need $\begin{cases} \text{never} \\ \text{hardly} \\ \text{scarcely} \end{cases}$ remind you.

or

I $\begin{cases} \text{hardly} \\ \text{scareely} \end{cases}$ need remind you.

A negation in a main clause may justify *need*, as a modal, in a dependent clause:

102   I am not sure that you need come,

as opposed to its use as a full verb in

103   I am quite sure that you need to study hard.

Didn't need to, needn't have
14.28

You didn't need to, as in

104   Did you buy those flowers for me? Oh, you didn't need to do that, can mean either (a) 'it wasn't necessary to buy them' or (b) 'you have bought them unnecessarily'. Meaning (a) is obviously intended in   - .

105   We didn't take an umbrella. We didn't need to. It wasn't raining.

Only meaning (b) is expressed in:

106   Oh, you needn't have done that.

Dare
14.29

a DARE, as a modal, occurs in negative contexts and in questions: *eg*

107   I can't look down. I $\begin{cases} \text{daren't. (modal)} \\ =\text{don't dare to. (full verb)} \end{cases}$

108   I couldn't look down. I $\begin{cases} \text{daren't. (modal)} \\ =\text{didn't dare to. (full verb)} \end{cases}$

109   $\begin{cases} \text{Dare we} \\ =\text{Do we dare (to)} \end{cases}$ go in yet?

110   I'm not sure that I dare go in yet.

111   How dare you speak to me like that?

DARE is a modal, with past reference, in

112   I never dare ask him

and a full verb in

113   I never dared (to) ask him.

It is a full, non-defective verb, in

114   She hesitated, not daring to go on.

Note the idiomatic use of *dare* in the affirmative in

115   I dare say you're right.

Used to
14.30

a In the six operations in 1.26, *used to* is used thus:

1 He $\left\{\begin{array}{l}\text{used not}\\\text{usedn't}\end{array}\right\}$ to smoke a pipe.

2 Used he to smoke a pipe?

3 Usedn't he to smoke a pipe?

4 He used to smoke, didn't he?

5 He *used* to smoke, I know.

6 He used to smoke, and so did she.

Used would sound very odd in modern English at the end of [4] and [6]; while *did* frequently occurs in informal, colloquial English in [2] and [3], in *Did he use(d) to? Didn't he use(d) to?* Feeling against those last two forms prompts 'careful' speaker to avoid *used to* in operations [2] and [3], by using a sentence like

116 Did you smoke a pipe? *or* 117 Didn't he usually smoke a pipe?

Note that *used to live* would not replace *lived* in *We lived in London for ten years*, ie when a definite period is stated.

b Distinguish *He used (not) to smoke*, as above, from *He's (not) used to smoking* (7.20).

Had better, had best, would rather, would sooner (3.2)
14.31

a *Had better, had best, would rather, would sooner* (informally *'d better, 'd best, 'd rather, 'd sooner*) only occur in the forms just given. *Had* $\left\{\begin{array}{l}better\\best\end{array}\right\}$ = should, would be advisable to; *would* $\left\{\begin{array}{l}rather\\=sooner\end{array}\right\}$ = prefer to, *eg*

118 A I think we had $\left\{\begin{array}{l}better\\best\end{array}\right\}$ stop now.

   B I would $\left\{\begin{array}{l}rather\\=sooner\end{array}\right\}$ go on.

These expressions are not used in the negative, though the infinitive can be negated, as in

119 A We 'd better not go on any farther.

   B I'd rather not stop yet.

Would rather and *would sooner* can occur in questions:

120 Would you $\left\{\begin{array}{l}rather\\=sooner\end{array}\right\}$ stay here?

b *Would rather* and *would sooner* can also be followed by a finite clause with a verb in the MODAL PAST indicating non-fact:

121 I'd $\left\{\begin{array}{l}rather\\=sooner\end{array}\right\}$ you $\left\{\begin{array}{l}\text{kept quiet about this.}\\\text{didn't say a word about it.}\end{array}\right\}$

May as well, might (just) as well
14.32

These expressions are used as follows:

122 A How shall we go? Shall we walk or go by bus?

   B We $\begin{Bmatrix} \text{may} \\ \text{might (just)} \end{Bmatrix}$ as well walk. That's what I suggest.

123 A Isn't the traffic slow today?

   B Yes, we might (just) as well $\begin{Bmatrix} \text{walk} \\ \text{have walked} \end{Bmatrix}$ It would be just as quick.

   A I agree. We might (just) as well not $\begin{Bmatrix} \text{take} \\ \text{have taken} \end{Bmatrix}$ a bus at all. It's so slow.

$\begin{Bmatrix} May \\ Might \end{Bmatrix}$ *as well* has no question form, and no negative; though the following infinitive can be negated, as in [123]. However, a question, affirmative and negative, can be formed with *It might be (just) as well to*, as in

124 Might it (not) be (just) as well to send a telegram?

Chapter Fifteen

Adverbials

A Form
15.1
a Many adverbs are formed by the addition of the suffix *-ly* to an adjective, *eg*

> 1 Your writing is clear. You write *clearly*.
> 2 Frequent accidents are those that happen *frequently*.
> 3 Recent events are those that have occurred *recently*.

b The addition of *-ly* results in *-ll* when the base ends in *-l*: .
careful(ly)   skilful(ly)   civil(ly)   cool(ly)
Final *y* after a consonant or vowel changes to *i*:
(busy) busily   (happy) happily   (dry) drily   (day) daily   (gay) gaily
However, in monosyllables, *dryly* is also acceptable, and *slyly* is normal.

c Final *e* in the base, after consonant + *l*, is regularly omitted:
(able) ably   (suitable) suitably   (gentle) gently   (simple) simply
Otherwise, it is retained, *eg*
(wise) wisely   (sole) solely
except in
(due) duly   (true) truly   (whole) wholly

d The addition of *-ally* is normal when the base ends in *-ic*:
automatic(ally)   basic(ally)   scientific(ally)
EXCEPTION: public/publicly

e A number of words beginning with *a-* are adverbs, *eg aboard, abreast, abroad, afar, afresh, aloud, anew, apart, ashore, aside, astray*, as in

> 4 They have gone $\begin{cases} \text{aboard} \\ \text{abroad} \\ \text{astray} \end{cases}$

Distinguish such words from adjectives beginning with *a-* (7.17b, c)

f *Well* is an adverb corresponding to *good* in

> 5 Your writing is good. You write well.

But *well*, and old fashioned *goodly* are adjectives in

> 6 I am not (feeling) well. (7.17a)
> 7 John Halifax was a goodly (=kind or handsome) man.

15.2
The adverbial suffix *-ly* is not added to, adjectives already ending in *-ly* (7.1). Corresponding to an *-ly* adjective we must use an adverbial phrase as follows:

8 They were very friendly (*adj*). They welcomed us in a very friendly
$\left\{\begin{array}{l} \text{way.} \\ =\text{manner.} \end{array}\right\}$

15.3

A number of adverbs have the same form as the corresponding adjectives,
eg

$\left.\begin{array}{l} \text{Daily} \\ 9 \quad \text{Weekly} \\ \text{Quarterly} \end{array}\right\}$ newspapers are published $\left\{\begin{array}{l} \textit{daily.} \\ \textit{weekly.} \\ \textit{quarterly.} \end{array}\right\}$

10 An early riser gets up *early*.
11 A fast-train travels *fast*.
12 This is hard work. We have to work *hard*.
13 An ambitious man has high aims. He aims *high*.
14 A late starter starts *late*.
15 He gave a low bow. He bowed *low*.
16 Run in a straight line. Run *straight* to the tape.

For *hardly*, see 15.27; *highly* is dealt with in 15.28 and *lately* in 15.18b.
Lowly is an adjective, as in 7.1.

15.4

a *Clear* is an adjective in [17] below; *clearly* an adverb in [18]:

17 Wipe the windscreen clear. (Verb Pattern D2b in 10.1)
18 I can't see the road clearly.

Only *clear*, whether one calls it an adjective or an adverb, occurs in

19 Stand clear of the gates!

b Note whether an adverb with or without -*ly* is used in:

20a A sharp knife cuts cleanly.
  b The bullet went clean through the wall.
21a These new laws concern us all directly (=in a direct way).
  b Let's meet $\left\{\begin{array}{l} \text{directly} \\ =\text{straight} \end{array}\right\}$ (=immediately) after lunch,
  cp I'll tell you directly (=as soon as) he comes. (conjunction)
22a You have answered fairly (=in a fair or just way).
    Your answer was fairly good. (see 15.27)
  b Being a sportsman can mean playing fair(ly).
23a Don't drop that vase. Hold it firmly.
  b Hold this post firm(ly) while I hammer it into the ground.
    The enemy is advancing. Stand firm.
24a We shouted loudly for help, but nobody came.
  b Don't speak so loud(ly). Someone will hear you.
25a Mary dresses very prettily.
  b She's pretty good. She dances pretty well.

26a The car turned sharply and drove away.

I spoke to the driver sharply.

b At the crossroads, we turned sharp (to the) left.

We arrived at ten o'clock sharp.

27a Speak slowly please. Drive slowly onto the ferry.

b Slow! Go slow(ly): we're coming to a crossroads.

Comparison of adverbs

15.5

Many adverbs are gradable, can be modified by *very, so* and *too*, and can be compared. They include:

a Most adverbs of manner, *eg clearly, carefully, well*;

b *often, frequently, seldom, rarely* (adverbs of frequency);

c *early, late, recently, soon* (adverbs of relative time);

d *near, far* (adverbs of relative place).

15.6

a Monosyllabic adverbs, *eg hard, fast, soon, late, near,* also *early,* form their comparison with the addition of *-er, -est,* as in 7.5, other adverbs with *more, most,* as in 7.9. Either *oftener* or *more often* is acceptable. Comparison at the same degree is expressed by *as – as,* as in 7.11; to a lower degree by *not* $\left\{ \begin{array}{c} as \\ so \end{array} \right\}$ *– as,* or *less . . . than,* as in 7.12. Thus:

28 Tom writes $\left\{ \begin{array}{l} \text{faster} \\ \text{more neatly} \\ \text{more often} \end{array} \right\}$ than I do.

29 He doesn't work as untidily as you do.

b Note the following irregularities:

	COMPARATIVE	SUPERLATIVE
well	better	best
badly	worse	worst
far	farther *or* further	farthest *or* furthest

B Adjuncts

Adverbs of manner

15.7

a The normal position for adverbs of manner is at the end of a clause (1.49b), though, if there are two or more types of adverbial at the end of a clause, manner will come before place and time:

30 George played very $\left\{ \begin{array}{l} \text{well} \\ \text{badly} \end{array} \right\}$ in the match yesterday.

In passive constructions, the adverb can precede or follow the past participle

31 This house was $\left\{\begin{array}{l} \text{built badly.} \\ = \text{badly built.} \end{array}\right\}$

Notice the possible positions with prepositional verbs, verb + adverb particle, and phrasal verbs (12.1).

32 We looked $\left\{\begin{array}{l} \text{into the problem carefully.} \\ = \text{carefully into the problem.} \end{array}\right\}$

33 He walked on quietly.[1]

34 He brought $\left\{\begin{array}{l} \text{his children up} \\ \text{them up} \\ = \text{up his children} \end{array}\right\}$ strictly.

35 Go $\left\{\begin{array}{l} \text{on with your work quietly.} \\ = \text{quietly on with your work.[1]} \end{array}\right\}$

15.8

Adverbs of manner saying *how* an action is performed can freely occur with action verbs (13.5), as in examples [30–35], but not with stative verbs (13.2). Thus we could not replace *prepared* by *knew* in

36 George prepared his lesson carefully.

However, there are certain adverbs of manner that answer the question *How well?*: these can be used with stative verbs and can be placed *before* the verb. Notice the difference between

37 I write clearly. (That is *how* I write)
   and

38 I remember that day clearly *or* I clearly remember that day. (That is *how well* I remember it)

Similarly, notice the difference between

39 You write well. (That is *how* you write)
   and

40 I remember your father well *or* I well remember your father.

Well can only come before *believe, eg*

41 I can well believe it.

15.9

Notice the difference, in meaning and position, between adverbs of manner and VIEWPOINT ADVERBS that answer the question *From what point of view?* For example:

42 The expedition was planned scientifically? (How was it planned.)
   and

43 Scientifically, the expedition was a success.

---

[1] *He walked quietly on* is also possible, but *He walked on quietly* is a safer model to imitate.

In [42], *scientifically* could be paraphrased by *in a scientific manner*; in [43], by *from a scientific point of view*. A viewpoint adverb could also come at the end of a sentence, after a break in intonation and a comma in writing:

43a The expedition was a success, scientifically.

Other viewpoint adverbs would be

educationally   financially   practically   theoretically

Those same adverbs could also be used as adverbs of manner answering the question *How?*; and *practically* has a further use that will be explained in 15.27.

15.10

Then there is a difference in position and meaning between adverbs of manner that are closely associated with the verb, and similar ADVERBS CLOSELY ASSOCIATED WITH THE SUBJECT. For example:

44 George wrote to Mary foolishly. (He wrote in that way)
  and
45 George foolishly wrote her a letter.
  or
45a He has foolishly written her a letter.

Those last two examples could be rephrased *George* $\left\{ \begin{matrix} was \\ has\ been \end{matrix} \right\}$ *foolish to write to her* or *It* $\left\{ \begin{matrix} was \\ has\ been \end{matrix} \right\}$ *foolish of him to write* ... See 3.15d which gives a list of adjectives that could fit into the pattern *He was foolish to write to her*. Adverbs corresponding to those adjectives, *ie bravely, cleverly, cruelly, generously, kindly,* etc. could also be used as 'subject' adverbs replacing *foolishly* in example [45]. Note that *good* appears in 3.15d but that *well* could not replace *foolishly* as a 'subject' adverb. That is because *good* in 3.15d means 'kind'. We could therefore rewrite *It was good of George to write to her* by

46 George kindly wrote to her,

which does not mean the same as *George wrote to her kindly.*

15.11

There are other differences involving adverbs of manner. *eg*
a 47 You may answer the next question generally, not in detail.
  48 You generally (= usually) answer questions in too much detail.
  49 Generally (speaking), I think you have done very well.
  Generally in [47] is an adverb of manner answering the question *How?*; in [48] it is an ADVERB OF FREQUENCY; in [49] it is a DISJUNCT.
b In
  50 I spoke to the child simply *or* I spoke simply to the child
  simply is an adverb of manner answering the question *How?* But in

51 I simply spoke to the child,

simply is a FOCUSING ADVERB (15.21), replaceable by *only*.

c *Badly* is an adverb of manner answering the question *How?* in

52 That hairdresser cut your hair badly.

The same word is an INTENSIFIER, emphasising *needs* in

53 Your hair needs cutting badly;

and, in that sense, *badly* could occupy a medial position, *eg*

53a Your hair $\begin{cases} \text{badly needs} \\ \text{has badly needed} \end{cases}$ cutting.

Adverbials of time and place
15.12

TIME ADVERBIALS could answer the following types of question:

 a When, in past or future or neither?

 b Since when?

 c For how long?

a TIME-WHEN adverbials are freely used with past tense, as in 13.16; with past perfect as in 13.21; and with the 'future tenses' as in 13.25–35. A special set of time adverbials can be used with the present perfect, as in 13.19.

b SINCE-WHEN adverbials (*ie since* + point in time, *eg since yesterday, since last year, since 1971*, etc) are used with present perfect or past perfect, as in 13.9, 13.13, and 13.21.

c FOR-HOW-LONG adverbials can be used with any tense, *eg*

54 $\begin{cases} \text{We stayed there} \\ \text{We have stayed here} \\ \text{We go away every year} \\ \text{We shall stay there} \end{cases}$ for six weeks.

Note the use of *I have* $\begin{cases} lived \\ been\ living \end{cases}$ *here for six years* (13.9a, 13.13b); and note that *for-how-long* adverbials can only be associated with verbs of duration, as in

55 $\begin{cases} \text{We stayed (}ie \text{ our stay lasted)} \\ \text{We did not leave (}ie \text{ our not-leaving lasted)} \end{cases}$ for six weeks.

Left could not replace *stayed* in [55], without making the sentence mean 'We left intending to be away for six weeks'.

15.13

When a series of time adverbials occurs in a sentence, the more detailed information is normally given first, as in

56 I landed in America at six o'clock in the morning on the twenty-fifth of June (*or* on June the twenty-fifth) 1959.

That order might be changed, but a break in intonation would then usually result, as indicated by the oblique strokes in

56a I landed in America in 1959, / in June, / on the twenty-fifth / to be exact, / at six o'clock in the morning, I think.

15.14

Any time adverbial, or a series of time adverbials, could come at the beginning of a sentence, if emphasis were needed on the time of an event or state, *eg*

56b $\left\{\begin{array}{l} \text{In 1959} \\ \text{At six o'clock} \\ \text{At six o'clock in the morning on June 25th} \end{array}\right\}$ I landed . . .

15.15

ADVERBIALS OF PLACE can refer to POSITION, as in

57 I met George Lamb in Paris,

or to DIRECTION, as in

58 We used to go to the same school.

Adverbials of position may be obligatory in a sentence, *eg*

59 We $\left\{\begin{array}{l} \text{were} \\ \text{lived} \end{array}\right\}$ in the same house;

or they may be optional adjuncts, as in example [57]. If they are obligatory, they would remain at the end of a sentence. If optional, they could come at the beginning so as to emphasise the place of an event or state, as in

57a In Paris, I met George Lamb.

Note the adverbs of direction ending in *-ward(s)*, *eg backward(s)*, *forward(s)*, *upward(s)*. Adverbs of direction would not normally begin a sentence.

15.16

As with adverbials of time, when a series of place adverbials occurs in a sentence the more detailed information comes first, *eg*

60 We lived at number 35, Woodstock Road, Harlow.

Commas are conventionally written in an address, as in [60], though there need be no break in intonation. There *would* be breaks in intonation, as indicated by the oblique strokes, if the order were changed, as in

60a We lived $\left\{\begin{array}{l} \text{at} \\ \text{in} \end{array}\right\}$ Harlow, / in Woodstock Road, / at number 35.

15.17

An adverbial of place usually precedes one of time, if both occur in the same clause, as in

[30] George played very well in the match yesterday.

The order could be reversed for the sake of balance or emphasis.

Adverbials of frequency and of relative time
15.18
a ADVERBIALS OF FREQUENCY include
always   ever   frequently   generally   occasionally   often   never
rarely   seldom   sometimes   usually   several times a week
A phrase, eg *several times a week*, will normally come at the end of a
sentence; or, for emphasis, at the beginning. A single word adverb, eg
always, will normally occupy the medial position explained in 1.50, eg

61 We $\left\{\begin{array}{l}\text{have often seen him}\\ \text{are always tired}\\ \text{sometimes go to Spain.}\end{array}\right\}$.

Ever is usually restricted to questions:

62 $\left\{\begin{array}{l}\text{Do you ever go}\\ \text{Have you ever been}\\ \text{Did you ever go}\end{array}\right\}$ skiing?

Ever is normal after *hardly* and *scarcely* but *not ever* is usually replaced by
never:

63 I $\left\{\begin{array}{l}\text{don't ever}\\ =\text{never}\end{array}\right\}$ go there now.

Never, rarely and *seldom* are negators (1.59) and therefore do not
normally occur in the same clause as *not* or another negator; they attract
any, as in 6.42, and its compounds (6.47e); and in rhetorical style they can
come at the beginning of a sentence, provided inversion of subject and
operator follows:

64 $\left\{\begin{array}{l}\text{Never}\\ \text{Rarely}\\ \text{Seldom}\end{array}\right\}$ have we seen such a spectacle as this!

b ADVERBS OF RELATIVE TIME include
just (=in very recent time or in time very soon after now)
lately (=recently)   recently   soon   still (=as late as now or then)
suddenly[1]   yet
Just occupies only the medial position mentioned above, as in

65 We $\left\{\begin{array}{l}\text{have}\\ \text{are}\end{array}\right\}$ just $\left\{\begin{array}{l}\text{seen}\\ \text{going to see}\end{array}\right\}$ the exhibition.

Still would normally occupy that position, eg
66 Are you still waiting?
though it could also come at the end, as in
67 Are you waiting still?
Still at the beginning of a sentence would usually be a conjunct, frequently
occurring in informal style, as in
68 I've never met George. Still, I know a lot about him.

[1] *Suddenly* is an adverb of manner in *He came in suddenly* but an adverb of relative time in
I've suddenly thought of an idea.

Already, lately, recently, soon and *yet* tend to come at the end of the sentence, though they also occur in the medial position.

15.19

A single-word adverb of frequency or of relative time may come before the operator, including DO, in an emphatic assertion, especially in reply to a negative:

69 A This train $\begin{cases} \text{is never late.} \\ \text{never arrives late.} \end{cases}$ (normal)

    B I beg your pardon. It always $\begin{cases} \textit{is} \text{ late.} \\ \textit{does} \text{ arrive late.} \end{cases}$

    It never *did* arrive on time.

70 A Why don't you mend that fuse?

    B But I already *have* mended it.

In B's response in [69] and [70], the operator (*is, does, did, have*) is strongly stressed.

15.20

In the negative, the operator + not will come before *always* but after *sometimes*:

71 This train isn't always late. It doesn't always stop here.

72 It sometimes doesn't stop at every station.

Other adverbs of frequency can precede or follow operator + *not*:

73 This train isn't $\begin{cases} \text{often} \\ \text{generally} \\ \text{usually} \end{cases}$ late, *ie* It seldom *is* late.

74 It $\begin{cases} \text{often} \\ \text{generally} \\ \text{usually} \end{cases}$ isn't early, *ie* It's often late.

Focusing adverbs
15.21

a These focus attention on one item of information contained in the clause. They are of two main kinds, exemplified by *only* (meaning 'that item and nothing else') and *even* (meaning 'and that item in addition to others'), as in

75 I spoke to John only (= to him and no one else).

76 I spoke to Mary even (= to her as well as the others).

b In normal conversation, these two adverbs usually come between the subject and the verb. Thus:

75a I only spoke to John

    and

76a I even spoke to Mary,

with an intonation that starts on a relatively high note on *only* and *even*, drops on *spoke*, and has a nuclear fall on *John* and *Mary*, will produce a meaning equal to that of [75] and [76]. In formal, or 'careful' writing, [75a] and [76a] could be interpreted as '*I spoke*, but took no other action with regard to John and Mary'; and then they could be read with an initial high rise in intonation on *spoke*, followed by an immediate fall.

c In a longer sentence than [75] or [76], *eg*

77 I only spoke to John during the lunch-hour yesterday,

there is more scope for uncertainty as to exactly what item of information is being brought into focus. In speech, we can make our meaning clear by intonation and stress. In writing, we can try to make it clear by putting *only* as near as possible to the item emphasised, or by using a cleft sentence (2.51). Thus:

IN SPEECH

  i I only *spoke* to John . . . (I did nothing else)

  ii I only spoke to *John* . . . (to no one else)

  iii I only spoke to John during the *lunch*-hour yesterday.

  iv I only spoke . . . during the lunch-hour *yesterday*.

IN SPEECH OR WRITING

  i I only spoke to John during the·lunch-hour yesterday.

  ii I spoke only to John . . .

or It was only John that I spoke to during etc.

  iii I spoke to John only during the lunch-hour yesterday.

or It was only during the lunch-hour that I spoke to him.

  iv I spoke to John during the lunch-hour only yesterday.

or It was only yesterday that I spoke to John during the lunch-hour.

In (iv) *only* could come before or after *yesterday*; but in any case (iv) could mean either 'yesterday and no other day' or 'as late as yesterday'.

Note: If [77] were re-phrased so as to begin with *Only yesterday* . . . , inversion of subject and verb would occur, *eg Only yesterday did I speak to John.*

15.22

Only, as in [77], restricts the meaning of part of the sentence. Other adverbs that serve this purpose are

  just   merely   simply

which precede the item focused, and *alone*, which only follows it:

78 I $\left\{\begin{array}{l}\text{just}\\\text{merely}\\\text{simply}\end{array}\right\}$ said 'Hullo' to Mary, that's all.

79 I said 'Hullo' just to Mary (to no one else).

80 We can't afford that rent on my salary alone.

Exactly is often used as a focusing adverb, before or after a *wh*-question word, as in

81 $\begin{Bmatrix} \text{Exactly what} \\ \text{What exactly} \end{Bmatrix}$ are you trying to tell me?

15.23

Also, too and *as well* are frequently-used adverbials that focus attention on additional information, thus:

82 $\begin{Bmatrix} \text{John bought a book.} \\ \text{I borrowed a book.} \\ \text{I bought a pen.} \end{Bmatrix}$ I also bought a book.

Like *only, also* can be ambiguous. By itself, the second sentence in [82] could mean either

82a I, as well as someone else, bought a book.

82b I bought, as well as, *eg* borrowed, a book.

82c I bought a book, as well as something else.

In speech, those differences in meaning could be made clearer by means of stress:

82a I *also* – bought a book.

82b I also *bought* a book.

82c I also bought a *book*.

We could equally well say

83 I bought a book also,

with the same range of meanings. *Too* and *as well* could freely replace *also* in [83]. *Too*, between commas, could replace *also* in [82a] (*I, too, bought a book*); but *too* could not replace *also* in [82b] or [82c]. *As well* could not replace *also* in any of those examples except [83].

15.24

Remember that the negative of *I bought a book* $\begin{Bmatrix} also \\ too \\ as\ well \end{Bmatrix}$ would be *I didn't buy a book either*.

Adverbials of degree, including intensifiers
15.25

Consider the following example:

84 I've nearly finished your story. It's very exciting.

Both *nearly* and *very* can be considered as adverbials of degree, but of a different kind. *Nearly* could not be deleted from [84] without a substantial change of meaning: it indicates a degree along a scale which can be measured by the number of pages in the story. *Very exciting* suggests 'exciting to a high degree'; *very* can be deleted without substantial change of meaning. The speaker could convey the same idea by saying *It is exciting*. He uses *very* to make his remark sound enthusiastic. We shall therefore call *nearly* an ADVERB OF DEGREE, and *very* an INTENSIFIER.

15.26

Different adverbials of degree and different intensifiers modify different classes of word. To understand these differences we must consider:

a whether the word being modified is an ADJECTIVE; an *-ed* PARTICIPLE USED AS AN ADJECTIVE, as in 7.2; an *-ed* PARTICIPLE *not* USED AS AN ADJECTIVE; an ADVERB; or a VERB;

b whether an adjective or *-ed* participle refers to a permanent QUALITY or to a temporary STATE;

c whether the word modified suggests something desirable or POSITIVE on the one hand, or undesirable or NEGATIVE on the other;

d whether the word modified is GRADABLE (*eg good*) or UNGRADABLE (*right*); and, if ungradable, whether it refers to a STANDARD (*eg good enough*) or to an ABSOLUTE (*eg perfect*);

e whether the modifier expresses the idea of UPGRADING or of DOWNGRADING.

These criteria are illustrated in the Table below

Table 14

WORDS MODIFIED

	Adjective	-ed as adjective	Other -ed forms	Adverb	Verb
quality	good				
state	busy	married	completed		
positive	good	pleased	completed	well	like
negative	bad	displeased	uncompleted	badly	dislike
gradable	good	pleased		well	like
ungradable	perfect	married	completed	perfectly	know
upgrade	(very) good	(very) pleased		(very) well	like (very much)
downgrade	(not) good (at all)	(not) pleased (at all)		(not) well (at all)	(not) like (at all)

Degree
15.27

The following are among the frequently-used adverbials of degree:

ALMOST frequently occurs before an ungradable adjective or adverb, whether standard or absolute, and before a non-adjectival *-ed* form. It does not normally occur with a negative; *eg*

85 This is almost $\left\{ \begin{array}{l} \text{completed} \\ \text{perfect} \\ \text{straight} \end{array} \right\}$. It is almost good enough.

ALTOGETHER, meaning '100 per cent', is frequently used with *not* before a negative adjective; also before a positive or negative verb; sometimes before an adjective expressing an absolute; *eg*

86   Your work is not altogether $\begin{cases} \text{bad.} \\ \text{(un)satisfactory.} \end{cases}$

87   I don't altogether $\begin{cases} \text{like} \\ \text{dislike} \end{cases}$ him.

88   Your work is altogether perfect.

BARELY downgrades an adjective referring to a standard; before an ungradable verb, it suggests that the standard required is not fully satisfied, or only just satisfied; *eg*

89   I'm afraid your work is barely good enough. (=a little less than good enough).

90   I can't tell you anything about George. I barely know him. (=I have only just made his acquaintance)

FAIRLY downgrades a positive adjective, an *-ed* participle used as adjective, or an adverb:

91   Bob and I are fairly good friends. (less than very good)

92   I know him fairly well – not very well.

93   I'm fairly satisfied with your work. It could be better.

HARDLY could replace *barely* in [89] and [90] and would be the more likely to occur in normal speech. In addition, it would occur in

94   You can hardly (=not really) expect me to believe that.

As a negator it means *only just* in

95   I had hardly left the house when the telephone rang,

which could be re-worded as

95a   Hardly had I left the house when the telephone rang.

A LITTLE, meaning 'more than zero', is often found before certain negative adjectives and adjectival *-ed* forms, but comes after verbs.

96   I'm feeling a little $\begin{cases} \text{sad} \\ \text{worried} \end{cases}$ this morning.

97   You've made a little progress. (*a little* is there a determiner) You are improving a little. (adverbial of degree)

LITTLE, meaning 'almost zero' and usually modified by *very*, occurs after verbs:

98   People seem to read very little these days.

NEARLY can replace *almost* in [85]; but unlike *almost* it can be preceded by *not*:

85a   This is not nearly straight, not nearly good enough.

Our work is not nearly $\begin{cases} \text{completed} \\ \text{finished} \end{cases}$. We have a lot to do yet.

PRACTICALLY could replace *almost* in [85], but not *nearly* in [85a].

QUITE means 'moderately' when it occurs before a gradable adjective, adjectival *-ed* form, adverb or verb, as in

99   Your work is quite good. You have done quite well. I am quite pleased with it. I quite like it.

Depending on the intonation, *quite* in those examples could suggest either 'below the maximum' or 'approaching the maximum'. Before an ungradable word, *quite* means '100 per cent', as in

100 You are $\left\{\begin{array}{l}\text{quite}\\=\text{perfectly}\end{array}\right\}$ right. I $\left\{\begin{array}{l}\text{quite}\\=\text{entirely}\end{array}\right\}$ understand.

Quite can be used, as in [99] before ENJOY; and, as in [100], before APPRECIATE, BELIEVE, FORGET, REALISE, RECOGNISE.

Not quite occurs before a 'standard' or an 'absolute' to suggest that the required level is a little below 100 per cent, as in

101 You are not quite right. Your answer is not quite good enough.
       I don't quite understand.

RATHER could replace *fairly* in [91], [92] and [93], *eg*

[91a] Bob and I are rather good friends. I know him rather well.

But in those examples *rather good, rather well* etc. do not mean 'less than good, less than well' but indicate an upgrading towards 'good', 'well' and 'satisfied'. *Rather* is also used before a negative adjective or adverb to suggest 'on the way towards that undesirable state', as in

102 I'm feeling rather $\left\{\begin{array}{l}\text{unwell}\\\text{depressed}\end{array}\right\}$. I've done rather badly in my exams.

Rather would not be replaced by *fairly* in that example.

Fairly and *rather* could both occur in

103 That is a $\left\{\begin{array}{l}\text{fairly}\\\text{rather}\end{array}\right\}$ long story.

But only *rather* is acceptable in the structure of

104 That is rather a long story. It's rather a story.

Rather a story = a remarkable or complicated story. *Rather*, not *fairly*, is also acceptable in

105 I rather $\left\{\begin{array}{l}\text{like}\\\text{sympathise with}\end{array}\right\}$ him. I rather doubt it.

SCARCELY could replace *barely* in [89] and [90] and *hardly* in [94], [95] and [95a].

SOMEWHAT could replace *rather* in [102] and *a little* in [96]. Another example would be

106 He was $\left\{\begin{array}{l}\text{rather}\\=\text{somewhat}\end{array}\right\}$ surprised and looked around him

$\left\{\begin{array}{l}\text{rather}\\=\text{somewhat}\end{array}\right\}$ anxiously.

TOO, before an adjective, adjectival *-ed* form or an adverb, suggests a degree higher than necessary or desirable, *eg*

107 This is too hard: I can't do it. I'm too tired: I must have a rest.
       You have tied this too tightly: I can't undo it.

Too can be modified by *much* or *far*, eg *This is* $\left\{\begin{array}{l}much\\far\end{array}\right\}$ *too difficult.*

Intensifiers
15.28
A BIT, informal, is often used after a verb in the negative, as in
108 I don't like this a bit.
ABSOLUTELY occurs before non-gradable adjectives, adverbs and verbs which suggest an extreme positive or negative degree:

109 This is absolutely $\begin{Bmatrix} \text{magnificent} \\ \text{awful} \end{Bmatrix}$. You've done absolutely

$\begin{Bmatrix} \text{splendidly} \\ \text{appallingly} \end{Bmatrix}$. I absolutely $\begin{Bmatrix} \text{adore} \\ \text{detest} \end{Bmatrix}$ him.

AT ALL, neutral in style, could replace *a bit* in [108]. It could come before or after a gradable adjective or adverb, *eg*

110 This is not $\begin{Bmatrix} \text{good at all.} \\ \text{at all good.} \end{Bmatrix}$ You haven't done $\begin{Bmatrix} \text{well at all.} \\ \text{at all well.} \end{Bmatrix}$

111 I don't like it at all.

I don't at all like it is also possible.

BADLY upgrades NEED and WANT, making them more emphatic, as in

112 You badly $\begin{Bmatrix} \text{need} \\ \text{want} \end{Bmatrix}$ a haircut *or* You $\begin{Bmatrix} \text{need} \\ \text{want} \end{Bmatrix}$ a haircut badly.

It can also modify negative *-ed* forms, as in

113 Several people were badly $\begin{cases} \text{frightened.} \\ \text{hurt (physically).} \\ \text{injured.} \end{cases}$

very hurt is acceptable when *hurt* refers to personal feelings.

COMPLETELY is frequent before non-gradable adjectives and verbs:

114 This is completely $\begin{Bmatrix} \text{empty} \\ \text{right.} \end{Bmatrix}$ I $\begin{Bmatrix} \text{agree} \\ \text{understand} \end{Bmatrix}$ completely.

DEEPLY occurs with negative verbs and negative *-ed* forms; referring to personal feelings; *eg*

115 I deeply resent your remarks. I am deeply $\begin{cases} \text{disappointed.} \\ \text{hurt.} \\ \text{offended.} \end{cases}$

ENTIRELY: use in the same way as *completely*.

EXTREMELY serves as an emphatic replacement for *very*, as in

116 I am extremely $\begin{Bmatrix} \text{busy.} \\ \text{tired.} \end{Bmatrix}$ You work extremely $\begin{Bmatrix} \text{hard.} \\ \text{fast.} \end{Bmatrix}$

GREATLY often occurs before *-ed* forms to suggest that a considerable change in the state of affairs has been effected, as in

117 He was greatly $\begin{cases} \text{changed.} \\ \text{encouraged.} \\ \text{mistaken.} \end{cases}$ His story was greatly $\begin{Bmatrix} \text{admired.} \\ \text{exaggerated.} \end{Bmatrix}$

HIGHLY is used before adjectives and *-ed* forms, especially those referring to personal feelings and qualifications:

118 He was highly $\begin{cases} \text{sensitive about his weakness.} \\ \text{suspicious of strangers.} \end{cases}$

119 He was highly $\begin{cases} \text{delighted.} \\ \text{qualified.} \\ \text{trained.} \end{cases}$

INDEED reinforces *very* or *very much*, as in

120 He $\begin{cases} \text{is very good} \\ \text{played very well} \end{cases}$ indeed.   I like him very much indeed.

It reinforces agreement to the use of a word already mentioned, as

121 A Is that correct?   A Do you object?

    B It is indeed correct.   B I do indeed object.

IN THE $\begin{cases} \text{LEAST} \\ = \text{SLIGHTEST} \end{cases}$ is a stronger expression than *at all* in [111]:

111a I don't like it in the $\begin{cases} \text{least.} \\ \text{slightest.} \end{cases}$

MOST (not to be confused with the superlative, as in 7.9 and 15.6) is an enthusiastic replacement for *very* before certain positive adjectives expressing subjective feelings; *eg*

122 Thank you very much. You are most $\begin{cases} \text{kind} \\ \text{generous} \end{cases}$, and I am most grateful to you.

MUCH is used as an intensifier, in rather formal style, in

123 We much $\begin{cases} \text{appreciate} \\ \text{prefer} \end{cases}$ your offer.   They were much $\begin{cases} \text{admired.} \\ \text{mistaken.} \end{cases}$
A much improved offer.

Very before *much* would make the examples in [123] less formal; and *very* before *much* is obligatory when the intensifier follows the verb, as in

123a We appreciate your offer very much.

PARTICULARLY occurs before a gradable adjective, *eg particularly good*;
PERFECTLY is commonly used before a positive adjective or adverb, whether gradable or ungradable: *eg*

124 This is perfectly $\begin{cases} \text{sound} \\ \text{right} \end{cases}$. You know that perfectly well.

It can also precede a negative adjective expressing an extreme, *eg*

125 I think this is perfectly $\begin{cases} \text{awful} \\ \text{terrible} \end{cases}$. (informal)

POSITIVELY can, paradoxically, modify a strongly negative adjective or verb, as in

126 I find him positively dishonest. I positively dislike him.

PRETTY serves as a mild and informal replacement for *very*
REALLY can modify an adjective, adverb or verb, as in

127 The place is really beautiful, I really like it.

128 You have done that really excellently.

SERIOUSLY modifies negative adjectives and adjectival -ed forms:

129 He was seriously $\left\{\begin{array}{l}\text{hurt (physically)}\\\text{injured}\\\text{worried}\end{array}\right.$

TERRIBLY is frequently used in informal style as a strong replacement for *very*, as in *terribly busy, terribly worried*. It can be used, again informally, with certain gradable verbs, as in

130 Do you mind terribly if we don't come with you?

THOROUGHLY intensifies a positive or negative adjective or verb:

131 He is thoroughly $\left\{\begin{array}{l}\text{happy.}\\\text{lazy.}\\\text{selfish.}\end{array}\right\}$ I thoroughly $\left\{\begin{array}{l}\text{approve.}\\\text{disapprove.}\end{array}\right\}$

It is commonly used before an -ed form expressing physical feelings or personal emotions, as in

132 She was thoroughly $\left\{\begin{array}{l}\text{annoyed.}\\\text{exhausted.}\\\text{upset.}\end{array}\right\}$

UTTERLY intensifies negative adjectives, -ed forms and verbs, eg

133 He is utterly mad. We utterly reject his accusations.

134 We are utterly $\left\{\begin{array}{l}\text{opposed to}\\\text{bored with}\end{array}\right\}$ the whole idea.

VERY modifies adjectives and adverbs, not verbs. It can be duplicated for emphasis, as in *It's very, very hot today.*

Modifiers of comparatives and superlatives
15.29

a What has been said about adjectives in 15.27–28 applies only to the positive degree (1.44a). Adjectives in the comparative degree take a different set of modifiers. These can upgrade, thus:

135 This is $\left\{\begin{array}{l}\text{much}\\\text{very much}\\\text{far}\end{array}\right\}$ better. (neutral) It's a lot better. (informal)

Superior and *inferior* are normally treated as comparatives. *Much superior* is formal, but *very much superior* or *far superior* would be neutral in style. Commonly-used downgraders are *hardly any* and *no*, eg

136 This is $\left\{\begin{array}{l}\text{hardly any}\\\text{no}\end{array}\right\}$ better.

A little and *rather* can modify comparatives, but not *fairly*.
Any would occur in questions, eg *Is this any better?*

b *Very* modifies a superlative, as in

137 This is the very $\left\{\begin{array}{l}\text{best.}\\\text{first.}\end{array}\right.$

C, Disjuncts and conjuncts
15.30
DISJUNCTS (1.52), expressing the speaker's or writer's attitude or approach
to the statement he is making, include
a single-word adverbs:

briefly	certainly	frankly	generally
honestly	perhaps	personally	really

b phrases:

in a few words	in all fairness	in short	of course

c non-finite clauses:

speaking frankly   to tell you the truth   to cut a long story short

d finite clauses:

if I may say so   if you don't mind my pointing it out
Examples:

138 $\begin{cases} \text{Honestly,} \\ \text{In short,} \\ \text{To tell you the truth,} \\ \text{If I may say so,} \end{cases}$ we knew nothing about it.

The disjunct can come at the end of the sentence:
139 I believe him, personally;
or it can come after the subject, as in
140 I honestly don't remember.
Notice the difference between the adverb of manner and the disjunct in
the following:

141 He was speaking $\begin{cases} \text{frankly.} \\ \text{honestly.} \\ \text{personally.} \end{cases}$ (adverbs of manner)

142 $\begin{cases} \text{Frankly,} \\ \text{Honestly,} \\ \text{Personally,} \end{cases}$ I don't trust him. (disjuncts)

Also notice the difference between *really* as an intensifier, meaning *very*
or *very much* (as in examples [127] and [128]) and *really* as a disjunct,
meaning 'I am telling the truth when I say', as in
143 Really, I didn't do it. I really didn't do it.
A difference of that kind becomes apparent in brief negative answers, *eg*
144 A Is the water hot?

B Not $\begin{cases} \text{really.} \\ \text{terribly.} \\ \text{very.} \end{cases}$ (intensifiers)

145 A Did you take my newspaper?

B $\begin{cases} \text{Certainly} \\ \text{Honestly} \\ \text{Really} \end{cases}$ not. (disjuncts)

15.31

CONJUNCTS (1.52), introducing a new sentence in a series and linking it logically with what has been said before, include:

a altogether (meaning 'in all')   besides   consequently   however   moreover   nevertheless   therefore   yet

b as a result   in any case   on the other hand

c considering all that   to conclude   all things considered

d that is to say   what is more   what is more important

Examples:

146 Production, gentlemen, has increased by twenty per cent this year.

$$\left\{ \begin{array}{l} \text{Altogether,} \\ \text{As a result,} \\ \text{Considering all that,} \\ \text{That is to say,} \end{array} \right\} \text{we can present the nation with a very}$$

satisfactory report.

Like disjuncts, conjuncts can come at the end of a sentence, after a comma, as in

147 Our report is very satisfactory, $\left\{ \begin{array}{l} \text{therefore.} \\ \text{that is to say.} \end{array} \right\}$

Or they can come after the opening phrase:

148 We still, $\left\{ \begin{array}{l} \text{however,} \\ \text{though,} \end{array} \right\}$ have a lot of work to do.

Note the use of *though* as a conjunct, not replaceable by *although*. In this role, *though* is typical of informal rather than formal style. It can come at the end of the sentence:

149 We still have a lot of work to do, though.

Finally, note the difference between the adjunct *yet* (15.18) and the conjunct (2.3) *yet*:

150 I have not had the pleasure of meeting you yet (*adjunct*). Yet (*conjunct*) I have heard so much about you that I feel I know you well already.

Appendix One

Summary of spelling rules

For the spelling of individual words, the reader is referred to a good dictionary. The following is a summary of spelling rules which come within the scope of this Grammar:

1 NOUNS, PLURAL
  a Regular, *eg boys, matches, gases, potatoes, countries*: see 1.11.
  b Irregular: nouns ending in *o*: 5.15; in *f* or *fe*, 5.16; *men, women* etc., 5.17; Latin, Greek and French plurals, 5.22.
  c Compound nouns: 5.25–26.
  d Proper nouns: 5.27.
2 NOUNS ENDING IN *-er*, *-or* or *-ar*, *eg employer, writer, runner, occupier, flier* or *flyer, actor, beggar*: 5.1.
3 VERBS, 3RD PERSON SINGULAR, PRESENT TENSE, *eg plays, wishes, goes*: 1.11.(2).
4 VERBS, *-ed* FORMS, *eg played, stopped, gassed, tried, occurred, offered*: 1.16.(3) and 9.4.
5 VERBS, *-ing* FORMS, *eg waiting, writing, stopping, gassing, beginning, offering, dying, dyeing*: 1.16.(5), 9.3.
6 ADJECTIVES ENDING IN *-able*, *eg comfortable, preferable, regrettable, reliable, agreeable, manageable*: 7.1.
7 ADJECTIVES ENDING IN *-ous*, *eg courageous, dangerous, spacious, vigorous, piteous, gaseous*: 7.1.
8 ADJECTIVES ENDING in *-ful*, *eg careful, beautiful, skilful*: 7.1.
9 ADJECTIVES ENDING IN *-y*, *eg dirty, muddy, icy*: 7.1.
10 COMPARATIVE AND SUPERLATIVE OF ADJECTIVES, *eg faster, bigger, wider, happier, happiest*: 7.5 and 7.8.
11 ADVERBS ENDING IN *-ly*, *eg carefully, happily, drily, truly, wholly*: 15.1.

CHANGES IN THE BASE WHEN AN ENDING IS ADDED TO IT
12 BASE ENDING IN *e*. Delete the *e* before adding *-ed*, *-en*, *-er*, *-ing* or *-y*:
  pleased, widen, wider, writing, stony
  Before *-able*, the final *e* is optionally deleted, *eg sal(e)able.* but it is retained in any case after *c, g* or *e*:
  peaceable, manageable, agreeable
  Before *-ous*, final *e* is retained, but it changes to *i* after *c*:
  courageous, spacious.
  Before a suffix beginning with a consonant sound, final *e* is retained:
  careful, careless.

Note *dying, lying, ageing, agreeing, dyeing, hoeing, singeing, swingeing*:
9.3b.

13 BASE ENDING IN *-y* PRECEDED BY A CONSONANT. Change the *y* to *i* before
any ending except *-ing* and *-ous*:
   occupied, occupier, reliable, beautiful, beautify, pitiless.
But *occupying, piteous*. For *flier, flyer, drier, dryer*, 5.1; 7.5

14 BASE ENDING IN A SINGLE CONSONANT LETTER PRECEDED BY A SINGLE
VOWEL LETTER. Double the consonant before *-able, -ed, -en, -er, -ing*
and *-y* in any monosyllable and in the final syllable, if stressed, of a
longer word. Note: (i) final *s* is not doubled in the plural of nouns;
(ii) final *p* and *t* are doubled in words ending with *-quip* and *-quit*;
(iii) in British English final *l* and *p* are usually doubled even when the
last syllable is unstressed:
   regrettable, stopped, fatten, runner, running, muddy;
   acquitted, equipped, quitted; travelled, traveller, travelling.
But *buses, gases, raining, offering*. For *picnicking*, see 9.3e.

15 SINGLE OR DOUBLE CONSONANT AFTER A PREFIX. The consonant at the
beginning of the ROOT of a word is doubled only if the prefix ends in a
consonant; but the consonant ending the prefix is usually assimilated
to the consonant that begins the root. Thus:

PREFIX	EXAMPLES
a-	*alight, alike, alone*, as in 7.17: *aboard, afar, aloud*, as in 15.1
ad- (=to)	*addict, addition, address* The *d* of *ad-* is assimilated to roots beginning with *c, f, l, n, p, r, s, t*, as in *accord, accustomed; afford; allocate, allow; announce; appeal, appoint, apposition; arrange; assemble, assent, assign; attach, attack, attempt, attract, attribute*
com- (=with)	*communicate* NOTE *ac-* + *com-* in *accommodation* The *m* of *com-* is assimilated to roots beginning with *l, n, r* as in *collide, collision, collocate, colloquial; connect, connive; correspond*
de- (=from)	*decrease, degrade, deliver, depart*
dis- (=apart)	*dissect, dissent, dissolve* The *s* of *dis-* is assimilated to the root beginning with *f* in *different*
e- (=out)	*emerge, eminent* (=standing out), *emit*
in- (=not)	*incomplete, ineligible, innocent* The *n* of *in-* is assimilated to roots beginning with *l, m, r*, as in

	illegal, illegible, illegitimate; immature, immediate,
	imminent, immovable; irregular, irrelevant
pre- (= before)	*preface, prejudice, prepare, preposition*
pro- (= for)	*proclaim, produce, pronoun*
sym- (= with)	as in *symmetrical*. The *m* is assimilated to *l* in *syllable*.
un- (= not)	*unnatural, unnecessary*

Appendix Two

Notes on punctuation and the use of capital letters

1 FULL STOP

a Obligatory at the end of a complete sentence, provided that the adjuncts and dependent clauses belonging to that sentence have been included. See the numerous examples in this Grammar.

b Often used in abbreviations consisting of single letters, as in *i.e.*, abbreviation for the Latin *id est* = *that is*, and *e.g.*, abbreviation for the Latin *exempli gratia* = *for example*. However, abbreviations on the model of U.N.E.S.C.O. (United Nations Educational Scientific and Cultural Organisation) may become new words, still spelt with capital letters, thus: UNESCO.

c Normal with abbreviations on the model of *adj.* for *adjective* and *Dept.* for *Department*. The full stop is optional if the last letter of the abbreviation is also the last letter of the word, as in *Dr(.)* for *Doctor*.

2 COMMA

a Obligatory in separating non-restrictive apposition (1.33f) and non-restrictive relative clauses (2.26) from the rest of the sentence in which they occur. See the examples in 1.33f and in 2.30 etc.

b Obligatory in order to avoid misunderstanding in sentences such as the following:

According to Jack, London is far too crowded.

He left early, because I saw him go. (See 2.45f)

He left us, to pay the bill. (See 3.12)

c Normal in separating conjuncts and disjuncts from the rest of the sentence in which they occur, as in

However, there may be a few exceptions.

There may, however, be a few exceptions.

There may be a few exceptions, however.

Naturally, that is not the whole story.

He did not speak to the President, naturally.

d Normal in marking the beginning and end of a phrase that is inserted into the structure of a sentence, as in

London, according to Jack, is far too crowded.

e Normal at the end of a non-finite clause that begins a sentence

Having been invited, I intend to stay.

Built in 1468, this castle was the scene of many battles.

To see Inca building at its most impressive, one should go to Machu Picchu.

Never at a loss for a word, Jackson held us all spell-bound.

f Usual at the end of an adverb phrase or of a dependent clause beginning a sentence.

In search of gold, my great-grandfather landed in America.

As soon as he had settled down, he sent for his family to join him.

g Normal when a comment clause (2.10) follows a main clause, and obligatory when a comment clause interrupts a main:

He was the first man to swim the Bosporus, I believe.

He was the first man, I believe, to swim the Bosporus.

h Useful in making the distinction between a purpose clause (2.48) and a result clause (2.49):

We turned up the radio so that everyone could hear. (purpose)

We turned up the radio, so that everyone could hear. (result)

i *Note*: Unless there is an interruption in the clause, as in *d* and *g*, no comma or any other punctuation mark must separate the verb and its object, whether the object is a noun phrase, a finite (*that-* or *wh-*) clause, or a non-finite clause. Thus:

He told me
{ the truth.
{ that he knew exactly what to do.
{ where he was going.
{ to send him a telegram.

3 SEMICOLON

a A means of separating an additional clause from the rest of the sentence to which it belongs, as in

Soon, indeed, it will be only by their situations that cities can be distinguished; but therein Istanbul is unrivalled.

A semicolon, rather than a comma, makes that sentence easier to read: it indicates that, whereas the *that*-clause is dependent on the main, the *but*-clause is not.

b Usual in marking off each of a succession of dependent clauses, finite or non-finite, which are all dependent on an initial main clause:

The Committee therefore agreed(:) that Mr Abbott be invited to attend the next meeting; that, in the meantime, no action should be taken on the basis of his report; and that a more detailed estimate should be prepared.

You are kindly requested(:) to complete the enclosed form; to post it at once in the envelope provided; and to notify this office at once of any change in your address.

4 COLON

a Usual after an introductory clause or phrase as in the example in [3b] above.

b Serves to separate two finite clauses, when the second provides an explanation, expansion or modification of what is said in the first, and when there is no subordinating conjunction linking the two. A colon could replace the semicolon in the example in [3a] above: the effect would be to make a contrast between *(un)distinguished* and *unrivalled*. Another example:

We must sell this property: maintenance costs are far too high.

5 QUOTATION MARKS (OR INVERTED COMMAS)

a Either single or double quotation marks are obligatory at the beginning and end of direct speech (2.11). Note the use of the comma (replaceable by a colon) before the quotation begins, and the use of a comma before a reporting phrase that follows the quotation:

The guard shouted, 'The road is closed'. *or* 'The road is closed,' the guard shouted.

b Inverted commas are often used to indicate that a word is being used in a special, not generally accepted, sense:

Would you call *be going to* and *be to* 'future tenses'?

c Two sets of inverted commas may occur, as in

I heard that man say, 'The guard shouted "The road's closed"'.

Leech speaks of 'five types of "future tense"'.

6 APOSTROPHE

a Obligatory with the possessive form described in 5.31–38.

b Obligatory with the contractions listed in 1.31.

7 EXCLAMATION MARK

a Normal after exclamations, as in 1.61, and after vigorous commands as in *Get down! Take cover!*

b Often used in intimate correspondence, especially in a feminine style, as in *Guess what! Sue's married!*

8 QUESTION MARK. Obligatory at the end of direct questions, as in 1.58.

9 DASH. Dashes could replace the commas before and after the kind of interruption exemplified in 2d above.

10 CAPITAL LETTERS are obligatory at the beginning of:

a the first word of a sentence;

b personal names, *eg Mr George Lamb*;

c the names of roads, streets, towns, villages, countries, etc. and geographical features, *eg North Road, High Street, Boston, Japan, Mount Everest, Lake Ontario, the Pacific Ocean*;

d names of the days of the week, months, special festivals, *eg Monday, March, Christmas, Easter*;

e nouns and adjectives referring to nationality, *eg He is French, two Frenchmen, They have French passports*;

f names of languages, *eg Do you speak English?*

g names of institutions, *eg the British Museum, the United Nations*;

h The first person singular, *I*, is always spelt with a capital;

i A capital is normal at the beginning of a title referring to a particular person. Compare these two sentences:

A republic usually elects a president.

John Roberts, President of the Union, will address the assembly;

j Words like *committee, government, school, union, university,* are normally spelt with a capital when they refer to a particular institution. Compare these two sentences:

A committee is a group of persons elected or appointed to undertake certain duties.

The (Executive) Committee will meet again on May 10th.

Bibliography

Principal works consulted, and recommended for further reference. These are listed in chronological order of publication so as to illustrate traditional and modern influence on the present book, although the overlap between traditional and modern is considerable.

1891   SWEET, H. *A New English Grammar*, (Oxford)

1909   JESPERSEN, O. *A Modern English Grammar on Historical Principles*, (London and Copenhagen)

1924   PALMER, H. E. and BLANDFORD, F. G. *A Grammar of Spoken English*, rev. R. Kingdon, 1969 (Cambridge)

1933   *The Shorter Oxford English Dictionary*, ed. C. T. Onions, (Oxford)

1933   JESPERSEN, O. *Essentials of English Grammar*, (London)

1948   HORNBY, A. S., GATENBY, E. V. and WAKEFIELD, H. *The Advanced Learner's Dictionary of Current English*, (London): see also 1974

1952   FRIES, C. C. *The Structure of English*, based on *American English Grammar*, (New York, 1940)

1953   WEST, M. *A General Service List of English Words*, (London)

1954   HORNBY, A. S. *A Guide to Patterns and Usage in English*, (London)

1957   CHOMSKY, N. *Syntactic Structures*, (The Hague)

1957   ZANDVOORT, R. W. *A Handbook of English Grammar*, (London)

1962   STRANG, B. M. H. *Modern English Structure*, (London)

1962   CLOSE, R. A. *English as a Foreign Language*, (London)

1962   QUIRK, R. *The Use of English*, with a supplement on *Notions of Correctness*, J. Warburg, (London)

1965   FOWLER, H. W. *A Dictionary of Modern English Usage*, rev. Sir Ernest Gowers, (Oxford)

1965   CHOMSKY, N. *Aspects of the Theory of Syntax*, (Massachusetts)

1965   PALMER, F. R. *A Linguistic Study of the English Verb*, (London)

1967–8   HALLIDAY, M. A. K. *Notes on Transitivity and Theme in English*[1]

1968   SCOTT, F. S., BOWLEY, C. C., BROCKETT, C. S., BROWN, J. G. and GODDARD, P. R. *English Grammar*, (Auckland)

1968   RUTHERFORD, W. E. *Modern English*, (New York)

1972   LEECH, G. N. *Meaning and the English Verb*, (London)

1971   CLOSE, R. A. *The English We Use*, (London)

1972   QUIRK, R., GREENBAUM, S., LEECH, G. N. and SVARTVIK, J. *A Grammar of Contemporary English*, (London)

1972   SINCLAIR, J. MCH. *A Course in Spoken English: Grammar*, (London)

[1] Papers published in the *Journal of Linguistics*.

1973   QUIRK, R. and GREENBAUM, S. *A University Grammar of English,* (London)

1974   HORNBY, A. S. *Oxford Advanced Learner's Dictionary of Current English,* third edition, (London)

1975   LEECH, G. N. and SVARTVIK, J. *A Communicative Grammar of English,* (London)

1975   COWIE, A. P. and MACKIN, R. *Oxford Dictionary of Current Idiomatic English,* (London)

1976   HALLIDAY, M. A. K. and HASAN, R. *Cohesion in English,* (London)

1978   *Longman Dictionary of Contemporary English* (London)

1976   HALLIDAY, M. A. K. and HASAN, R. Cohesion in English, (London)

1978   *Longman Dictionary of Contemporary English* (London)

Index

Grammatical terms are entered in small capitals (*eg* SUBJECT). Other subjects and notions appear in ordinary type (*eg* Abstractions). Individual words treated in the Grammar are printed in italics (*eg abandon*).

Numbers refer to chapter section and sub-section. More important sections are indicated in bold type (*eg* **1.47**;).

Abbreviations: ADJ = ADJECTIVE; ADV = ADVERB; CONJ = CONJUNCTION; DET = DETERMINER; N = NOUN; PREP = PREPOSITION; V = VERB; *passim* = everywhere (in many parts of the book).

Shape 1.44; 5.6; 7.16
share 10.8
shark 5.19
sharp(ly) 15.4
shaven 3.38
she **1.5**; 1.10; 1.32; 4.36; **6.28**
sheaf 5.16
shear, sheared 9.8
sheath -s 5.14
shed (v) 9.6
sheep 5.20
sheer 7.14
sheet 5.9
shelf 5.3; 5.16
shelter 10.8
shelve 5.3
shew(n) see *show*
shield (v) 10.8
shine 9.7; 10.8
ship, by - 8.9
ship's 5.36
Ships 6.27; 6.28
shocked 7.2; 7.20
shocking 7.2
shone see *shine*
shook see *shake*
shoot, shot 9.7; 10.8
shorn see *shear*
SHORT RESPONSES 1.1; 1.15; **1.60**;
  2.8(footnote); 2.26(footnote); 3.8; 3.9;
  4.42
short, in - 8.9
shortcomings 5.23
shorts 5.23
should **1.15**; 1.31; **2.17**; 2.38(footnote);
  2.42; 3.1; 13.37; **14.8**; **14.23–6**
    - beginning a Conditional clause
    2.42
    - *have -ed* 14.10–11; 14.26
shouldn't 1.31
shout 2.11; 10.4(B11b)
  - *out* 10.4(B11)
show, showed, shown 9.8; 10.4(B11); 10.5;
  10.8
shrink 9.8
shrunk 3.38 (see *shrink*)
shut (v) 9.6; 10.2(O2)
  - *up* 12.3
Sibilant 1.11; and page xi
sick 7.17; 7.20
  the - 7.21

side 8.1
-*side* 5.34
sight, by/in/out of - 8.9
signal 9.3; 9.4
silly 3.15; 7.20
similar 7.20
SIMPLE PAST (tense) **1.16**; 1.28; **13.16–19**
  - PRESENT (tense) **1.16**; 1.28; **13.7**
  - SENTENCE **1.2**; **Chapter One**; 2.1; 4.1
  - VERB 1.14; 1.16; 1.50; 2.12
simple 7.8
simply 15.22
since (Time) 1.58; **2.40**; 4.7; 4.18; 13.9;
  13.13; **13.19**; **13.21**
    (Reason) **2.45**; 4.7
sincere 7.20
sing 9.3; 9.8; 10.5
singe -ing 9.3
singer 7.5
SINGULAR 1.10; 1.12
sink 9.8
-*sion* 5.1
sit 1.46; 9.7
sit-in(s) 5.26
Size 1.44; 7.16
skilful 7.1; 7.20
slay, slain 9.8
sleep, slept 9.7
slew see *slay*
slice 5.9; 6.34
slide, slid 9.7
sling 9.7
slink 9.7
slit 9.6
slow 3.15; 7.20
slow(ly) 15.4
slung see *sling*
slunk see *slink*
small 7.8
smell, smelt 9.7; 10.4(B9); 10.8; 13.2
smile (N & V) 5.2
  (v) 10.8
smite, smote, smitten 9.8
so (Conjunct or Conjunction) 2.3; 2.45
  - +ADJ/ADV +*that* 2.49
  - +ADJ +*as to* 3.14; 4.24
  - *as to* 3.12; 4.24
  - *far* (ADV) 1.23; 13.9; 13.19
  - *have I, - I have* 4.40–1
  - *long as* 2.43
  - *much/many* 6.38; 6.51